THE NEW CAMBRIDGE COMPANION TO

ST. PAUL

St. Paul was a pivotal and controversial figure in the fledgling Jesus-movement of the first century. *The New Cambridge Companion to St. Paul* provides an invaluable entryway into the study of Paul and his letters. Composed of sixteen chapters by an international team of scholars, it explores some of the key issues in the current study of his dynamic and demanding theological discourse. The volume first examines Paul's life and the first-century context in which he and his communities lived. Contributors then analyze particular writings by comparing and contrasting at least two selected letters, while thematic chapters examine topics of particular importance, including how Paul read scripture, his relation to Judaism and monotheism, why his message may have been attractive to first-century audiences, how his message was elaborated in various ways in the first four centuries, and how his theological discourse might relate to contemporary theological discourse and ideological analysis.

Bruce W. Longenecker is the Melton Chair of Religion and Professor of Christian Origins at Baylor University.

CAMBRIDGE COMPANIONS TO RELIGION

This is a series of companions to major topics and key figures in theology and religious studies. Each volume contains specially commissioned chapters by international scholars, which provide an accessible and stimulating introduction to the subject for new readers and nonspecialists.

Other Titles in the Series

AMERICAN ISLAM Edited by Juliane Hammer and Omid Safi

AMERICAN JUDAISM Edited by Dana Evan Kaplan

AMERICAN METHODISM Edited by Jason E. Vickers

ANCIENT MEDITERRANEAN RELIGIONS Edited by Barbette Stanley Spaeth

AUGUSTINE'S "CONFESSIONS" Edited by Tarmo Toom

KARL BARTH Edited by John Webster

THE BIBLE, 2ND EDITION Edited by Bruce Chilton

THE BIBLE AND LITERATURE Edited by Calum Carmichael

BIBLICAL INTERPRETATION Edited by John Barton

BLACK THEOLOGY Edited by Dwight N. Hopkins and Edward P. Antonio

DIETRICH BONHOEFFER Edited by John de Gruchy

JOHN CALVIN Edited by Donald K. McKim

CHRISTIAN DOCTRINE Edited by Colin Gunton

CHRISTIAN ETHICS Edited by Robin Gill

CHRISTIAN MYSTICISM Edited by Amy Hollywood and Patricia Z. Beckman

CHRISTIAN PHILOSOPHICAL THEOLOGY Edited by Charles Taliaferro and Chad V. Meister

CHRISTIAN POLITICAL THEOLOGY Edited by Craig Hovey and Elizabeth Phillips

THE CISTERIAN ORDER Edited by Mette Birkedal Bruun

CLASSICAL ISLAMIC THEOLOGY Edited by Tim Winter

JONATHAN EDWARDS Edited by Stephen J. Stein

EVANGELICAL THEOLOGY Edited by Timothy Larsen and Daniel J. Treier

FEMINIST THEOLOGY Edited by Susan Frank Parsons

FRANCIS OF ASSISI Edited by Michael J. P. Robson

THE GOSPELS Edited by Stephen C. Barton

THE HEBREW BIBLE/OLD TESTAMENT Edited by Stephen B. Chapman and Marvin A. Sweeney

THE JESUITS Edited by Thomas Worcester

JESUS Edited by Markus Bockmuehl

JUDAISM AND LAW Edited by Christine Hayes

C. S. LEWIS Edited by Robert MacSwain and Michael Ward

(continued after index)

THE NEW CAMBRIDGE COMPANION TO

ST. PAUL

Edited by

Bruce W. Longenecker

Baylor University

CAMBRIDGE
UNIVERSITY PRESS

CAMBRIDGE
UNIVERSITY PRESS

University Printing House, Cambridge CB2 8BS, United Kingdom

One Liberty Plaza, 20th Floor, New York, NY 10006, USA

477 Williamstown Road, Port Melbourne, VIC 3207, Australia

314–321, 3rd Floor, Plot 3, Splendor Forum, Jasola District Centre, New Delhi – 110025, India

79 Anson Road, #06–04/06, Singapore 079906

Cambridge University Press is part of the University of Cambridge.

It furthers the University's mission by disseminating knowledge in the pursuit of education, learning, and research at the highest international levels of excellence.

www.cambridge.org
Information on this title: www.cambridge.org/9781108423700
DOI: 10.1017/9781108529204

First published 2020

A catalogue record for this publication is available from the British Library.

Library of Congress Cataloging-in-Publication Data
NAMES: Longenecker, Bruce W., editor.
TITLE: The new Cambridge companion to St. Paul / edited by Bruce W. Longenecker, Baylor University, Texas.
DESCRIPTION: Cambridge ; New York : Cambridge University Press, 2020. |
SERIES: Cambridge companions to religion | Includes bibliographical references and index.
IDENTIFIERS: LCCN 2019058879 (print) | LCCN 2019058880 (ebook) | ISBN 9781108423700 (hardback) | ISBN 9781108438285 (paperback) | ISBN 9781108529204 (epub)
SUBJECTS: LCSH: Bible. Epistles of Paul–Criticism, interpretation, etc. | Bible. Epistles of Paul–Theology. | Paul, the Apostle, Saint.
CLASSIFICATION: LCC BS2650.52 .N48 2020 (print) | LCC BS2650.52 (ebook) | DDC 225.9/2–dc23
LC record available at https://lccn.loc.gov/2019058879
LC ebook record available at https://lccn.loc.gov/2019058880

ISBN 978-1-108-42370-0 Hardback
ISBN 978-1-108-43828-5 Paperback

For Ed Sanders

who opened vistas for fresh conversations

Contents

Map

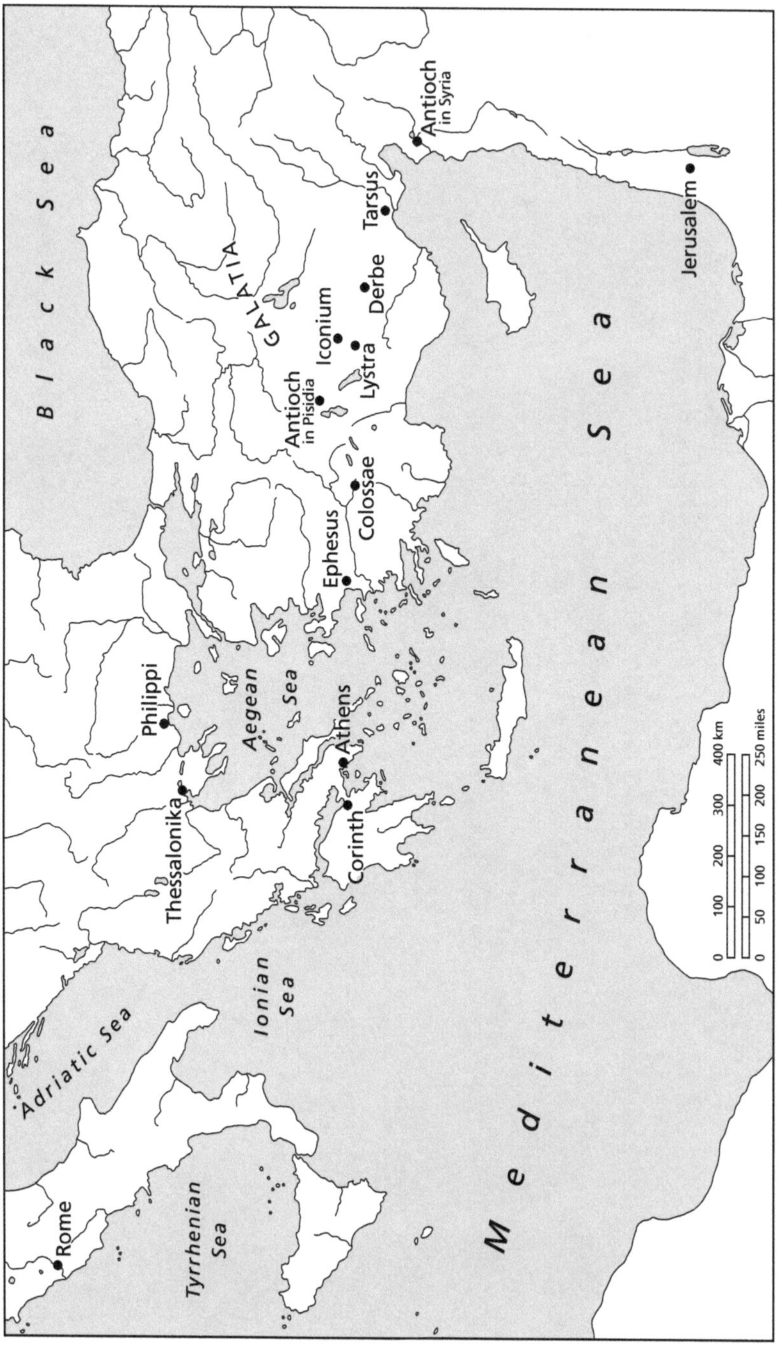

Cities of the Roman World and Paul's Mission

Contributors

James W. Aageson is Professor of New Testament and Early Christianity emeritus at Concordia College, Moorhead, Minnesota. His publications include *Written Also for Our Sake: Paul and the Art of Biblical Interpretation* (1993), *In the Beginning: Critical Concepts for the Study of the Bible* (2000), *Paul, the Pastoral Epistles, and the Early Church* (2008), and *Windows on Early Christianity: Uncommon Stories, Striking Images, Critical Perspectives* (2016). He is a former associate editor of the *Catholic Biblical Quarterly*.

Richard S. Ascough is a professor in the School of Religion at Queen's University in Kingston, Canada. His research focuses on the formation of early Christ groups and Greco-Roman religious culture, with particular attention to various types of associations. Among other publications, he is the author (with John Kloppenborg and Philip Harland) of *Associations in the Greco-Roman World* (2012) and *1 and 2 Thessalonians: Encountering the Christ Group at Thessalonike* (2014).

John M. G. Barclay is Lightfoot Professor of Divinity at Durham University. His recent publications include *Paul and the Gift* (2015), *Paul: A Very Brief History* (2017), and *Pauline Churches and Diaspora Jews* (2011). He is series editor for the new Cambridge University Press series, New Testament Theology.

Douglas A. Campbell is Professor of New Testament at Duke Divinity School. His recent publications include *Pauline Dogmatics: The Triumph of God's Love* (2020), *Paul: An Apostle's Journey* (2018), *Framing Paul: An Epistolary Biography* (2014), and *The Deliverance of God: An Apocalyptic Rereading of Justification in Paul* (2009). A book of essays has been published analyzing his critical approach to justification: *Beyond Old and New Perspectives on Paul: Reflections on the Work of Douglas Campbell* (2014).

Susan Grove Eastman is Associate Research Professor of New Testament at Duke Divinity School. Her research and teaching focus on personhood and participation in the letters of Paul and in interdisciplinary perspective. Her publications include *Paul and the Person: Reframing Paul's Anthropology* (2017), "Galatians," in *The New Interpreter's Bible One Volume Commentary* (2010), *Recovering Paul's Mother Tongue: Language and Theology in Galatians* (2007), and numerous articles and essays.

Paula Fredriksen, Aurelio Professor of Scripture emerita at Boston University, is currently Distinguished Visiting Professor at the Hebrew University, Jerusalem, and a member of the American Academy of Arts and Sciences. She has published on Jesus: *From Jesus to Christ*, 2nd ed. (2000), *Jesus of Nazareth, King of the Jews* (1999); on Augustine: *Augustine on Romans* (1986), *Augustine and the Jews* (2010); on Paul: *Paul, The Pagans' Apostle* (2017); and most recently on the earliest community in Jerusalem: *When Christians Were Jews* (2018).

Michael J. Gorman holds the Raymond E. Brown Chair in Biblical Studies and Theology at St. Mary's Seminary & University in Baltimore, Maryland. His publications include *Participating in Christ: Explorations in Paul's Theology and Spirituality* (2019), *Abide and Go: Missional Theosis in the Gospel of John* (2018), *Apostle of the Crucified Lord: A Theological Introduction to Paul and His Letters*, 2nd ed. (2017), *Becoming the Gospel: Paul, Participation, and Mission* (2015), *Inhabiting the Cruciform God: Kenosis, Justification, and Theosis in Paul's Narrative Soteriology* (2009), and *Cruciformity: Paul's Narrative Spirituality of the Cross* (2001).

David G. Horrell is Professor of New Testament Studies and Director of the Centre for Biblical Studies at the University of Exeter, UK. Among his recent publications are *An Introduction to the Study of Paul*, 3rd ed. (2015), *Solidarity and Difference: A Contemporary Reading of Paul's Ethics*, 2nd ed. (2016), and *The Making of Christian Morality: Reading Paul in Ancient and Modern Contexts* (2019).

Sylvia C. Keesmaat is Adjunct Professor of Biblical Studies at Trinity and Wycliffe Colleges at the University of Toronto, and Biblical Scholar in Residence at St. James Anglican Church in Fenelon Falls. She is the author (with Brian Walsh) of *Romans Disarmed: Resisting Empire, Demanding Justice* (2019), (also with Brian Walsh), *Colossians Remixed: Subverting the Empire* (2004), and *Paul and His Story: (Re)Interpreting the Exodus Tradition* (1999).

David Lincicum is the Rev. John A. O'Brien Associate Professor of Theology at the University of Notre Dame. He is the author of *Paul and the Early Jewish Encounter with Deuteronomy* (2010), and co-editor of several books, including *Ferdinand Christian Baur and the History of Early Christianity* (2017) and *Law and Lawlessness in Early Judaism and Early Christianity* (2019).

Bruce W. Longenecker is the Melton Chair of Religion at Baylor University. His recent publications include *In Stone and Story: Early Christianity in the Roman World* (2020), *The Cross before Constantine: The Early Life of a Christian Symbol* (2015), and *Remember the Poor: Paul, Poverty, and the Greco-Roman World* (2010). He is co-editor of the *Paideia* commentary series.

Margaret Y. MacDonald is Dean of Arts and Professor of Religious Studies at Saint Mary's University in Halifax. Her publications include *The Power of Children: The Construction of Christian Families in the Greco-Roman World* (2014), (with Carolyn Osiek and Janet Tulloch) *A Woman's Place: House Churches in Earliest Christianity* (2006), *Colossians and Ephesians* (2000), *Early Christian Women and Pagan Opinion: The Power of the Hysterical Woman* (1996), and *The Pauline Churches: A Socio-Historical Study of Institutionalization in the Pauline and Deutero-Pauline Writings* (1988).

Margaret M. Mitchell is the Shailer Mathews Distinguished Service Professor of New Testament and Early Christian Literature at the University of Chicago. She is the author of numerous books and articles on Paul and his ancient interpreters (e.g., Origen, Chrysostom, Gregory of Nyssa), including *Paul, the Corinthians, and the Birth of Christian Hermeneutics* (2010) and *The Heavenly Trumpet: John Chrysostom and the Art of Pauline Interpretation* (2000; 2002).

Matthew V. Novenson is Senior Lecturer in New Testament and Christian Origins at the University of Edinburgh, where he is also Director of the Centre for the Study of Christian Origins. He is the author of *Christ among the Messiahs* (2012), *The Grammar of Messianism* (2017), and *The End of the Law* (forthcoming). Presently, he is editing the *Oxford Handbook of Pauline Studies* and writing a critical commentary on the Letter of Paul to the Philippians.

Peter Oakes is Professor of New Testament at the University of Manchester. His publications include *Philippians: From People to Letter* (2001; 2007), *Reading Romans in Pompeii* (2009; 2013), and *Galatians* (2015). He is editor of *Journal for the Study of the New Testament Booklist.*

Abbreviations

Adv. Haer.	Irenaeus, *Adversus haereses* or *Against Heresies*
Adv. Marc.	Tertullian, *Adversus Marcionem* or *Against Marcion*
AJ	Josephus, *Antiquitates judaicae* or *Jewish Antiquities*
Ber.	*Berakot*
BJ	Josephus, *Bellum judaicum* or *Jewish War*
CIL	*Corpus Inscriptionum Latinarum*
Clem	*De clementia*
Col	Colossians
Cor	Corinthians
Dan	Daniel
Deut	Deuteronomy
En	Enoch
Eph	Ephesians
Exod	Exodus
Ezek	Ezekiel
Gal	Galatians
Gen	Genesis
Hab	Habakkuk
Heb	Hebrews
Ign. *Magn.*	Ignatius, *To the Magnesians*
Ign. *Phld.*	Ignatius, *To the Philadelphians*
Ign. *Smyrn.*	Ignatius, *To the Smyrneans*
Ign. *Trall.*	Ignatius, *To the Trallians*
Isa	Isaiah
Jer	Jeremiah
Lev	Leviticus
m.	Mishnah
Macc	Maccabees (1, 2, 3, or 4)
Mart. Scil.	*Acts of the Scillitan Martyrs*
Matt	The Gospel of Matthew

NETS	New English Translation of the Septuagint
NIV	New International Version
NRSV	New Revised Standard Version
Num	Numbers
Pet	Peter (1 or 2)
Phil	Philippians
Phlm	Philemon
Pol. *Phil.*	Polycarp, *To the Philippians*
Ps	Psalms
Rom	Romans
Sam	Samuel (1 or 2)
Thess	Thessalonians (1 or 2)
Tim	Timothy (1 or 2)

Part I

Paul, Letters and Communities

1 What Do We Find in Paul's Letters?

BRUCE W. LONGENECKER

Whatever else he might have been, the apostle Paul was resolute, daring, and audacious. By comparison with many others of his day, he lived his life at breakneck speed – always digging deeper, moving forward, adding more to the agenda. Throughout the short span of time that he is viewable on the screen of world history, Paul passionately advocated a configuration of devotion that was new to the Roman world – the worship of the God of Israel through the one Paul called "our Lord Jesus Christ." That passion, captured in the letters he wrote to struggling young Jesus-groups, resulted in an impressive amalgam that combined the spirited novelty of Jesus-devotion with the robust resources of Paul's Jewish heritage – with different mixtures of the two at any given time, and often with an eye on the socio-religious structures that animated the Roman world.

Writing letters was Paul's way of guiding fledgling communities of Jesus-followers – communities that he had founded (usually) that lay dotted around the eastern Mediterranean basin. In those early days when many aspects of Jesus-devotion were in their infancy and in some state of flux, Paul had a mixed reputation because he advocated views and practices that were controversial. Sometimes members of early Jesus-groups held Paul in high esteem, supporting his cause to the extent of sponsoring it financially from their own limited resources. But some people in communities he had founded (and beyond them as well) began to wonder whether Paul might be something of a charlatan, extracting money from those on whom he preyed; or a dangerous maverick, striking out on his own while devising theological discourse that was ethically defective and theologically problematic; or unreliable, given to changing his mind about plans he had already devised.[1] Some

[1] For discussion of Paul's critics, see Patrick Gray, *Paul as a Problem in History and Culture: The Apostle and His Critics through the Centuries* (Grand Rapids, MI: Baker Academic, 2016).

thought there was an imbalance in his self-presentation, with his letters being powerful but his personality being weak and unimpressive.[2] Even someone who admired Paul nonetheless admitted that some things in his letters are "hard to understand" (2 Pet 3:16).

As hard as they might be to understand, Paul's letters have been formative in the shaping of history, especially ecclesial history – contributing much to defining the contours of Christian discourse and identity for two millennia. In theological debates strewn throughout Christian history, it is only a slight overstatement to say that all parties have wanted to conscript Paul as an advocate for their cause, to legitimate their respective viewpoints. Even in the early twenty-first century, a leading philosopher (in the process of abandoning the atheism he had long advocated) gave Paul a ringing endorsement of high honor, describing him as "a first class intellectual" who "had a brilliant philosophical mind."[3]

This description of Paul's intellectual credentials might come as some surprise to those who imagine that Paul advocated a simple view that faith is all that's needed to enable the Christian soul to enter through the heavenly gates at the point of death. There are many reasons why this simplistic impression of Paul has taken hold in popular form, and many reasons why it is a truncated and unsatisfactory understanding of the letters from which we derive our knowledge of his life and theological discourse. Whatever we might think of Paul, his message was anything but simple. Paul was an expert at what we might call "thick description" – that is, he was able to see deeply into a situation, constructing its terms of engagement and assessing what he deemed to be the contours of its deepest theological significance. He interpreted the past, the future, the present; he interpreted the lives of individuals, of communities, of cultures. In all these ways, he was a dynamic lifelong learner, "constantly learning from, and deploying, a variety of sources and strategies in a complex, shifting, and challenging environment" of the Roman world.[4]

WHY DID PAUL WRITE LETTERS?

Paul's letters are the earliest Christian documents in existence. Although timelines for his life and letters are inevitably open to

[2] These questions about Paul derive largely from Paul's self-defense in 2 Cor 10–13.

[3] Anthony Flew (or his ghost writer), *There Is a God: How the World's Most Notorious Atheist Changed His Mind* (San Francisco, CA: HarperOne, 2007), 157, 186.

[4] Paul M. Robertson, *Paul's Letters and Contemporary Greco-Roman Literature: Theorizing a New Taxonomy* (Leiden: Brill, 2016), 219.

discussion and debate, most scholars place his letters generally within the 50s – with some scholars placing a few texts into the 60s. By comparison, the canonical gospels began to circulate a few decades later: Mark's Gospel in the early 70s; Matthew's Gospel and Luke's Gospel in the 80s or 90s; John's Gospel in the 90s – all these dates being rough estimates. When Paul founded groups of Jesus-followers in urban centers of the Roman world, those groups had few of the resources to support a robust corporate life as devotees of Jesus Christ. It is hard to imagine that these groups would have known much more than the outline of Paul's story about Jesus's death and resurrection and, perhaps, some of Jesus's sayings (although even that is open to question).[5] Having access only to some oral traditions, young Jesus-groups could not draw on an established tradition of theological reflections embodied within Christian canonical texts. When Paul left one city in order to bring his "good news" (or "gospel") elsewhere, the groups he left behind were outfitted with very few traditional resources. If he was confident that those fledgling communities would survive without his direct oversight, this was probably because he believed that the Spirit of God was enlivening all aspects of their corporate life (e.g., 1 Thess 5:12–22).

Paul's letters were not exercises in "systematic theology," sorting out theological intricacies for successive Christian generations. We don't find in them a theological system packaged in a precisely ordered, well-defined, immaculately structured presentation of "doctrinal truths." Paul would not even have seen the need to set out an exhaustive systematic articulation of Christian doctrine to enhance the theological discourse of the Christian church for generations to come; such a thing would have been unnecessary. Paul's letters often give the impression that the culmination of all time would soon be dawning on this world, perhaps within his own lifetime or in the not-too-distant future (e.g., 1 Thess 4:16–17; 1 Cor 7:26, 29–31; 15:51).

Written in Greek to Jesus-followers in specific first-century situations, Paul's letters were meant to guide particular Jesus-followers who, in his view, needed theological fine-tuning – or, at times, a more radical overhaul. Sending letters was his way of assisting struggling communities, trying to get them through to the next stage of their development, seeking to ensure that their devotion to Jesus Christ would stay focused within certain

[5] On the sayings of Jesus in Jesus-groups established by Paul, see Heinz Hiestermann, *Paul and the Synoptic Jesus Tradition* (Leipzig: Evangelische Verlagsanstalt, 2017); Michael B. Thompson, *Clothed with Christ: The Example and Teaching of Jesus in Romans 12:1–15:13* (Eugene, OR: Wipf & Stock, 2011).

theological parameters before the imminent coming of their Lord. As such, Paul's letters generally engaged in issues that, in his mind, were on the near horizon for Jesus-groups and for his own ministry.

Not a systematic theologian, Paul was more like a pastoral theologian, teaching Jesus-followers to think theologically about who they were – how their story was animated by the story of God's engagement with the world, how they were developing in their devotion to Jesus Christ, how they differed from the "pagan" environment all around them, and how they were to engage with each other and with others beyond their corporate gatherings. Doing theology "on the move," Paul was a master of pastoral "theologizing" in an effort to help communities of Jesus-followers shape their identities in relation to a worldview of what God has already done in Christ and would bring to completion through Christ.[6]

WHAT LETTERS DID PAUL WRITE?

When we study Paul's letters, we are, in one sense, studying a collection of diverse texts that early communities of Jesus-followers kept, copied, and circulated among themselves (and with others) – evidently finding those letters to be important for their self-understanding. When later Christian leaders compiled lists of the standard texts that were expected to edify Christian faith and practices (i.e., the "canon"), many letters with Paul's name on them were placed within that diverse library.[7] But not all of Paul's letters have survived; some letters seem to have fallen out of circulation (one of which is referenced in 1 Cor 5:9; see also 1 Cor 16:1; Col 4:16).[8] By contrast, some texts were written in Paul's name after his death – such as the second-century texts known as *The Letter to the Laodiceans* and *3 Corinthians*.[9] These are instances in which

[6] On Paul's theological discourse in relation to situations, see (for instance) J. C. Beker, *Paul the Apostle* (Minneapolis, MN: Fortress Press, 1980), 23–108; Calvin Roetzel, *The Letters of Paul: Conversations in Context*, 5th ed. (Louisville, KY: Westminster John Knox, 2009).

[7] Those letters were usually ordered from longest to shortest, first in relation to letters sent to communities (Romans through 2 Thessalonians, with only Ephesians being out of order in terms of length) and then in relation to letters sent to individuals (1 Timothy through Philemon).

[8] The same thing may have been the case for writings by other New Testament authors, as illustrated by 3 John 9: "I [previously] wrote to the church" – a comment that seems to reference a letter that has not survived.

[9] On the theological discourse of the *Letter to the Laodiceans*, see Bruce W. Longenecker and Scott C. Ryan, "Presenting the Pauline Voice: An Appreciation of the Letter to the Laodiceans," *New Testament Studies* 62 (2016): 136–148.

later authors used Paul's name to authenticate certain theological convictions that they thought could be attributable to Paul, at least by extension – even doing so "out of love for Paul," as one such writer from the late second century seems to have professed.[10] In the process, various texts were written that expanded the narrative of what Paul stood for.[11] As a consequence, Paul came to be memorialized across a spectrum of views, placed as an apostolic fountainhead for diverse trajectories of Christian identity.[12]

Many scholars think this same process of extending the Pauline voice (or, in a sense, writing "speech in character") applies to some texts contained within the New Testament itself. Of the thirteen New Testament texts that have Paul's name on them, seven are "undisputed," being recognized as authored by Paul. In canonical order, these are: Romans, 1 Corinthians, 2 Corinthians, Galatians, Philippians, 1 Thessalonians, and Philemon. The other six are "disputed" in terms of their authorship: 2 Thessalonians, Colossians, Ephesians, 2 Timothy, 1 Timothy, and Titus (listed in impressionistic order from most likely to least likely to have been authored by Paul).[13] Scholars will differ as to whether any or all of these six are to be included in attempts to discern the theologizing of Paul himself.[14] The practice of "allonymity" or

[10] Tertullian says that this motivation was declared by the person who wrote the popular second-century story of Paul and Thecla in the *Acts of Paul and Thecla*; see Tertullian, *On Baptism*, 17.

[11] Laura Salah Nasrallah (*Archaeology and the Letters of Paul* [Oxford: Oxford University Press, 2019], 253–254) proposes that "we should not define as forgeries or deceptions writings in Paul's name but not from Paul's pen. Rather, we should understand them as part of a larger literary tendency in antiquity, that of producing an 'epistolary narrative' to flesh out the life of a great man .... The afterlives of Paul make sense as early Christian improvisations of history rooted in the growing sainthood of this man."

[12] See, for instance, Richard I. Pervo, *The Making of Paul: Constructions of the Apostle in Early Christianity* (Minneapolis, MN: Fortress Press, 2010); Benjamin L. White, *Remembering Paul: Ancient and Modern Contests over the Image of the Apostle* (Oxford: Oxford University Press, 2014); Jens Schröter, Simon Butticaz, and Andreas Dettwiler, eds., *Receptions of Paul in Early Christianity: The Person of Paul and His Writings through the Eyes of His Early Interpreters* (Berlin: deGruyter, 2018); Isaac Oliver and Gabriele Boccaccini, eds., *The Early Reception of Paul the Second Temple Jew: Text, Narrative, and Reception History* (New York: T&T Clark, 2018).

[13] In the early centuries of Christian history, the Epistle to the Hebrews was occasionally thought to have been written by Paul, although many other authors were also proposed. While the letter may have been influenced somewhat by Pauline thought, there is nothing to suggest that Paul himself was involved in authoring it.

[14] Making decisions on these matters is more of an art than a science, but neither is it without some controls. Decisions take into account certain aspects of the texts, such as the linguistic style, the way ideas are expressed, the theological content, and the

"allepigraphy" (writing in the voice of another; usually referred to as "pseudonymity" or "pseudepigraphy") means that any or all of these six texts need to be used with some caution when reconstructing Paul's own theological discourse.[15] Several scenarios illustrate the point.

(1) Should we use both the undisputed 1 Thessalonians and the disputed 2 Thessalonians to reconstruct the Thessalonian situation and Paul's response to it, or only 1 Thessalonians?
(2) Was Colossians authored by Paul, with an earnest disciple refreshing Paul's letter by writing a similar letter (Ephesians, which reuses about two-thirds of Colossians) in order to bring together a number of strands of Paul's thought and represent them?[16] Or were both letters written by Paul himself? Or were they both allonymous?
(3) Should we link Colossians and Philemon to the same historical situation, or are the two letters only artificially related, one being authored by Paul (Philemon) and the other by an earnest disciple seeking to extend Paul's voice into a new day and a new context (Colossians)?[17]

It is not necessary to lay out all the permutations of how the six disputed letters might be analyzed in relation to the seven undisputed letters of Paul. These are simply three scenarios illustrating that reconstructing the theology of Paul is not a simple task, even with regard to the sources available to us for that task.

DID OTHER PEOPLE CONTRIBUTE TO PAUL'S LETTERS?

A number of letters in the Pauline corpus suggest that they were sent under the authority of Paul together with other people. In canonical order, the Pauline letters that list more than one sender include:

manner in which the author engages with opposition. The case of 1 Timothy is especially interesting, since it seems to be cognizant of the Lukan Gospel (with 1 Tim 5:18 and Luke 10:7 sharing a saying word-for-word; cf. Matt 10:10) – a gospel that most scholars would date in the 80s or 90s.

[15] On the issue of allonymity or allepigraphy (both from the Greek *"allos,"* meaning "other"), see especially I. Howard Marshall, *The Pastoral Epistles* (Edinburgh: T&T Clark, 1999), 79–92.

[16] On this reading of Ephesians, see Carey Newman, "Narrative Cross, Apocalyptic Resurrection: Ephesians and Reading Paul," in *One God, One People, One Future*, eds. John Anthony Dunne and Eric Lewellen (Minneapolis, MN: Fortress Press, 2018), 493–512.

[17] The first of these approaches appears in Douglas Campbell's essay in this book. For an earlier version of the same approach, see Jerome Murphy-O'Connor, *Paul: His Story* (Oxford: Oxford University Press, 2004), 147–157.

- 1 Corinthians, sent by Paul and Sosthenes (1 Cor 1:1)
- 2 Corinthians, sent by Paul and Timothy (2 Cor 1:1)
- Galatians, sent by Paul "and all the members of God's family who are with me" (Gal 1:1–2)
- Philippians, sent by Paul and Timothy (Phil 1:1)
- Colossians, sent by Paul and Timothy (Col 1:1)
- 1 Thessalonians, sent by Paul, Silvanus, and Timothy (1 Thess 1:1)
- 2 Thessalonians, sent by Paul, Silvanus, and Timothy (2 Thess 1:1)
- Philemon, sent by Paul and Timothy (Phlm 1:1)

How are we to interpret these lists of senders at the start of these letters? Were the letters written jointly, with Paul sharing authorial rights equally with the others? Were the letters the "product of a complex exchange of ideas of which Paul was a key contributor, but not the only one whose ideas were reflected in the final product"?[18] Was Paul the leader of a small group of associates, some of whom served as Paul's assistants in preparing his letters?[19] Or was this co-author/co-sender convention merely a formality – nothing more than a kindly inclusive gesture, perhaps, or more likely, a rhetorical device used simply to bolster the authority of the letter (by enlarging the authorial voices)? Was Paul always the main author of these letters, even if there were co-senders at times?[20]

One recent study has suggested that the most likely situation was something like this: A scribal secretary (perhaps someone like Tertius, who introduces himself in Rom 16:22 as "the writer of this letter") would have taken notes while listening to Paul and any others who might have contributed ideas regarding what should be included in the letter. From these preliminary notes, the secretary would have prepared a rough draft of a letter, which was read to Paul and his team, who collectively would make corrections and additions along the way. This editing process would have continued until Paul and the others were

[18] See Richard S. Ascough, *1 & 2 Thessalonians: Encountering the Christ Group at Thessalonike* (New York: Bloomsbury T&T Clark, 2017), 22. Relatedly, Murphy-O'Connor (*Paul: His Story*, 165–166) hypothesizes that, when we consider factors why Paul's relationship with the Corinthians derailed after the writing of 1 Corinthians, one factor might be that Sosthenes had given him bad advice about the "unChristian" approach Paul should take when writing 1 Corinthians.

[19] For this view, see E. Randolf Richards, *Paul and First-Century Letter Writing: Secretaries, Composition, and Collection* (Downers Grove, IL: InterVarsity Press, 2004), 155, where Paul's letters are called "team letters."

[20] For this view, see Markus Bockmuehl, *The Epistle to the Philippians* (London: A & C Black, 1998), 86.

satisfied with a final product. For some of the longer letters (such as Romans and the Corinthian letters), the process might have taken about two weeks to complete.[21] Then the letter would have been sent with a letter carrier to its intended audience.[22]

Paul's letters give different impressions about their authorship. In a letter like 1 Thessalonians, for instance, there is little indication that Paul took the lead as the primary authorial voice. That letter includes numerous references to its three senders through the use of first-person plural referents ("we," "our," "us"), while first-person singular referents that highlight Paul appear only rarely throughout the five chapters (2:18; 3:5; 5:27). It might be that Paul's was, in fact, the primary authorial voice of that letter, but that impression does not emerge as clearly as we might otherwise expect. On the other hand, in a letter like Galatians, there is very little sense that all those whom Paul refers to as co-senders ("all the members of God's family who are with me") contributed much to the letter. In that letter, virtually everything seems to be flowing from the mind of Paul, with first-person singular referents appearing throughout its six chapters. (First-person pronouns appear approximately 40 times in Galatians, and there are also first-person singular verbal forms to add to that number.)[23]

The influence of other people may be evident in some of the Pauline letters in another manner as well. Some letters have features that leave them vulnerable to theories of textual compilation. It is sometimes suspected that some letters are not in the same form now as they were when originally composed; instead, two or more of Paul's letters may have been joined together to form the unified text that we now have. The people who combined the letters are usually thought to have been

[21] Richards, *Paul and First-Century Letter Writing*, 93. In Richards's view (see 164–165), even copying the finished version of Romans would have taken nearly twelve hours (likely a three day process in itself); before that, the secretary's preparation of the various drafts of a letter like Romans might have taken twelve days, excluding the note-taking sessions and the final composition. As Richards notes, we should refrain from thinking "that Paul easily dashed off a letter over the weekend" (165).

[22] A common view of Paul's letter to the Romans, for instance, is that Phoebe, "the benefactor of many" (Rom 16:2), carried the letter from Corinth to Rome – probably even being involved in reading and explaining the letter to Jesus-groups in Rome. On the role of Phoebe (and her probable slave Tertius), see, for instance, Robert Jewett, *Romans: A Commentary* (Minneapolis, MN: Fortress Press, 2007), 22.

[23] Compare the early Christian document called 1 Clement (c. 80–110). It purports to have been written by the collective members of the church in Rome, but its writing style gives no evidence of multiple authors; instead, it seems to have been composed by one person, who was later identified as Clement (rightly or wrongly).

some of Paul's co-workers, editing his work after his death. The letter that is most likely to be a compilation is 2 Corinthians (which is sometimes thought to be an amalgamation of between two and five separate letters). Occasionally, Philippians is said to be a composite text as well.[24] There is little agreement among scholars on these matters (although probably more scholars imagine Philippians to be a single text than a composite).

Relatedly, in the earliest extant manuscripts of Romans (from the third century and beyond), the contents of Romans 15–16 are structured with enough variation to show that the letter survived in different arrangements in those chapters. Explanations as to why this might have been include (1) the possibility that the letter's contents were abridged in some manuscripts because of the influence of popular "Marcionite" movements in the second century (which may not have appreciated the way Paul's good news was linked to the God of the Judeans, as in Rom 15:7–13), (2) the possibility that the letter's final chapter was removed from the letter originally sent to the assemblies in Rome since it seemed too personal to be included in the final canon of Paul's letters, or (alternatively), (3) the possibility that the letter's final chapter of personal greetings was added to a single copy of the letter that was sent to Jesus-followers in Ephesus (where Paul had spent roughly three years, presumably knowing more people there than he knew in the Jesus-groups of Rome), and made its way into the textual history of the letter through that route. Even if the order of Romans as presented in Bibles today is representative of the ordering of the letter that Paul originally sent to Jesus-followers in Rome (as seems likely), the textual tradition nonetheless makes it clear that, on occasion, people after Paul handled his letters in ways that sometimes shaped them this way or that way.

This same phenomenon may come into play with regard to a closely related issue – that is, the possibility that "interpolations" were inserted into Paul's letters at a later time. Some letters lend themselves to the view that small sections have been added at some point after the letters were sent out. Two of the more important passages that are sometimes thought to be post-authorial interpolations include 1 Cor 14:34–36 (about women needing to be silent, in contrast to Paul's own affirmation of head-covered women praying and prophesying in the gathered community, as in 1 Cor 11:1–16) and 1 Thess 2:14–16 (about God's wrath falling upon "the Jews who killed both the Lord Jesus and the

[24] Paul writes "finally" in 3:1, as if the letter is coming to an end, although there are two more chapters to follow (3:2–4:23).

prophets").[25] The way these two passages are adjudicated will influence our view of Paul one way or another. Other possible interpretations have been proposed over the years, but usually with less significant impact on how we view Paul and his theology.

To What Extent Is Paul's Theological Discourse Stable?

Because Paul always wrote into situations, and because situations always differ, Paul's theologizing took on different contours in each of his letters. One example of this pertains to Paul's pronouncements about "the law" (or God's instructions to the people of Israel). In Galatians, Paul's statements about the law carry an overwhelmingly negative force. This kind of forceful rhetoric was, in his view, required by the situation, since some gentile Jesus-followers in Galatian Jesus-groups were under the impression that they needed to incorporate "law observance" within their devotion to Jesus Christ. In order to counter that perception, Paul's discourse in Galatians followed lines that give a largely unfavorable impression about the law. In Romans, however, when the pressure of the Galatian situation had dissipated somewhat and when other factors were in play, Paul was more nuanced in his pronouncements, adding a more favorable strand to his discourse about the law. In that context, Paul felt able to pronounce the law to be "holy" and "spiritual" (Rom 7:12, 14), while "the commandment" is said to be "holy, righteous, and good" (Rom 7:12). The tone and content of Paul's discourse differ somewhat in these two letters, emerging from two different situations. Is there a stable theological construct that unites these moments of theologizing? Does Galatians represent "raw Paulinism," while Romans represents "refined Paulinism"? Might Romans be "one of the earliest interpretations of Galatians," as one interpreter has suggested?[26] How are these things to be negotiated?[27]

Embedded within this example is a thorny question that arises in relation to a number of issues in Paul's letters – whether Paul's

[25] On 1 Cor 14:34–36, see the fuller discussion in Bruce W. Longenecker and Todd D. Still, *Thinking through Paul: A Survey of His Life, Letters, and Theology* (Grand Rapids, MI: Zondervan, 2014), 126–132.

[26] J. Louis Martyn, "Romans as One of the Earliest Interpretations of Galatians," in *Theological Issues in the Letters of Paul*, ed. J. Louis Martyn (Edinburgh: T&T Clark, 1997), 37–46.

[27] For one take on this complex issue, see Bruce W. Longenecker, "Sharing in Their Spiritual Blessings? The Story of Israel in Galatians and Romans," in *Narrative Dynamics in Paul: A Critical Assessment*, ed. Bruce W. Longenecker (Louisville, KY: Westminster John Knox Press, 2002), 58–84.

theologizing developed in some fashion over the years, and whether presentational development is evident within his letters. Perhaps Paul adjusted some theological components within his worldview at various points, articulating new layers of theological content as a result of his engagement with fresh situations or thinking things through in further ways as time went on. Or perhaps he simply adjusted his theological discourse to do better justice to his theological worldview, refracting his discourse through new forms of expression in order to give greater clarity to the theological content of his thought. Of course, these two forms of development ("theological change" versus "presentational variation") could easily go hand in hand. In this regard, we might listen to a master of Pauline interpretation, E. P. Sanders, who offered this assessment of the issue of development in Paul's letters:

> Of course Paul's thought developed. How could it not? He was an intelligent and reactive human .... Only a dullard would repeat time after time what he had previously thought or refuse to think back through some of his opinions as issues and objections arose during his ministry. Adaptation must have been his watchword .... As problems shifted, and as his understanding of them advanced, he made adjustments.[28]

Here again, though, the issue is complicated by different determinations regarding the extent of the Pauline letter collection. The notion of "development in Paul" would look one way if only the undisputed letters are taken into account, while looking much different if all thirteen letters are placed in the mix. And since scholars often disagree on the sequential ordering of the letters they deem to be relevant, the issue is open to a number of different interpretations of the data.

Take, for example, statements about widows in the Pauline letter corpus. In 1 Corinthians, the advice to all widows is that it is best if they "remain unmarried" so that they can dedicate themselves fully to the work of their Lord without being distracted once again by the obligations of household management (7:8, 39–40). In 1 Timothy, however, the advice is for younger widows to "marry, bear children, and manage their households" (5:14). Part of the difference behind these two pronouncements may well have to do with the perception of time that is informing them. In 1 Corinthians, there is cognizance of "the impending crisis" (7:26, referring to the return of the Lord Jesus Christ);

[28] E. P. Sanders, "Did Paul's Theology Develop?," in *The Word Leaps the Gap*, eds. J. R. Wagner et al. (Grand Rapids, MI: Eerdmans, 2008), 334–335.

in view of that imminent event, getting distracted by household duties would impede the urgent need to spread the good news. In 1 Timothy, however, there is less of a sense of the imminent return and more of a sense of the need to embed Christian devotion in the life of Christian households of the Roman world. It is possible to see the distinct pronouncements in 1 Corinthians and 1 Timothy as both being embedded in missional concerns while illustrating a difference in their missional strategies. If we imagine both texts to have been written by Paul, this would be an example of development in his theologizing; if, however, these two texts have different authors, they would illustrate development within the Pauline trajectory, with different forms of instruction being given in different contexts by different authors.

One aspect of Paul's theological discourse, however, seems to have been consistently articulated without much sense of development or adjustment. For Paul, the Christological pattern of self-giving was to serve as the moral compass for all Jesus-groups. This is one of the threads that runs most consistently throughout the majority of the Pauline letters in one way or another. It was almost the bedrock of his pastoral theologizing, something he returned to again and again, no matter the form of theological discourse he happened to be employing at any given point.

HOW MUCH DO WE KNOW ABOUT PAUL'S LIFE?

Much of Paul's life lies in murky darkness. At one end of things, we don't know when he was born and the situation of his early years; at the other end, we can't be sure when or how he died – other than the likelihood that he died as a martyr in Rome at some point in the sixties (a likelihood admittedly based primarily on ecclesiastical tradition).

In between those murky points, we know a few points of detail about Paul's life, but not much. In the early years, Paul dug deeply into the ancestral traditions of Judaism, or "Judeanism" as some are preferring to call it these days (since in Paul's day the term "Judaism" did not refer so much to a "religion" but to a posture of committing oneself to preserving the ancestral traditions of the Judean people with intentional zealous fervor, over against any perceived threats to Judean identity).[29]

[29] In this, the young Saul may have idealized Phinehas, a hero of Judean history who was remembered for his "zeal" (1 Macc 2:54; cf. Gal 1:14) when he ran a spear through the bodies of a mixed-race couple when a Hebrew man took a woman from a foreign race into his household (Num 25:6–13) – an act that preserved Israel

Identifying with the Pharisaic branch of Judeanism (Phil 3:5), Paul probably never encountered Jesus of Nazareth during the years that the Nazarene was active in Galilee and Judea.[30] At some point in the early 30s, however, he had an experience of encountering the one he would thereafter proclaim as the risen Lord (1 Cor 15:8; Gal 1:15–16; Phil 3:6). As part of that experience, he felt himself called to be an apostle for the risen one, whose assemblies he had previously persecuted (1 Cor 15:9; Gal 1:13–14). In fact, instead of expending his energies in efforts to preserve the integrity of Judean identity and practice, Paul's life now became redirected toward those beyond the boundaries of Judeanism – the gentiles, or "the nations" (*ta ethnē*). The good news needed to go out to them; the God of all creation had acted definitively in the life, death, and resurrection of Jesus Christ, and all the world needed to hear the message and to see its transforming power at work.[31]

In the early stage of his mission to spread the good news, Paul was part of a missionary team in which he was closely associated with a man named Barnabas (Gal 2:1–10). That team had success in various places, including a few groups of Jesus-followers who resided in Galatia. At some point, that partnership broke up (probably as a result of tensions arising from a highly-charged incident at Antioch, described in Gal 2:11–14). Paul now (probably from the late 40s onwards) struck out to places further afield, without Barnabas but with a team of close associates who seem to pop in and out of our picture – including Timothy, Titus, and Silvanus (or Silas). In this phase of his mission, Jesus-groups (perhaps comprising some three dozen members, roughly speaking) were founded in cities dotted around the Mediterranean basin of the Roman world – such as Galatia, Philippi, Thessalonica, Corinth, and Ephesus. It was in this phase of Paul's mission (probably throughout much of the 50s) that a substantial body of his letters were written. And we know from several of those letters that Paul's gospel was looked upon with some suspicion, perhaps even antagonism – as some influential Jesus-followers found his good news to be plagued with certain

and was "reckoned to him as righteousness from generation to generation forever" (Ps 106:31).

[30] In *When Paul Met Jesus: How an Idea Got Lost in History* (Cambridge: Cambridge University Press, 2016), Stanley E. Porter revives the old theory that Paul did, in fact, encounter Jesus.

[31] The extent to which Paul himself continued to observe the ancestral practices of Judean devotion is currently a highly contested issue. What is clear is that gentile Jesus-followers themselves were to become more Judean in their convictions and practices (e.g., monotheism and morality) than in their previous "pagan" identities.

theological deficiencies. Paul's letters are frequently marked by attempts to bolster the legitimacy of his own apostleship, as well as attempts to bring theological clarity to situations on the ground. Throughout this period, Paul seems to have been tireless in his efforts, many of which are beyond our field of vision. For instance, when writing to Jesus-followers in Rome (perhaps in 57 or so), Paul mentions having completed a mission that we otherwise know nothing about – a mission to Illyricum (Rom 15:19; Croatia and Bosnia today, roughly speaking).

It was in his letter to Jesus-followers in Rome that Paul makes an intriguing comment, claiming that there was "no further place for me [to carry out my mission] in these regions" from Jerusalem to Illyricum (Rom 15:23). This declaration seems undergirded by the view that Paul sought to establish groups of Jesus-followers in main centers of the Roman world, from which the good news would spread further, as ripples spread outward. But with "no further place" to preach the "good news," Paul was now setting his sights on preaching in what he called "Spain," or the regions to the west of Italy (Rom 15:24–28). Prior to that, however, he committed himself to taking a collection of money to "the poor among the saints at Jerusalem" (Rom 15:26) – a collection he oversaw for a few years throughout the mid-50s, ensuring that communities founded among the gentiles were seen to support communities of Judean Jesus-followers (so, 1 Cor 16:1–4; 2 Cor 8–9; Rom 15:14–33).

At this point the trail starts to go cold, depending on how one estimates the dates of certain letters and how one judges the extent of the Pauline corpus.[32] One way or another, however, Paul died prior to the destruction of the city of Jerusalem by Roman forces in 70 CE – his death preceding that event by almost a decade in one reconstruction of his life or by three or so years in another reconstruction. And depending on one's reconstruction of the final years of his life, Paul may have lived long enough to see the "governing authorities" of Rome undertake a pogrom of slaughtering Jesus-followers in Rome (starting in 64 CE). These were the same Jesus-followers to whom Paul had said that the ruling authorities had been "instituted by God" and were acting as "the servant of God to execute wrath on the wrongdoer" (Rom 13:1, 4). We may wonder how that text was heard in the light of the martyrdom of many to whom this text was originally sent.

[32] For surveys of the possible endings of Paul's life, see the essays in *The Last Years of Paul*, eds., Armand Puig i Tàrrech, John M. G. Barclay, and Jörg Frey (Tübingen: Mohr Siebeck, 2015).

TO WHAT EXTENT CAN WE MAKE USE OF THE ACTS OF THE APOSTLES?

The very brief reconstruction of Paul's life undertaken in the previous section has not been informed by data from the Acts of the Apostles – a text that dedicates roughly half of its narrative to events in the life of Paul (who is especially prominent throughout Acts 13–28, with cameo appearances prior to that). But the presentation of Paul's life that we find in Acts is somewhat problematic. Sometimes data about Paul's life gleaned from the Pauline letters diverges from data about Paul's life gleaned from Acts. For instance, in Galatians Paul testifies that after encountering the risen Lord, he did not go to Jerusalem to see "those who were already apostles before me"; instead, he went directly "into Arabia, and afterwards I returned to Damascus" (Gal 1:17). Without any mention of Jerusalem in his account, Paul can say that later in his ministry he "was still unknown by sight to the churches of Judea [i.e., Jerusalem]" (1:22). The narrative of Acts is quite different, however. After encountering the risen Lord, Acts depicts Paul returning to Jerusalem and trying "to join the disciples" (9:26); in fact, Barnabas "took him and brought him to the apostles," so that Paul "stayed with them and moved about freely in Jerusalem, speaking boldly in the name of the Lord" (9:27–29).

For many interpreters, divergences in detail of this kind require us to give precedence to Paul's first-person accounts, and to see the Acts narrative as informed by the interests of the author who narrated events through particular filters. For instance, the author of Acts does not concentrate much on disputes that arose within the Jesus-movement, preferring to show that movement as fairly unified in its focus and mission. Instead, there are several ways in which the Paul of Acts is sometimes thought to diverge from the Paul of the undisputed letters in order to merge with the ecclesiastical interests of the author of Acts. Three examples illustrate the point.

(1) The description of Paul going to Jerusalem immediately after his encounter with the risen Lord (as noted above) links Paul and the Jerusalem apostles at the earliest possible opportunity. In this way, it fits well with the narrative's portrait of general harmony among the leadership of the early Jesus-movement, even though that aspect of Acts seems to run in the opposite direction to Paul's own testimony in Galatians 1.

(2) The split between Paul and Barnabas was probably acrimonious and related to a key theological difference between them (probably

rooted in the divisive event recounted in Gal 2:11–14). In Acts, however, that split seems to be sanitized, being presented simply as a difference in opinion over the personality of a potential co-worker (Acts 15:36–41).

(3) Paul's theological interests in Acts seem to be more in accordance with Peter's theological discourse in Acts than the theological discourse of the undisputed Pauline letters.[33]

We might conclude, then, that evidence from Acts is not to be used in a reconstruction of the life, letters, and theology of Paul, since it would just get in the way of reliable historical reconstruction. For most, however, it is not prudent to completely write off Acts as a resource for historical reconstruction, even if it needs to be used cautiously for historical purposes. For instance, the general details that Acts gives when recounting Paul's move from Macedonia to Achaia corresponds relatively well to the data of Paul's letters, so that the general outline of Paul's movements from Thessalonica to Athens and then Corinth is fairly consistent in each.[34] Most scholars, then, find the historical presentation of Acts to be conflicted to some degree – useable at times, perhaps, but only with discretion. Even then, however, some scholars prefer to use that presentation only when it corroborates other data from Paul's letters, while other scholars use that presentation to fill in extra details or to add to our understanding of Paul's letters, as long as the presentation in Acts does not run contrary to the data of the letters themselves.[35] Often, decisions will be made on a case by case basis.

[33] On issues of this kind, see (for instance), J. C. Beker, *Heirs of Paul: Paul's Legacy in the New Testament and in the Church Today* (Minneapolis, MN: Fortress Press, 1991); Richard Pervo, *Luke's Story of Paul* (Minneapolis, MN: Fortress Press, 1990).

[34] Compare Acts 17:1, 17:15, and 18:1 with 1 Thess 2:2, 3:1, Phil 4:15–16, and 2 Cor 11:7–9. But even then there are differences, with Acts depicting Timothy as staying in Thessalonica while Paul moved south (Acts 17:14), whereas 1 Thessalonians depicts Timothy as having left Thessalonica and accompanying Paul south, only going back to Thessalonica (being sent by Paul) after arriving in Athens (1 Thess 3:1–2).

[35] For instance, Acts alone tells us that Barnabas had strong connections with the Jerusalem community (Acts 4:36–37; 9:27; 11:22). If this is right, it would seem to add further contours to the shape of Paul's ministry; that is, once Paul and Barnabas broke their association in the late 40s, Paul could more easily be depicted by those antagonistic to him as something of a maverick after that break, since Paul's links to the "mother church" in Jerusalem were less obvious than had previously been the case.

WHAT WILL YOU FIND IN THIS BOOK?

Much more could be said in order to give an orientation to the study of Paul and his letters, but enough has been said to introduce a few general issues and to lay some foundations that will be elaborated and enhanced in the essays that follow in this book. It remains only to explain something about the character and contents of this book.

The first thing to note is that this book is primarily meant to service introductory explorations of the theological discourse of Paul's letters. Accordingly, the *New Cambridge Companion to St. Paul* is intentionally compact in its coverage rather than expansive. There is no intention to cover every possible topic in the study of Paul; if this book provokes interest to study Paul further, with other books servicing those expanding interests, that is to be welcomed. But for the purposes of this book, the essays that follow are not research essays, even if they are informed by the latest currents in Pauline studies. Instead, these essays are intended to capture a sense of Paul's theological vision in its complexity, its challenge, perhaps its contestability, and at times even its genius.

Second, like all *Cambridge Companions,* this is a multi-authored volume. Fifteen scholars have written fresh essays on topics selected for this introductory volume. Their task was not to coordinate their understanding of Paul at some point in the collective middle, so that they all end up saying roughly the same thing. If that had been the task, none of them would have accepted the invitation to write for this book. Instead, their assignment was to write stimulating essays that spur readers to think about major issues in ways that are deemed to be most beneficial, according to their own judgment regarding coverage and presentation. As a consequence, there is at times some diversity in the views expressed. That diversity simply reflects some of the state of play within current academic discussion and debate. But even when differences of opinion might be evident within the covers of this book, no view contained in this book falls beyond the diverse bounds of responsible discussion in contemporary academic contexts.

Third, this book is divided into three parts, with each part serving different purposes. The three essays of the first part of the book help to set the scene – with this brief introduction to the study of Paul and his letters being followed by an interpretation of what Paul stood for ("Who Was Paul?" by Paula Fredriksen in Chapter 2) and an overview of the world in which Paul's communities lived ("What Kind of World Did Paul's Communities Live in?" by Richard S. Ascough in Chapter 3).

The second part of the book contains five essays that discuss the thirteen letters within the Pauline corpus. The authors in this second part have been asked to write about two or more letters within their essays, in an effort to help the reader learn through comparison and contrast.

- The first of these essays discusses the texts that, through their commonalities and differences, illustrate various ways in which early forms of Jesus-devotion were relating to their contexts within the Roman world and how Paul addressed particular issues that arose within those communities ("The Thessalonian and Corinthian Letters" by Margaret Y. MacDonald in Chapter 4).
- The two letters that have generated the most theological discourse over the centuries (not least with reference to justification, faith, the law, and sin) are dealt with next ("Galatians and Romans" by Peter Oakes in Chapter 5).
- Two letters written from prison are then given consideration, each being linked further by the fact that they are two of the most personal and autobiographical letters in the Pauline corpus ("Philippians and Philemon" by Douglas A. Campbell in Chapter 6).
- Attention then turns to two letters whose content overlaps significantly in linking both big-picture theology to the practicalities of everyday life in the Roman world ("Colossians and Ephesians" by Sylvia C. Keesmaat in Chapter 7).
- The final chapter of the second part of this book explores the three pastoral letters that give instruction about Christian leadership in the Roman world ("The Pastoral Epistles" by James W. Aageson in Chapter 8).

The eight essays in the third part consider some of the big questions pertaining to Paul's theological discourse – its contours, commitments, and contributions (including its contributions beyond the first-century world).

- The first essay of this section captures Paul's vision of the problems that plague God's world ("What Did Paul Think Is Wrong in God's World?" by Bruce W. Longenecker in Chapter 9).
- The next essay collects a variety of theological threads from Paul's letters to reconstruct the matrix of his theological discourse about God's initiative in Christ ("What Did Paul Think God Is Doing about What's Wrong?" by Michael J. Gorman in Chapter 10).
- Discussing God's initiative in Christ involves further consideration of God's initiatives within communities of Jesus-followers – the

focus of an essay inevitably paired with the previous one ("What Did Paul Think God Is Doing in Christian Communities?" by Susan Grove Eastman in Chapter 11).

- The extent to which Paul's theological discourse was shaped by an engagement with scripture (the Hebrew Bible or Old Testament) is given attention in the subsequent essay ("How Did Paul Read Scripture?" by David Lincicum in Chapter 12).
- A related topic is then treated, examining the complexities of Paul's relationship to his ancestral traditions ("Did Paul Abandon either Judaism or Monotheism?" by Matthew V. Novenson in Chapter 13).
- If Paul's message was "a stumbling block" to some and "foolishness" to others (1 Cor 1:23), the next essay asks what attraction Paul's message might have had for some of his contemporaries in the Roman world ("Why Were People Attracted to Paul's Good News?" by David G. Horrell in Chapter 14).
- Consideration is then given to the recasting of Paul in early Christian literature, noting the different ways in which Paul was remembered and rebranded by others after his death ("How Was the Reception of Paul Shaped in the Early Church?" by Margaret M. Mitchell in Chapter 15).
- A final essay reflects on ways in which Paul's discourse submits contestable, provocative, and perhaps even fruitful theological resources for contemporary theological reflection in the twenty-first century ("What Makes Paul Challenging Today?" by John M. G. Barclay in Chapter 16).

* * *

Over the centuries, many people have admired Paul, many people have found him problematic, many have done both. The chapters of this book have been written for people who want to assess his contributions afresh, exploring the complexities of his letters and deliberating the intricacies of his vision.

Further Reading

Barclay, John M. G. *Paul: A Very Brief History*. London: SPCK, 2018.
Fredriksen, Paula. *Paul, the Pagan's Apostle*. New Haven, CT: Yale University Press, 2017.
Gorman, Michael J. *Apostle of the Crucified Lord: A Theological Introduction to Paul and His Letters*. 2nd ed. Grand Rapids, MI: Eerdmans, 2017.

Gray, Patrick. *Paul as a Problem in History and Culture: The Apostle and His Critics through the Centuries*. Grand Rapids, MI: Baker Academic, 2016.
Horrell, David G. *An Introduction to the Study of Paul*. New York: Bloomsbury T&T Clark, 2015.
Longenecker, Bruce W. and Todd D. Still, *Thinking through Paul: A Survey of His Life, Letters, and Theology*. Grand Rapids, MI: Zondervan, 2014.
Roetzel, Calvin. *The Letters of Paul: Conversations in Context*. Louisville, KY: Westminster John Knox, 2009.
Sanders, E. P. *Paul: The Apostle's Life, Letters, and Thought*. Minneapolis, MN: Fortress Press, 2015.
White, Benjamin L. *Remembering Paul: Ancient and Modern Contests over the Image of the Apostle*. Oxford: Oxford University Press, 2014.

2 Who Was Paul?

PAULA FREDRIKSEN

Paul's letters stand at the heart of the Christian canon. Through his seven uncontested epistles, we can trace the arc of Paul's life from outsider, hostile to the Jesus-movement, to committed insider, dedicated to spreading the "good news of Jesus Christ."[1] Who was Paul? How do we know? And what, through him, can we learn about the message of this late Second Temple Jewish movement that formed in the wake of Jesus of Nazareth's mission and memory? These issues will be explored here by examining four dimensions of Paul's life: Paul the persecutor, Paul the "convert," Paul the apostle, and Paul the persecuted.

PAUL THE PERSECUTOR

It was only midway through his life that Paul adhered to the good news of the crucified and returning messiah. When first encountering that message, he reacted negatively against it (Gal 1:13; 1 Cor 15:9; Phil 3:6). This strong reaction eventually gave way to an equally strong advocacy. If Jesus died about 30 CE, then the change in Paul's attitude probably occurred, at the earliest, about late 32 CE.[2] After that, his trip to Jerusalem to meet with Peter "after three years" (Gal 1:18) would have been in the year 35 or so.

Before the change in Paul's attitude, Damascus seems to have been where his efforts against "the *ekklēsia* of God" were concentrated. After receiving his commission "to proclaim him [God's son] among the

[1] The uncontested letters are (in one reconstruction of their historical sequence): 1 Thessalonians, 1 Corinthians, Galatians, 2 Corinthians, Philippians, Philemon, and Romans.

[2] This allows time for Jesus's original followers to regroup after his execution, to resettle in Jerusalem, to consolidate as a community, and then to conceive the idea of taking the gospel message out on the road beyond Judea and the Galilee to the cities of the Diaspora.

gentiles," Paul narrates his transition from opponent to apostle saying, "I did not confer with flesh and blood, nor did I go up to Jerusalem ... but I went away into [Roman] Arabia, and again *I returned to Damascus*" (Gal 1:16–17). Damascus, then, seems to have been where Paul initially "persecuted" the young assembly.

Even this brief description of a very thin slice of Paul's life raises essential questions both about his hostile past and about his subsequent apostolic mission and message. First, *what* did Paul do in Damascus when he "persecuted the assembly of God to the utmost and tried to destroy it" (Gal 1:13)? And, second, *why* did he do this?

The "What" of "Persecution"

Acts depicts lurid violence against Christ-followers. "Saul" consents to Stephen's lynching (8:1) and later, deputized by the high priest, he tears off from Jerusalem to Damascus, "breathing threats and murder," intending to bind and drag offenders out of their Diaspora homes back to the holy city for punishment (9:1–2).

Luke takes liberties with his topic here that today we would grant only to the historical novelist. No high priest ever had jurisdictional authority over Jewish life in the Diaspora. Moreover, even within Judea vigorous variety flourished among Jews holding differences of opinion, without resorting to "threats and murder." Within Jerusalem itself, Pharisees argued with each other and kept and cultivated practices and beliefs (especially about resurrection) that differed notably from those of aristocratic priestly Sadducees. A short several miles outside of the city, an entire community by the Dead Sea, committed to a revelation of what would happen at the End-Time, generated its own practices, prayers and commentaries, followed a different liturgical calendar, and held the Jerusalem priesthood in contempt. The priests in Jerusalem never lifted a finger against these disputatious others. Whatever actions Paul took against the Christ-assembly in Damascus in the early thirties, then, these were certainly not coordinated with Caiaphas, Jerusalem's then-high priest.

But what would Paul have meant by "persecution" (*diōgmos*)? If not lynchings, coercive violence, and imprisonments (as Acts would have it), then what? Alas, Paul nowhere says. Elsewhere in his letters, however, Paul laments his own hardships as an apostle. "For the sake of Christ, I am content with weaknesses, insults, hardships, persecutions (*diōgmoîs*), and calamities" (2 Cor 12:10). His preceding chapter provides detail:

> Five times I have received at the hands of the Jews forty lashes less one. Three times I have been beaten with rods; once I was stoned. Three times I have been shipwrecked, a night and a day I have been adrift at sea; on frequent journeys, in danger from rivers, danger from robbers, danger from my own people and danger from pagans, danger in the city, in the wilderness, and at sea; danger from false brethren, in toil and hardship. (2 Cor 11:24–27)

Striking in this list is the variety of Paul's "persecutors." More than just Jews reacted negatively to Paul. "Beaten with rods" is a Roman juridical punishment. "Stoning" seems to imply violence performed by an urban mob (cf. "danger in the city"): although the ethnicity of the perpetrators is opaque, Diaspora cities obviously held more non-Jews than Jews (cf. v. 26: "danger from my own people, danger from pagans"). "False brethren" is Paul's term of choice for those other members of the Christ-movement with whom he disagreed (cf. Gal 2:4). He feels threatened by them, too. Strong winds, shipwreck, and high water are suggestive of the domain of lower, hostile gods, about whom Paul elsewhere complains (cf. 2 Cor 4:4; Gal 4:3; 1 Cor 15:24–25).

Most pertinent to our current question about what Paul himself did to "persecute the *ekklēsia*" in Damascus are Paul's own encounters with "the thirty-nine lashes," receiving them no fewer than "five times" (2 Cor 11:24). "Thirty-nine lashes" was specifically an *intra-Jewish* disciplinary practice, derived from Deut 25:1–3. Its social context was the synagogue, which had a consensual authority only over other Jews. Further, those on the receiving end of the lash had to willingly accede to it. (Otherwise, the perceived offender could always just walk away.) "*Punishment implies inclusion.*"[3] If synagogal lashes had been the discipline conferred on Paul by the Jewish community, then perhaps they were the same form of discipline that Paul originally gave to other (Jewish) apostles, acting on behalf of Damascus synagogue authorities. And note that he did so "to the utmost" (*kath' hyperbolēn*; cf. the NRSV's translation, "violently"). To the maximum number of thirty-nine lashes? To the maximum number of perceived offenders? Paul does not say. We cannot know.

[3] E. P. Sanders, *Paul, the Law, and the Jewish People* (Philadelphia: Fortress Press, 1983), 192, italics original. On voluntary submission, Anthony E. Harvey, "Forty Strokes Save One: Social Aspects of Judaizing and Apostasy," in *Alternative Approaches to New Testament Study* (London: SPCK, 1985), 79–86.

The "Why" of "Persecution"

Why did Paul "persecute the assembly (*ekklēsia*)"? What offense had its members committed? And why, later, was he himself persecuted as an apostle of Jesus Christ? Again, he does not say. Absent evidence, speculations abound. Four explanatory scenarios currently predominate: (1) the scandal of the crucified messiah; (2) the scandal of devotional practices; (3) the scandal of legal laxity: Jews mingling with Gentiles; and (4) the scandal of legal laxity: levels of apostolic observance. We consider each of these in turn.

Some scholars contend that the core message of the new movement (the proclamation of a *crucified* messiah) would have religiously scandalized any and all Jews everywhere (cf. 1 Cor 1:23). In Gal 3:13, Paul cited Deut 21:23 ("Cursed be everyone who hangs on a tree") to explain how the blessing of Abraham, through Christ, now encompassed non-Jews as well. Focusing on this verse, scholars have speculated that the message of a messiah dying a shameful death "cursed of God" (and, by implication, of the messiah's himself being accursed by God) was an unthinkably scandalous thought. Paul earlier, and other Jews later, would violently censor any such proclamation.

This "scandal of the crucified messiah" is one of those tropes of New Testament scholarship that refuses to go away, despite all its problems as historical reconstruction. The text of Deuteronomy, first of all, describes not a method of capital punishment (death by hanging) but a post-mortem display of the executed criminal's body, a form of publication of the offender's death. By the first century of the Roman period, "hanging on a tree" could indeed refer to crucifixion.[4] But outside of Paul's snarled passage in Galatians, no Jewish source speaks of hanging in general or of crucifixion in particular as signaling death under a divine curse.

Other Jewish texts actually belie this interpretation. 2 Samuel recounts that the bodies of Saul and of Jonathan were hanged, but nowhere in this text or in any other is this taken to imply that the two men died a death cursed by God (2 Sam 21:12). Closer to our period, Josephus relates the deaths of thousands by crucifixion. The Hasmonean king Alexander Janneus crucified eight hundred Pharisees (AJ 13.380). Later, Rome similarly executed Judah the Galilean's sons (AJ 20.102). During the troubles after Herod the Great's death, the Roman legate Varus crucified two thousand rebels in Judea (BJ 2.75; AJ 17.295).

[4] We see this interpretation, for instance, in the Dead Sea Scrolls, 11Q Temple.

And prosecuting the siege of Jerusalem in 70, Titus affixed thousands of Jews to crosses outside of the city walls (BJ 5.449–51). But Josephus says nothing about a divine curse, and neither does anyone else.

In brief, nothing in Judaism holds that a man who died by crucifixion was therefore cursed by God, and we have no evidence of any Jews ever having done so. The experience of the original apostolic community, moreover, presents further counter-evidence: it resided in Jerusalem for decades largely unmolested by Jewish religious authorities, and it too proclaimed a crucified messiah. Paul's deployment of Deut 21:23 to construct a sequence of verbal chiasms around the idea of blessing and curse should not and cannot be generalized into a widespread (and only seemingly explanatory) Jewish fixed idea. The argument that first-century Jews everywhere would be actively and aggressively scandalized by the message of a crucified messiah should be retired from introductory books on Paul (like this one) and from New Testament scholarship *in toto*.

Perhaps the scandal involved devotional practices – a second explanatory interpretation. If actions speak louder than words, then possibly it was not only the gospel message, or claims made about Jesus as messiah, that scandalized the larger Jewish community in Damascus ca. 32 and prompted opposition there. The devotional behaviors associated with that message may have inspired these other Jews to oppose evangelizing apostles. Practices of Christ-devotion included the assembly's ritual acclamation of Jesus as "lord," with a connotation usually reserved in scripture for God (Phil 2:10–11); giving benedictions intimately linking Christ and God (Rom 16:20); summoning and calling upon Jesus in group worship (*Marana tha*!, "our lord, come!"; 1 Cor 16:22) and being immersed in his name as the entrance ritual for believers (e.g., 1 Cor 1:2; Rom 10:9–13). This "binitarian" or "dyadic" worship pattern of prayer and praise happened so early (as Paul's initial hostility witnesses) and so intensely that it might fairly be deemed a "radical mutation" that seemed to other Jews to trespass the bounds of normative cultic practices.[5]

This conjecture explains both Paul's giving and getting the lashes: such devotional practices seem implicitly to elevate Jesus's divine status to uncomfortable heights. Complicating this conjecture, however, is one thing that we know and one thing that we do not know.

[5] For these early devotional practices and their implicit Christology, see especially Larry Hurtado, *Lord Jesus Christ: Devotion to Jesus in Earliest Christianity* (Grand Rapids, MI: Eerdmans, 2003).

What we *do* know is that Second Temple Judaism evinced belief in a wide variety of divine mediatory figures: archangels, divine-human hybrids, the super-celestial population of God's heavenly court. In magical texts, these figures, too, are summoned, not unlike how Jesus Christ is summoned by members of the *ekklēsia*. Some Diaspora synagogue manumission inscriptions even call upon *pagan* gods as witnesses.[6] Late Second Temple Judaism, in short, seems to have been comfortable with a broad range of divine beings, some of whom functioned in ways not unlike Jesus Christ in groups of his followers.

What we do *not* know is the actual devotional practices that were enacted on these occasions in comparable Jewish groups: exorcizing demons, casting spells, freeing slaves. Absent that knowledge, we cannot build a clear picture of "normative" Jewish cultic practice. And finally, once again, we have the counter-example of the Jerusalem community, the early and original source of this "dyadic" devotion. No Christ-follower there was ever subject to thirty-nine lashes – a disciplinary option that the city's religious authorities had forty years to exercise. Evidently the community's pattern of devotion was never thought to fall beyond the bounds of acceptability within the broader context of Jewish liturgical practices.

A third interpretation sees the scandal to involve legal laxity, as Jewish Christ-followers had close social interaction with gentile Christ-followers. If Christ-following Jews were mingling with, praying with, and eating together with the uncircumcised (so goes this argument), that activity would have scandalized the broader Jewish community (cf. Gal 2:11–13). The synagogue in Damascus regarded this inter-ethnic mixing as an intolerable social and religious affront, and Paul reacted accordingly by disciplining them; later, Diaspora synagogue communities, for the same reason, "persecuted" (that is, disciplined) him.

This "explanation" stumbles fatally against all of the other notable data evincing the extent to which Jews mixed with non-Jews throughout the Hellenistic and Roman periods – not only within Diaspora synagogues, but also (before 70) within Jerusalem's temple complex itself. For that matter, their Diaspora cities of residence were themselves premier pagan religious institutions. Jews living there mingled intimately with their pagan neighbors: in public baths, in gymnasia, in

[6] Synagogue inscriptional material, with discussion, is reviewed in Lee I. Levine, *The Ancient Synagogue: The First Thousand Years* (New Haven: Yale University Press, 2000), and in Irena Levinskaya, *The Book of Acts in Its Diaspora Setting* (Grand Rapids, MI: Eerdmans, 1996).

theaters and stadia and amphitheaters (as actors, athletes, and gladiators, not only as spectators), in hippodromes and in urban libraries, odeons, and museums, and at the meals regularly given by various trade associations.

Moreover, evidence both literary and inscriptional, both Jewish and pagan, conveys a picture of active gentile involvement in and benefaction to these Diaspora Jewish communities. Pagan sponsors built and refurbished synagogue structures; they subvened Jewish charities; they participated in Jewish festivals;[7] they sent votive offerings to the temple in Jerusalem. No less a pagan than the divine emperor Augustus paid for sacrifices on his own behalf to be offered at the temple's altar (Philo, *Embassy to Gaius*, 317). And Jews as soldiers, athletes, spectators, ephebes (young men in civic and military training), and town councillors would have been present at pagan liturgical acts, most specifically at sacrifices to urban or imperial deities.

In brief, Jews and pagans throughout the ancient Mediterranean routinely interacted socially and, thus, what we would term "religiously" – in Jerusalem and its temple precincts; in Judean cities such as Caesarea; in the cities of the western Diaspora. Why, then, would the synagogue, whether in Damascus or anywhere else, object specifically to the *ekklēsia*'s very same social permeability? The fact that gentiles were present in Diaspora Christ-assemblies explains nothing about synagogue resistance to and rejection of the gospel.[8]

Then perhaps the scandal was a different kind of legal laxity, one that involved levels of apostolic observance – a fourth common interpretation. In this view, the problem was that Christ-following apostles, speaking to gentiles as well as to fellow Jews, were lax in their personal observance of Jewish law.[9] Such Jews would accordingly be regarded as "sinners" by their more rigorous coreligionists. As such, they would have been the object of muscular disapprobation – in Paul's language, they (and later he) would have been "persecuted."

This explanation for synagogue resistance to the gospel relies upon an idea of consistent and trans-local standards of Jewish practice. But local variety and variability characterized Jewish life whether in the

[7] For example, consider the Alexandrian "interfaith" meal celebrating the translation of Jewish scriptures into Greek mentioned by Philo, *Life of Moses*, 2.41.

[8] On this inter-ethnic, thus inter-religious Mediterranean mixing, see Paula Fredriksen, *Paul: The Pagans' Apostle* (New Haven, CT: Yale University Press, 2017), 32–60.

[9] Some scholars, such as Martin Hengel, ascribe such lax practices specifically to the "Hellenists," that is, to the Greek-speaking Jews resident in Jerusalem and represented in Acts particularly by Stephen.

Diaspora or in Judea alone. Sadducees had major disagreements with Pharisees, who themselves were split on how to interpret the law, while the community of the Dead Sea busily developed its own traditions and practices, and the more learned questioned the practices of the un(der) educated "people of the land" (*amme ha-aretz*). None of these significant differences, whether theological or practical (such as whether to follow a lunar or a solar calendar) led to violent confrontation or to juridical punishments. As in the homeland, so too in the Diaspora: some Jews did things in one way, others in another way.[10] Different Jews, in antiquity no less than now, interpreted Jewish ancestral traditions differently. Diversity of practice was not the exception but the rule.

We are still left, then, with pressing questions that none of these four prominent interpretations satisfactorily explain: Why did Paul persecute fellow Jews who were members of the early Jesus assembly in Damascus? And why, later, did diaspora synagogue communities persecute him? Attempts to reconstruct a plausible and a specifically *intra-Jewish* reason for the administration of the thirty-nine lashes have foundered once we placed Paul's own letters within the context of what we know from other sources about ancient diaspora communities, and about Mediterranean urban society more generally.

This then allows us to frame the question differently: Did Jewish opponents of the early gospel movement *share* motivations with those other "persecutors" whom Paul names: Roman magistrates, pagan city-dwellers, rival apostles, and pagan gods? As we follow Paul from Damascus out into the broader Greek-speaking Diaspora, we will investigate his relations with all of these various antagonists, in the effort to find an answer to this question. But before that, a prior question looms: How did Paul come to realign his allegiances so radically in the first place?

PAUL THE "CONVERT"

Into Paul's synagogue community, sometime in the early 30s of the first century, came apostles proclaiming the good news: Jesus the messiah had been crucified, then raised from the dead, and was *therefore* shortly to return to establish God's kingdom. These emissaries of the new messianic movement would have formed a small assembly within the larger urban Jewish community comprising themselves, some local Jews, and perhaps some local gentiles variously affiliated with the

[10] This is evident, for instance, from Philo, on no less essential an issue than Jewish circumcision (*Migration of Abraham*, 89–93).

synagogue. Presumably as an agent of the synagogue authorities, Paul would have "persecuted" the Jewish members of this group, subjecting them to disciplinary lashing.

But then, unexpectedly, Paul received his own vision of the risen Christ. It transformed him from adversary to apostle. Indeed, he insisted in his letter to the Galatians (dictated some twenty-plus years after the event), that God's purpose in revealing Christ "his son" to Paul was specifically so that Paul "might proclaim him among the gentiles" (Gal 1:16). His vision of Christ, his allegiance to the gospel, and his vocation to summon the nations came all at once (or so Paul implies).

What was this vision? What sort of experience did Paul undergo? In Galatians, he says elliptically only that God revealed "his son in me" (*en emoi*): an interior, psychological event might seem to be implied (such as that conveyed by Caravaggio's famous painting, *The Conversion of St. Paul*). In 1 Corinthians, however, Paul emphasizes visual experience, "seeing." The risen Christ "was seen" by Peter, then by a series of other witnesses and, "last of all ... he was seen by me" (1 Cor 15:8). "Have I not seen Jesus our Lord?" (1 Cor 9:1). This language implies a visual object.

What did Paul think that he saw? He does not say. We need to infer from other places in Paul's letters where he speaks of Jesus and of raised bodies. In Philippians, Paul describes Jesus as having preexisted super-celestially, "in the form of [a] god" (Phil 2:6), which might imply an angelic, glorious body.[11] Whatever and however he imagined this glorious superhuman substance to be, that was how Paul "saw" the risen Christ – not in a body of "flesh and blood" (a concept that Paul heatedly rejects, 1 Cor 15:50), but in a "spiritual body" (*sōma pneumatikon*, 1 Cor 15:44–50). Christ's earthly body (Phil 2:7–8), through resurrection, had transformed from flesh and blood (back?) into a rarefied material substance, *pneuma*, "spirit" – the same sort of body that those "in Christ," whether living or dead, Paul insists, would also attain once Christ returned (1 Cor 15:51–54).

Church tradition has long identified Paul's visionary experience and change of heart as his "conversion." That word choice complicates historical reconstruction. Conversion implies that Paul had two clearly demarcated religious choices before him, Judaism and Christianity, and that his vision moved him from the former to the latter. In becoming Christianity's premier convert, Paul thereby becomes, as well,

[11] For this translation of Phil 2:6, see Fredriksen, *Paul*, 133–141; on angelic body, see Paul Holloway, *Philippians* (Minneapolis, MN: Fortress Press, 2017), 114–124.

religiously, an "ex"-Jew or, at least, an ex-Pharisee (Phil 3:6; cf. Gal 1:14). Drawing on all the harsh things that Paul has to say about the law throughout his letters, many scholars accordingly assume that Paul himself, after his conversion, repudiated Jewish practices. To be a Christian meant and means to abandon the observance of Jewish law.

But in the early thirties of the first century, and in fact for the whole course of Paul's lifetime, Christianity as a movement separate from and even antagonistic toward Judaism did not yet exist. There was, then, no entity separate from Judaism for Paul to convert to. For this reason, prominent scholars in the twentieth century issued a fundamental challenge to this traditional construct of conversion when interpreting Paul's experience. Emphasizing the vibrant eschatology of the first generation of the Jesus-movement, which expected Christ's return within its own lifetime, Albert Schweitzer, Johannes Munck, and Krister Stendahl urged that the gospel represented an apocalyptic form of Judaism, not a new and different religion outside of and opposed to it. Munck and Stendahl further argued that Paul's own language indicates that he thought of his apostleship not as involving a change of religion but as a prophetic "call" or "commission" like that of Isaiah (Isa 49:1–6) and of Jeremiah (Jer 1:4). Paul asserted that God "called" him (*kalesas,* Gal 1:5) to preach the good news about the impending return of the eschatological messiah, David's "son" and thus the "son" of Israel's god.[12]

Joining this movement did entail a radical adjustment for pagans, of course. They changed gods; they ceased sacrificing before their images and ceased participating in urban cults; and they assumed new behaviors. For Jews, however, joining the Jesus-movement involved something more like a shift in perspective, and the adoption of a foreshortened timeframe, since what they expected to happen at the End-Time was said to already be happening among them. So too for Paul: even after his life-changing vision, Paul worshiped the same god as before; he read the same scriptures as before; and he valued the same ethical standards as before. And, without the presupposition that being a Christ-follower is intrinsically incompatible with Jewish practice, there is no reason to think that Paul did not continue to live according to the same ancestral traditions as before. He speaks of himself as an Israelite, a biological descendant of Abraham, a member of the tribe of

[12] For a review of a century of scholarship on this issue, see Paula Fredriksen, "Paul the 'Convert'?," in *The Oxford Handbook of Pauline Studies*, eds. R. Barry Matlock and M. Novenson (Oxford: Oxford University Press, forthcoming).

Benjamin, a Hebrew, a Pharisee, and an exemplarily zealous keeper of Jewish traditions (Rom 11:1; Phil 3:5; Gal 1:14). He nowhere renounces these identities; he simply values their benefits less than he values "the surpassing worth of knowing Christ Jesus my lord" (Phil 3:8). Paul valued Christ more than anything else, but that does not mean that he jettisoned everything else.[13]

If we suppose that Paul continued to live as a Jew, why did he speak so harshly about Jewish law? He says that the law effects a curse (Gal 3:10–14); it is a form of slavery (Gal 4 passim); it is a medium of selfish desire, sin, and death (Rom 7). Yet Paul also speaks very positively of Jewish law. It is one of Israel's divinely granted privileges (Rom 9:4); it is the measure of community love and the standard for community decency even for gentiles (Rom 13:8–9; 1 Cor 7:19); it is a pathway to Christ (Rom 10:4). "The law is holy, and the commandment is holy and just and good" (Rom 7:12). Though at one point Paul says that no one is made righteous before God by the law (Gal 3:11), at another point he says that he himself was "blameless" with respect to just such righteousness (Phil 3:6).

What role, then, does Jewish law play in Paul's gospel? What was this great apostle to the gentiles saying to gentiles? And for that matter, why was he taking this Jewish message to gentiles to begin with?

PAUL THE APOSTLE

Two recent trends in Pauline scholarship have helped to resolve the seeming paradox of Paul's attitude toward Jewish law and, thus, have helped to clarify Paul's own practice of Jewish law: attention to Paul's rhetoric, and attention to ancient constructions of peoplehood, "ethnicity."

The rhetorical work has taken seriously the fact that Paul addressed all of his extant letters to gentiles. Jewish law affects Jews and non-Jews in radically different ways, Paul insists. But why should this be so? To answer this question, we first must consider our English translation of Paul's Greek term, *ethnē*. Up to this point in this essay, I have toggled

[13] 1 Cor 9:20–21 is often read as if Paul easily slipped between identities, acting "as if" a Jew or a gentile in order to "win" some from each group. But while no one thinks that Paul sacrificed to pagan gods while becoming "as one outside the Law" (v. 21), many assume that Paul's acting "as a Jew" implies that, otherwise (that is, when not pitching to Jews), Paul was not Law-observant. This to me seems to rest on a prior presupposition, namely that law-observance is intrinsically incompatible with "Christian" belief. I will address this presupposition further below.

between translating *ethnē* as "nations," "gentiles," and "pagans." But the connotations of these three English terms differ in ways that matter acutely for understanding Paul.

The words "nations" and "gentiles" seem to imply religiously neutral ethnicity: the people so described are simply not Jews. In Paul's lifetime, however, there was no such thing as a religiously neutral ethnicity. In the ancient Mediterranean, gods came bundled together with places and peoples. To put this point otherwise: peoples were born into their relations with, and thus their obligations to, their gods – as indeed Jews were to theirs. Gods and their humans formed family groups, in which gods were the senior members to whom correct deference and the display of affection and respect were due. Ancestral customs (or what moderns think of as "religion") choreographed these protocols of respect. Pantheons were an ethnic patrimony.

In other words, for ancient peoples, ethnicity coordinated heaven and earth.[14] Citizens of cities considered themselves family, both "horizontally" (in relation to human contemporaries) and "vertically" (in relation to their ancestors and gods). Particularly in the urban context, gods were important celestial patrons, attending to the well-being of the city to the degree that the city solicited their good will (through urban festivals, sacrifices and liturgies). Alexandrians worshiped Alexandrian gods. Romans worshiped Roman gods. Athenians worshiped Athenian gods. In short, and *by definition,* non-Jews worshiped non-Jewish gods. For these reasons, when translating Paul's letters, *ethnē* is best rendered not by the religion-neutral term "gentiles," but by the religion-specific term "*pagans*."

The Synagogue Context

How then should we regard the *theosebeis*, the "god-fearers" who, as non-Jews, participated variously in synagogue life? These god-fearers were active pagans – priests in the imperial cult, town councilors responsible for urban liturgies. Acts delicately avoids mentioning that these Judaizing "gentiles" were pagans, and this reticence has confused historical scholarship to no end. Many scholars have simply assumed that if gentiles frequented synagogues, then of course they would have stopped worshiping idols and their own native gods – whether on their own initiative or by demand of the Jewish congregation. But as our wealth of synagogue inscriptions and literary evidence attests, this is

[14] Paula Fredriksen, "How Jewish Is God? Divine Ethnicity in Paul's Theology," *Journal of Biblical Literature* 137 (2018): 193–212.

nonsense. God-fearers were Judaizing *pagans* – ethnic and religious outsiders who voluntarily associated, in ad hoc ways, with Diaspora synagogues. They simply added the Jews' god to their native pantheons.[15]

Synagogues evidently had no problem with such arrangements. Diaspora communities not only welcomed such sympathetic pagans: they publicly acknowledged them, leaving the record of their gratitude in mosaic and on stone. No pressure was brought to bear on these Judaizing outsiders to make an exclusive commitment to the Jewish god. (Later Christian authors criticize synagogues for this.) If pagan men did wish to make such a commitment, they underwent proselyte circumcision, thereby "becoming" Jews of a special sort.[16] Most pagans, however, affiliated with synagogue communities *as* pagans. This was a very long-lived and socially stable arrangement: from the Hellenistic period on through centuries after the accession of Constantine, synagogues continued to accommodate sympathetic outsiders.

But in first-century rural Judea and Galilee (Jesus's regular ambit), pagans had been thin on the ground. Jesus of Nazareth had taken his message of the impending Kingdom of God for the most part exclusively to fellow Jews. The variegated traditions associated with this eschatological expectation had relevance for pagans as well: the triumph of good over evil; the revelation of the messiah (in those texts that mention a messiah); the resurrection of the dead; the judgment of the wicked; the ingathering of the exiles and restoration of Israel to its Davidic plenum of twelve tribes; the final glorification of Jerusalem and especially of the temple. At the End-Time, when God established his rule, sang inclusive prophetic texts, pagans too would play a part. "All the *ethnē* and tongues" would stream to God's "holy mountain, Jerusalem"; this was foreseen by Isaiah, with the phrase "all the *ethnē*" referencing the seventy nations descended from Noah, as enumerated in Genesis 10 (Isa 66:18–20). At the End-Time, all humanity together, both Israel and the nations, would gather in the temple.[17]

[15] Fredriksen, *Paul*, 49–60; Fredriksen, "If It Looks Like a Duck, and It Quacks Like a Duck . . . : On *Not* Giving Up the Godfearers," in *A Most Reliable Witness: Essays in Honor of Ross Shepard Kraemer*, eds. Susan Ashbrook Harvey et al. (Providence, RI: Brown Judaic Studies, 2015), 25–34.

[16] Pagan women "became" Jews through marriage (the biblical paradigm), as well as by assuming Jewish practices.

[17] On the eschatological plenum of humanity, see especially James M. Scott, *Paul and the Nations: The Old Testament and Jewish Background of Paul's Mission to the*

With God's final revelation, in other words, pagans would smash their idols and turn to worship Israel's god alone (e.g., Tobit 14:6). In some iterations of this story line, even the pagans' gods would join in the worship of Israel's god: "All gods bow down before him" (Ps 97:7). This turning of the pagan nations would be a capstone End-Time miracle. In his mission, Jesus had concentrated on Jews. God himself would take care of the pagans. Jesus had framed no "gentile policy."[18]

Neither did that small society, post-resurrection, that gathered around the memory of Jesus's mission and message. Nor, as long as they stayed in Jerusalem, would they have had to: the city's population was overwhelmingly Jewish. Eventually, however, some members of this messianic community took the message of the Kingdom, now linked with expectations of Jesus's glorious second coming (his *parousia*) into new territory: the great coastal cities, like Joppa and Caesarea, and on into the cities of the Greek-speaking West. Working their way via the network of urban Jewish communities in the mixed cities of the Diaspora, these apostles encountered something previously unknown to them: pagans present in synagogue communities too.[19]

It is on this sociohistorical point that our literary, epigraphical, and archaeological evidence converges to support the depiction of Paul's mission in Acts, and helps us to read Paul's own letters in their historical context. As soon as the Christ-apostles went out from Jerusalem to other (mixed) urban synagogues, they would have encountered these Judaized pagans – pagans, that is, who *as pagans*, through their contact with these synagogue communities, would have been familiar to some degree with biblical terms and concepts, and piously inclined toward Israel's god in some fashion or other. The post-crucifixion movement that formed around Jesus's mission and message, in other words, did not have to wait for Paul to become involved with interested gentiles. These populations were already there, in the Diaspora synagogue communities that served as the gospel's conduits. This would eventually grow to become the "gentile mission" – the particular focus of Paul's efforts by mid-century, as

Nations with Special Reference to the Destination of Galatians (Tübingen: Mohr Siebeck, 1995).

18 Of course, the four canonical gospel writers told the story of Jesus's life in ways that tipped its relevance to the later gentile communities of Christ-followers.

19 On the ways that the seriatim delays of the *parousia* eventually propelled the good news out from Jerusalem, see Paula Fredriksen, *When Christians Were Jews: The First Generation* (New Haven, CT: Yale University Press, 2018), 74–143.

well the focus of his competitors, the apostles advocating proselyte circumcision. What we think of as "the gentile mission" was an early if inadvertent side effect of the movement's spread through Diaspora synagogues.

In his own letters, Paul nowhere states forthrightly that he evangelized within synagogue networks. This has left some scholars to surmise that he recruited pagans in other ways, perhaps simply by holding forth in various urban public venues or by waiting for them to wander in while he sat at work. Were that the case, he would have been making things much more difficult for himself than they needed to be. Why start from scratch, explaining to non-oriented pagans the identity of Israel's god, or the importance of Jewish scripture or of the figure of Abraham or of David or of a messiah, or the idea of the resurrection of the dead, when Diaspora synagogues already held a Judaized pagan population who could attend to the gospel message with a much higher level of understanding?

Also, Paul's letters do convey oblique acknowledgments of synagogue activities. He received synagogue disciplinary lashing at least five times (2 Cor 11:24). In the Diaspora, he interacted with Jews both within the Jesus-movement (2 Cor 11:22–23; Gal 2 passim, Antioch) and outside of it (1 Cor 9:20; cf. 2 Cor 11:26). He conceptualized the message of the movement as "good news" for Jews first as well as for gentiles (Rom 1:16; 2:9–10). By mid-century, Paul may have seen himself as preeminently the "apostle ... [to] all the [gentile] nations" (Rom 1:1–6); but along the way, he certainly interacted with, and evangelized, fellow Jews also. It would have been very odd indeed if Paul regarded the coming of Israel's messiah as good news only for pagans: the impending establishment of God's kingdom was good news for Jews as well. The trans-local matrix for all of these multi-ethnic interactions was to be found in the indigenous synagogues that throve in the rich religious ecosystem of Mediterranean culture.

Ethnic Essentialism

"We are Jews *physei*," Paul said to Peter in Antioch, "and not gentile sinners" (Gal 2:15). The New Revised Standard Version translates the Greek word *physei* as "by birth." What that word means, however, is "by nature" (*physis*). For Paul as for most of his contemporaries, a human group, an *ethnos* or *genos*, had certain hardwired characteristics: different peoples were what they were and behaved as they behaved because that was their "nature." Classical ethnographers tirelessly stereotyped the behaviors of different foreign groups. People were as they were because that's how they were. Even the stereotypes were stereotyped.[20]

As Paul's statement to Peter reveals, Paul thought of pagans as sinners "by nature," and he assumed that Peter would agree with him. Pagans worshiped gods other than the god of Israel, and they did so by making offerings before images ("idols" in the language of Jewish anti-pagan rhetoric). In the biblical view, this fundamental act of religious malfeasance, which was seen as descriptive of the entire non-Jewish world, invariably led to a cascade of other sins: sexual misconduct (*porneia*), lying, theft, violence, murder, sacrilege. Time and again in his letters, in long, lush sin lists, Paul indicts pagans for these behaviors (Rom 1:18–32; 1 Cor 9:9–11; Gal 5:19–21).

Paul's moralizing represents one extreme of a spectrum of Jewish attitudes toward pagan culture. It was not the only one. Jews in the western empire also greatly admired the Greeks. Many got good gymnasium educations, mastered the curriculum, forged Homeric hexameters praising Jewish cult and culture, took Greek names, and gave philosophy the ultimate compliment, claiming its origins for themselves. Pious legend sanctioned the translation of Israel's scriptures into Greek. Synagogue and city provided wide zones of social and religious interaction between pagans and Jews.[21]

But Paul's apocalyptic framework precluded such comfortable intercultural ecumenism. He thinks and speaks urgently, prophetically. As with his great scriptural mentor and model, Isaiah, so also with Paul: his intense apocalyptic expectation propelled his high-contrast depiction of Israel and the nations. The narrative function of the pagan nations in apocalyptic traditions is precisely to represent "*not*-Israel" – that is, all those other peoples who have not known God and who do not know God but who will come to know God at the End-Time. This theological distinction, in short, echoes and even emphasizes this ethnic distinction.

[20] Gideon Bohak, "The Ibis and the Jewish Question: Ancient 'Anti-Semitism' in Historical Context," in *Jews and Gentiles in the Holy Land in the Days of the Second Temple, the Mishnah and the Talmud: A Collection of Articles* (Jerusalem: Yad Ben-Zvi Press, 2003), 27–43; Benjamin H. Isaac, *The Invention of Racism in Classical Antiquity* (Princeton, NJ: Princeton University Press, 2004).

[21] See especially Erich S. Gruen's two studies, *Heritage and Hellenism: The Reinvention of Jewish Tradition* (Berkeley, CA: University of California Press, 1998), and *Diaspora: Jews amidst Greeks and Romans* (Cambridge, MA: Harvard University Press, 2002).

Paul's prophetically-girded ethnic essentialism in turn accounts for all the negative things that he has to say about pagans, about the law, and most emphatically, about proselyte circumcision. Left to their own devices, pagans worship idols, indulge in bad sex, lead distempered family and social lives, and in general behave abominably (e.g., Rom 1:18–32, though cf. 2:14–15). All such behaviors, starting with worshiping "false" gods and idols, are condemned by Jewish law.

But what if a pagan attempts to live according to the precepts of Jewish law (as, for example, a god-fearer might do)? What if, indeed, he even goes so far as to receive proselyte circumcision, through this ritual act changing ethnicity and "becoming" a Jew? These circumstances, interestingly, call forth Paul's harshest statements about the law. In his letters, all of which were addressed to the *ex*-pagan pagans of the Jesus-movement, Paul stridently insists that the law is a curse – that is, a curse *for gentiles/pagans.* The law brings death – *for gentiles/pagans.* The law only makes sin worse – *for gentiles/pagans.*

Even more extreme (and indeed, a minority opinion within Roman-period Judaism and thereafter), Paul the ethnic essentialist rejects proselyte circumcision as a means for a male pagan to become a Jew, for two reasons. First, according to the law, covenantal circumcision occurs on the male's eighth day of life (cf. Phil 3:4, boasting of his own eighth-day circumcision); by contrast, an adult pagan deciding to convert to Judaism clearly does so long after this mandated period. Second, for Paul ethnicity is hardwired, *physei.*[22] This sheds light on Paul's comment in Rom 2:17 regarding the non-Jew who "calls [him]self a Jew." This person, presumably a gentile who has received circumcision, nonetheless invariably and inevitably commits "gentile/pagan" sins (Rom 2:21–26, a reprise of the "pagan" sins listed in Romans 1). Even if such a person "knows the law," he still, helplessly, violates the law (the rhetorical "I" of Romans 7). For Paul, circumcision cannot "fix" gentile nature.[23]

In other words, Paul does not reject (proselyte) circumcision because he thought that pagans *should not* become Jews. Paul rejects such circumcision because he thought that pagans *could not* become Jews. Even when pagans receive circumcision, they are still pagans "by

[22] Even when, through Christ, the ex-pagan is grafted into the olive tree (of Israel? of eschatological redemption?), he is engrafted *para physin*, "against nature" (Rom 11:24).

[23] Matthew Thiessen, *Paul and the Gentile Problem* (Oxford: Oxford University Press, 2016); Matthew V. Novenson, "The Self-Styled Jew of Romans 2 and the Actual Jews of Romans 9–11," in *The So-Called Jew in Paul's Letter to the Romans*, eds. Rafael Rodriguez and Matthew Thiessen (Minneapolis, MN: Fortress, 2016), 133–162.

nature." By mid-century other apostles of Christ were making inroads into Paul's ex-pagan communities, as we see, for instance, in his letter to the Galatians. This development drove Paul to the intemperate language of that letter. But his reasoning on proselyte circumcision emerges more calmly elsewhere – in both 1 Corinthians and Romans.

In 1 Cor 7:18–19 (a much-misinterpreted passage), Paul states:

> Was anyone called who was already circumcised? Let him not surgically remove his circumcision. Was anyone called while in foreskin? Let him not seek circumcision. Circumcision is nothing, and foreskin is nothing. What matters is keeping God's commandments.

Circumcision, of course, *is* one of God's commandments – to Israel (Gen 17:14). And as we know from his remarks in Philippians, Paul thought highly of his own circumcision (3:4). Speaking specifically of Jews and Judaism in Romans, Paul says, "What is the advantage of the Jew? What is the value of circumcision? Much in every way" (Rom 3:1–2). And in the same letter he asserts that the law is one of the divinely-granted privileges that distinguishes Israelites, his "family" (*syngeneis*, Rom 9:4). In 1 Corinthians 7, then, Paul is not talking about Jews (those who were "already circumcised") and gentiles (those "in foreskin"); instead, *he is talking about two different kinds of ex-pagan Christ-followers*. Some of these at some earlier point had received proselyte circumcision; some had not. Both kinds of ex-pagans were now enabled to fulfill the law ("keeping God's commandments") by being in Christ (cf. Rom 13:8–9, where Paul lists laws from the Ten Commandments). Circumcision had not enabled them to do so; the spirit of Christ did.

Paul's mid-century mission, in his own view, uniquely enabled ex-pagan pagans to become law-obedient. In this sense, Paul's was a *Judaizing* mission. Through his work, he gets pagans to live according to the standards of idealized Jewish behaviors: chaste marriages, self-control, community consciousness, generous charitable giving.[24] Unlike the pagans who do not know God, Paul's ex-pagan pagans have "turned to God from idols, to serve the living and true god, and to wait for his son from heaven" (1 Thess 1:9). And especially in respect of the first two of Sinai's Ten Commandments (to have no other gods and to shun the worship of images – that is, idols), Paul's gospel was precisely *not* "law-free." During the brief charismatic interval between Christ's resurrection and his victorious Second Coming, Paul's gospel was producing "eschatological gentiles" in

[24] On Paul and generosity, see Bruce W. Longenecker, *Remember the Poor: Paul, Poverty, and the Greco-Roman World* (Grand Rapids, MI: Eerdmans, 2010).

advance of the Kingdom. Their very existence validated his conviction that the End-Time was truly, rapidly approaching – "closer to us now," he taught in Romans, "than when we first became convinced. The night is far gone. The Day is at hand" (Rom 13:11–12).

These eschatological gentiles were, before the coming of the Jesus-movement, only an apocalyptic trope, and an apocalyptic hope. Convinced by his vision of the risen Christ that the eschatological kingdom was about to dawn (e.g., 1 Cor 15 passim), Paul was only further confirmed in his conviction by the radical reformation of gentiles that the spirit, through his mission, was bringing into being.

These gentiles represent the "new creation" – a theme that Paul uses to conclude his letter to the Galatians: "Circumcision is not anything, neither is foreskin anything, but *kainê ktisis*, new creation" (Gal 6:15). Paul here speaks, again, not of Jews ("circumcision") and gentiles ("foreskin"); instead, he speaks of *proselyte*, that is, of gentile circumcision – the topic of this whole radioactively angry letter. The *only* way to affect this new gentile creation, Paul was convinced, was Paul's way – after all, it was for this purpose that God had formed him in his mother's womb (Gal 1:14; cf. Rom 1:1–6). Gentiles could be eschatologically re-formatted *not* by flesh (the site of circumcision), he insisted, but only through and by spirit, infused through immersion. According to flesh (*kata sarka*), gentiles were intrinsically of a different family. But according to spirit (*kata pneuma*), they could be brought into God's family. Spirit effected "adoption as sons" (*huiothesia*). On this most crucial aspect of his idiosyncratically Jewish message, Paul thought like a Roman – which, of course, he also was.[25]

The Spirit of Sonship

Roman legal culture had long availed itself of a particular form of fictive kinship – sons not begotten could nonetheless be made by means of adoption. This was a way to settle and to stabilize the next generation of "family." At issue were questions of the legal inheritance of property,

[25] J. Albert Harrill, *Paul the Apostle: His Life and Legacy in Their Roman Context* (Cambridge: Cambridge University Press, 2012). Paul is not gender-inclusivist here (or anywhere); at issue is specifically *male* legal inheritance. See Caroline Johnson Hodge, *If Sons, then Heirs: A Study of Kinship and Ethnicity in the Letters of Paul* (Oxford: Oxford University Press, 2007). On ex-pagan pagans (only) as the Pauline *kainē ktisis*, see Paula Fredriksen, "'Circumcision is Nothing and Foreskin is Nothing': A Non-Reformation Reading of Paul's Letters," *Protestant Bible Scholarship: Antisemitism, Philosemitism and Anti-Judaism*, edited Arjen Bakker, René Bloch, Yael Fisch, Paula Fredriksen and Hindy Najman, JSJ Supplements (Leiden: Brill, forthcoming 2020).

and of the continuation of lineage through the creation of "new" ancestry for the adopted son, which entailed new obligations to the patrilineal cult. Paul creatively repurposed these Roman legal protocols to articulate Jewish eschatological ends.

Israel was (already) God's "son," and God was (already) Israel's "father." Paul simply repeats and assumes this biblical commonplace in Romans 9:4. In terms of earthly lineage, Israel "according to the flesh" had descended from "the forefathers": Abraham, Isaac, Jacob, and the eponymous founders of the twelve tribes. To this family God had given many irrevocable gifts and had made many promises (Rom 9:6; 11:29). Indeed, the reason that Christ had come, Paul insisted, was on account of God's truth, to confirm God's promises to Israel (15:8) – including the promise of final redemption. Gentiles, by contrast, had no "fleshly" connection (that is, family connection) to Israel. Toward them, God acted with mercy (15:9). Through immersion into Christ, ex-pagan pagans in Pauline communities received *pneuma*, variously described as the "spirit of God" or as the "spirit of Christ" or simply as "holy spirit." Spirit made "sons."

The spirit changed everything. By receiving the "spirit of adoption," these ex-pagans became adopted "brothers" (*adelphoi*) of Christ, pneumatically knit into Abraham's lineage. (Jews already shared a family relation with Christ, Rom 9:6.) This eschatological "son-making" (*huiothesia*) rendered these ex-pagans (now as adopted sons) equally legitimate heirs to the redemptive promise God had made to Abraham (see Gal 3–4 and Rom 4). Together with Israel, they could also inherit the Kingdom. Even more radically: their new "father" was not, or not only, Abraham: it was Israel's god. Thanks to their adoption, and like Israel "according to the flesh," these ex-pagan pagans, too, could now call God, "Abba, Father" (Gal 4:6–7; Rom 8:15). They had been brought into God's family through Christ, "the first born of many brothers" (Rom 8:29).

Paul had seen empirical proof of the spirit's presence in the charismatic empowerment of his congregations. His assemblies now spoke words of wisdom and knowledge. Inspirited ex-pagans could heal, work miracles, and prophesy. They were able to distinguish between kinds of spirits. And they could speak the speech of angels as well as interpret that speech (1 Cor 12:8–13; cf. 14:18 and 2 Cor 12:12, on Paul's own spirited powers). By loving their neighbor (that is, their brother in community), they fulfilled the law (e.g., Gal 5:14; Rom 13:8–9). The spirit accomplished what mere flesh (thus, circumcision) never could. Spirit enabled ex-pagan pagans to stop acting like pagans.

But adoption by spirit demanded more than ethical behaviors, more than charismatic expertise, more than new community consciousness. Sonship had a public face. As adopted heirs, these ex-pagans had specific responsibilities to their (new) patrilineal cult and to their new family's god – the same, indeed, as those of "born" sons, Israel. Like Jews in the Diaspora, then, so too God's "new" sons: these people could no longer participate in civic cult to local deities, nor sacrifice before those deities' images. In the eyes of the *ekklēsia*, they may have been "eschatological gentiles," but in the eyes of their unaffiliated neighbors, they were deviant pagans. In this way they threatened majority culture's "friendly agreement" between heaven and earth. For this, Paul paid a price.

PAUL THE PERSECUTED

We return, then, to Paul's list of human antagonists in 2 Cor 11: synagogue authorities (the source of thirty-nine lashes, no fewer than five times); Roman magistrates (three times beating Paul with rods); hostile city-dwellers (stoning Paul); rival apostles who also, like Paul, evangelized pagans ("false brethren" who avoided "persecution" by "preaching circumcision," Gal 6:12, cf. 5:11). We failed to find a plausible, specifically intra-Jewish reason for Paul's being lashed by other Diaspora Jews. If we integrate this disciplinary punishment back into his longer list of persecutors, however, a common motivation for all these hostile acts begins to emerge: fear of the gods.

Earthquake. Flood. Famine. Plague. These were not religiously neutral events; they were registers of divine discontent. Happy gods made for happy humans, which is why Greco-Roman cities spent so much time and effort honoring their gods. Public acts of piety secured heaven's goodwill. Gods were more than distant immortal powers. They were powerful social agents, very sensitive to slights from humans who should be giving them their due respect.

The pagan gods of Paul's letters easily become invisible to modern readers. After all, as modern readers know, Paul was a Jew, and Jews were monotheists. But Paul, like his fellow coreligionists, was an *ancient* monotheist. This meant that his allegiance fastened on a single god, his own god, the highest god, the god of Israel. But, as he forthrightly told his Corinthian congregation (and as they already knew), the world teemed with other gods and superhuman powers as well. "Idols," those man-made representations of pagan gods, might be "nothing"; but gods, even if lower and less powerful than Israel's god (*daimonia*, Paul sneers; "godlings") were still definitely something. "Even if there are so-called gods, whether in heaven or on the earth – *as indeed there are many gods and many lords* – for us there is one god, the Father ... and one lord, Jesus Christ" (1 Cor 8:4–6; cf. 10:20).

Diaspora synagogues had long accommodated pagan interest in Israel's god by welcoming such people into their community as god-fearers. But Paul, and those other apostles who coordinated their missions with his, upended the social and religious equilibrium that these synagogues embodied and maintained. In Christ's name, they demanded a much more radical form of Judaizing of these pagans than the synagogue had ever requested or required. Once "in Christ," these people in principle could no longer show respect to their old gods (cf. 1 Cor 5:11: some baptized god-fearers evidently were confused). They were to act as if they had "become" Jews (for men, via circumcision), when in fact they had not.

Conversion to Judaism was a known phenomenon, grudgingly tolerated.[26] But it was a bizarre and alarming novelty to find ex-pagan pagans committing themselves exclusively to Israel's god, without circumcision. It was dangerously disrespectful to the established gods of the family and the city – in our terms, it was a public health risk and a security threat. What if the gods, insulted and angry, struck back at the city? What if the pagan majority, insulted and angry, struck back at the synagogue, the obvious source of this disruptive new movement?

Hence Paul's woes: the insults, the beatings, the imprisonments. Acts narrates the afflictions that Paul lists. There, itinerant apostles are repudiated by their host synagogues, run out of town by irate pagan citizens, and occasionally punished by Roman authorities attempting to keep the peace.[27] The floggings that Paul both gave (back in Damascus) and later submitted to should be seen within this context. They were the synagogue's effort at damage control, its attempt to contain the gospel message because it was so socially destabilizing – *not* for other Jews, for whom affiliation with the Christ-movement mid-first century meant a lateral move from one kind of Jewishness to another, but for affiliated ex-pagan gentiles.

Angry gods harassed Paul too. The "god of this world" frustrated his mission (2 Cor 4:4). Hostile elements derailed his movements (2 Cor 11:27). Cosmic deities threatened to seduce his gentile assemblies (Gal

[26] For this reason, perhaps, the "false brethren" who urged circumcision on Christ-following pagans had avoided "persecution" (Gal 6:12).

[27] See, for instance, Acts 13:50; 14:2, 4–6, 19; 16:20–24; 17:5–9; 18:12–17; 19:23–41; cf. 2 Cor 4:8–9; 6:4–5; 11:24–26; cf. also Mark 13:6, 11.

4:8–11). But Paul (and his assemblies) knew something that his "persecutors" both human and divine did not: the power of these gods was about to cede forever to the returning, conquering Christ. Angels, principalities (*archai*), celestial and terrestrial and subterranean beings (Phil 2:10), cosmic elements (*stoicheia*, Gal 4:9) – all of these "rulers of this age" (who themselves were the responsible parties for Christ's crucifixion; 1 Cor 2:8) would soon kneel to the messiah and to God his father (Phil 2:11).

Pagan gods, in brief, not only serve as Christ's apocalyptic resistance. They were necessary in order to cement Jesus's identity as the final Davidic warrior, the eschatological champion "descended from David according to the flesh," the messianic "root of Jesse" who will arise to rule the nations (Rom 1:3; 15:12, cf. Isa 11:10).[28]

The warrior Christ must first defeat or destroy "every ruler (*archê*) and every authority (*exousia*) and power (*dynamis*)" before final redemption can occur (1 Cor 15:24). Paul's language here resonates with Davidic enthronement psalms: the messiah will reign "until he [God] has put all his enemies [that is, the enemies of the Davidic king] under his feet" (v. 25; cf. Ps 110:1).[29] Christ as the Davidic messiah will subdue these cosmic powers. In 1 Cor 15:24, he "destroys" or "abolishes" them. In 1 Thessalonians, Christ descends from heaven "with a cry of command, with the archangel's call and the sound of the trumpet of God" (4:16). In Philippians 2, Christ subjugates these gods (knees above the earth and upon the earth and below the earth all "bend" to him at his *parousia*, ultimately acknowledging the god of Israel; cf. Ps 97:7). In Romans, Paul seems to speak of these cosmic entities with more sympathy: together with the rest of creation they "groan," awaiting the victorious return of Christ (8:19–22; though cf. 8:38, where they seem still to be part of the resistance).

Once "the redeemer" comes "from Zion" (that is, once the returning Christ manifests from the temple mount), human redemption will be secured (Rom 11:25–26). At this point in Romans 11, reprised at his finale in Romans 15, Paul's vision seems altered from that of his previous statements. He makes no mention of impending wrath or of the doom of unbelievers (cf. 1 Thess 1:9; Rom 1:18). But neither does he

[28] On the necessity of pagan gods to establish Jesus's role as (returning) Davidic messiah, see Fredriksen, *When Christians Were Jews*, 147–156.

[29] Matthew V. Novenson, *Christ among the Messiahs: Christ Language in Paul and Messiah Language in Ancient Judaism* (New York: Oxford University Press, 2012), especially 137–173.

still combine humanity into one family of ethnic and pneumatic brothers united under Abraham (a typical misreading of the "Israel of God" in Gal 6:16). Instead, echoing Isaiah, Paul presents redeemed humanity in two ethnically distinct families – Israel "according to the flesh" (*kata sarka*), Paul's kinsmen, and *ta ethnē*, everybody else, all the other nations.[30]

Paul here invokes biblical eschatological arithmetic: Christ is about to save the seventy nations descended from Noah ("the fullness of the nations," a nod to Genesis 10 in Rom 11:25) and the plenum of Davidic Israel (the twelve tribes, "all Israel," itself an eschatological idea; Rom 11:26). The collection of scriptural verses that closes his remarks in Romans 15:9–12 repeats this bicameral eschatological unity: the nations rejoice *with* Israel. They praise God *with* Israel. The nations join *with* Israel. But they do not *join* Israel.

In Paul's inflection of apocalyptic redemption in Christ, Israelite identity perdures as a central component. Paul catalogs its compositional elements in Rom 9:4–5: sonship, the divine presence in Jerusalem's temple ("glory" in the NRSV), the covenants (with Abraham, Isaac, and Jacob), the giving of the law (to Moses on Sinai), the cult of offerings enacted in Jerusalem's temple ("worship" in the NRSV), the promises, the forefathers, and the family relationship to and with the messiah. If, according to Paul, this God-granted identity would continue into the Kingdom, why would we assume that he suspended it, or rejected it, or made it peripheral in the interim?

* * *

Did Paul achieve his goal of visiting the Christ-assemblies in Rome (Rom 1:13; 15:22–24)? Was he able thereafter to press on to Spain (Rom 15:24, 28)? We do not know. With the seven undisputed letters, Paul passes from history – or at least, beyond our vision. The Paul of Acts does arrive in Rome. Still later tradition asserts that he died there, martyred under Nero. Claiming the relics of both chief apostles, Peter and Paul, Rome's imperial and apostolic prestige synergistically bolstered its assertions of authority over all other Christian communities both East and West. With Constantine, that authority was wedded to political power, thus to the exercise of coercive force. Paul's seven letters, with their kinetic summons to an impending messianic

[30] J. Ross Wagner, *Heralds of the Good News: Isaiah and Paul "In Concert" in the Letter to the Romans* (Leiden: Brill, 2002).

redemption, were now institutionally harnessed and eschatologically quieted (with Acts on one side and the pseudepigraphical epistles on the other). In these ways, the apostle of the messianic End-Time empowered the new arm of late antique government, the Roman imperial church.

Further Reading

Bohak, Gideon. "The Ibis and the Jewish Question: Ancient 'Anti-Semitism' in Historical Context." In *Jews and Gentiles in the Holy Land in the Days of the Second Temple, the Mishnah and the Talmud: A Collection of Articles*, 27–43. Jerusalem: Yad Ben-Zvi Press, 2003.

Fredriksen, Paula. "How Jewish Is God? Divine Ethnicity in Paul's Theology." *Journal of Biblical Literature* 137 (2018): 193–212.

Fredriksen, Paula. *When Christians Were Jews: The First Generation*. New Haven, CT: Yale University Press, 2018.

Fredriksen, Paula. *Paul: The Pagans' Apostle*. New Haven, CT: Yale University Press, 2017.

Fredriksen, Paula. "'Circumcision is Nothing and Foreskin is Nothing': A Non-Reformation Reading of Paul's Letters." In *Protestant Bible Scholarship: Anti-semitism, Philosemitism and Anti-Judaism*, edited Arjen Bakker, René Bloch, Yael Fisch, Paula Fredriksen and Hindy Najman. Leiden: Brill, forthcoming.

Harrill, J. Albert. *Paul the Apostle: His Life and Legacy in Their Roman Context*. Cambridge: Cambridge University Press, 2012.

Hurtado, Larry. *Lord Jesus Christ: Devotion to Jesus in Earliest Christianity*. Grand Rapids, MI: Eerdmans, 2003.

Isaac, Benjamin H. *The Invention of Racism in Classical Antiquity*. Princeton, NJ: Princeton University Press, 2004.

Levinskaya, Irina. *The Book of Acts in Its Diaspora Setting*. Grand Rapids, MI: Eerdmans, 1996.

Novenson, Matthew V. *Christ among the Messiahs: Christ Language in Paul and Messiah Language in Ancient Judaism*. New York: Oxford University Press, 2012.

Novenson, Matthew V. "The Self-Styled Jew of Romans 2 and the Actual Jews of Romans 9–11." In *The So-Called Jew in Paul's Letter to the Romans*, edited by Rafael Rodriguez and Matthew Thiessen, 133–162. Minneapolis, MN: Fortress Press, 2016.

Sanders, E. P. *Paul, the Law, and the Jewish People*. Philadelphia: Fortress Press, 1983.

Stendahl, Krister. "The Apostle Paul and the Introspective Conscience of the West." In *Paul among Jews and Gentiles*, 78–96. Philadelphia: Fortress Press, 1976. Originally published in *Harvard Theological Review* 56 (1963): 199–215.

Thiessen, Matthew. *Paul and the Gentile Problem*. Oxford: Oxford University Press, 2016.

Wagner, J. Ross. *Heralds of the Good News: Isaiah and Paul "In Concert" in the Letter to the Romans*. Leiden: Brill, 2002.

3 What Kind of World Did Paul's Communities Live In?

RICHARD S. ASCOUGH

From the perspective of modern life in the West, life for the majority of inhabitants of the Roman empire at the time of Paul was "poor, nasty, brutish, and short" (to invoke Thomas Hobbes). People struggled to make ends meet, their surroundings were dirty and noisy, work was menial and took a physical toll, and medical knowledge was rudimentary. Life expectancy was on average only about twenty years or so, and those who lived longer could expect a continued struggle through their thirties with infectious diseases, malnutrition, parasites, rotting teeth, and declining eyesight. And this is only those who survived infancy, for which there was a very high mortality rate. Although not much of this sounds desirous, the contrast was not as sharp as we might expect; this was considered "normal" in much the same way we accept our own situations and limitations as normative. The real contrast, both then and now, was socioeconomic, with a small minority who had both economic and political power and whose lives could be seen in contrast to the day-to-day living of the majority. These elite (who in today's terms we might refer to as the "top one percent") enjoyed access to political and economic resources well beyond those below them, most of whom faced a daily struggle to survive.

The communities to which Paul wrote his letters were all located in urban environments and thus in this essay, we will look at the sociocultural codes and contexts of daily living that filled the Roman cities during the first century. This is not to relegate the rural context completely to the background. Many city-dwellers either had their roots in the non-urban environment and/or continued to work in agriculture outside of the city gates. Yet as city-dwellers, their identity as individuals and as a small community would have been framed by the urban setting. It is important to keep in mind, however, that city- dwellers represented only about ten percent of the population of the Roman empire, which is estimated to have been somewhere between fifty and eighty million in the first and second centuries CE. Rome itself was by far the largest metropolis, with 700,000–800,000 inhabitants (sometimes thought to be closer to one million). Most of the other cities would have been well under 100,000 in total population. No matter their size, however, urban centers tended to be compact, with dense concentrations of people in a small area. If the city was rebuilt under Rome, it tended to be laid out in a grid pattern; otherwise, it followed the layout of its predecessor, which often in the eastern empire was modeled on the Greek city plan. In all cases, the forum/agora (market) was centrally located.

It is tempting, of course, to think of the ancient Roman cities as comparable to those of our own day. And to a degree there are overlaps. They were centers of commerce, full of bustling movement, constant noise, and pervasive smells. And they were multicultural on different levels. Although in this essay I will refer to them as "Roman" cities, since that is the historical time period in which Paul's letters are situated, the cities themselves had a mixed heritage. Most of them were previously "Greek" cities insofar as they had been (re)settled by Greeks or Macedonians in earlier centuries. Thus, they retained much of their Greek cultural heritage, and east of Italia, the lingua franca in all of the cities was Greek, which is why Paul wrote his letters in this language. Buildings retained their Greek style, in part because they were built earlier and in part due to Roman elites' adulation of all things Greek. Nevertheless, underneath the Roman veneer and the Greek structure lay a local foundation – perhaps in some architectural styles from an earlier ethnic group, or sometimes in the form of a continuation of an indigenous language or worship of a local deity (albeit sometimes under the guise of a Roman or Greek god). For example, in Philippi, which was a city colonized and thus settled by Roman soldiers, there is inscriptional evidence for the coterminous use of Greek and Latin[1] and expressions of devotion to the Thracian deities alongside the Greek and Roman pantheon.

SOCIAL STRATIFICATION AND STATUS

In the modern western context, we tend to think about social "class" primarily in economic terms with the "elite" being those who have the most money, whereas in the Roman period one's social status was determined by where one fell within the Roman *ordo*, the classification

[1] See Peter Pilhofer, *Philippi. Band I. Die erste christliche Gemeinde Europas* (Tübingen: Mohr Siebeck, 1995), 85–87.

given in the official census that was conducted on a regular basis. Although grounded in economic privilege, one's place was also linked to one's political standing and to a larger degree to one's ancestry. The three basic divisions were patricians, plebeians, and non-citizens. The patricians were the elite – they had ancestral lines purporting to go back to the founding of Rome. The bulk of the population, however, either held Roman citizenship (the plebeians or plebs) or were non-citizens or slaves. This generalized tripartite division also represented a decrease in the power and privilege accorded to those of each rank.

At the very top of the hierarchical pyramid was the senatorial rank, comprising a small minority of the population. Men from these families held positions of power and influence in Roman politics. Immediately below them, but still a small, elite circle, were the equestrians, men of equally important ancestry. To remain in either the senatorial or equestrian rank, one's property value had to meet a minimum threshold, a value that was reformed upwards by Augustus in the early imperial period. Males in either of these ranks made their careers by moving through a series of public offices, called the *cursus honorum*, in which they held military and administrative posts that gave them leadership experience, not to mention opportunities to increase their power by forging networks and alliances and to build wealth through taxation and, at times, extortion. As a result, the senators and equestrians were extremely wealthy and very powerful in civic politics across the empire, and were unlikely to have been affiliated with any of the groups to which Paul's letters were addressed.

The plebeians were free Roman citizens who had neither the ancestry nor the wealth to rise to the higher rank. Within this census designation, however, there continued to be a hierarchical structure, with wealth providing the basis for the divisions. For the most part, however, the plebeians worked in all but the most menial of occupations or served in the military, albeit with no hope of rising to the high officer ranks. There were some opportunities for political office for the plebs, although again their status would prove to be a limiting factor. According to the Book of Acts, Paul had been granted Roman citizenship, the privileges of which he invoked in order to avoid corporal punishment and also to make an appeal to appear before the imperial courts in Rome (Acts 22:25–29). Non-citizens had no such rights and privileges. At the very bottom of the citizen rank were the *proletarii*, the landless poor who had so little by way of wealth that they did not even qualify for military service and tended to work as manual laborers.

A third broad category in the Roman social stratigraphy was that of non-citizen. Although technically members of this rank were "lower" on the social scale, we cannot think in terms of economic distinctions, since some non-citizens accumulated great wealth. And, as with the other two broad categories, there were subdivisions within this rank. At the top were the free persons, people who were born free, either within the Roman empire or as foreigners (*peregrini*). Much like the citizens, free persons were in the working class, making a living in a vast range of occupations in the cities or perhaps as farmhands in the rural lands outside the gates. They did not, however, enjoy the rights of citizenship and thus could not vote and were subject to harsher punishments for crimes. It was possible to purchase Roman citizenship, but this was costly and thus rare. Of lesser status were the freedpersons, those who had formerly been slaves and had been manumitted (freed), either through the goodwill of their master or by purchase of their freedom. They had even fewer rights than free persons, although their children would be regarded in the latter category and be granted citizenship. Many freedpersons were highly educated and experienced and thus were given positions in the civil government. It was also possible, as some cases attest, for freedpersons to amass great wealth, although this did not provide them with accompanying high status in the eyes of the elite.

At the bottom of the social hierarchy were the slaves, who were not even accorded personhood. Under the law, slaves were considered property and treated as such. Slaves, for the most part, came into their position after amassing unrepayable debt or as the spoils of war, or they were descendants of such people. Although legally not permitted to marry, many slaves did have families and were encouraged to do so by their masters. And although not an enviable status by any stretch of the imagination, how one was treated by one's master would make all the difference in the life of a slave. That said, even well-treated slaves would have sought manumission or emancipation at their first opportunity. It is curious, then, that Paul advocates that slaves remain in such a position (1 Cor 7:21–24), although this likely reflects his anticipation of Jesus's return and the end of the world order rather than an affirmation of slavery itself. And when it came to a slave he knew personally, Paul had no qualms about helping others to rethink that slave's status, as we see in his appeals on behalf of Onesimus in the letter to Philemon.

Thus, in Roman society social status was the primary structuring element among people and one's status determined where and with whom one might socialize. There was an empire-wide concern around establishing and maintaining the social order and thus, in general there were strong boundaries between each of the hierarchal social divisions. Nevertheless, the boundaries between them became more porous over time, particularly from the late republican period and early part of the Imperial period with the rise of "newly monied" merchants, those who had acquired great wealth but whose ancestry was that of the *proletarii*.

In a patriarchal society such as ancient Rome, women and children would have shared the social rank of their male guardian, usually either their father or their husband. That said, some of the rights accorded to those of particular ranks (such a voting, for example) would not have been extended to women. Nevertheless, women from the senatorial class would have been accorded much more social status than a man of a lower rank. For example, if walking toward one another on the street, a freedman would be required to give way to an upper-ranking woman, in recognition of her higher status.

It is unlikely that anyone in the groups to which Paul's letters were addressed were from the upper ranks of Roman society – certainly not senators and almost equally certainly not equestrians. It is possible, however, that some members could be counted among the *humiliores*, a category of people who controlled considerable amounts of money, whether citizen or not, free or freed.[2] For example, Paul claims to have baptized Stephanus and his entire household in Corinth (1 Cor 1:14–16), suggesting he was a person of wealth.[3] And Phoebe of Cenchrea is named as Paul's patron, a clear indication that she is a woman with some disposable income (Rom 16:1–2; see below). For the most part, however, members of the Pauline communities were likely the poor – manual workers and small business owners or unskilled laborers[4] and slaves (1 Cor 7:21).

HONOR AND SHAME

In the Roman world, every person was vigilant about how they were being evaluated by everyone else, whether positively or negatively. And of primary concern was positive validation, the estimation of a person's

[2] Dale B. Martin, *The Corinthian Body* (New Haven, CT: Yale University Press, 1995), xvi.

[3] This might also be the case for Gaius, whose household Paul mentions in Rom 16:23. The verse is usually translated as "Gaius, who is host to me and to the whole church, greets you," but recent arguments have been put forward that suggest that the Greek word "*xenos*" should be rendered "guest" not "host." In this reading, Gaius is not, or at least not necessarily, a wealthy patron. See John S. Kloppenborg, "Gaius the Roman Guest," *New Testament Studies* 63 (2017): 534–549; Richard Last, *The Pauline Church and the Corinthian Ekklēsia: Greco-Roman Associations in Comparative Context* (Cambridge: Cambridge University Press, 2016), 62–71.

[4] Martin, *Corinthian Body*, xvii.

honor by peers. First and foremost was ascribed honor, which was granted primarily through one's genealogy and social standing (as discussed in the previous section). Even among the elites it mattered greatly to which family line one belonged, with patricians claiming greatest honor for a lineage that stretched back to the founding of Rome itself. Acquired honor was more flexible as it was directly linked to one's actions. For example, hosting a successful banquet in which one's peers were well-fed and amply entertained would garner accolades that would bring about increased honor.

In practical terms, those who were delegated more honor received greater respect and better treatment in public. At the same time, honor was understood to be a limited good; there was only "so much" to go around and thus honor could be gained or lost at any given time. If one person gained more honor, it must be at the expense of someone else. Thus, each social engagement was an opportunity for social equals to compete with one another for honor. In such exchanges, men would vie with one another in the court of public opinion. For example, a man might have issued a challenge with a pointed verbal barb directed against his opponent's character, or unleashed a rhetorical flourish against his opponent's recent actions or that of his family. In his riposte, the man challenged must have not only defended himself but offered a countervailing attack against his challenger, showing the accusations not only to be unfounded but also ill-conceived. As the exchange drew to a close, the audience of the exchange would determine which man lost face and which had thus increased his honor. Competition for honor was not simply verbal, however. We noted above that a successful banquet would gain the host greater honor, but it came at the expense of the honor of others. As a result, people went to great expense to host increasingly lavish meals to indicate they deserved the greatest honor. Indeed, gaining such honor (what we might call social capital, since it resulted in more social engagements) was more important than economic capital, and there are stories of people nearing financial bankruptcy in pursuit of such acquired honor.

The preceding paragraph has been deliberately gendered since in the Roman world, honor was the purview of adult males. As with social standing, women and children were normally tied to the honor of their male guardian, usually their husband but also their father or brothers.[5] They were expected to be virtuous and pious, closely following

[5] See David A. deSilva, "Paul, Honor, and Shame," in *Paul in the Greco-Roman World: A Handbook*, 2nd ed., vol. 2, ed. J. Paul Sampley (London: Bloomsbury, 2016), 32–33.

sociocultural conventions, particularly around sexuality. Any break from societal norms would result in their bringing dishonor to their male guardian in the court of public opinion. In this way, "shame" was considered a good thing as it helped a woman to know her place in and out of the public eye. As a result, women predominantly occupied private spaces and spent their time in the company of other women. If they ventured out in public, they would often ensure that a male relative accompanied them.

Although such patriarchal restrictions are now rightly viewed in the West as oppressive, such gendered assumptions pervade the letters of Paul. Properly understanding ancient cultural practices can go a long way in redressing the prescriptive use of such texts in the past and present to repress the public roles of women in Christendom. Even more importantly, and not unrelatedly, it is also noteworthy that women do have some public presence in Paul's letters and so attention must be given to how these texts can be understood with respect to ancient cultural expectations. Indeed, as we shall see below, many women could and did participate in some aspects of the public acquisition of honor but in so doing "were crossing boundaries that a good part of the society held sacred."[6]

One of the primary mechanisms to attain honor in the Roman world was patronage. Wealthy men and women would give money to a person or group, but not as a loan. In exchange for their financial benefaction, the recipient would publicly honor the donor. We have an extensive database of inscriptions giving accolades and listing all the great deeds of patrons. For example, an inscription from Bruttium and Lucania, Italy dating from the late first century CE, honors an elite patron who has donated land to an association dedicated to the god Silvanus:

> Lucius Domitius Phaon, in order to assure for all time the cult, the maintenance and the sacrifices for the members who are now in the association (collegium) of Silvanus and who will be in the future, has allotted his own estates ... along with their villas and enclosed territories. He has also stipulated that the income that comes from the aforementioned estates shall be used on the following days .... They shall do everything mentioned above without deceit, and so that all know that it is for the welfare of our most excellent leader

[6] Wayne A. Meeks, *The First Urban Christians: The Social World of the Apostle Paul* (New Haven, CT: Yale University Press, 1983), 23.

> and lord that the estates listed below have been dedicated and the days of sacrifice fixed. (*CIL* X 444)[7]

Although less common, women also could be honored for their benevolence. This is seen, for instance, in a mid-second century CE inscription from Rome that recognizes Salvia Marcellina as a woman who

> donated as a gift to the association (collegium) of Aesculapius and Hygiae the land for a chapel with a pergola and a marble statue of Aesculapius and an attached covered solarium in which the membership (populi) of the above-named association can hold a banquet .... Likewise the same Marcellina donated to the 60 members of the above-named association 50,000 sesterces. (*CIL* VI 10234)[8]

Just as the association of Aesculapius and Hygiae benefited from donations given by a female benefactor, so too Paul identified Phoebe of Cenchrea as having acted as a "patron" to him and many others (Rom 16:1–2). Paul's letters also indicate that he had received funding from some members of his Christ groups, in particular those at Philippi and Thessalonica (see Phil 4:15; 2 Cor 11:9). And there is some indication that people such as Philemon (Phlm 17, 22) opened their homes to Paul as an act of support.

HOUSING AND ENVIRONMENT

Until recently the household dominated the interpretive imagination when it came to thinking about where groups to which Paul wrote might have met.[9] In such cases, the architectural structure of the house would have provided a room in which a group could gather to talk and even to share a meal together. At best these would have been modest homes since even the wealthiest adherents at this early stage were not likely to have been part of the elite but rather of the "middling" social

[7] Richard S. Ascough, Philip A. Harland, and John S. Kloppenborg, *Associations in the Greco-Roman World: A Sourcebook* (Waco, TX: Baylor University Press, 2012), no. 308.

[8] Ascough, Harland, and Kloppenborg, *Associations in the Greco-Roman World*, no. 322.

[9] See Edward Adams, *The Earliest Christian Meeting Places: Almost Exclusively Houses?* (London: Bloomsbury T&T Clark, 2013), 1–5.

strata with incomes slightly above subsistence level.[10] As such, their houses would have been modest.[11]

Yet there are times in which houses and households were not directly evoked by Paul. And even in mentioning a particular "household" he may not have been referencing the location of a meeting (a "house") but rather the dominant social configuration of the group (familial), which might have resided in an apartment. Given the low socioeconomic status of the majority of Christ-adherents, tenement housing in apartment blocks is a realistic setting for gatherings of Christians in some cities.

Ancient cities were crowded. Streets were narrow and buildings could be up to six or seven stories high in large cities, cutting out much of the natural light during the day, and making it particularly dark at night. Most of the population lived in apartment buildings (*insula*), which generally were poorly constructed and prone to fires or collapse. Multiple apartment blocks could be built around an inner courtyard and shared staircases. The upper floors of the buildings were less desirable, in part due to the need to navigate stairs and in part because they were smaller. The bigger, but costlier, accommodations were closer to the ground. There were no apartments on the ground level itself as that space was given over to shops and taverns.

Apartments were small and cramped with little natural light or fresh air, save for that which came through the small, uncovered windows. A large, open space served as the main gathering area for the family and if there were rooms to the sides, they were tiny and used only for sleeping. Otherwise, bedding was rolled out onto the central floor space, where members of the extended family would spend the night sleeping amidst the noise from the streets below.

Most apartments would have neither running water nor toilets. For the latter, public latrines were available in the city, although inside the apartment, buckets were used (and dumped into the streets below). Public latrines were not particularly private by modern standards. Open stone benches had small holes over a drain that was flushed with water, often coming directly out of the nearby baths, and a sponge could be

[10] See Bruce W. Longenecker, *Remember the Poor: Paul, Poverty, and the Greco-Roman World* (Grand Rapids, MI: Eerdmans, 2010).

[11] An example of such a residence is the house of a cabinet maker in Pompeii, which might have accommodated up to forty people gathered at meetings; for an imaginative reconstruction along these lines, see Peter Oakes, *Reading Romans in Pompeii: Paul's Letter at Ground Level* (Minneapolis, MN: Fortress Press, 2009), 80–83.

wetted from a small channel at one's feet and used for cleaning afterwards. The openness of the space and seating (which could be for as many as twenty-five or more) suggests that relieving oneself was also a time to engage in social discourse and networking with people who were doing the same in close proximity.

In urban centers that had aqueducts, fresh water was brought into the city and made available at public fountains, having then to be carried up into the apartment with buckets. Due to the risk of fire, not to mention the discomfort of smoke, little cooking was done in apartments themselves. Rather, people would cook outdoors in the inner courtyard or take advantage of the cheap, simple meals of bread, chickpea cakes, and porridge, accompanied by wine, which were purchased from street vendors and taverns.

The "typical" Pauline community was small relative to the population density of the urban environments in which they were located. How small, however, remains somewhat disputed. Many scholars agree that no single group was larger than perhaps forty to fifty members. In cities in which there were more than one group, such as in Corinth and in Rome, the combined total of the groups might well exceed fifty, although was not likely to be more than one hundred in total. Recently, however, some scholars have argued that the groups were much smaller in size, perhaps closer to twelve to fifteen members in each, given the capacity of the most likely meeting places – an apartment, a room in a home, a tavern.[12] Thus, when we imagine an audience gathered to hear a reading of one of Paul's letters, there were not likely to be more than a small circle of extended family, friends, and acquaintances, the latter perhaps forged through network connections and, particularly, occupational or religious associations.[13]

Also of interest is the title of the Pauline groups, which in Greek is *ekklēsia*. Although in most English translations this word is rendered "church," we must not imagine that it is any sort of dedicated building – that is, it is not an independent architectural structure and it is certainly not something designed for a religious purpose, at least not one centered on Christ. Rather, *ekklēsia* indicates the group itself, the individuals who together comprised the community to which Paul wrote. In the

[12] See Richard S. Ascough, "Reimagining the Size of Pauline Christ Groups in Light of Association Meeting Places," in *Scribal Practices and Social Structures among Jesus Adherents: Essays in Honour of John S. Kloppenborg*, eds. William E. Arnal et al. (Leuven: Peeters, 2016), 547–565.

[13] See Richard S. Ascough, "Paul and Associations," in *Paul in the Greco-Roman World*, vol. 1, 68–89.

Greek political system, the *ekklēsia* was the central governing body of a city, comprising democratically elected, elite men. This more restrictive delineation should not, however, govern how we imagine the composition of other types of groups given this moniker, nor should the etymology of the word. Literally, *ekklēsia* means "called out," which some have interpreted to be indicative of Christ-followers being "called out" from their broader cultural context. All indications are to the contrary, however, as Christ-followers seem to have been very much embedded in their urban environment, sometimes struggling to navigate it while staying faithful to their commitments to God (as suggested by some of the social issues that Paul addressed in his letters).

WORK AND LEISURE

Work life was difficult for the majority of the population in the Roman world and particularly horrible for those who were slaves. Although most people could find work, it was most often manual labor of some sort. The workday would begin at dawn and continue through until dusk and required much physical output. Many inhabitants of cities worked outside the walls on farms taking care of crops or animals. Vineyards likewise provided opportunities for daily work. Inside the city industries of all sorts flourished, some demanding skilled labor. For example, carpenters, blacksmiths, or masons could be apprenticed from a young age. Unskilled labor was also plentiful, however, such as working in a laundry facility or on the docks and in the warehouses. In all such occupations, freemen, freedmen, and slaves would rub shoulders working together, although the slaves would be assigned the least desirable (and often most unhealthy) tasks.

Non-slaves would receive a daily wage for their work, although it was not a substantial sum of money. In general, people made enough to cover their daily expenses (food, accommodation, basic clothing) and any extraordinary purchases were intermittent. From the elite perspective, this kind of subsistence living, along with the sweat that would accompany much manual labor, was viewed as a source of dishonor. Among the workers themselves, however, there was likely a much more positive attitude when not in the company of the elite, with pride being taken in their various skills and crafts.

Life was not complete drudgery, however. The urban environment provided opportunities for various forms of leisure activities. First and foremost was the theater, a civic structure often centrally located or easily accessible in the city. By Paul's time the theater was used for a range of events that included drama and dance performances as well as literary and sporting competitions. Although Greek drama was translated and adapted for Roman audiences, the Romans also developed their own literary tradition of tragic and comedic plays that would be performed in Latin. Performances were generally undertaken by professional actors, many of whom belonged to guilds dedicated to the god Dionysus. Indeed, such performances were never separated from their origins or function as cult acts, meant to honor or pacify the gods and ensure divine blessings on the city. While theater attendance was affordable for the general population, it was subsidized heavily by the administration or elite patrons.

Other forms of theater entertainment included sporting events, such as wrestling and gladiator fights. These latter in particular seemed to have been wildly popular in the first century CE. Although there were professional gladiators who chose to fight in the arena, most combatants were war captives, criminals, or slaves, and thus had little choice. Great honor could be gained from victory, but death was never far away. Similarly, great honor and the threat of death surrounded the chariot races that took place in another popular entertainment venue, the circus. These elongated oval structures (based only in the largest of Roman cities) lent themselves well to high-speed competitions and spectacular crashes.

Since houses and apartment complexes rarely had their own baths, most people bathed in the public establishments. Men could go to the bath complex to exercise with weights or aerobically, or perhaps even play some ball games. Eventually they would enjoy a cleansing progression through pools that got increasingly hotter, heated by a complex hypocaust system, to open up the body's pores and wash away the dirt and grime. This was followed by a plunge into a cold pool to close the pores, and perhaps a massage. Women could also go to the baths, although they had their own separate baths or they went to the public baths during designated times during the day, usually morning, so as to be apart from the men; mixed-gender bathing was rare. But like the men, women would partake of a series of pools, all the while relaxing and socializing with one another.

Other forms of entertainment could punctuate the day. Adult leisure time might be spent playing games, some involving dice, bones, or marbles, the gameboards for which have been found scratched into the stones at marketplaces or on theater seats and in the bath complexes. Such games were often accompanied by gambling. Archaeologists have found numerous children's toys in Roman homes, such as dolls, pull carts, and even wooden swords.

GODS AND CULT

According to the prevailing worldview in Paul's time, all of life was controlled by superhuman forces. Each event, no matter how large or small, had some divine agent behind it. For example, the weather was controlled by sky gods while the sea was controlled by water gods. These deities could be the well-known, "universal" gods of the Romans, such as Jupiter, Neptune, Juno, or Apollo. Or they could be local deities, such as the Anatolian Sabazios, Agdistis, and Ma. Alongside these deities were a plethora of minor deities (good and malevolent) that controlled all aspects of everyday life. Such deities (major and minor) needed to be honored and placated to ensure ongoing peace and security, both at the empire-wide level and on the personal level – and every level in-between.

Empire-wide there was keen attention to public cult. Professional colleges of priests or priestesses ensured that daily sacrifices took place. Ritual specialists sought the will of the gods, providing advice to governing authorities across the land. Public temples and the semi-public worship of local and foreign deities permeated the civic landscape. Major cult buildings, however, were most often located on the perimeter of the marketplace or nearby. In fact, these buildings served a purpose far beyond the primary cult acts that took place there. They were key components in the economic life of the city, serving roles that today we would associate with banks – providing financial and cultural support to individuals and merchants through loans, savings, and sometimes insurance.

In the post-Augustan era, there was increasing attention to the cult of Roma, the deified personification of Rome itself and of the emperor. In the late first century BCE, the Senate at Rome recognized that the gods sanctioned the current ruler, which led to the granting of divine status to emperors and sometimes members of their families. The inclusion of the emperor (or his divine spirit) in the pantheon of the gods in temples throughout the empire served to reinforce both the political agenda of Rome and as a reminder of the subjection of the local populations.[14] Even the coins used for everyday commercial exchange carried this political message, often depicting divine images of the ruling emperor and inscriptions citing his honor, power, or benevolence.

[14] See Bruce W. Winter, *Divine Honours for the Caesars: The First Christians' Responses* (Grand Rapids, MI: Eerdmans, 2015), 11.

In the temples themselves, priests offered up prayers to the emperor and sacrifices on his behalf, and also drew attention to the emperor's own intercessions to the gods on behalf of the empire.[15] Although there was no formal requirement that men and women were to participate in the imperial cult during the first century, there was significant pressure to do so. Failure to participate could have resulted in social ostracism or, worse, suspicion of treason, since the emperor was the protector of the empire and of the Pax Romana (the Roman peace) throughout the land. For members in Christ-groups, this would mean keeping a low profile and perhaps even tacitly acknowledging the gods, including the emperor.

The situation in the home would be different for Christ-adherents. Residences of all sorts normally included shrines or altars that recognized the divine spirits that watched over the household:[16] the Penates, which were family deities and heroized ancestors, and the *genius*, a divine representation of the head of the household. All members of the household were expected to venerate these deities on a daily basis. The Lares were likewise recognized as the spirits within the house, although they could be found in many public places as well, providing divine protection for such things as travel routes, entryways, or even entire cities. The Lares themselves were permanent residents of places, remaining as the protectors of a house even when the occupants departed with their Penates and the representation of the *genius*. Nevertheless, within the domestic sphere, Christ-adherents would likely have removed all such deities in light of their turning to "the one true God" (1 Thess 1:9). For Judeans this was not an issue since Torah prohibited the representations of gods in their houses. But for non-Judeans such a radical break with ritualized practices and the deeply-rooted cultural beliefs could be difficult, even traumatic.[17] It is no wonder, then, that in the Pauline letters we find admonitions to vigilance in remaining

[15] See Winter, *Divine Honours for the Caesars*, 49.

[16] James B. Rives, *Religion in the Roman Empire* (London: Routledge, 2007), 118–119. See further Harriet I. Flower, *Dancing Lares and the Serpent in the Garden: Religion at the Roman Street Corner* (Princeton, NJ: Princeton University Press, 2017).

[17] See for instance, Natalie R. Webb, "Powers of Protection in Pompeii and Paul: The Apotropaic Function of the Cross in the Letter to the Galatians," in *Early Christianity in Pompeian Light: Texts, People, Situations*, ed. Bruce W. Longenecker (Minneapolis, MN: Fortress Press, 2016), 93–122; and Jeremiah N. Bailey, "Spheres and Trajectories: The Angels of the Churches (Revelation 1–3) in Context," in *Early Christianity in Pompeian Light* (Minneapolis, MN: Fortress Press, 2016), 167–192.

faithful to monotheism, an indication of the residual effects of the cultural presumption of the presence of deities in multiple spheres of life.

One of the pressing community issues that Paul addressed revolved around eating and drinking. Food is a basic human necessity, but many cultures have boundaries around what can and cannot be consumed. Because of their origins in the Judean milieu, early Christ-groups found it challenging to decide whether or not Judean food restrictions applied to non-Judeans who became Christ-followers. Of particular note was "food sacrificed to idols" – that is, anything to be consumed that had been ritually dedicated to a deity prior to its being brought to the table. Such food, particularly meat, was common in the Roman world. Every temple had some manner of ritual sacrifice that often involved grains or animals. For example, a lamb could be sacrificed on the altar that stood before a temple of Isis but only part of the entrails and meat were actually burned on behalf of the god. What remained would be used for a feast at the temple or sold to the general public in the marketplace for consumption at home. In either case, but particularly with meat, the food could be considered "polluted" by those who opposed such cult practices. Most meat, in fact, had its origins in cultic circumstances, thus necessitating guidance on whether or not it could be consumed by Christ-adherents (see 1 Cor 8:1–10:31; Rom 14:1–23). For the most part, however, meat was expensive, and many Christ-adherents would probably have relied on simpler fare to meet their daily caloric needs.

FREELANCE RELIGIOUS EXPERTS AND TRAVEL

People living in Greek and Roman cities often encountered freelance religious experts – as those who "earned their recognition and legitimacy through demonstrations of skill and learning" rather than having it ascribed to them through social or political status.[18] These people, predominantly men, traveled from city to city proclaiming their particular message with rhetorical flourish. Through a variety of differing skills and tactics such as magic, astrology, divination, philosophy, or cult, these purveyors of "religion" drew individuals and groups into their own particular sphere of influence. Although some experts were focused on the dissemination of practices and texts linked to ancient religion (e.g., Judean, Egyptian), others (including Paul) formed and

[18] Heidy Wendt, *At the Temple Gates: The Religion of Freelance Experts in the Roman Empire* (Oxford: Oxford University Press, 2016), 10.

supported individuals as well as communities of like-minded adherents by offering specific services such as "purification, character reform, essence change and divinization, the acquisition of specialized religious skills, care for ancestors, salvation or escape from eschatological judgment, and ultimately deification and immortality."[19]

The ability of such freelance religious experts to travel widely across the empire was largely facilitated by the extensive roads built and maintained by the Romans, primarily by the military. The key to maintaining the Pax Romana was the ability to move a large number of troops efficiently from one spot to another in response to real or perceived threats. When not deployed in war or peacekeeping, soldiers worked on repairing or building roads. These roads were constructed to allow fast passage of carts, horses, and troops, and often had adjoining footpaths for pedestrians. By placing rectangular stone blocks atop layers of stone, rubble, and cement, and by cambering the surface for drainage, the Romans ensured that the roads were built to last; some of them are even usable today in parts of Europe. Dotted along the major arteries between cities were inns that provided basic food and lodging for the night. And although banditry could be a problem on the roads, traveling as part of a group (as Paul did) provided safety in numbers.

In addition to the roads, travelers could also take to the sea, where the Roman navy had the threat of piracy well in hand. Often trade ships would take on extra passengers, allowing quicker travel between major port cities. At the same time, sea travel was more fraught with danger than the roads because of the unpredictability of the weather. And during the winter months, all but the most brave or foolhardy tended to stick to the roads in order to be safer.

It is within this broad context that we can situate Paul. The skills, discourses, and practices reflected in his letters show him to have been a freelance expert in Judean religion; yet in contrast to other Judeans, he maintained a somewhat distinctive emphasis on Jesus as the Messiah, or "Christ." But for his audiences (both those who heard him speak and those to whom he wrote), he would have been clearly identified as educated and attempting to attract a following. Thus, in addition to imagining that Paul founded Christ-groups by working with extant groups of one sort or another (such as occupational or religious associations in Macedonia),[20] it is also clear that he spoke with individuals

[19] Wendt, *At the Temple Gates*, 187.

[20] See Richard S. Ascough, *Paul's Macedonian Associations: The Social Context of Philippians and 1 Thessalonians* (Tübingen: Mohr Siebeck, 2003).

and their households in order to influence them to adhere to the promise God provided through Christ (see, for example, 1 Cor 1:14, 16; Philemon).

DEATH AND BURIAL

A significant aspect of the world in which Paul's communities lived was the pervasiveness of death. Not only was life short compared to modern standards (as we noted earlier), but death, or more accurately the dead, were always present. Whereas today we tend to marginalize death, pushing it into funeral homes and cemeteries tucked away behind churches or in fenced-off portions of the city, in the Roman world reminders of death abounded.

Funerary practices differed regionally and over time. During the early imperial period Romans tended to favor cremation, at least up until the second century CE. In the eastern regions of the empire, however, the majority of ethnic groups, including Greeks and Jews, buried their dead.

Inhumation was disallowed within the walled boundaries of the city, so people buried the remains of their loved ones on the outskirts. When approaching the main gates of most cities, one passed through the necropolis, "the city of the dead." The elite tended to have large, ostentatious burial plots. In fact, "rather than creating cemeteries set off from the noise and movement of life, they vied for the most public and visible plots, those closest to the city gates or at least in the first row of tombs along the principal road."[21] Proximity to the city gate and the main road was an indication of family status and honor – the closer the better. Family mausoleums could be multiple stories and be ornately decorated with reliefs and accompanying inscriptions honoring the deceased. For those who could not afford a mausoleum, a sarcophagus would suffice. These rectangular stone receptacles were decorated to the degree that the deceased or family could afford and placed above ground as a way of honoring the dead. As with the mausoleum, an inscription would generally not only name the deceased but also laud his or her deeds and family honor, perhaps also expressing the grief of those still alive. Some tombs included a semicircular bench that invited family and strangers to sit and reflect on the memory of the deceased,

[21] John R. Clarke, *Roman Life: 100 B.C. to A. D. 200* (New York: Harry N. Abrams, 2007), 147.

while others included altars where offerings could be made to the memory of the deceased.[22]

Of course, this kind of honorific display was only available to the wealthy. For the vast majority, such ostentatious presentation was out of the question. The best one could hope for was a small commemorative inscription by which one would be remembered. For those who were too poor to afford their own plot, a pauper's grave was the inevitable end. However, the horror of this dishonor of not being remembered led some religious and occupational groups to use their collective funds to purchase plots in which their members could be buried and memorialized.

Although grave markers were an important aspect of remembering the dead, more significant honor came through post-mortem graveside commemorations. Living family members, or friends, or even fellow group members, regularly gathered at the graveside to undertake sacrifices or share a meal in honor of their ancestors and their deceased loved ones. In some regions these were more formally prescribed rituals held on specific days, such as the *rosalia* or the *parentalia*. In other cases, the inscription itself delineates the terms for such commemorations, sometimes even setting aside a portion of the estate funds to be invested so that proper rites might continue regularly. Such concerns for memorialization may not have disappeared within the Christ-groups, but were mitigated by the promise of deliverance from death through a post-mortem existence with the risen Christ himself (e.g., 1 Thess 4:13–18; 1 Cor 15:51–56).

* * *

The early Christ-adherents clearly lived in a world different than our own, yet they still faced challenges that occur in many urban environments even now – such as earning sufficient income for basic sustenance, finding shelter, navigating social relationships, and reflecting on death. There are, however, some fundamental differences from life in the modern West. There was no social safety net in place to help the poor and oppressed, incomes tended to be only slightly higher than subsistence level, housing was uncomfortable and sometimes dangerous, social hierarchies were entrenched in ways that governed daily interactions, and death was present all around. And, more foundationally, we tend no longer to think of all of life being in the control of divine

[22] Clarke, *Roman Life*, 147.

beings that must be placated through regular ritual actions, with threats of punishments lurking close by. All of these and more are issues that Paul must address when writing letters to his communities in their first-century urban contexts.

Further Reading

Adams, Edward. *The Earliest Christian Meeting Places: Almost Exclusively Houses?* London: Bloomsbury T & T Clark, 2013.

Ascough, Richard S. "What Are They Now Saying about Christ Groups and Associations?" *Currents in Biblical Research* 13, no. 2 (2015) 207–244.

Ascough, Richard S. "Paul and Associations." In *Paul in the Greco-Roman World: A Handbook*. Vol. 1, edited by J. Paul Sampley, 68–89. London: Bloomsbury, 2016.

deSilva, David A. "Paul, Honor, and Shame." In *Paul in the Greco-Roman World: A Handbook*. 2nd ed., vol. 2, edited by J. Paul Sampley, 26–47. London: Bloomsbury, 2016.

Harrison, James R. "The First Urban Churches: Introduction." In *The First Urban Churches 1: Methodological Foundations*, edited by James R. Harrison and L. L. Welborn, 1–40. Atlanta, GA: SBL Press, 2015.

Longenecker, Bruce. *Remember the Poor: Paul, Poverty, and the Greco-Roman World*. Grand Rapids, MI: Eerdmans, 2010.

Meeks, Wayne A. *The First Urban Christians: The Social World of the Apostle Paul*. New Haven, CT: Yale University Press, 1983.

Sampley, J. Paul, ed. *Paul in the Greco-Roman World: A Handbook*. 2nd ed., 2 vols. London: Bloomsbury, 2016.

Wendt, Heidi. *At the Temple Gates: The Religion of Freelance Experts in the Roman Empire*. Oxford: Oxford University Press, 2016.

Winter, Bruce W. *Divine Honours for the Caesars: The First Christians' Responses*. Grand Rapids, MI: Eerdmans, 2015.

Part II

The Pauline Letter Collection

4 The Thessalonian and Corinthian Letters

MARGARET Y. MACDONALD

Paul's letters to Corinth and Thessalonica offer us some of the most important early evidence of the community life of Jesus-followers in the urban centres of the Roman world. Paul founded the communities of both Thessalonica and Corinth, and Acts 16–18 sets the establishment of these communities (together with missionary activities in Philippi, Beroea, and Athens) within the context of Paul's first mission to Europe. When this group of four letters (1 Corinthians, 2 Corinthians, 1 Thessalonians, 2 Thessalonians) is read together, we get a sense of the varying responses of community members to gospel themes – along with the related beliefs, ethical positions, and ritual practices introduced by Paul himself. In an atmosphere of newness and enthusiasm, there was much to work out. Reading this collection of letters together also enables us to appreciate the flexibility of Paul's own responses to the issues that arose in his absence. Depending on the circumstances, we hear him emphasize one aspect of an emerging belief more than another aspect, and we catch glimpses of him working out approaches and setting forth norms for the first time (and he sometimes admits this!).[1] The reaction of the neighbours of the newly committed Jesus-followers also emerges as an important factor in the analysis of these letters, as we detect some of the issues and tensions that arose in the communities' social relations with outsiders.

Recent research has emphasized that various lenses or methodological approaches can bring out elements that might otherwise go undetected in these letters – both in seeking to understand Paul's own voice in them and in the effort to uncover the shape of community life for the Jesus-followers with whom he interacted. For the purpose of the

[1] In 1 Cor 7:10–12 Paul distinguishes between the command against divorce based on the teaching of Jesus (the Lord gives this command) and his own directive concerning marriage between believers and unbelievers, which he states explicitly does not come from the Lord.

study of these letters, three things have been especially fruitful in this regard: (1) an awareness of their setting in the Roman empire, (2) an awareness of ancient rhetorical conventions, and (3) an awareness of the diversity of membership within Paul's communities (including the presence of women, slaves, children, and people of varying socioeconomic status). Much of this essay is shaped by the work of scholars who have used these approaches to uncover the meaning and social context of these documents.

WRITING THE THESSALONIAN AND CORINTHIAN LETTERS

The urban setting of Paul's correspondence and the geographical proximity of the two cities of Thessalonica and Corinth forms our starting points for outlining the situation in which Paul wrote this body of letters. Understood to be the earliest of Paul's letters, 1 Thessalonians was addressed to a community that was located in the capital of the Roman province of Macedonia and was strategically important for both land and sea routes in the regions of the Eastern Mediterranean. Paul's brief reference to having been 'mistreated in Philippi' (1 Thess 2:2) confirms the picture in Acts where he and his fellow-worker Silas are accused of disrupting the city including market interests (Acts 16:19–40) before moving on to Thessalonica (Acts 17:1–9), where he 'declared the Gospel of God in spite of great opposition' (1 Thess 2:2). Paul presents his relationship with the Thessalonian community as being close and emotionally charged, and we hear of his repeated attempts to return to them after separation ('Satan blocked our way!' 1 Thess 3:18). From his location in Athens, he sent Timothy to the Thessalonian community (1 Thess 3:1–2), making his way to Corinth. It was while he was in Corinth that Paul wrote the first letter to the Thessalonians around 50 CE, seemingly only a number of weeks (or perhaps a few months at most) after he left Thessalonica. In this way, the two communities were bound together in Paul's missionary activities, with the founding of the community in Corinth very close in time frame to the composition of 1Thessalonians.

Paul's second letter to the Thessalonians may also have been written in the early 50s, shortly after he wrote 1 Thessalonians. There are many similarities between the two letters, including expressions of hostility experienced at the hands of outsiders. But about half of all scholars today believe that the letter is pseudonymous, written in Paul's name shortly after his death. With a focus on the outline of the letters, some have argued that the parallels are so close that the second letter appears to be an imitation of the first. At the same time, as will be discussed below, thematic similarities shared by the two letters are obscured by differences in their perspectives, with the questions and outlook of community members being noticeably different in the two letters, especially with respect to the timing and nature of the return or coming of Christ (*parousia*; 2 Thess 2:2). Some have suspected 2 Thessalonians to be pseudonymous because (among other things) the author's approach seems to differ from Paul's – such as the inclination to describe the punishment of persecutors (2 Thess 1:5–10) in greater detail than is characteristic of Paul's undisputed letters.

Turning to the Corinthian letters, 1 Corinthians offers some of the most important evidence regarding the way of life and concerns of early Jesus-followers in the Roman world. The work was written from Ephesus (1 Cor 16:8–9; cf. Acts 18:1–7) around 54 CE. It is Paul's response to information that came to him from three sources: (1) a letter from the community itself (1 Cor 7:1), (2) reports from members of the household of Chloe (1 Cor 1:11), and (3) a visit to Ephesus by three men from Corinth (Stephanus, Fortunatus, and Achaicus; 1 Cor 16:17). Paul does not seem to have experienced the hostility and harassment in Corinth that was typical of his experience in Thessalonica; in Corinth, he was able to win adherents, both Jews and gentiles (1 Cor 1:22–24; 7:18), in a relatively peaceful environment. But Paul's ongoing relations with the new Jesus-followers were far from easy. The itinerant nature of Paul's leadership meant that his communities easily came under the influence of other leaders, and the early stages of socialization of new (and often independent-minded) Jesus-followers meant that group dynamics and practices often evolved in a way that troubled Paul. Moreover, the letters to the Corinthians reveal an intensely personal relationship between Paul and the communities. In 1 Corinthians 9:1–2, for example, the existence of the Corinthian community is depicted as proof of the legitimacy of his apostleship.

Paul wrote several letters to the Corinthians, one of which predated 1 Corinthians but has since been lost (1 Cor 5:9; some scholars have identified this to be 2 Cor 6:14–7:1). The events that led to the composition of 2 Corinthians are the subject of great debate together with the nature of the composition of itself, with most scholars understanding the work to be a composite of more than one letter (all written eighteen to twenty-four months after the composition of 1 Corinthians). In terms of a sequence of events, it is clear that interactions between the Corinthians and Paul deteriorated between the time of writing

1 Corinthians and 2 Corinthians, with many of Paul's most impassioned entreaties being found in 2 Corinthians (or fragments thereof). It seems that in the interim between these letters, Paul had paid 'a painful visit' to Corinth (2 Cor 2:1), which was probably his second visit to the community (cf. 2 Cor 12:14; 13:1). This was subsequently followed by a 'tearful' letter (2 Cor 2:1–4), which some have identified with 2 Cor 10–13, but probably is now lost. With improved relations, from Macedonia Paul apparently wrote 2 Corinthians 1–9 (or some argue 1–7 or 1–8) about 55 CE (2 Cor 7:5; cf. 2 Cor 2:12–13; 8:1; 9:2). But the situation seems to have deteriorated again leading to the fiery and often sarcastic entreaties of 2 Cor 10–13. While this reconstruction of events is based on a two-letter hypothesis, some scholars have argued that 2 Corinthians consists of five or even six letter fragments. 2 Corinthians, then, permits a number of different situational scenarios.

GOSPEL IRONIES IN THE ROMAN WORLD

The Corinthian and Thessalonian correspondence contain Paul's reactions to questions and problems those communities had. Paul tended to frame his answers to community concerns by reiterating his gospel message. This message emerges especially clearly in 1 Thessalonians, which he frames directly in response to the community's experience of persecution shared with Paul himself. In the opening thanksgiving of 1 Thessalonians, Paul describes a powerful and transformative gospel, not only transmitted with words, but also in power and in the Holy Spirit – perhaps a sign that miracles and other dramatic manifestations of the Spirit accompanied Paul's preaching (1 Thess 1:5). Paul talks of the Thessalonians receiving the word of the Lord in spite of persecution and suffering (1 Thess 1:6–7). The Thessalonians are said to build upon Paul's example of preaching and are conduits of the word not only in Macedonia and Achaia but even beyond those regions (1 Thess 1:8) – offering us a window into early evidence of networks of communication where Paul, his fellow-workers, and community members contributed to the expansion of the movement.

It is crucial to observe that 1 Thessalonians offers the earliest evidence of the content of the gospel Paul preached in the cities of the eastern Mediterranean, including these three components: (1) a call to serve 'the true and living God' because (2) God raised his Son Jesus from the dead and believers now wait for his return from heaven, and (3) Jesus is the one who will rescue believers from the wrath that is to come (1 Thess 1:9–10). Later in the epistle, Paul reiterates that Jesus died and rose again (1 Thess 4:14). He speaks of believers obtaining salvation through our Lord Jesus Christ and who also died for them (1 Thess 5:9–10). We know that acceptance of Paul's gospel message called for Jesus-followers to reorient their lives – not least in turning to God from idols (1 Thess 1:9). This is a shorthand way of highlighting how gentile Jesus-followers (who seem to have made up the majority of the Thessalonian community) had breached the religiopolitical system that fused together religious, familial, economic, and political elements of the empire.

Scholars who have explored Paul's attitude toward the Roman empire have uncovered some anti-imperial nuances of his gospel proclamation, which stand out especially clearly in 1 Thessalonians. At this early stage of Christian origins, Jesus-followers were not recognized as members of a separate religion (i.e., Christianity) that would be persecuted by political authorities in the empire; but even in this period Jesus-followers were often viewed as trouble-makers in their neighbourhoods. To turn from idols to worship the one God meant the cessation of worshipping the gods that not only protected the empire but also their cities, their places of work, and even their homes – since every aspect of daily life was infused with the presence of the Greco-Roman gods. We do not know what form of persecution the Thessalonians were experiencing exactly, but it seems to have involved elements of suffering and isolation. Perhaps it was related to the accusation that the gospel interfered with business success – the very thing Paul is blamed for in Acts 16:19–40 (cf. Acts 17:16–34; in Acts 19:23–41, the profits related to the production of statues of the goddess Artemis are in view).

Scholars have noted the anti-imperial connotations alive in the notion of 'gospel' itself, which means literally 'good news', but was used to celebrate successes in the imperial political context. It is not surprising that Paul in the Corinthian correspondence turns to the irony of a gospel message rooted in the life of a crucified messiah proclaimed by a 'weak' messenger like the apostle himself. As a leader in a new movement proclaiming Jesus as messiah, Paul found himself in conflict with synagogue authorities in addition to local leaders. He speaks of floggings and beatings, and 'five times' having received the 'forty lashes minus one' (2 Cor 11:24). The Corinthians were seemingly spared from such harsh treatment and even from the neighbourhood hostilities experienced by the Thessalonians. With great rhetorical flourish (including a catalogue of suffering in 2 Cor 11:21–28), Paul criticizes the boastful attitude of community members by speaking with irony of Corinthian wisdom in contrast to his own foolishness (2 Cor 11:19–20) and weakness (2 Cor 11:21).

In the first four chapters of 1 Corinthians, such ironic contrasts based on the content of the gospel (and Paul's experiences in proclaiming it) become part of a framework for a rudimentary, but provocative, theology of the cross. Because the Corinthians were bickering over the status of various prominent apostles, Paul called them to consider a perspective on the world that stands in sharp contrast to the usual definitions of prestige and success. Paul announced that God's wisdom is opposed to the wisdom of this age and the rulers of this age. Deep ignorance and misunderstanding on the part of the rulers of this age (i.e., the Roman empire) had led to the crucifixion of the 'Lord of glory' (1 Cor 2:6–8). From an imperial perspective, the 'Lord of glory' was a crucified criminal or insurrectionist. It is not surprising, therefore, that Paul can confidently assert that 'the message about the cross is foolishness to those who are perishing' (outsiders to the assembly of Jesus-followers), while for those who are being saved it is a message bestowing the power of God (1 Cor 1:18). Christ sent Paul to proclaim the gospel 'not with eloquent wisdom' (1 Cor 1:17). Paul draws upon the irony of the transformative power of the proclamation of the crucified Christ to challenge the conventional (and completely human) perspective of elitist and competitive Corinthians (cf. 1 Cor 1:10–31). While his preaching to the Corinthians does not seem to have enraged the wider Corinthian community, there was much in the broad shape of Paul's preaching that could be heard as subversive. At the very least, Paul's proclamation of the mystery of God and God's dealing with the world led to many questions among the Corinthians about daily interactions with their family members and neighbours.

APOCALYPTIC EXCITEMENT

Soon after turning to God from idols, the Thessalonian Jesus-followers began to have questions about the return of Jesus. In the opening thanksgiving of 1 Thessalonians, Paul mentions that the Jesus-followers are eagerly awaiting God's son from heaven; Thessalonian believers were living in an atmosphere of anticipation wrapped up in a strong conviction of a final judgement where they will be 'rescued' or 'delivered' from the 'wrath that is coming' (1 Thess 1:10). The Thessalonian correspondence provides us with some of the best evidence of apocalyptic excitement in the earliest forms of Christianity. With dramatic imagery, Paul states that the Lord Jesus will appear 'like a thief in the night' (1 Thess 5:2) and his followers are to stand prepared wearing an armour of faith, love, and hope (1 Thess 5:8). And at his coming, the Lord Jesus will apparently be accompanied by angelic helpers (cf. 2 Thess 1:7).[2] But it would be misleading to think of this apocalyptic fervour as merely a set of beliefs or attitudes about the return of Christ; for Paul, it clearly had ethical implications. The followers of the Lord Jesus were to be 'blameless before our God and Father at the coming of our Lord Jesus Christ with all of his saints' (1 Thess 3:13). Experiencing God's presence was paramount, and this required a holy and blameless life.

These convictions and attitudes of anticipation among the Thessalonians were accompanied by uncertainties about the future, most especially the fate of community members who died before the imminent coming of the Lord Jesus, the *parousia*. It seems that these early followers of Jesus viewed his resurrection as the beginning of the resurrection of the dead that was understood to characterize the end times. The Thessalonians understood Paul's initial preaching to mean that the end would come soon and they would live to see the Lord Jesus's return. Therefore, they were alarmed when some community members began to die, wondering about their fate and worrying they had no hope for the afterlife and the glory of the *parousia*. Paul's message of comfort in 1 Thess 4:13–5:11 (framed in terms of traditional Jewish apocalyptic motifs) continues to present an expectation of imminence (1 Thess 4:15,17) but makes it plain that that those who have died in Christ will certainly share in the blessings of the end times. In fact, those who have already died will be raised up to join Christ before the living (1 Thess 4:13–15). In response to Thessalonian speculation, Paul stresses that the precise timing remains unknown and is not ultimately important; rather one must focus on being prepared (1 Thess 5:1–11).

The different issues raised in 2 Thessalonians and the different way those issues are handled have led some scholars to adopt the view that 2 Thessalonians is pseudonymous (as noted above). In this letter, the addressees have accepted that 'the day of the Lord is already here', apparently reinforced by a letter purporting to be from Paul (2 Thess 2:2). In this letter, the Thessalonians seem to have adopted what some have called an 'over-realized eschatology', in which the future dimensions of the dawning kingdom are excluded altogether. In addition,

[2] Angels are associated with the final judgement in apocalyptic literature of the Hebrew Bible and Jewish intertestamental literature (e.g., Dan 7:10, 18; 1 En 1:9), as well as in the Synoptic Gospels (e.g., Mark 8:38; 13:27; Matt 13:41; 25:31).

some community members have excessive confidence in their own gifted status and receipt of divine favour and presence – to the point where they appear to have quit their jobs, demanding financial support for a type of ministry based on superior qualifications (2 Thess 3:6–13). By contrast, 2 Thessalonians places firm emphasis on the future and (in a manner that some have identified as departing from Paul) stresses the severity of future judgement on those who afflict community members (2 Thess 1:5–10). But as in 1 Thessalonians, we can find evidence of corollaries between apocalyptic excitement and an ethical stance – both in terms of (1) the attitudes and behaviours of community members (2 Thess 1:5, 11–12), and (2) Paul's recommendation that disruptive, busybody activity should be avoided in favour of quietly working for a living (2 Thess 3:10–11).

In hearing Paul's voice in these letters, we get a sense of the apostle's innovative contribution to the development of early Christian belief. He is laying the foundation for much reflection on resurrection, the second coming, life after death, and balance between present salvation and future expectation – all of which would be formulated in later Christian doctrine. Here we sense the sparks of community life that were integral to this creative enterprise, culminating in a vision of salvation through Jesus Christ whose death enabled life with him to be shared both by those who are awake (i.e., alive) upon his return and by those who are asleep (i.e., dead; 1 Thess 5:10–11).

Some of this same creativity can be sensed in 1 Corinthians where we also find evidence of strong evidence of a realized (perhaps 'over-realized') eschatology. In that letter, Paul often argues against a sense of superiority among some of the Corinthians – a superiority that was tied (at least to some degree) to the belief that Jesus-followers already share in the fruits of salvation. With discourse dripping in poignant irony (including a use of kingdom language with political overtones designed to shake any sense of privilege), Paul proclaims in 1 Cor 4:8: 'Already you have what you want! Already you have become rich! Quite apart from us you have become kings!' Aiming to dampen such attitudes, the dominant approach that Paul takes in 1 Corinthians is to stress the future dimensions of eschatological convictions, highlighting concepts of revelation and disclosure of divine mystery and knowledge associated with some types apocalyptic thought. In the opening thanksgiving of the letter, for example, Paul refers to the spiritual gifts of believers, while at the same time referring to a time of expectation as they 'wait for the revealing (*apokalypsis*) of our Lord Jesus Christ' (1 Cor 1:7–8; cf. 2:7–10; 4:5; 7:26–31).

As will be discussed below with respect to some of his ethical directives, Paul clearly seeks to shake the Corinthians out of a stance of confidence and complacency with respect to the status quo, leading to inadvertent slippage into the standards of the world. The kingdom of God will certainly not be inherited by the unrighteous (1 Cor 3:10–15; 5:5; 6:2, 3, 9; 11:27, 32) and Paul's strongest statements suggest that every earthly stronghold, including dominant political powers, are doomed (1 Cor 15:24; 16:22). Such bold statements have invited speculation about the anti-imperial aspects of Paul's thought.[3] Paul is responding, however, to the Corinthian interpretations of the gospel, which may well have been varying and are difficult to unpack. As in the Thessalonian correspondence, Paul speaks of physical death, the resurrection, and the end of time in a way which attempts to place each in temporal relationship to one another. Once again, he appeals to vivid apocalyptic imagery: 'Listen, I will tell you a mystery! We will all not die, but we will all be changed, in a moment, in the twinkling of an eye, at the last trumpet' (1 Cor 15: 51–52). Throughout 1 Corinthians 15 Paul appears to reply to some Corinthians who thought there was no resurrection of the dead (1 Cor 15:12). Given some of the dualistic philosophical notions at the time that purported a strong distinction between body and soul, it would not be surprising if bodily resurrection had been difficult to accept. Such hesitancy could be bolstered by experiences of the Spirit that reinforced the confidence of those who thought they were spiritually rich and already living a transcendent/heavenly life in glory. But against those who may have held such attitudes and beliefs, Paul continues to insist (as he does in 1 Thessalonians) that there will be a resurrection of the dead. Here, however, he goes even further, suggesting that this bodily resurrection will involve a transformed body: 'For this perishable body must put on imperishability and this mortal body must put on immortality' (1 Cor 15:53).

THE ROLE OF THE SPIRIT

Both Paul and the communities with which he interacted appealed to apocalyptic concepts as a 'warrant for innovation'.[4] These concepts

[3] On this theme see, for example, Richard A. Horsley, ed., *Paul and Empire: Religion and Power in Roman Imperial Society* (Harrisburg, PA: Trinity Press, 1997).

[4] On this concept and the diverse use of apocalyptic notions in relation to various social settings in Paul's communities, see Wayne Meeks, *The First Urban Christians: The Social World of the Apostle Paul* (New Haven, CT: Yale University Press, 1983), 178–179.

played a key role in the development of beliefs and communal stances – the creative pulses of emerging Christianity. As noted above, in 1 Corinthians Paul appealed to apocalyptic notions to call for dissociation from the standards of the broader society, but also to push to new levels of development ideas that were related to resurrection and life beyond death. Sometimes Paul used notions about the dawning of the new age to moderate tendencies that were moving in innovative directions that he found problematic. In 1 Corinthians 7, for example, Paul emphasized the future to curtail extreme tendencies to break up or devalue marriages. Although radically ascetic views would have disordered the communities and disrupted the families within them, Paul nonetheless gave this counsel to virgins: 'in view of the impending crisis, it is well for you to remain as you are' (1 Cor 7:26). As can be detected in 1 Corinthians 7, the experiences of the Spirit are closely associated with these dynamics toward asceticism. The unmarried woman and virgin are said to be anxious about the affairs of the Lord so that they may be holy 'in body and spirit' (1 Cor 7:34). For Paul, remaining unmarried is mostly desirable for women. But he also asserts that there are circumstances when young women should go on to marry, not remaining 'as they are' in an unmarried state (1 Cor 7:32–38). In other words, 'being anxious about the affairs of the Lord' is a determinative, but not always purely positive, consequence of an ascetic lifestyle for women. Paul's response concerning the remarriage of widows (perhaps in response to those who ban widows from remarrying altogether) offers an indication that different interpretations of experiences of the Spirit were at play in the Corinthian communities. One detects a note of sarcasm in Paul's voice when he says, 'And I think that I too have that Spirit of God' (1 Cor 7:20).

This retort provides a vivid example of how an appeal to the Spirit could be used to assert authority in the strongest possible terms – even bolstering views that could not otherwise be derived from Jewish scripture or Jesus's teaching (1 Cor 7:10–12). The Spirit was apparently at the heart of battles to determine authentic forms of teaching and practice. For instance, the false teaching purporting that the Day of the Lord is already here was bolstered by an appeal to the guidance of the Spirit (2 Thess 2:2). In Corinth, receipt of the Spirit was a powerful source for defining community life, for sanctioning certain forms of leadership and influence, and sometimes promoting elitism. The experience of baptism and the reception of the Spirit (Paul ties both closely together in 1 Cor 6:11) seem to have given some members great conviction in their superior insight into divine mysteries. With a certain amount of irony, in 1 Cor 2:6–3:3 Paul addresses those who prided themselves on being 'spiritual' (the *pneumatikoi*), thinking themselves to have special status bestowed by the Spirit. In general, Paul sought to bring people down to earth by highlighting what still lies ahead in the future.

We see another side of things in 1 Corinthians 11–14, which provides fascinating insight into the role of the Spirit as the motivator and perhaps also the catalyst to commitment and growth in the Corinthian communities. There is evidently great interest in a type of Spirit-induced ecstatic or mystical speech known as *glossolalia* or tongues – the speaking of words which are not generally understood to be in a human language and therefore require the gift of interpretation. But Paul sought to squelch over-enthusiasm for this spiritual gift, perhaps because he saw it as leading to a type of spiritual elitism. His famous speech about love in 1 Corinthians 13 is meant to engender perspective, grounding the community in appropriate ethical norms. When it comes to inspired speech among the spiritual gifts, he prefers the gift of prophecy that the Spirit also inspires, because that gift leads to the edification of the community (1 Cor 14:1–12). The gift of prophecy is shared by both men and women, even if Paul expressed the need for decorum in prophecy and a recognition of God-ordained hierarchy in relations between men and women (1 Cor 11:12–16; see further below).

The kind of rarefied atmosphere of worship described in 1 Corinthians may not have been present at all times in every place. But we know that demonstrations of the power of the Spirit were sometimes presented by Paul as key to his own mission. Much of 2 Corinthians concerns the apostle's authority in relation to rivals, even though here, as in 1 Corinthians, he sought to moderate elite and extreme tendencies with a theology of the cross. In 2 Corinthians, true authority, including apostolic authority, lies ironically in weakness (2 Cor 4:7–15) echoing the weakness/strength of the crucified/resurrected Christ. Through such rhetorical devices as parody in 2 Corinthians 10–13, we catch a glimpse of the great significance of miracles and demonstrations of power in the competition to gain the allegiance of community members through public performance. While rivals may have largely been exacerbating tendencies that existed in the community already, it is clear that Paul responds to external rivals in 2 Cor 10–13, whom he labels as 'super-apostles' (2 Cor 11:5; 12:11) and 'false apostles' (2 Cor 11:13). In 2 Corinthians 12, Paul presents himself (sometimes speaking in the third person) as the recipient of heavenly revelations of the greatest magnitude (2 Cor 12:1–10). Reacting to the draw of the super-apostles, he explains with biting sarcasm: 'The signs of a true apostle were performed among you with utmost patience, signs and wonders and mighty works. How have you been worse off than the other churches, except that I myself did not burden you? Forgive me this wrong!' (2 Cor 12:12–13).

In the earlier letter of 1 Thessalonians, the fact that Paul proclaims his gospel not only verbally but also through various 'charismatic' acts is stated neutrally – simply as a matter of fact, without the polemical tone we find in 2 Corinthians. This reminds us that routes the Corinthians sometime chose to take were not completely different from the pathways presented by Paul to demonstrate his own authenticity as an apostle.

The situation is slightly different among Thessalonian Jesus-followers. On the one hand, Paul explicitly associates his gospel and ministry with the Spirit: 'our message of the gospel came to you not in word only, but also in power and in the Holy Spirit and with full conviction; just as you know what kind of persons we proved to be among you for your sake' (1 Thess 1:5; cf. 1 Cor 2:4; Rom 15:19). But in 1 Thessalonians we find no evidence of believers claiming special insight or claims to authority based on their possession of the Spirit, in contrast to the situation in Corinth where such tendencies clearly play a role in the myriad of opinions and divisions. Nevertheless, their reception of the Spirit was central to the Thessalonians' conviction that they were living in the 'last days' as well as other aspects of their situation – their questions about death and their impatience that the end (with its vindication of the followers of Jesus) had not yet come.

SOCIAL INTEGRATION AND INTERACTION

In the Thessalonian correspondence, the community is bolstered and consolidated by notions of vindication in the last days – vindication in response to suffering caused by a sinful and corrupt society. In keeping with dualistic notions found in other Pauline works (cf. Ephesians), Paul distinguishes between (1) the destruction that will befall those who belong to the darkness on the day of the Lord and (2) the salvation experienced by the children of light (1 Thess 5:1–11). This distinction is meant to encourage and build up the community (1 Thess 5:11). There are indications that both Paul and the community members have suffered at the hands of outsiders and can identify directly with the promises of judgement on others and recompense for Jesus-followers.

Paul speaks of having been abused at Philippi and of having the courage to preach the gospel in the face of great opposition (1 Thess 2:2;

cf. Acts 17:1–9); he may also have been subject to slanderous attacks in Thessalonica (1 Thess 2:3–16). Drawing connections between the Thessalonians, himself, and the crucified Lord, Paul addresses the situation in the community. Affliction (*thlipsis*, probably some type of persecution) characterized the environment within which they received the word (1 Thess 1:6) and will continue to characterize their lives until the last days. Paul sends Timothy back to Thessalonica because he is concerned that they will be shaken by such afflictions (1 Thess 3:2–5). Unfortunately, Paul does not tell us what these afflictions involved. Yet the way he connects them to his own experience and that of the Lord (1 Thess 1:6) suggests that we should think of strong social harassment, perhaps caused by withdrawal from some of the normal social and business activities that believers came to associate with an evil idolatrous world (cf. Acts 16:19–40). The issues are not explicitly mentioned here, but we know from second-century sources that the desire to remain unmarried and marriage to non-believers (issues discussed already in 1 Corinthians 7) could lead to great friction in families and neighbourhoods.[5]

With the composition of the Thessalonian and Corinthian correspondence, we are at a time well before Roman authorities set out to persecute believers. But for those who had 'turned to God from idols' (1 Thess 1:9) there were plenty of opportunities to appear suspicious during fiery debates and the probing of unusual behaviour. (Perhaps there were even occasions when Jesus-followers were tempted 'to return evil for evil', 1 Thess 5:15.) Paul reacts by counselling Jesus-followers 'to aspire to live quietly, to mind your own affairs, and to work with your hands, as we directed you, so that you may behave properly towards outsiders and be dependent on no one' (1 Thess 4:11–12).

In contrast to 1 Thessalonians, in 1 Corinthians Paul does not hesitate to call for dissociation from outsiders in very strong terms, while at the time same time allowing for some carefully scrutinized elements of engagement. As in 1 Thessalonians, Paul emphasizes his own suffering at the hands of authorities and members of the public in the Corinthian correspondence (e.g., 1 Cor 4:9–13; 15:30–32; 2 Cor 11:23–28). And especially when drawing upon apocalyptic imagery, he does not hesitate to emphasize the doom that will befall the unrighteous of the world (e.g., 1 Cor 6:2, 3, 9; 11:26, 32; 15:24). But the Corinthian correspondence gives no hint (unlike 1 Thessalonians) that

[5] Sexual control and proper decorum in marriage (in contrast to the Gentile non-believers) may be in view, however, in 1 Thess 4:3–5.).

community members are themselves being harassed by outsiders. In fact, instead of social alienation, there are 'signs suggesting the social acceptability of the Corinthian Christians'.[6]

In order to caution and stabilize the Corinthians, Paul offers several instructions related to their interaction with 'outsiders'. For instance, in 2 Cor 6:14–7:1 (often viewed as a fragment of an earlier letter; cf. 1 Cor 5:9–13) Paul offers an especially strong call to disassociate from outsiders. Yet, in contrast to such advice, many of the Corinthians seem to have continued with 'business as usual', seeing their dealings with outsiders and societal institutions as 'unproblematic', whereas Paul himself and perhaps some Corinthians had more scruples and reservations. With a proclivity to be divisive, some Corinthians did not hesitate to take their disputes to law-courts (1 Cor 6:1–6). They continued to dine in the houses of non-believers (1 Cor 10:27) and outsiders could be present to witness worship activities (1 Cor 14:23–25). Most alarmingly of all from Paul's perspective (and probably because of the business networking opportunities they provided), believers continued to attend the banquets and gatherings held in the temples dedicated to the worship of the gods and goddesses of the Roman world (1 Cor 8:10). The use of such spaces for a variety of civic, club, and business purposes was widely accepted in this era and some Corinthians, perhaps especially the more affluent ones, saw no reason to cease such practices.

Sociologists have regularly noted varying degrees of withdrawal from the world among a variety of sectarian groups. For instance, the Jewish communities associated with the Dead Sea Scrolls and perhaps some groups of Jesus-followers (such as those associated with Johannine literature) seem to have opted for high degrees of withdrawal from the world around them.[7] Paul and members of his communities may not always have agreed on the level of dissociation required in this new age. Through Paul's voice, we detect a certain tension between openness to outsiders and distinction from outsiders (whom God will ultimately judge! 1 Cor 5:13). Paul pushes back hard when he thinks fundamental beliefs and moral stances have been compromised, especially with respect to idolatry (1 Cor 10:1–22; cf. 1 Cor 8) and sexual morality

[6] This has been observed by John M. G. Barclay in "Thessalonica and Corinth: Social Contrasts in Pauline Christianity," *Journal for the Study of the New Testament* 47 (1992): 58. He offers a detailed comparison that has been particularly valuable for this study.

[7] See Margaret Y. MacDonald, *The Pauline Churches: A Socio-Historical Study of Institutionalization in the Pauline and Deutero-Pauline Writings* (Cambridge: Cambridge University Press, 1988), 32–42.

(1 Cor 5:1–13). But committed to winning as many adherents as possible especially among the gentiles of the ancient Mediterranean world, he recognizes the value of ongoing interaction. His responses to dining in the houses of outsiders and to the issue of mixed marriage are particularly illuminating when seeking to understand this tension.

In contrast to actually participating in activities in the temples of the Roman world, Paul advises the Corinthians to continue to accept dinner invitations in private homes and to 'eat whatever is sold in the meat market without raising any question' (1 Cor 10:25). He nevertheless places strict boundaries around activities, protecting those of weaker conscience (perhaps of lower social status) who may be offended by such dining. The issue involves 'idolatrous' meat potentially previously used in sacrifices. Such meat would be avoided by Jews or perhaps gentile Jesus-followers who ate meat more rarely and associated it directly with idolatrous festivals and activities. Paul's advice is to continue to partake if no objections are raised (1 Cor 10:27–30) – advice that is no doubt shaped by the very real possibility that such interactions could eventually lead to the expansion of the community.

The household setting of these communities was incredibly important to their life and growth (as will be discussed further below). Very early in the history of this movement, some individuals chose to accept the gospel while their partners did not. In 1 Cor 7:12–16, Paul responds to this new problem by making the deciding factor the willingness of the unbeliever to stay married. With no guidance from the words of Jesus, Paul thought those established marriages between a believer and a non-believer should not be terminated by the believer, unless interrupted by a challenge by the unbeliever. We can only surmise the nature of the context here, but the references to the need for 'peace' may offer an early indication of the strife and hostility that later characterized mixed marriages, especially for women. Paul's rhetorical question about the possibility of 'saving' a husband or wife (1 Cor 7:16) may offer an indication of an 'evangelical' motive – the possibility that the family will provide an atmosphere conducive to becoming a Jesus-follower. This idea may also underlie the unusual reference to the 'holiness' of the children who are products of such mixed marriages (1 Cor 7:14). The advice supports remaining married within a potentially tense and complicated situation, in a world where the head of the household should determine religious allegiance. In this context, Paul seeks to stabilize community members within their families, offering a chance for the expansion of the community by maintaining good relations with outsiders where possible. The approach is quite similar to the advice he gives with respect to dining in the homes of non-believers. Circumstances may dictate greater separation from outsiders, but if possible, peaceful coexistence should be maintained. Famously, Paul proclaims: 'Give no offense to Jews or to Greeks or to the church of God, just as I try to please everyone in everything I do, not seeking my own advantage, but that of many, so that they may be saved' (1 Cor 10:32–33).

The emphasis is much more on reducing harassment than on winning new members, but the sentiment of not giving offense is also crucial to 1 Thess 4:11–12 where believers are encouraged to live quietly, minding their own business, working with their hands, in order that they may 'behave properly towards outsiders and be dependent on no one'. Even where relations were strained the advice given seems to leave open the possibility of making an impression through moral behaviour and general demeanour.[8]

FAMILIES

An awareness of these issues is in keeping with the growing appreciation of family life for understanding a number of features of Paul's correspondence and the community life of Jesus-followers. These features include: (1) Paul's use of familial imagery and the techniques he uses to persuade his audiences, (2) the ethics he propounds in relation to issues arising in the communities, and (3) the leadership of communities and the atmosphere of gatherings – issues that are given consideration here.

Concepts and symbolism related to master-slave relationships, parenting, childhood, and marriage abound in his letters. Pointing especially to Paul's abundant use of sibling language to address communities and collaborators (brothers and sisters in Christ), scholars have argued that Paul makes use of a 'fictive kinship' concept to reinforce the bonds of community life. In other words, the community identity is being bolstered by a commitment that competes with or even replaces the family or household as typically defined.

In 1 Thessalonians Paul speaks passionately about the love he has for the Thessalonian community (1 Thess 2:8). For example, Paul draws on images from his work as an artisan to address his great efforts on

[8] We detect such dynamics even more strongly in 1 Pet 3:1–6 where marriage between believing women and unbelieving men is the subject of concern and wives are counselled to submit to the authority of their husbands so that some of them will be won over by their wives' reverent conduct (1 Pet 3:1–2).

behalf of the community before he turns to images of parenting that are rooted in the involvement of slaves in the care of children in the Roman world. Both the appeal to manual labour and to the work of slaves are part of a rhetorical strategy where Paul reverses the values of elite society (which found such efforts demeaning) and ultimately places him in the role of servant to his communities. In 1 Thess 2:5–8, Paul represents his interaction with them as being as gentle as a wet nurse caring for her own children (the Greek text may also be translated simply as a nurse with her children).[9] The use of such imagery draws on the presence of slaves in households and the potential presence of slaves who acted as wet nurses within the communities. Slaves frequently acted as wet nurses in the Roman world, continuing on as the nannies of very young children – a phenomenon that was recognized by ancient authors who gave advice on how to carefully select a wet nurse, the first teachers of children. The formative influence of the wet nurse on her babies may also underlie Paul's metaphorical references to weaning and spiritual milk in 1 Cor 3:1–2. While the gap between slave and free children certainly widened greatly with the passing years, at a young age slave children and free children were often playmates, being watched and cared for by the same slave caregivers.

If Paul is indeed referring in 1 Thess 2:5–8 to the equalizing care offered by a wet nurse to her own children as well as to her charges, he is potentially using the mothering efforts of a slave as a model for his love for the community because those efforts were known to surpass social stigmas and boundaries – a feature that would mesh well with his theology. But even if Paul did not use the image of a nurse's love for her charges for this purpose, that imagery remains a powerful 'mothering' symbol to reinforce his bond with the community. It is also important to observe the shift from maternal to paternal love in the same text, where Paul describes his relationship to the Thessalonians as being like that of a father to his own children (1 Thess 2:11).[10] Elsewhere he makes use of a family metaphor to convey his most poignant emotions of betrayal and jealousy, likening himself to a parent who whose

[9] On this topic see Jennifer Houston McNeel, *Paul as Infant and Nursing Mother: Metaphor, Rhetoric and Identity in 1 Thessalonians 2:5–8* (Atlanta, GA: SBL Press, 2014); Beverly Roberts Gaventa, *Our Mother Saint Paul* (Louisville, KY: Westminster John Knox, 2007); Carolyn Osiek and Margaret Y. MacDonald (with Janet Tulloch), *A Woman's Place: House Churches in Earliest Christianity* (Minneapolis, MN: Augsburg Fortress, 2006), 63–67.

[10] It should also be noted that female and male expressions of familial authority and influence both play a part in this passage.

plans to present the community as a virgin bride to the bridegroom Christ were endangered by the community's disappointing behavior (2 Cor 11:2–3).

If we turn to the communities themselves, there is much evidence to suggest that the acceptance of the gospel was raising new questions and leading to challenges in relation to family life – despite the importance of the family and households for the infrastructure of the group. A fundamental question which surfaces in 1 Corinthians 7 is whether family life (especially marriage) should continue along the same lines as before. We have already seen that in 1 Corinthians 7 Paul is markedly reserved about any change of status in light of the rapidly approaching return of the Lord. It is generally accepted that Paul quotes ascetic extremists at the beginning of 1 Corinthians 7 when he states that 'it is well not to touch a woman'; these were Corinthians who thought marriage in the new age should be rejected altogether, most likely based on the authority they felt was sanctioned through their experience of the Spirit. In response, Paul maintains his preference for celibacy for those who possess the gift, but rejects the idea of sexual renunciation as permanent within marriages (as opposed to some later early Christians who supported 'spiritual marriage') or for those who did not possess the gift of celibacy given the ever-present danger of slipping into immorality.

As highlighted above, marriages between believers and unbelievers were one potential source of friction with society, but it is important also to acknowledge that Paul's own preference for celibacy in addition to the enthusiastic proponents of asceticism among the Corinthians could potentially be interpreted as anti-familial. This was a society where the speeches of politicians and philosophers together with imperial legislation encouraged marriage, procreation, and remarriage after divorce and widowhood. In particular, Paul's cautious support of widows remaining unmarried if possible (1 Cor 7:40) matched some of the patterns among well-to-widows, whose tendency to remain unmarried was subject to critique from some people who advocated more traditional practices of widows getting remarried. In fact, in 1 Corinthians 7 Paul shows particular concern with the ascetism of female believers. This is reflected especially in his use of the term 'virgin' (*parthenos*) which refers to women in all but one instance (1 Cor 7:28, 34, 36, 37; the exception being 7:25) – a word sometimes masked in English translations as 'girl', 'unmarried', or 'betrothed'. A focus on women is not surprising in an ancient Mediterranean culture that valued the virginity of daughters and the purity of monogamous wives.

We can get a sense of these pressures and the hierarchical arrangements of family life in Paul's recognition that virgins may have to sacrifice a commitment to celibacy in order to follow through with marriage to a partner who might otherwise 'lose control' (1 Cor 7:36–38).[11]

In keeping both Paul's views and the community of Jesus-followers in mind, we catch a glimpse of various attempts to redefine family life in 1 Corinthians. Some unmarried women, including widows, viewed their commitment as Jesus-followers as involving a commitment to celibacy and they would have found support in the words of Paul. Phoebe, the female church leader from Cenchrea, the seaport of Corinth, whom Paul praises in Rom 16:1–2 is probably a good example of this (since there is no reference to her having a husband). Chloe, mentioned in 1 Cor 1:11 (discussed further below), may offer a second example. But Paul in 1 Corinthians 7 makes it abundantly clear that marriage continues to play an important role in community life and indeed one married couple mentioned in 1 Cor 16:19, Prisca and Aquila, offers evidence of the importance of the leadership of a married couple both as Paul's collaborators and hosts of house churches in both Ephesus and Rome (1 Cor 16:19; Rom 16:3–5) – and possibly also in Corinth, since Acts describes them as having offered hospitality to Paul there (Acts 18:2–3).

COMMUNITY AND SPACE

Writing to the Corinthians from Ephesus, Paul sends greetings (1 Cor 16:19) from Aquila and Prisca, together with the church in their 'house' (*oikos*; the same term can be translated 'household'). This is one of several references in the New Testament to house churches, serving as reminders of the significance that families and the household atmosphere had for the life of these communities. Houses of various shapes and sizes were probably not the exclusive meeting places of these Jesus-followers, but houses are explicitly named as gathering places and associated with certain leaders. Scholars have speculated that some of the more economically secure believers may have owned a *domus* – a residence typically governed by a *paterfamilias* (the property owner and head of the household) and shared with his wife, children, slaves, and other tenants (who may have included former slaves and workers). But cramped apartment buildings (*insulae*) may have been common

[11] Determining the precise scenario behind this passage is unfortunately impossible.

meeting places as well. Texts such 2 Thess 3:6–13 have been viewed as offering a window into such contexts where subsistence was of very real concern and manual work was required for the sake of survival.[12] The world of work also introduces us to fact that workshops (often located on the ground floor of apartment buildings) have been identified as probable gathering spaces for Jesus-followers, together with other possibilities such as inns and rented dining rooms associated with temples (a common practice for the various associations in the Roman World). It is important to note that in contrast to the Corinthian correspondence, the Thessalonian correspondence makes no explicit references to the community meeting in houses; moreover, the likely presence of artisans and manual labourers (1 Thess 4:11; cf. 1 Thess 5:12) suggests rather that workshops were more typical meeting places for them.[13]

Community members are sometimes referred to in relation to their family circumstances. In a rare reference to the baptism of a whole family unit, Paul speaks of the baptism of the household of Stephanas (1 Cor 1:16) and he urges the Corinthians to recognize the leadership of these people based on the service they have provided to 'the saints' (or community members; 1 Cor 16:15); they were likely among the higher social status members of the community, much like Erastus the city treasurer (Rom 16:23, if that interpretation of his status is correct).[14] But perhaps on the lower end of the spectrum, we find a reference to 'Chloe's people' (1 Cor 1:11).

The expression 'Chloe's people' literally means the ones belonging to Chloe, indicating that she is the head of the household. Chloe is not the only example of a female head of the household being singled out in the New Testament; Nympha has a church that meets in her house (Col 4:15). But in contrast to Nympha, we cannot be certain that Chloe herself is a believer (though clearly members of her household are), and the lack of explicit mention of a house may indicate that the household lives in the modest accommodation of an ancient apartment

[12] See Robert Jewett, "Tenement Churches and Communal Meals in the Early Church," *Biblical Research* 38 (1993): 23–43. More broadly, see Edward Adams, *The Earliest Christian Meeting Places: Almost Exclusively Houses?* (New York: Bloomsbury, 2016).

[13] See Adams, *The Earliest Christian Meeting Places*, 33–34.

[14] The same has traditionally been said of Gaius who is presented in Rom 16:23 as sending greetings from Corinth to Rome and who is usually thought to be described as the host to Paul and to the whole church. That way of understanding Paul's reference to Gaius has recently been seriously challenged; see John Kloppenborg, "Gaius the Roman Guest," *New Testament Studies* 63 (2017): 534–549.

complex. Chloe's people have reported to Paul on one of the main issues that surfaces in the Corinthian correspondence: conflict based on division. While the source of division cannot be reduced to a single issue, it is likely that differing social statuses was a primary factor in causing division (1 Cor 1:26), as can be detected most obviously in Paul's response to the divisions at the Lord's Supper, with community members seeming to have access to different types of food and some community members refusing to share food (1 Cor 11:17–33).

Paul uses the powerful image of the harmony of the body of Christ in order to break down emerging hierarchies (1 Cor 12:12–31). Commentators have pointed out that body analogies were frequently employed in the ancient world to encourage social harmony, especially in the political realm. Seneca, for example, describes the emperor as the soul or head and the state as his body (*Clem.* 1.4.3–5.1). Scholars debate the extent to which Paul subverts imperial traditional motifs in the use of his body analogy, but there is no question that he calls for special consideration for the weak and less honourable (1 Cor 12:23–24). With a clear focus on the future and in anticipation of the reward of the end times (see above), it may be best to understand Paul's representation of the community as 'an imperfect anticipation, or foretaste, of this future reality in the present … [when] believers' statuses are radically redefined, regardless of whether their location in Greco-Roman social strata is changed'.[15]

1 Cor 12:12–31 is located within a broader textual unit of 1 Corinthians 11–14 – a textual unit that provides us with insight into ritual practices, meeting spaces, and the hierarchies that emerged within those activities and arrangements. This textual unit is also particularly important for understanding Paul's pronouncements on women and gender and the ritual activities of women within the community. A focus on the rhetorical situation created by Paul's arguments has led to the uncovering of the initiatives of women prophets in 1 Cor 11:2–16 who removed their head covering (whether veils or hair styles remains debated) while prophesying. The arguments in this text are somewhat convoluted, including Paul's use of Genesis to restore order and impose a divinely ordained hierarchy shaping relations between men and women, even while also acknowledging a fundamental equality of

[15] Helen Morris, "The City as Foil (Not Friend nor Foe): Conformity and Subversion in 1 Corinthians 12:12–31," in *The Urban World of the First Christians*, eds. Steve Walton, Paul R. Trebilco, and David W. J. Gill (Grand Rapids, MI: Eerdmans, 2017), 145, where a summary and discussion of scholarly perspectives is offered.

men and women before God. But this passage also offers a window into the fact that we cannot take for granted that Paul's theology was shared by all members of the community. Paul acknowledges the presence of women prophets within the community even as he seemingly seeks to restrict their authority. Meshing with the theological perspectives that shaped community life in other ways, it seems that the behaviour of the Corinthian women prophets can be understood as motivated by 'direct access to the resurrected life in Christ through God's Spirit'.[16]

The nature of concrete meeting places and notions of sacred space have been of great interest in the study of Paul's letters in recent years. One of the main questions concerns the relationship between the domestic spaces that were clearly used as meeting places and the assembly defined as 'sacred space' where ritual activities involving worship, dining, and teaching occurred. The domestic atmosphere must surely have infused the atmosphere of the community gatherings – such as the presence of children and slaves caring for them (which was simply taken for granted in this era). Paul has certain expectations concerning the proper behaviour of men and women during worship that ultimately posits men at the top of the hierarchy in defining the space of the assembly (*ekklesia*). Despite their highly visible presence and the evidence that they support the community in various ways, women find their place at the bottom of the hierarchy in this gender construction (1 Cor 11:1–3). While it is taken by some scholars to be a later addition to the text (in part because it has seemed contradictory to Paul's acknowledgement of women prophets), 1 Cor 14:32–34 points to a desire on the part of Paul to distinguish between household space where women can ask questions at home and the *ekklesia* space where women's behaviour should be carefully monitored and, in fact, where they should keep silent.[17]

Taken as a whole, 1 Corinthians 11–14 demonstrates the importance of the ritual context of meetings for defining theology and ethics. Paul uses an array of symbolism, tying the standards of community life both to creation and to the experiences of the Spirit that shape group interaction. His teachings on spiritual gifts provide insight into the values of the *ekklesia*, which he hopes will shape leadership (1 Cor 12: 27–31) and are tied to ethics, which should govern the community rooted in love (1 Cor 13:1–13).

[16] Antoinette Clark Wire, *The Corinthian Women Prophets: A Reconstruction through Paul's Rhetoric* (Minneapolis, MN: Fortress Press, 1990), 185.

[17] See Jorunn Okland, *Women in Their Place: Paul and the Corinthian Discourse of Gender and Sanctuary Space* (London: T&T Clark, 2004), 151, 178.

Above all, love emerges as the theme that ties the Corinthian and Thessalonian correspondence together. This is evident not only in the standard that Paul sets for himself in dealing with these communities, but also in the standard that transcends all others to direct the interactions among Jesus-followers. In an atmosphere of newness and enthusiasm, love seems to ground all things. In the apostle's view, without love there is nothing of value to be, to have, to gain, or to hold onto in these end times (1 Cor 13:1–3).

Further Reading

Barclay, John M. G. "Thessalonica and Corinth: Social Contrasts in Pauline Christianity." *Journal for the Study of the New Testament* 47 (1992): 49–74.
Collins, Raymond F. *Second Corinthians. Paideia.* Grand Rapids, MI: Baker Academic, 2013.
Gaventa, Beverly. *First and Second Thessalonians.* Louisville, KY: Westminster John Knox, 2012.
Horsley, Richard A., ed. *Paul and Empire: Religion and Power in Roman Imperial Society.* Harrisburg, PA: Trinity Press, 1997.
Jewett, Robert. "Tenement Churches and Communal Meals in the Early Church." *Biblical Research* 38 (1993): 23–43.
McNeel, Jennifer Houston. *Paul as Infant and Nursing Mother: Metaphor, Rhetoric and Identity in 1 Thessalonians 2:5–8.* Atlanta, GA: Society of Biblical Literature, 2014.
Meeks, Wayne. *The First Urban Christians: The Social World of the Apostle Paul.* New Haven, CT: Yale University Press, 1983.
Morris, Helen. "The City as Foil (Not Friend nor Foe): Conformity and Subversion in 1 Corinthians 12:12–31." In *The Urban World of the First Christians*, edited by Steve Walton, Paul R. Trebilco, and David W. J. Gill, 141–159. Grand Rapids, MI: Eerdmans, 2017.
Okland, Jorunn, *Women in Their Place: Paul and the Corinthian Discourse of Gender and Sanctuary Space.* London: T&T Clark, 2004.
Osiek, Carolyn and Margaret Y. MacDonald (with Janet Tulloch). *A Woman's Place: House Churches in Earliest Christianity.* Minneapolis, MN: Augsburg Fortress, 2006.
Thiselton, Anthony C. *The First Epistle to the Corinthians.* Grand Rapids, MI: Eerdmans, 2013.
Wire, Antoinette Clark. *The Corinthian Women Prophets: A Reconstruction through Paul's Rhetoric.* Minneapolis, MN: Fortress Press, 1990.

5 Galatians and Romans

PETER OAKES

After Paul wrote Galatians, he wrote at least one letter, 1 Corinthians, on different topics and in a different manner. He then wrote a letter to people in Rome that returned to many of the topics of Galatians and that, in significant ways, matched Galatians in its vocabulary, themes, and structure – this despite the fact that Romans appears to address a different situation from Galatians.

The most striking structural similarity between the letters is that, a fifth of the way through each (Gal 3:15–21 and Rom 3:19–31), Paul writes a short, intense, focal passage about *pistis* ('trust', 'loyalty'), righteousness, Christ, Christ's death, law and works. However, two further structural similarities follow. In each letter, the focal passage is followed by an extended discussion involving Abraham and the nature and identity of God's people, including issues of *pistis*, law, flesh, Spirit, Jews and gentiles. In Galatians this is primarily chapter 3, but, more broadly, runs through to Gal 5:12. In Romans, it is primarily chapter 4, but the issues of the identity of the people of God and the relationship of that to *pistis*, etc., run right through to Rom 11:36. A third structural similarity between the letters is the subsequent passages on living as the loving people of God: Gal 5:13–6:10 and Rom 12:1–15:13. The relationship between these two passages, and between each of them and other parts of the letter are reinforced by shared ideas such as love being the fulfilment of the law (Gal 5:14; Rom 13:8–9).

Romans is not a redaction of Galatians (although we cannot exclude the idea that some phrasing in Romans is a deliberate modification by Paul of phrasing that he may have used in Galatians or other contexts). An attempt to perform formal redaction criticism on Romans as if it were a version of Galatians would be unwise. However, the relationships between Romans and Galatians mean that comparison between the two does offer the promise of shedding light on what Paul is writing in Romans. In any case, the remit of the present chapter is to consider both letters. As we shall see, the process of comparison of the ways in which Paul handles related themes sheds light on his choices in expressing these themes in both Romans and in Galatians.

We will proceed by taking each section of the parallel structure and considering some potentially significant points of similarity and difference. As well as the three pairs of sections above, we will consider the three remaining pairs of sections, which are inherent in constructing Greek letters in general and Paul's type of letters in particular – namely, the letter opening (Gal 1:1–10; Rom 1:1–15), passages setting up the issues to be dealt with (Gal 1:11–2:14; Rom 1:16–3:18), and the letter closing (Gal 6:11–18; Rom 15:14–16:27). As we work through the six sections, we will particularly keep an eye on a number of the themes common to the two letters, again considering similarities and differences in how they are handled: Jews and gentiles; law, *pistis*, and Christ; sin, judgment, and righteousness; death and life; flesh and spirit; and love. We will consider how these similarities or differences shed light on Paul's meaning and aims in each letter and how these relate to similarities or differences of the contextual setting of the letters.

The structure of the letters for the purposes of our comparative study is as follows:

	Galatians	Romans
Letter opening	1:1–10	1:1–15
Setting up the issues	1:11–2:14	1:16–3:18
Righteousness not through works of law but through *pistis* of Christ	2:15–21	3:19–31
From Abraham to the identity of the people of God	3:1–5:12	4:1–11:36
Living as the loving people of God	5:13–6:10	12:1–15:13
Letter closing	6:11–18	15:14–16:27

LETTER OPENINGS: GAL 1:1–10; ROM 1:1–15

Letter openings and closings are distinguished from other parts of letters in two ways. First, and fundamentally, these sections contain the signals needed to start and stop the letter in a culturally appropriate manner. The second way is that, in any letter-writing culture, various forms of words and grammatical structures become typical of these sets of text as they perform this starting and stopping. These lexical and grammatical features can be used and adapted by letter writers for various purposes.

Features common to the letter openings of Galatians and Romans are: Paul's name; his self-description as *apostolos* ('emissary', 'apostle');

locating the recipients, in Galatia (Gal 1:2) and Rome (Rom 1:7) respectively; the identical greeting, 'Grace to you and peace from God our father and the lord Jesus Christ' (Gal 1:3; Rom 1:7); reference to 'the gospel' (Gal 1:6–9; Rom 1:1–5, 9, 15) and to the resurrection of Christ (Gal 1:1; Rom 1:4); and some kind of characterization of Christ (Gal 1:4; Rom 1:2–4) and of the recipients (Gal 1:6; Rom 1:6–8).

It is at this last point that the sharp differences between the letter openings become clear. Romans is fairly typical of Greek letters, including those of Paul, in praising the recipients, speaking warmly of their relationship with him, and expressing a keenness to meet: 'your faith is being proclaimed in the whole world' (Rom 1:8); 'I am longing to see you' (Rom 1:11). The Romans are also described as 'called by Jesus Christ . . . loved by God' (Rom 1:6–7). In contrast, and uniquely for Paul, the recipients of Galatians are simply 'the assemblies of Galatia' (Gal 1:2), with nothing about their calling, holiness, or links to Christ. In Gal 1:6, far from praising them, he attacks them, 'I am astonished that you are so quickly turning aside from the one who called you'. This is so far from the normal pattern of letter openings that Hans Dieter Betz is reasonable in seeing the opening as ending at 1:5, rather than including the whole of 1:1–10.[1] However, the contrast with Paul's other letters is so diametric that 1:6–10 is probably a deliberate change to the normal letter-opening pattern (and 1:11 looks like the start of a letter body, see below).

Paul's complaint about the Galatian Christians fits with his characterization of himself in Gal 1:1. Note its negative form: 'Paul, an emissary not from people, nor through a person, but . . .'. He is on the defensive, rebutting a relativization of his mission and message. He is also on the offensive, starting by making it clear to the Galatians that the gospel they are abandoning is not human, but divine. The opening of Romans shows no such defensiveness. Paul does assert his authority as an apostle, but his references to this quickly feed into explanation either of his gospel (1:2–4; 16–17), or of his enthusiasm to visit and communicate with the Roman Christians (1:9–15). In Rom 1:2–4, the gospel is of Christ, linked to God, David, the Spirit, and lordship. Galatians 1:4 characterises Christ in different terms, as redeemer, giving himself to rescue the sinful from 'the present evil age.' Both characterizations set up key elements of what is to come in the letters.

[1] Hans Dieter Betz, *Galatians: A Commentary on Paul's Letter to the Churches in Galatia* (Philadelphia: Fortress, 1979), 16.

SETTING UP THE ISSUES: GAL 1:11–2:14; ROM 1:16–3:18

There is much that is similar and much that is different between these Galatians and Romans passages. Note first the differences. The genres are different: the Galatians passage is entirely narrative, while Romans is largely diatribal argument – making a case by engaging one or more imagined interlocutors (2:1, 2:17, etc.). It does, however, include a fairly extensive narrative account (1:19–32) of some sort of moral decline from knowledge of God to idolatry, then of actions by God in response. There are also lexical and thematic differences between these sections of the letters. Notably, Galatians 1:11–2:14 does not use the language of trust (*pistis*), righteousness, law, and so on, that will feature heavily in the subsequent argument, although there is one reference to Paul preaching the *pistis*, usually translated here as 'the faith' (Gal 1:23). Romans, by contrast, deploys all the key terms that will be used in the following section of the letter, with 1:16–17 in particular acting as an anticipatory summary of ideas about trust and righteousness in 3:19–31 and other texts. More broadly, Rom 1:16–3:18 is full of terminology of sin and divine judgment, both of which are absent from the Galatians passage. The bulk of the Romans passage starts and ends with statements of human sinfulness: 1:18 speaks of the 'ungodliness and unrighteousness of people, who suppress the truth in unrighteousness'; and 3:18 quotes Ps 36:1, 'There is no fear of God before their eyes'. Much of the argument between these verses serves to establish the universality of this human condition. In contrast, in Gal 1:11–2:14, Paul narrates first the story of the divine origin of his gospel (1:11–24), then a visit to Jerusalem, during which his calling to the gentiles was acknowledged by the Jerusalem Christian leaders (2:1–10), then an incident at Antioch in Syria in which he opposed Peter publicly because, when some people had arrived from Jerusalem, Peter (and other Christian Jews) had withdrawn from their previous practice of eating with gentiles (2:11–14).

There are, however, crucial similarities between the passages, which in turn lead to structural similarities later in the letters: each passage begins with emphatic reference to Paul's gospel and has a key drive towards equalising the status of Christian Jews and Christian gentiles. We have already noted that each letter opening features references to Paul's gospel (*euangelion*) and his preaching of it. In each letter this becomes the axis on which Paul makes the turn into the body of the letter, setting a key topic.

> For I declare to you, brothers and sisters, that the gospel proclaimed by me is not a human opinion. For neither did I receive it from a person ... but I received it through a revelation (*apokalypsis*) of Jesus Christ (Gal 1:11–12).

> For I am not ashamed of the gospel, for it is power of God for salvation for everyone who trusts: for a Jew first and for a Greek. For righteousness of God is revealed (*apokalyptetai*) in it, on the basis of *pistis*, for *pistis*, as it is written, 'The one who is righteous on the basis of *pistis* will live.' (Rom 1:16–17, quoting Habakkuk 2:4)

In Galatians, Paul goes on to narrate how God 'was pleased to reveal (*apokalypsai*) his son to me so that I might proclaim (*euangelizōmai*) him among the gentiles' (Gal 1:16). In Romans, Paul shifts, by direct contrast with 1:16–17, to declare that the 'wrath of God is being revealed (*apokalyptetai*)' upon the sinfulness that Paul then sets out in Rom 1:18–3:18.

For many scholars, the link between gospel and revelation (*apokalypsis*) is the key factor for interpreting these letters. For J. Louis Martyn it defines the theology of each letter: each announces the apocalyptic intervention of God to recreate the Cosmos through the death and resurrection of Christ. For Martyn, Paul's terminology of righteousness ('rectification'), flesh, spirit, and so on, relates primarily to this cosmic change rather than to realms of individual decision and action.[2] For Stephen Westerholm, Paul's view of the inability of the law to save is something that Paul received by revelation, rather than Paul thinking that non-Christian Jews shared this view of the law.[3] Douglas Campbell goes a step beyond this in the centrality he attributes to revelation. For Campbell, Paul does not present Jewish law as defective but instead presents his opponents' view of law and salvation as defective specifically because it is at odds with the gospel revealed by God.[4] Among Campbell's most bold exegetical claims based on this is that much of

[2] J. Louis Martyn, "Apocalyptic Antinomies in Paul's Letter to the Galatians," *New Testament Studies* 31 (1985): 410–424; Martyn, *Galatians: A New Translation with Introduction and Commentary* (New York: Doubleday, 1997), appealing particularly to texts such as Gal 6:14–15.

[3] Stephen Westerholm, *Perspectives Old and New on Paul: The "Lutheran" Paul and His Critics* (Grand Rapids, MI: Eerdmans, 2004), 333.

[4] Douglas Campbell, "An Attempt to Be Understood: A Response to the Concerns of Matlock and Macaskill with *The Deliverance of God*," *Journal for the Study of the New Testament* 34 (2011): 173; more broadly Campbell, *The Deliverance of God: An Apocalyptic Rereading of Justification in Paul* (Grand Rapids, MI: Eerdmans, 2009).

Rom 1:18–3:20 represents Paul's opponents' view, rather than Paul's own view.[5]

In Galatians, Paul's motivation for focusing on his gospel is clear: the Galatians are abandoning it (1:6), so highlighting its divine origin and its validation by the Jerusalem apostles makes sense as a strategy for reversing that abandonment. Paul's motive for shaping the narrative towards his clash with Peter at Antioch, over Jewish practices in a gentile context, only becomes really clear towards the end of the letter where Paul indicates that some gentile Christian men are adopting circumcision (Gal 5:2) and that this is being encouraged by some people who have influenced the Galatians after Paul was there (Gal 6:11). Paul sees this as 'compelling' the Galatian Christian gentiles to Judaize (i.e., to adopt Jewish customs), a charge that he levels against Peter for what Paul sees as the effect of Peter's withdrawal, in Antioch, from eating with Christian gentiles (2:14, cf. 2:3).

In Romans, there is not the same sense of an obvious reason why Paul would start the body of the letter with assertions about his gospel. This uncertainty as to Paul's motivation is in fact characteristic of the letter as a whole, providing space for endless theories, classically set out in the essays collected in Karl Donfried's *The Romans Debate.*[6] One clue to Paul's motivation is provided by the fact that he sets out some key characteristics of his gospel from the outset of the letter (something he does not immediately do for the Galatians). There is some sense of Paul wanting to set out his message to the Roman Christians, most of whom he has not met. Another clue to Paul's motivation comes in his specifying in 1:16–17 that the gospel is for Jews and Greeks. This brings us to the second key commonality in the way in which the issues are set up in each of the two letters.

Despite the different genres of Gal 1:11–2:14 and Rom 1:16–3:18, and despite differing motifs and vocabulary, each aims at equalising Christian Jews and Christian gentiles. In Galatians this equalisation is a practical one: the status of Christian gentiles is such that Christian Jews should eat with them (Gal 2:11–14) and there is no need for the gentile men to be circumcised (Gal 2:3). In Romans, the equalisation is, in this part of the letter, a matter of ideas, a theological conclusion to be drawn: both Jews and gentiles relate to God's law and judgment in some sense (Rom 2:1–16); each group can be 'circumcised of heart' (Rom 2:29),

[5] Campbell, "An Attempt to be Understood," 188.

[6] Karl P. Donfried, ed., *The Romans Debate*, revised and expanded ed. (Peabody, MA: Hendrickson, 1991).

which matters more than physical circumcision; Jews and gentiles are both under sin (Rom 3:9–18). All this equalisation is more decisive than Jewish privileges that Paul acknowledges, such as having been 'entrusted with the oracles of God' (Rom 3:2).

For most of history, the expression 'Christian Jew' has been an oxymoron: in most contexts 'Christian' and 'Jew' have been identities defined over against each other, a pattern that also reflects a long history of tension and of Christian persecution of Jews. However, if we are to attach the term 'Christian' to the very earliest groups of Jesus-followers, we must remember that they were ethnically Jews. Some scholars argue against calling any first-century people 'Christians' or 'Jews' but the points of continuity between first-century groups and many current groups with those heritages appear sufficiently significant to allow such current groups to claim the kind of continuity with their first-century forebears that is signalled by using the same English words to represent them – although we do also need to remain aware both of discontinuities between then and now and of differences among first-century groups claiming any particular cultic or ethnic identity.

RIGHTEOUSNESS NOT THROUGH WORKS OF LAW BUT THROUGH *PISTIS* OF CHRIST: GAL 2:15–21; ROM 3:19–31

Commentators on Romans consistently begin a new section at 3:21. Reasons for this are clear. Thematically, it represents a clear turning point in the letter's argument. From 1:18–3:20 Paul mainly demonstrates sinfulness, while in 3:21 he turns to describing salvation. There is also a parallel between 1:16–18 and 3:21. After Paul has presented in 1:16–17 his opening summary of the gospel in which the righteousness of God is revealed in relation to trust (*pistis*), Paul announces the revealing of God's wrath (Rom 1:18); in Rom 3:21–22 Paul brings us back to the revealing of the righteousness of God in relation to trust, as in 1:16–17.

Comparison with Galatians suggests the need to slightly adjust this standard form of outlining the structure of Romans. Comparing Gal 2:16 with Rom 3:21–22 draws attention to one way in which Rom 3:21 develops beyond 1:17. Romans 3:21 focuses on a righteousness that is 'apart from law' or (according to most scholars) a righteousness that is 'made known apart from law' (but see discussion below). Law is a new element in this section, one not present in Rom 1:17. Once law is seen as a key topic in Rom 3:21, we are into the pattern of Gal 2:16 – namely, Paul arguing that law cannot bring righteousness without needing *pistis*

Iēsou Christou ('trust of Jesus Christ').[7] In that light, Rom 3:21 is closely associated with Rom 3:19–20, because that is where we find the statement about the law being unable to bring righteousness.

Considering Rom 3:19–20 further, we note some key parallels to Gal 2:15–16. The most specific is that Rom 3:20, like Gal 2:16, quotes Ps 143:2 (142:2 in the Septuagint Greek translation), even using a similarly modified form of the Septuagint text (he changes the Septuagintal expression equivalent to 'all living' into 'all flesh' in both letters). A more detailed point of comparison is the opening term of Rom 3:19, 'we know'. This is often overlooked in Romans but has a parallel in Galatians, which is very prominent in that text.

> We, Jews by nature and not sinners from among the nations, knowing that … (Gal 2:15–16)
>
> We know that …. (Rom 3:19)

In each letter what 'we' know is that the law cannot, on its own, bring righteousness to any person in the world, Jew or gentile. In Romans, Paul frames the knowledge indirectly: 'we know' that the law speaks to Jews so as to hold the world accountable to God because works of the law cannot bring righteousness. This allows him to also bring in other themes important to Romans: God's judgment and the function of law as revealing sin. However, what 'we know' reaches the same conclusion in each letter. The 'we' who know this are certainly Jews in Galatians. In Romans it makes sense for them to be Jews too: in both cases 'we' know about the law and about what it can and cannot do. In each letter, Paul effectively explains how Jews know this. They do so because they know the psalms, in particular Ps 143:2. In Paul's early Christian (revealed) reading of the scriptures, he sees the psalmist's despair about righteousness as an expression of the plight of all those whose only resources are those available to the psalmist – namely, the law. A major disadvantage of placing the start of a section of Romans at

[7] 'Trust of Jesus Christ' is a translation attempting to replicate the ambiguity of the Greek, *pistis Iēsou Christou*. Without contextual clues, the phrase could refer to 'trust in Jesus Christ' or 'Jesus Christ's trust' ('trust' might also be replaced by 'loyalty' or other terms). For discussion of *pistis Christou* in Galatians as a way of life of trust in and loyalty to Christ (and, just conceivably, Christ's loyalty to his people and/or people's trust/loyalty towards God through Christ), see Peter Oakes, "*Pistis* as Relational Way of Life in Galatians," *Journal for the Study of the New Testament* 40 (2018): 255-3–275. For a related social reading in Romans 'as broadly defined jargon for participation in the community of the converted', see Robert Jewett, *Romans: A Commentary* (Minneapolis, MN: Fortress Press, 2007), 277.

3:21 is that it masks the likelihood that Paul's thought in that verse runs straight on from 3:19–20, making the line of argument in 3:19–22 similar to that in Gal 2:15–16: 'We Jews know from Psalm 143:2 that no one has righteousness on the basis of works of the law (*ergōn nomou*) but God has now enabled this to happen through trust of Jesus Christ (*dia pisteōs Iēsou Christou*)'.

Seeing this sequence of Paul's argument in Rom 3:19–22 helps confirm that the 'knowing' at the start of Gal 2:16 is supposed to be derived from Psalm 143, even though that text is not quoted until the end of Gal 2:16. Of course, this accounts only for the negative side of what Gal 2:16 sees as being known. The broader sequence of Romans, with its citation of Hab 2:4 in Rom 1:17, lends weight to the idea that that Habakkuk text may be a significant element of what Jews know that contributes to the idea in Gal 2:16 that righteousness is available through *pistis Iēsou Christou* (as both Douglas Campbell and Francis Watson have argued, although with results differing sharply from each other).[8] The Habakkuk text gets quoted later in Galatians, in 3:11, where it is part of the argument applying the conclusions of 2:16 specifically to gentiles.

For Romans, an effect of considering 3:19–20 together with 3:21–31 is that it brings out the 'sandwiching' of the righteousness terms of 3:21–22 between those of 3:20 and 3:24 which, in turn, fits with use elsewhere in the letter and in Galatians. In Rom 3:25–26, Paul plays on an ambiguity in the Greek phrase *dikaiosynē theou*, the 'righteousness of God'. Paul unpacks the purpose of 'the evidence of his [God's] righteousness' as being 'so that he would be righteous (*dikaion*) and would consider righteous (*dikaiounta*) the person of "trust of Jesus"'. Paul sees 'righteousness of God' as a term appropriate both for God's character and for an aspect of God's action in providing righteousness to people. The sandwiching of the two occurrences of 'righteousness of God' in 3:21–22 between 3:20 and 3:24 implies that God's providing of righteousness is in view there. The sequence from 3:20–24 is as follows:

> [20] ... on the basis of works of law, no flesh is considered righteous (*dikaiothēsetai*) before him ... [21]but now righteousness of God (*dikaiosynē theou*) has been revealed ... [22]righteousness of God (*dikaiosynē theou*) through trust of Jesus Christ to all those who

[8] Douglas Campbell, *The Rhetoric of Righteousness in Romans 3.21–26* (Sheffield: Sheffield Academic Press, 1992), 204–213; Francis Watson, "By Faith (of Christ): An Exegetical Dilemma and Its Scriptural Solution," in *The Faith of Jesus Christ: Exegetical, Biblical, and Theological Studies*, eds. Michael F. Bird and Preston M. Sprinkle (Peabody, MA: Hendrickson, 2009), 147–163.

> trust. For there is no distinction, [23]for all sinned ... [24]and are considered righteous as a gift (*dikaioumenoi dōrean*) by his grace ...

The revealing of 'righteousness of God' answers the problem set by 3:20. The way that the 'righteousness of God' does this is then explained by 3:23–24, which gets the reader back to the key verb of 3:20 (*dikaioō*, 'consider righteous').

As well as fitting the argument of Gal 2:16, this connection of ideas also fits well with other important passages in Romans, including 5:17, 9:30, 1:17, and 3:28–30. Romans 5:17 speaks of 'those who receive the overflow of grace and of the gift of righteousness (*tēs dōreas tēs dikaiosynēs*)'. Romans 9:30 describes gentiles as having 'gained possession of righteousness, righteousness on the basis of trust (*katelaben dikaiosynēn, dikaiosynēn tēn ek pisteōs*)'. This coordinates with Rom 1:17, in which the 'righteousness of God' is characterised as being 'on the basis of trust' (*ek pisteōs*; and also 'for trust', *eis pistin*), which is then explained as fitting Hab 2:4, 'the one who is righteous on the basis of trust (*ek pisteōs*) will live'. These ideas of righteousness being given or gained, and being linked to *pistis* (trust) fit well with the *dikaiosynē theou* of 3:21–22 being the means of 'being considered righteous' in 3:24 and (negatively) 3:20. This is further reinforced by 3:28–30 ending (nearly) the passage by returning to the language of being considered righteous on the basis of, or through, trust.

This coordination between Gal 2:16, Rom 3:19–24 and the Romans texts about righteousness as a gift or something gained works very neatly if, in Rom 3:21–22, the Greek, *dikaiosynē theou*, might be read as 'righteousness from God' (taking the Greek *theou* as a 'genitive of origin'), rather than as 'righteousness of God'. This is supported by the occurrence of the explicit idea of origin in Phil 3:9, which refers to *tēn ek theou dikaiosynēn*, 'the righteousness from God'. It does, however, make Paul's idea of *dikaiosynē theou* a new creation by him, without evident precedent in Jewish texts. As Rudolf Bultmann (who advocates this view) points out unashamedly, such a meaning of the term is not to be found in the Septuagint or other previous Jewish literature.[9]

Two alternatives are better rooted in Jewish texts. N. T. Wright argues that *dikaiosynē theou* is God's 'covenant faithfulness', which reaches a climax in the faithful death of Christ that brings about the creation of God's whole 'righteous' people, Jew and gentile.[10] Ernst

[9] Rudolf Bultmann, "δικαιοσύνη θεοῦ," *Journal of Biblical Literature* 83 (1964): 16.

[10] N. T. Wright, *Paul and the Faithfulness of God* (Minneapolis, MN: Fortress Press, 2013), 804, 998.

Käsemann sees 'the righteousness of God' as God's 'power which brings salvation'.[11] Richard Hays supports Käsemann's view by appeal to the context of Ps 143:2. Psalm 143:2b (the text quoted in Rom 3:20) is immediately preceded (in Ps 143:1–2a) by calls for God to:

> Hear my prayer in your faithfulness (*alētheia*).
>
> Answer me in your righteousness (*en tēi dikaiosynēi sou*).
>
> And do not enter into judgment with your servant.

Linking this with Paul's assertion of God's righteousness in Rom 3:5, Hays sees 3:21 as the manifestation of God's saving righteousness of Ps 143:1 (also 143:11).[12] Hays' intertextual appeal to Ps 143:1 is problematised by the need to take *en tēi dikaiosynēi sou* instrumentally ('by means of your righteousness')[13] when the Psalmist looks more likely to be appealing to God's character ('in your righteousness'), as Wright argues when he too appeals to Ps 143:1 to support his reading.[14]

Wright does fit his understanding of *dikaiosynē theou* as covenant faithfulness into a reading of Rom 3:21–31 but it requires considerable exegetical complexity to do so.[15] It ought to be more straightforward to fit in Käsemann's idea of God's saving power. However, the idea is in fact part of Käsemann's overarching theory that *dikaiosynē theou* 'is for Paul God's sovereignty over the world revealing itself eschatologically in Jesus'.[16] This rather leads us away from righteousness as gift and from Rom 3:21–22 as a clear solution to the problem set in 3:19–20. It takes us more towards the cosmic apocalyptic ideas of Martyn.

Käsemann actually seeks to hold gift and action together, and does so in a way that looks valuable for our reading above. He writes that, 'the dominating sense of the divine righteousness in Paul is that of a gift … the sense 'the power which brings salvation' … qualifies throughout the sense 'divine gift' so that gift and Giver remain inseparable'.[17]

[11] Ernst Käsemann, *New Testament Questions of Today* (Philadelphia: Fortress, 1969), 168n*.

[12] Richard B. Hays, "Psalm 143 and the Logic of Romans 3," *Journal of Biblical Literature* 99 (1980): 115, citing Käsemann, *New Testament Questions of Today.*

[13] Jewett, *Romans*, 275.

[14] Wright, *Paul and the Faithfulness of God*, 995–996.

[15] Wright, *Paul and the Faithfulness of God*, 996–1000.

[16] Käsemann, *New Testament Questions*, 180.

[17] Käsemann, *New Testament Questions*, 168n*.

Käsemann draws on (among other texts) 2 Cor 5:21, in which Christians are communally described as being 'righteousness of God'. Rather than Bultmann's idea, in which 'righteousness from God' is righteousness given by God to people, for Käsemann the gift is 'righteousness of God' itself.[18] This reading makes considerable sense in Romans 3 if we detach it from Käsemann's attempt to bring it under the umbrella of his cosmic theory, which does not fit well with the idea of gift. In fact, we could probably say that the gift of God's righteousness is rather comparable to the presence of God's son and of God's Spirit in the Christian community.

One further point to deal with is that Douglas Campbell would object to our reading of Rom 3:22. He sees *dikaiosynē* there as being *revealed* through *pistis*, rather than *dikaiosynē* itself being characterised as 'through *pistis*'.[19] He sees the key issue as being the relationship between *pistis* and revelation rather than between *pistis* and righteousness. However, comparison with Galatians suggests that the relationship between *pistis* and righteousness is more likely to be the key issue. *Pistis* is related to righteousness eight times (Gal 2:16 [three times]; 3:6, 8, 11, 24; 5:5) and is only an object of revelation (3:2, 23), not a means of it. In Romans there is more of a case to be made for seeing *pistis* as a means of revelation (especially as one possible reading of Rom 1:17a; conceivably also 3:25). However, even in Romans *pistis* is far more often related to righteousness (1:17; [3:22]; 3:26, 30; 4:3, 5, 9, 11, 13, 22; 5:1; 9:30, 32; 10:4, 6, 10). It is the object of revelation in 10:8, 17. More decisive still is Paul's scriptural focus in both letters on Hab 2:4 and Gen 15:16. These central texts relate *pistis* to righteousness, not to revelation.

Galatians 2:15–21 and Rom 3:19–31 move apart somewhat after Gal 2:16 and Rom 3:22. In Gal 2:17–18, Paul speaks of his own pulling down and rebuilding, death and life. Romans 3:23–27 considers Christ's death as atoning sacrifice, then what God's actions convey about his character, then the wrongness of boasting. However, each passage speaks of Christ's death and comes back to the matter of law. Galatians 3:21 concludes the passage with the counterfactual, 'if there is righteousness through law' (supporting the link between 'righteousness' and 'being considered righteous'), and its implication, 'then Christ died for nothing'. Romans 3:28–29 is also emphatic that people are 'considered righteous by trust ... apart from works of law (*chōris ergōn nomou*)' (Rom 3:28). This last phrase corresponds to 'apart from law' (Rom 3:21) and

[18] Käsemann, *New Testament Questions*, 169.
[19] Campbell, *The Rhetoric of Righteousness*, 63.

also to 4:6, which speaks of God reckoning 'righteousness apart from works' (*dikaiosynēn chōris ergōn*). This fuels the idea that the King James Version might have been right all along in translating 3:21 as, 'But now the righteousness of God without the law is manifested' (contrary to most modern interpreters and translators), since the relevant topic of 3:19–31 is not the law's revelatory inability (as in the common translation 'manifested apart from law') but its inability to bring righteousness (as in the KJV).

Romans 3:29–30 focuses firmly on the agenda of the status of Jews and gentiles before God. Both groups (3:29–30) are now considered righteous on the basis of *pistis* – presumably the *pistis Iēsou Christou* of 3:22 – rather than works of the law. Galatians has not yet been directly arguing about the status of gentiles, although it is implicit in Paul's argument against Peter, and Galatians is about to turn to tackle it at length.

FROM ABRAHAM TO THE IDENTITY OF THE PEOPLE OF GOD: GAL 3:1–5:12; ROM 4–11

In both Romans and Galatians Paul moves from the intense passage on works, law, righteousness, trust, and Christ onto writing about Abraham, Jews, and gentiles (Gal 3; Rom 4). In each letter, this draws Abraham into the nexus of terms from the previous passage, using Genesis 15:6 to link him to *pistis* (Gal 3:6; Rom 4:3), then combining that with other scriptural texts to bring gentiles into the scope of his family and blessings.

As well as the fairly tight set of parallels between Gal 3 and Rom 4, there is an alternative, much looser structural parallel between much of Gal 3:1–4:6 and significant parts of Rom 4–11. To see this, we can begin by tracking the terms 'law' and 'righteousness' across Rom 4–11. Roughly, the pattern of this is:

Romans 4	Law, righteousness, *pistis*, Jews, gentiles
5:12–21	Law, righteousness, sin, obedience
6:12–23	Law, righteousness, sin
7	Law, sin, flesh, spirit
8	Law, righteousness, flesh, spirit
9:30–10:13	Law, righteousness, *pistis*, Jews, gentiles

If we compare Rom 4 with Rom 9:30–10:13, an interesting difference is in the role of Christ. Jesus Christ hardly appears in Rom 4, not coming into the argument until 4:24–25, the final two verses. In contrast, Christ plays the pivotal role in 9:30–10:13. He is *telos nomou*, the 'end' or 'goal' of the law, thus bringing righteousness to everyone who trusts (10:4), Jew or gentile (10:12). A major potential conceptual link between this and Galatians 3–4 is Christ's relationship to time. In Gal 3:19–4:6, Paul offers a narrative in which the event of Christ's arrival is the decisive change for law, righteousness, *pistis*, Jews, and gentiles. Christ's arrival that Paul signals in Rom 10:4 could perform the same function (i.e., decisive change) within the narrative of Rom 9:24–10:13. In tracking these issues, we will consider first the comparison between the two Abraham passages, Galatians 3 and Romans 4; then we will look at the second part of the looser parallel structure in which Gal 3:19–4:6 can be seen to relate to Rom 9:30–10:13 and to other texts in Romans about the function of the law. There are, of course, many sections of Rom 4–11 and Gal 3:1–5:12 that are much more divergent, although there would be quite a few points at which comparison would be interesting, e.g., on the status of Israel (Rom 9–11), to which we will return when considering Gal 6:16.

In the discourse about Abraham in both Romans 4 and Galatians 3, Paul uses Gen 15:6 as his starting point.

> Just as Abraham 'trusted God and it was reckoned to him as righteousness', know then that those who are of trust, these are sons of Abraham. (Gal 3:6–7)

> For if Abraham was considered righteous on the basis of works, he has a boast. But he doesn't have one before God because what does the scripture say? 'Abraham trusted God and it was reckoned to him as righteousness'. (Rom 4:2–3)

In Galatians 3:6–14, Paul moves very directly from Abraham's *pistis* (3:6) to the nature of the gentile Christian community (3:7–9). Paul is explaining the Galatian gentiles' experience of the Spirit (3:2–5) by showing from scripture how their trust in Christ can be the basis of righteousness (3:8, 11), which equates to evading the law's curse (3:10, 13) and inheriting Abraham's blessing (3:8–9, 14), which equates to receiving the Spirit (3:14).[20] In contrast, Romans 4 takes longer to get

[20] For discussion of how Gal 3 presents a theology of gentile reception of the Spirit, see Oda Wischmeyer, "Wie kommt Abraham in den Galaterbrief? Überlegungen zu Gal 3,6–29," in *Umstrittener Galaterbrief: Studien zur Situierung der Theologie des Paulus-Schreibens* , eds. Michael Bachmann, and Bernd Kollmann (Neukirchen-Vluyn: Neukirchener Verlag, 2010), 130, 135. See also Peter Oakes, *Galatians* (Grand Rapids, MI: Baker Academic, 2015), 100–115.

from Gen 15:6 to the gentiles. Paul reflects first on law, works, trust, and forgiveness, drawing in other scriptural texts in support (4:1–8). This enables him to address the topic of sin (three times in 4:7–8), which is a major topic in Romans (esp. Rom 1–3, 5–7) but is almost entirely absent in Galatians. Paul turns to the community issue in Rom 4:9. He points to the timing of Gen 15:6 as having been prior to Abraham's circumcision (4:9–10). Paul uses this to argue that Abraham is father of both Jews who have *pistis* and gentiles who have *pistis* (4:11–12). Galatians 3:17–18 also uses an argument from temporal priority that heads in the same direction but less directly. The covenant involving promise was given 430 years prior to the law, so the law cannot annul the promise (3:17), which means that the Abrahamic inheritance cannot be on the basis of law (3:18). This heads towards enabling gentile inclusion via arguments of types that Paul deploys in both letters, about the modes of operation of law and promise (Gal 3:18, 21; Rom 4:14–15).

An argument that Paul makes in each letter is that both Jewish and gentile followers of Christ are Abraham's seed. However, he follows differing intertextual directions to arrive there. In Rom 4:17–18, Paul takes the direct approach of drawing on Gen 17:5 (with help from the wording of 15:5), which promises that 'many nations/gentiles (*ethnē*)' will be Abraham's seed. Galatians takes two less direct routes. First, Gal 3:8 uses Gen 12:3 and 18:18, which say that 'all nations/gentiles' will be blessed 'in' Abraham. Paul effectively equates this to being 'sons of Abraham', a status that the gentile Christians have through sharing the trust of Gen 15:6 (Gal 3:7–9). Second, Paul launches a protracted Christological argument in Gal 3:16, using Gen 13:15 (and/or 17:8; 24:7) to declare Christ the single seed of Abraham. The punch line of the arguments is that all those 'in Christ', Jew or gentile, are 'one', hence Abraham's seed (3:28–29).

The differences between Paul's strategies in Romans 4 and Galatians 3 relate, to an extent, to the different roles of *pistis* at the ends of each argument. In Gal 3:25, the arrival of *pistis* is an event marking the change of the age. It is the arrival of Christ and offers righteousness through incorporation into Christ (Gal 3:23–29). In Rom 4:17–24, *pistis* picks up a more particular characteristic of Abraham, his trust specifically in the birth of a child from bodies that were reproductively dead (Rom 4:17–21). This enables Paul to return again to Gen 15:6 in Rom 4:22, but this time with a sharp twist.

> Therefore 'it was reckoned to him as righteousness'. It was not written on his account only that, 'it was reckoned to him', but also

on our account, to whom it will be reckoned, to those trusting in the one who raises Jesus our lord from the dead. (Rom 4:22–24)

The *pistis* that brings righteousness is now defined as trust in the God who raised Jesus from the dead (Rom 4:22–25).

These differences relate to the aims of the letters. Galatians aims to defend the unity of Jew and gentile in Christ, as equal members. The key effect of this is seen in the use of the Antioch incident (Gal 2:11–14) to launch Paul's key argument. He seeks oneness and constructs his argument about Abraham's seed in such a way as to make oneness essential to it. The aims of Romans appear more diffuse, including teaching quite a range of key ideas, such as aspects of the resurrection of Christ. In Romans 4, this is enabled by the specific focus that Paul gives to Abraham's *pistis*, a focus absent from Galatians. The emphasis on Christ's resurrection at the end of Romans 4 then fits with the later focus on it in passages such as 6:1–11.

Let us turn to the looser structural parallel that covers the longer range of material between Gal 3:1–5:12 and Rom 3–11. Both Galatians and Romans have a section on law, righteousness, *pistis*, Abraham, Jews, and gentiles (Gal 3:1–16 and Rom 4) and another section that brings together most of the same topics but features a decisive intervention by Christ (Gal 3:25–4:6; Rom 9:30–10:13).[21] In each letter, between the two passages Paul has offered extensive reflection on the significance of Law.

Romans 9:30–10:13 is in the middle of what is explicitly a discussion of Israel (a topic introduced in 9:1–3). Gentiles slip into the argument at 9:24. They will end up being warned against arrogance (11:18–20) and being co-opted into a strange argument that their incorporation into the Christian community will cause jealousy that will lead Jews to accept something like Paul's message (11:13–14). Before reaching this point, Paul again puts Jews and gentiles on a level in terms of salvation. Romans 9:30–33 presents the law as a risky matter for Jews. Paul sees the route to righteousness as via *pistis*. Gentiles attained this righteousness (9:30) but the law offered Israel the alternative of seeking righteousness on the basis of works, which Israel pursued (9:31–32). Paul saw this as Israel's stumble over a stumbling stone laid by God.

What shall we say then? That the gentiles that were not pursuing righteousness obtained righteousness, righteousness which is on

[21] There is also a key intervention relating to Christ in Gal 3:13 but it is not used to mark a change of time period in the way that happens in 3:25–4:6.

> the basis of trust. Israel, pursuing a law of righteousness, did not reach the law. Why? Because not on the basis of trust but as if on the basis of works. They stumbled over the stumbling stone. As it is written, 'See, I lay in Zion a stumbling stone and a rock that causes trouble, yet the one who trusts in him will not be put to shame'. (Rom 9:30–33, quoting Isa 28:16)

Paul expresses a deep concern for Israel's salvation (10:1). He praises their zeal but sees it as uninformed (10:2), arguing that the righteousness that Israel was pursuing was 'their own', rather than 'the righteousness of God' (Rom 10:3).

Romans 10:4, 'Christ is the *telos* of the law, for righteousness for everyone who trusts', appears to throw the reader into the world of Gal 3:23–25. Whether *telos* is taken as 'end' or 'goal', Christ's arrival, as in Gal 3:24–25, is the arrival of *pistis* that brings righteousness. In the scheme of Galatians, it means the end of the role of the law, which was as *paidagōgos* (Gal 3:24–25), a slave who looked after children during their education. How well would this work as an understanding of Rom 10:4? The answer is, rather poorly. In Romans 9, the law has nothing like a *paidagōgos* role. A role that the law does have here is as the route by which Israel pursued righteousness by works.[22] This equates to the misunderstanding of the law that Rom 3:19–20 seeks to combat: that works of the law could bring righteousness. Taking the 'but now' of Rom 3:21 in a temporal sense,[23] we can read Rom 3:19–22 as carrying the same kind of Galatians-type sequence as Rom 10:2–4, with both Romans passages announcing the righteousness-bringing event of the arrival of Christ and *pistis*, as seen in unambiguously temporal terms in Gal 3:24–25.

Galatians also offers the idea that this sequence could be drawn from Paul's experience. In Gal 2:15–16 Paul reminds Peter that they both trusted in Christ because they had become aware that Christ, not law, was essential to righteousness: their encounter with Christ led them to stop misusing the law in the manner of Rom 9:32. In Gal 2:19 Paul goes on to describe his experience as having 'died to the law', which freed him up to 'live to God'. In Rom 10:4 Paul could also be thinking more broadly of his experience of groups of Christian Jews in

[22] There is attractiveness in N. T. Wright's argument that somehow the 'stumbling stone' quotation from Isaiah merges the stone as the law and, in the second line, the stone as Christ (*Paul and the Faithfulness of God*, 1179).

[23] Contra Jewett (*Romans*, 272), who sees the contrast as more a logical than a temporal one.

general, leading to the conclusion that works of the law were not the route to righteousness, and consequently building a communal life that they and he saw as, in a sense, fulfilling the law: an experience of the law's *telos* in both senses (the telic 'goal' and the temporal 'end').

In Rom 10:5, Paul turns to Lev 18:5, a verse he also cites in Gal 3:12. In Galatians, this Leviticus text (which suggests that life flows from doing) is used to distinguish law from the action of *pistis* in bringing life, as in Hab 2:4, cited in the previous verse of Galatians. In Rom 10:5, Lev 18:5 is used to distinguish law from 'the word ... in your mouth and in your heart' (Rom 10:8, quoting Deut 30:14). Paul identifies this with 'the word of *pistis* that we preach' (Rom 10:8). This takes him to the second line of the Isaiah stumbling text, which goes on to commend 'trusting in him/it' (Rom 10:11, from Isa 28:16). Paul sees a combination of this and Joel 2:32, about calling 'on the name of the lord' (Rom 10:13), as bringing Jews and gentiles onto the same, secure level in terms of salvation (Rom 10:12). Paul arrives at a similar leveling of Jews and gentiles in both letters through repeatedly linked, but strikingly different, routes.

LIVING AS THE LOVING PEOPLE OF GOD: GAL 5:13–6:10; ROM 12:1–15:13

Both Galatians and Romans wait until very late in the letter before offering anything like detailed moral instruction: Gal 5:13; Rom 12:1. Galatians does not even use an imperative until 4:12 (apart from 'performative' ones such as 'know that' in 3:7). Romans uses them earlier, although as general, rather than specific, exhortations (e.g., 6:13). Neither letter centres on moral exhortation. Nor does Paul give the impression that either Gal 1:1–5:12 or Rom 1–11 are building towards the subsequent ethical sections as the aim of the arguments of the earlier chapters. For Galatians, a substantial proportion of scholars in the twentieth century even saw Gal 5:13–6:10 as addressing a different set of issues from the rest of the letter, although this interpretation has been relatively rare recently.[24] For Romans, apart from the return to issues about Jews and gentiles in 15:7–12, the section 12:1–15:13 has been largely ignored when considering the overall argument of the letter.

[24] This shift is due in no small measure to the cogent arguments in John M. G. Barclay, *Obeying the Truth: A Study of Paul's Ethics in Galatians* (Edinburgh: T&T Clark, 1988).

It does look unlikely that every part of Gal 5:13–6:10 and Rom 12:1–15:13 can be fit into a clear relationship with the rest of their respective letters, especially because each includes instructions that appear somewhat miscellaneous (e.g., Gal 6:3–6; Rom 12:11–21). However, some of the commonalities between the passages in Galatians and Romans do relate in interesting ways to the main lines of the letters' arguments. These commonalities revolve around the theme of love. Theologically, a key shared issue is love as the fulfilment of the law. Practically, a key shared issue is the outworking of each letter's argument in terms of a shared life of mutual welcome.

Love (*agapē*) is a central term in both Gal 5:13–6:10 and Rom 12:1–15:13. Galatians 5:6 has already set up the alternative to a strong circumcision/uncircumcision divide as being 'trust working through love'. Then, in Gal 5:13, love acts as the hinge to turn from a discourse about freedom to one about service: 'through love, be slaves to one another'. Loving your neighbour fulfils all the law (5:14). Discussion then focuses on the contrast between flesh and Spirit, with the first fruit of the Spirit being love (5:22). Much of the rest of the discourse relates conceptually to love but without further use of the term *agapē*. In Romans, the first concrete moral exhortation is to sincere love (12:9). Christians should have a continuing debt to love one another because love, in particular loving your neighbor, is the fulfilment of the law (13:8–10). Love is a key moral benchmark in 14:15 and, again, much of the rest of the discourse relates conceptually to love.

Martin de Boer offers a bold reading of the citation of Lev 19:18 in Gal 5:14. He takes the text as prophetic, arguing that what Paul means to say in Gal 5:14 is this:

> All that God promised in the Scripture concerning Christ and his Spirit has become concrete, visible reality for us in the actualization of the *one* word of promise articulated in Lev 19:18, that in the new creation inaugurated by Christ, you will truly love your neighbour as yourself.[25]

De Boer is, on the one hand, seeking to defend Martyn's 'apocalyptic' view, in which Christ has ended the cosmos in which law had force, so Paul cannot be seeing fulfilment of the law as now happening. On the other hand, de Boer wants to correct Martyn's unconvincing temporal resolution of this which sees Paul distinguishing between 'the enslaving

[25] Martinus C. de Boer, *Galatians: A Commentary* (Louisville, KY: Westminster John Knox, 2011), 350.

voice of the Sinaitic Law' and the promissory voice of the earlier, 'Abrahamic Law'. As de Boer notes, a problem with Martyn's scheme is that Lev 19:18 is Sinaitic.[26] De Boer's alternative is that *nomos* ('law') in Gal 5:14 refers, like in 4:21, to the books of scripture and not to the law code: 'Paul evidently does not regard the content of Lev 19:18 as part of the Mosaic legal code'[27]. However, an obvious problem for this is that it does not work in the Romans parallel. In Rom 13:9, Lev 19:18 is set off against a string of legal commands: 'Do not commit adultery, do not kill, do not steal, do not covet.' Here, Paul is clearly using Lev 19:18 as a part of the law code that sums up the law code. Since Paul uses *nomos* of Lev 19:18 as part of the law code in Romans, it is not plausible to argue that he could not have done this in Galatians. De Boer is aware of the tension between his reading and Romans; he makes a comment on this that we will return to in our concluding reflections. A problem with the particularly 'hard-edged' apocalyptic readings such as those of Martyn and de Boer is that they make Paul more uncomfortable with law than he actually is in either Galatians or Romans. Both letters show Paul writing that works of law cannot bring righteousness but neither shows Paul presenting the law as inherently negative so that a life that fulfilled the law would be wrong if, as Gal 5:14 and Rom 13:9 both indicate, that fulfilment primarily consists of love – a type of fulfilment which, valuably for Paul, does not require pursuit of food laws that would keep Jews and gentiles apart.

Having said all this, de Boer is rightly bringing to light something that Paul is doing conceptually in both letters, alongside what is implied by the more conventional reading in which Paul is seen as exhorting the recipients of each letter to practice love. Paul is undoubtedly doing this. As we will see shortly, maintenance or improvement of communal life is a practical aim of these sections of each letter. However, there is a significant extent to which Paul is also being descriptive. In each letter, his exhortations flow from his experience of loving Christian communities. In Galatians, this includes experience shared with his audience; he calls them back to (or calls them not to abandon) the loving life of the Spirit that they have already experienced, including while Paul was among them (esp. 3:2–5; 4:12–19; 5:7). In Romans, what Paul seeks to extend to his audience is undoubtedly what he has experienced elsewhere – a corporate life of love that, in fact, they are already familiar with (15:14).

[26] Martyn, *Galatians*, 505–508, 511, 558); de Boer, *Galatians*, 344n467.
[27] de Boer, *Galatians*, 345.

This effectively creates a letter-capping argument from experience of a communal life that, by its love, can be seen to fulfil the law. In Galatians, this has very direct purchase: their current life of Spirit-filled love fulfils the law; if they follow Paul's opponents into a law-dependent life they are, in his view, turning to the flesh, away from the Spirit, hence away from the very life that fulfils the law (esp. 3:2–5). In Romans, there is not the same sense of the letter being a fierce argument against opponents (pace Douglas Campbell; also see below). Any payoff is therefore probably subtler than in Galatians. It is, however, very important to Paul in Romans that his argument upholds the law (esp. 3:31). A presentation of Christian communal life as a fulfilment of the law through love is a powerful way of bringing such an argument to a close.

Rom 12:1–15:13 ends on a clear practical note.

> Therefore welcome one another, just as also Christ welcomed you, to the glory of God. For I say that Christ has become a servant of 'the circumcision' for the sake of the truth of God, so as to confirm the promises that were made to the patriarchs, and so that the gentiles will praise God for his mercy. (Rom 15:7–9)

The moral exhortation calls for a mutual welcome that has particularly in view a welcome between Jews and gentiles. Galatians too has an extensive concern for mutual relations. The term 'one another' (*allēloi*) occurs six times in 5:13–6:10 (excluding a nonpersonal use in 5:17). It occurs nine times in Rom 12:1–15:13. The passages in each letter also contain substantial other terminology carrying the idea.

Unlike Romans, in Galatians there is not a 'punch line' that Jews and gentiles in the community are to welcome one another. However, as we have seen, the main argument of the letter was launched by the account of the Antioch incident, which centres on Jews and gentiles eating together in the Christian community. Galatians 5:13–6:10 is full of exhortation to mutual love (5:13–14, 22; 6:1–2, 10), with warnings against the dangers of division (5:15, 20–21, 26). Paul may be concerned to heal divisions caused by the arrival of his opponents. Another possibility would be to encourage unity in the Christian community between Jews and gentiles. However, the clarity of Paul's expression of this in Romans 15 makes it striking that Gal 5:13–6:10 lacks direct reference to Jews or gentiles. Paul's aims here could be more general than either of these possibilities. In Gal 4:15, remembering an earlier time, he asks plaintively, 'Where then is your happiness?' As in 3:2–5, he appeals to their experience of the blessings of the life in the Spirit, life that flowed from their acceptance of his gospel of trust in Christ. The mixture of indicative and imperative in 5:13–6:10 could suggest that he hopes for a recovery of the full life of mutual love among them, while also appealing to the experience that they still have.

In Romans, Peter Lampe and many others have tied the ethics of welcome in 12:1–15:13 to the scenario suggested by Wolfgang Wiefel, in which the aim is specifically for Christian gentiles to welcome Christian Jews (including those who formerly had been community leaders) back to Rome after the expiry of an edict of emperor Claudius expelling Christian Jews from the city in 49 CE.[28] That is a conceivable scenario, but the probability of the chain of evidence used to support it is very low. The evidence centres on one passage from the Roman author Suetonius (*Claudius* 25.4). In a list of Claudius' actions towards various ethnic groups, Suetonius writes that he 'expelled the Jews at the instigation of Chrestus continually rioting' (*Iudaeos impulsore Chresto assidue tumultuantis expulit*). With about three alterations, this could be taken as evidence that Claudius expelled Christian Jews because of rioting among Jews over allegiance to Christus, a figure no longer around and never having been in Rome. Each misunderstanding by Suetonius (or his source) that is needed to sustain this reading is possible but each significantly reduces the probability of it as evidence for Wiefel's suggestion. This, and other issues, make it too weakly supported a hypothesis to be used as a major basis for interpretation of Romans.[29]

However, this hypothesis is not actually the main thrust of Wiefel's article. The main thrust was to demonstrate the pervasiveness of anti-Semitism in Roman culture at the time of Paul's letter. This broader idea is much more likely as a context for understanding Paul's rhetoric of mutual welcome. As Wiefel points out, combating of anti-Semitism fits well with the rhetoric of Rom 9–11. In Rom 9–11, Christian gentiles are called to react positively to Jews who are not Christians. Romans 12:1–15:13 would fit with that, although the rhetoric of especially Romans 14 implies that relationships among Christians are primarily in view. Despite the ambiguity of the food and calendrical issues in

[28] Wolfgang Wiefel, "The Jewish Community in Ancient Rome and the Origins of Roman Christianity," in *The Romans Debate*, ed. K. P. Donfried (Peabody, MA: Hendrickson, 1991), 92–96; Peter Lampe, *From Paul to Valentinus: Christians at Rome in the First Two Centuries* , trans. Michael Steinhauser (Minneapolis, MN: Fortress Press, 2003), 11–14.

[29] For a fuller argument see Peter Oakes, "Using Historical Evidence in the Study of Neronian Christian Groups and Texts," in *The Last Years of Paul's Life: Essays from the Tarragona Conference, June 2013*, eds. Armand Puig i Tàrrech, John M. G. Barclay, and Jörg Frey (Tübingen: Mohr Siebeck, 2015), 138–141.

Romans 14, a key issue in Rom 12:1–15:13 is evidently that of Jews and gentiles welcoming each other in the house churches of Rome. Galatians makes us ask whether the welcome in Romans is the Antioch issue of Jews and gentiles eating together. However, Romans does not indicate a danger (from Paul's perspective) of gentiles adopting Jewish laws and customs. The issue at stake could be a less heated one of relationships between various of the several house churches greeted in Romans 16.

LETTER CLOSING: GAL 6:11–18; ROM 15:14–16:27

As with the letter openings, the tonal difference between Galatians and Romans is particularly stark in the two letter closings. Apart from the closing grace wish, all the usual closing politenesses or expressions of affection are missing from Galatians, whereas they are more fully expressed in Romans than in any other of Paul's letters. Having said this, the closing of Galatians is far from being as aggressive towards the recipients as is the opening. By the time he reaches the closing, Paul has turned his fire from the recipients to very firmly focus on his opponents. Whereas in the opening it was, 'I am astonished that you are so rapidly turning away' (1:6), in the closing it is, 'Those who want to make a good showing in flesh, these are the ones compelling you to be circumcised' (6:12). The ending of Romans does also go beyond politeness and affection. There is a rationalisation of the sending of the letter (15:14–15) and, consequently, of Paul's ministry (15:16–21), leading onto explanation of his planned visit and some requests in relation to it and to Paul's other plans (15:22–33).

Romans, like Galatians, also ends with a resumption of some key areas of argument and, unusually for Romans, like Galatians it includes a warning against people who Paul sees as being dangerous.

> I urge you, brothers and sisters, to watch out for those who create divisions and obstacles, contrary to the teaching that you learned, and turn away from them. For such people are not enslaved to our lord Jesus Christ but to their own stomach, and through pleasant and fine words they deceive the innocent. (Rom 16:17–18)

There are various questions about which parts of the ending of Romans are original.[30] However, we have seen from this comparison of

[30] See, e.g., Douglas J. Moo, *The Letter to the Romans*, 2nd ed. (Grand Rapids, MI: Eerdmans, 2018), 5–8.

Galatians and Romans that, in either letter, unexpected fragments of tone or teaching can turn up that look more like the other letter. In this case, the warning about people who cause divisions would complement well Paul's call to mutual welcome among the Roman house churches. Romans 16:17–18 would be suggesting that he is addressing what he sees as a danger of lack of mutual welcome, either because he has heard of some people in Rome causing division, or he has a general fear of such people through his experience elsewhere.

An unusual aspect of the ending of Galatians, sounding more at home in Romans than in Galatians, is the introduction of the topic of boasting.

> They want you to be circumcised so that they might boast in your flesh. May I never boast except in the cross of our lord Jesus Christ, through whom the world was crucified to me and I to the world. (Gal 6:13–14)

In Romans, boasting is a result of works:

> Where then is boasting? It is excluded. Through what law, a law of works? No, but through a law of trust. For we reckon a person to be considered righteous by trust apart from works of law. (Rom 3:27–28)

> If Abraham was considered righteous on the basis of works, he has a boast. (Rom 4:2)

In Gal 6:13, Paul connects boasting with flesh (cf. also 6:11: 'they wish to make a good showing in the flesh'). In Romans, boasting is connected with works. This connection fits Galatians too, because Paul links works with flesh, particularly in Gal 3:3, where he parallels the hearers' adoption of works of the law with 'ending in flesh'. Conversely, the link between 'boasting' and 'flesh' in Galatians increases the likelihood of Paul having 'flesh' in mind when writing about boasting in Romans. This strengthens the likelihood of Wright's translation of Rom 4:1 as, 'What shall we say? Have we found Abraham to be our forefather according to the flesh?'[31] since Paul goes straight on to say, 'For if Abraham was considered righteous on the basis of works, he has a boast'.

A final point at which Romans should shed light on Galatians is the blessing of Gal 6:16: 'And to as many as walk by this rule, peace be upon them and mercy and/even/also (*kai*) upon the Israel of God'. There is far

[31] Wright, *Paul and the Faithfulness of God*, 1003.

more discussion of Israel in Romans than in Galatians. It would be foolish not to take Romans into account in trying to understand both the only direct reference to Israel in Galatians and the ambiguous syntax of the blessing. The argument of Romans 9–11 (and indeed of Galatians) makes it look unlikely that 'of God' is meant to qualify 'Israel' in such a way as to stop it referring to Jews as a whole people, so 'Israel of God' here probably refers to the ethnic people of Israel. The more natural point for complexity in the blessing is in the word 'mercy'. Both Galatians and Romans show that what Paul considers 'mercy' on Israel could refer to various things, including some that most Jews would disagree with. In view of this, the blessing looks best read as, 'And to as many as walk by this rule, peace be upon them, and mercy even upon the Israel of God'.[32]

CONCLUDING REFLECTIONS

Anyone of my generation attempting a comparison between Galatians and Romans feels Hans Hübner looking over their shoulder. His 1978, *Die Gesetz bei Paulus* (later translated into English as *Law in Paul's Thought*) forced apart the harmonised mixture between the two letters that interpreters often produced without much thought. Hübner portrayed a fiercely law-critical Paul of Galatians coming, through experience, to a much more nuanced position in Romans. Paradoxically, Hübner's work, although based on the axiom that Galatians and Romans should be treated as distinct texts, shows the value of setting the two texts beside each other to consider their similarities and differences. We can see this repeatedly illuminating his discussions (for instance, in his consideration of how fulfilment of the law, in Rom 13:8, relates to fulfilment of 'the whole law' in Gal 5:15).[33]

How far should we go in using the two letters to interpret each other? De Boer (defending his reading of Gal 5:14) offers this estimation:

> This interpretation of the referential meaning of the phrase 'the entire law' is perhaps not easily supported by the texts from Romans cited above. Galatians 5:14, however, must be interpreted on its own terms, as part of that letter. In Galatians, in contrast to Rom 13:8–10, Paul avoids the term 'commandment' and does not

[32] For discussion see Oakes, *Galatians*, 191–192.

[33] Hans Hübner, *Law in Paul's Thought: A Contribution to the Development of Pauline Theology* (Edinburgh: T&T Clark, 1984), 83–87.

> characterise Lev 19:18 as 'summing up' the law. Furthermore, when Paul writes Galatians, he has not yet written Romans, which will represent a further development and refinement of his thinking about the law for a very different audience. The churches of Galatia and the new preachers active in them, therefore, do not have access to Romans to assist in the interpretation of Paul's letter to them.[34]

Two letters, a few years apart, different circumstances, same writer. As, probably, in the case above, there are many specific points at which Paul is very likely to have the same view in both letters: Rom 13:9 is good evidence that he probably saw Lev 19:18 in Gal 5:14 as part of the Mosaic law code (in fact, if pushed, de Boer is inclined towards reading both texts the same way as in his reading of Gal 5:14).[35] What about broader patterns – such as the strongly temporal pattern in Gal 3:19–29 that (as we have seen) appears to shed light on the less explicitly temporal sequence of Romans? Is this interpretative move acceptable? This is undoubtedly a subtler, more arguable decision. However, even if we decide against seeing that sequence at work in Romans, it is clear that the exercise of comparing Galatians and Romans both raises significant questions about each letter and offers some valuable resources for tackling those questions.

Further Reading

Barclay, John M. G. *Obeying the Truth: A Study of Paul's Ethics in Galatians.* Edinburgh: T&T Clark, 1988.

Betz, Hans Dieter. *Galatians: A Commentary on Paul's Letter to the Churches in Galatia.* Philadelphia: Fortress Press, 1979.

Campbell, Douglas A. *The Deliverance of God: An Apocalyptic Rereading of Justification in Paul.* Grand Rapids, MI: Eerdmans, 2009.

de Boer, Martinus C. *Galatians: A Commentary.* Louisville, KY: Westminster John Knox, 2011.

Donfried, Karl P., ed. *The Romans Debate.* Revised and expanded ed. Peabody, MA: Hendrickson, 1991.

Hays, Richard B. "Psalm 143 and the Logic of Romans 3." *Journal of Biblical Literature* 99 (1980): 107–115.

Hübner, Hans. *Law in Paul's Thought: A Contribution to the Development of Pauline Theology.* Translated by J. C. G. Greig. Edinburgh: T&T Clark, 1984.

[34] de Boer, *Galatians*, 345.

[35] de Boer, *Galatians*, 345 after the above quote and n468.

Jewett, Robert. *Romans: A Commentary*. Minneapolis, MN: Fortress Press, 2007.

Käsemann, Ernst. *New Testament Questions of Today*. Philadelphia: Fortress Press, 1969.

Martyn, J. Louis. *Galatians: A New Translation with Introduction and Commentary*. New York: Doubleday, 1997.

Oakes, Peter. *Galatians*. Grand Rapids, MI: Baker Academic, 2015.

Oakes, Peter. "Using Historical Evidence in the Study of Neronian Christian Groups and Texts." In *The Last Years of Paul's Life: Essays from the Tarragona Conference, June 2013*, edited by Armand Puig i Tàrrech, John M. G. Barclay, and Jörg Frey, 131–151. Tübingen: Mohr Siebeck, 2015.

Oakes, Peter. "*Pistis* as Relational Way of Life in Galatians," *Journal for the Study of the New Testament* 40 (2018): 255–275.

Wiefel, Wolfgang. "The Jewish Community in Ancient Rome and the Origins of Roman Christianity." In *The Romans Debate*. Revised and expanded ed. Edited by K. P. Donfried, 85–101. Peabody, MA: Hendrickson, 1991.

Wright, N. T. *Paul and the Faithfulness of God*. Minneapolis, MN: Fortress Press, 2013.

6 Philippians and Philemon

DOUGLAS A. CAMPBELL

Comparing the letters to the Philippians and to Philemon brings to light important aspects of Paul's thought and practice – in particular, how certain key theological commitments are practically enacted when they encounter situational differences. Capturing a sense of what Paul is doing in these letters is best done by grasping what the problems were that he was addressing and considering how the letters deploy a set of rhetorical strategies to resolve those problems. These letters were documents of crisis! So the first step in our analysis must be a careful sleuthing through the letters to discover what specific dysfunctions are reflected in them.

THE PROBLEM AT PHILIPPI

Three clues point toward a particular problem at Philippi:[1]

(1) After the formal beginning of the letter, Paul spends some time talking about how the Philippian Christians should avoid competing for higher status with one another and, conversely, should lower themselves and act humbly. "Do nothing out of selfish ambition or vain conceit. Rather, in humility value others above yourselves, not looking to your own interests but each of you to the interests of the others" (2:3–4, NIV). This emphasis is present through all of chapter two until Paul pivots in 3:2 to address certain "enemies."

(2) In 4:2 Paul writes, "I plead with Euodia and I plead with Syntyche to be of the same mind in the Lord." Since Paul never admonishes individuals by name in the main body of any other letter in this negative way, there must be something here that reveals the situation that Paul is addressing in Philippians.

[1] See Holland L. Hendrix, "Philippi," in *Anchor Bible Dictionary*, vol. 5, ed. David Noel Freedman (New York: Doubleday, 1992), 313–317.

(3) It is not uncommon for Paul to address his letters to "the holy ones in Christ Jesus" who live in a certain city, in this case, "Philippi," but it is uncommon, and in fact unique, for him to address the community's "overseers and ministers" (*episkopois kai diakonois*, 1:1). Two of those "overseers and ministers" are likely to be referred to in 4:3: Clement and someone whom Paul refers to as his "fellow soldier," who was possibly the veteran Epaphroditus (named in 2:25 but here referred to in 4:3 with this military term).[2] In the same verse, Paul requests that the situation between Euodia and Syntyche should be monitored by this "fellow soldier."

Putting these clues together, we begin to see the problem that gave rise to much of Paul's letter. The Christian community is being torn apart by a conflict between two of its female leaders.[3] Refusing to adopt a proper attitude in relation to one another, Euodia and Syntyche are in some sort of destructive competition for status. Moreover, others among the community's elders seem unable to resolve this dysfunctional situation.

Significantly, this situation matches the information supplied by Acts in 16:12–40. The community began, Acts tells us, when Paul met a "God-fearer," Lydia, at a Jewish place of prayer just outside the city gates. She was an independent businesswoman working in the purple cloth industry, and was probably a freed slave. Her name, "Lydia," could simply be a woman's name, but it was also a region known for its work on textiles and dyeing.[4] In fact, Acts states that she originally came from a city in that region, Thyatira (16:14). Philippi, where she now resided, was a little Rome, which copied its exemplar assiduously. Purple dye of various qualities would have been needed to mark the togas of the city's officials, along with the other purple robes that were in fashion among the Roman elite.[5] It is entirely plausible, then, that this woman was a former slave who was brought from Lydia (her home region that she was originally named after) in order to manufacture purple cloth in Roman

[2] The Greek word *suzugos* was used for the Latin *commilito*, which meant "fellow soldier."

[3] More details can be found in my *Paul: An Apostle's Journey* (Grand Rapids, MI: Eerdmans, 2018), esp. 44–50.

[4] Lydia was located in the Roman province of Asia, presently in western Turkey. See Barbara Kelley McLaughlin, "Lydia (Place)," in *Anchor Bible Dictionary*, vol. 6 (New Haven, CT: Yale University Press, 1992), 423–425.

[5] A definitive study is David E. Graves, "What Is the Madder with Lydia's Purple? A Reexamination of the Purpurarii in Thyatira and Philippi," *Near East Archaeological Society Bulletin* 62 (2017): 3–28.

Philippi. As a free woman, however, it seems likely that she would take the more dignified name of a free woman – a name like Euodia or Syntyche. This suggests, and Paul's later letter largely confirms, that Lydia's small group of co-workers in the purple dye industry were the original nucleus of the Christian community in Philippi, together with a couple of veterans (see again 2:25) who doubtless knew the nameless jailer whom Paul converted (Acts 16:23–34). And, irrespective of exactly how we calculate specific dates on Paul's lifeline, this small community would have formed about ten years prior to the writing of this letter. The passage of time has clearly eroded the relationships at the heart of the community.

Anthropologists denote the ancient culture that Paul and his converts lived in an "honor-shame" society in which competitions for status were central.[6] Success in the form of honor and glory was craved, and defeat or ignominy, which activated the acute experience of shame, was abhorred – possibly to the point of committing suicide rather than enduring its agonies. An intense competition for status and honor extended from the highest levels (including the emperor) down through all the other socioeconomic levels that made up the empire in the cities and groups of the Roman world. And this competition involved not just rivals but their supporters who formed partisan cliques. Hence Greco-Roman society was a battleground between jostling leaders and their supporters who, up to the threshold of violence (which was frequently crossed) employed all manner of aggressive verbal tactics to advance – including slander, ridicule, and parody. Clearly, if any of this toxic partisanship leaked into Christian communities, trouble would follow, and yet this seems to have been the case at Philippi. Two of the community's leaders were clearly not getting on, and Paul's strong emphasis on "lowering" as against self-promotion suggests that a typical Greco-Roman competition for status was taking place between the two women who were leaders of the church.

If a key problem at Philippi was a competitive, fracturing leadership, a complementary problem is also apparent in the letter, namely, pressures from outside. These two challenges (internal and external) could easily compound each other. Without relational reconciliation between its leaders and a resulting unity, any external intervention could break

[6] The society's dynamics are usefully introduced by Bruce J. Malina, *The New Testament World: Insights from Cultural Anthropology*, 3rd revised and expanded ed. (Louisville, KY: Westminster John Knox, 2001), esp. 1–107.

the community apart along its internal fault lines, and Paul had already experienced this painful scenario at Corinth.

Interpreters have long noted how Paul shifts abruptly at 3:2 into a section characterized by much more aggressive language than he has previously been using. Indeed, this change of tone is so abrupt that scholars have often supposed that two different letters have been blended together into a single letter that we now read in the Bible. In this theory, the distinctive section finishes in 4:3 (having started at 3:2), with Paul's comments in 4:4 picking up from the thought of 3:1: "rejoice in the Lord." However, there is no evidence that ancient editors of letter collections actually did this, inserting one piece of one letter inside another. A mistaken interpolation into the middle of the letter is an even less likely scenario. And neither theory can explain the repetition and neat resumption of the phrase "rejoice in the Lord" in 4:4 (echoing 3:1). A more plausible suggestion is that from 3:2 to 4:4 Paul himself quotes from a previous letter he had written to the Philippians. Paul highlights precisely this in 3:1, saying that he is writing "*the same things*," and that doing so is "*not burdensome* but *a safeguard*." Ancient letter writers did do this, and Polycarp even knows that the Philippians received more than one letter from Paul (Phil 3:2).[7] So we will proceed on the assumption that this section is quite intentional, and is being quoted because it remains relevant.

It continues, "keep careful watch for those dogs, those evil workers, those mutilators!" (3:2). This seems to be an attack on those who try to force gentile Christians to follow Jewish customs. No matter how good such people are, Paul has better Jewish qualifications – but even so, he regards those status indicators as "excrement" in comparison to knowing Jesus (3:4–8). Paul goes on to describe these figures as "enemies of the cross of Christ" (3:18) who are destined for destruction and who worship their stomachs.[8]

We need to be careful here. Although these people are Jewish, there is no need to suppose that Paul is attacking all Jews generically. If we make this assumption, we risk basing Christianity on a negative prior construction of Judaism, raising all sorts of acute theological problems in due course, not the least of which is an unavoidable anti-Judaism.

[7] See my fuller discussion in *Framing Paul: An Epistolary Biography* (Grand Rapids, MI: Eerdmans, 2014), esp. 125–133. See also E. Randolph Richards' helpful account of writers copying their own material: *Paul and First-Century Letter Writing: Secretaries, Composition and Collection* (Downers Grove, IL: InterVarsity Press, 2004).

[8] A reference used by philosophers to denigrate people who were enslaved to their base appetites.

This is not an interpretation we should follow blithely after the Holocaust. And we do not have to follow it. Paul is attacking potential interlopers into his community who are far more likely to be messianic Jews than non-believing Jews. In contrast to non-believing Jews, Christ-believing Jews would have had easy access to an early Christian community and would presumably be more interested in visiting it in the first place.[9] So the target of Paul's hostility here is most likely a group of rival teachers proclaiming a gospel that intertwines the significance of Jesus with Jewish practices in a way that he thinks is invalid for gentile believers. It is insufficiently committed to sharing in Christ's death and resurrection. Participating in Christ's death and resurrection is always central for the rather mystical Paul, as he notes in this very context:

> I want to gain Christ and I want to be found 'in' him . . . [which means] knowing him, both the power of his resurrection and the companionship of his sufferings, being conformed to his death so that I might attain to that resurrection from the dead." (3:8, 10–11, author's translation).

Paul is clearly concerned that the Philippians stand unified against the possible arrival of these rivals, if they are not already in town (1:27–30). And the Philippians are probably under pressure in any case, being perceived by their non-Christian neighbors as religious deviants worshipping the one God who is foreign to the panoply of Greco-Roman gods. Philippi's great love of all things Roman, including worship of the emperor, also offered particular challenges to a community based in part on former soldiers, who had previously sworn allegiance to the Roman gods. Paul's unusual reference to Christ as "savior" in 3:20, in the context of a "heavenly citizenship," suggests a deliberate counterpoint to their previous emperor worship.[10]

With this rather complex set of challenges at Philippi in mind (relational dysfunction at the leadership level, and pressure from false teachers, coupled with the hostility of many surrounding pagans), we can turn to investigate the challenge that lay behind Paul's letter to Philemon. Although that letter presents in a different way, ultimately we will find that the same basic problem lies beneath the situation's surface.

[9] It is plausible in my view to link the hostile preachers of 1:15, 17, and 18 with the enemies of the cross attacked from 3:2. Occam's razor suggests keeping explanations as simple as possible, and data from Paul's other letters affirm this identification. See further my *Framing*, 133–142.

[10] Emperor worship is introduced usefully by Donald L. Jones, "Roman Imperial Cult," in *Anchor Bible Dictionary*, vol. 5 (New Haven, CT: Yale University Press), 806–809.

THE PROBLEM AT COLOSSAE[11]

Paul's shortest letter primarily addresses a man named Philemon. Two other people are also addressed specifically: a woman named Apphia and a man named Archippus, and they are not unimportant. But since the letter consistently uses second-person singular and masculine grammar ("you," etc.), Philemon seems to be the person who Paul has in his sights most definitively.

Another person is clearly in view in this letter, however. Philemon owns a male slave called Onesimus, a common Latin name for a slave, meaning "Useful," or more colloquially, "Handy." Slave owners generally renamed their slaves at purchase with the ancient equivalent of a pet name or with something impersonal.[12] But it is clear from this letter that Handy is an unhappy slave and is seeking Paul's help.

Many interpreters suppose that Handy had run away, seeking to escape from Philemon's household; this scenario is unlikely, however. Runaway slaves do not seek out friends of their owners for help, especially if those friends are in Roman custody at the time. Instead, they run. If they are caught, the consequences could be horrific – mutilation, punishment, and/or execution.[13] Rather than trying to escape from his master, it seems that Handy is pursuing a less drastic course of action, and one known to us from a few ancient sources.[14] Unhappy slaves could seek an intervention with their owners from important friends or associates of their owners.[15] Philemon is a member of a small Christian community, most probably located at Colossae, which had been founded by one of Paul's converts, Epaphras (Col 1:7).[16] So Paul is a spiritual authority figure who carries considerable weight. And Handy

[11] See Clinton E. Arnold, "Colossae," in *Anchor Bible Dictionary*, vol. 1, ed. David Noel Freedman (New York: Doubleday, 1992), 1089–1090.

[12] For instance, Paul refers to slaves called "Third" and "Fourth" (usually translated "Tertius" and "Quartus") in Rom 16:22–23.

[13] Jennifer A. Glancy provides details in *Slavery in Early Christianity* (Oxford: Oxford University Press, 2002).

[14] This realization must be credited to Peter Lampe. His research, published in 1985, is summarized by S. Scott Bartchy in "Philemon," in *Anchor Bible Dictionary*, vol. 5, ed. D. N. Freedman (New York: Doubleday, 1992), 307–308.

[15] Pliny the Younger (*Letter* 103) undertook this sort of intervention with his friend Sabinianus on behalf of another troubled slave (although the tone of his letter is rather different than that of Philemon).

[16] Argued in detail in my *Framing*, 254–309. Paul's letters to Philemon and to the community at Colossae are too closely and accurately intertwined for one of them (Colossians) to be the work of a forger.

has left Colossae in order to seek Paul's help, locating him in a nearby detention.[17]

It is impossible to determine from Paul's letter to Philemon exactly what Handy had done, but perhaps Colossians implies subtly that Handy has been lazy and dishonest, probably thieving. Paul warns against laziness extensively in 3:22–24.

> Slaves, obey your earthly masters in everything; and do it, not only when their eye is on you and to curry their favor, but with sincerity of heart and reverence for the Lord. Whatever you do, work at it with all your heart, as working for the Lord, not for human masters, since you know that you will receive an inheritance from the Lord as a reward. It is the Lord Christ you are serving. (NIV)

Paul then writes sternly, "Anyone who commits a crime will be repaid for their offending, and there will be no favoritism!"[18]

Masters do not receive as much attention from Paul in Colossians, but in 4:1 they are briefly urged to be *fair*, "providing your slaves with what is right and equivalent (*ton isotêta*) (i.e., to what they have done and what they deserve)."

If Paul's letter to the Colossians helps to shed light on the situation in Philemon, we can infer that Handy is feeling exploited and is responding with standard tactics that low-status people employ to get back at their superiors; he is not working hard when he is out of sight, which is, from Philemon's point of view, being lazy.[19] And the usual response to laziness in a slave is a beating – something that would also follow detection of a theft, thieving being another retaliatory tactic used by the oppressed. And things have recently reached such a point, Handy has fled to Paul for help. This is the problem, then, that Paul's letter to Philemon addresses, and clearly it will be a tough nut to crack.

COMPARING THE PROBLEMS

It is worth pausing to note how, despite the differences in detail, a similar underlying issue is present at both Philippi and Colossae. Both communities are being challenged *by internal breakdowns in key*

[17] Paul is possibly imprisoned in Apamea, the town on the border between Asia and Galatia. I recommend exploring possible locations on http://orbis.stanford.edu/.

[18] NIV modified. Note that Paul uses legal language here (Greek, *adikaioô*) to denote a legal offense or crime, as he does in 1 Cor 6:1–11.

[19] See James C. Scott, *Domination and the Arts of Resistance: Hidden Transcripts* (New Haven, CT: Yale University Press, 1990).

relationships. Relational dysfunction is the common factor. Female leaders are bickering and fighting at Philippi, and an owner and his slave are alienated at Colossae. Moreover, these relational breakdowns are sending ripples of destruction out through the rest of the community. The Philippians cannot now stand unified against external threats. In Colossae, a low-status slave has had a dysfunctional relationship with his master, a situation the Colossian Christian community has not been able to address.

With the sheer depth of these challenges now in sharp relief, we might well ask, how on earth is Paul going to fix these situations simply by sending a letter? As we'll see, each letter launches a carefully coordinated strategy designed to reorient dramatically the problematic relationships at both Philippi and Colossae.

Paul's Strategy at Philippi

Paul's main strategy for healing the fractured relationships at Philippi is a powerful recall of everyone there (including the community's jostling leaders) to the humility of Jesus. But this basic strategy is effected in multiple ways.

First, Paul reinserts a description of Jesus's own humility into the situation by writing one of the most profound paragraphs he ever penned: 2:6–11. Jesus's humility is depicted in the first half of this paragraph, with Paul describing Jesus's abandonment of life with God when he takes on a human body, and then, beyond this, when he accepts the fate of death, and a death by shameful execution at that. Paul describes this extraordinary, voluntary abandonment by Jesus of status and power as "emptying himself" (in a probable echo of the "suffering servant" depicted in Isaiah 53).[20] The first half of Paul's poem is as follows (author's translation):

Christ Jesus ...
being in form of God,
did not consider equivalence with God something to be grasped;
rather, he emptied himself
by taking the form of a servant,
being made in human likeness.
And being found in form as a person,

[20] For connections of this passage to Isaiah, see Richard Bauckham, "Paul's Christology of Divine Identity," in *Jesus and the God of Israel* (Grand Rapids, MI: Eerdmans, 2008), 182–232.

he humbled himself,
being obedient to the point of death –
death on a gallows!

Scholars have long detected something unusual about this paragraph. The prose Paul uses, evident even in translation, is a dense series of pregnant clauses. Because of this, some have thought that Paul is reproducing an important creed or hymn composed by the early church. But both the vocabulary and the message of the passage are typical of Paul himself. So a better explanation is that Paul himself composed the paragraph, quite possibly as a song, just as he recommends in 1 Cor 14:26 and Col 3:16. And like all good songs, this song tells a story – and a story must be told in order to speak of Jesus's character. We only know what people are like as we see them acting in relation to other figures and events over time.[21]

We need now to envisage the Philippians hearing this song, learning it, and singing it to one another. And the first half of their song is a story about Jesus's humble abandonment of status and power and converse embrace of shame – the exact reverse of their toxic surrounding culture and of some of their own behavior. Consequently, the singing of this song *introduces the mind of Christ into their minds*, as verse 5 commands: (paraphrasing) "Have *this* mind-set within you, this entire way of thinking and acting – the mind that was in Christ Jesus ... [the one who] emptied himself."

We should also notice that Paul's strategy is more complex and powerful than a mere narration of Jesus's humility and its transmission through song. A key additional component is the introduction of this humility into the community concretely through a trusted mediator. Paul exhorts the Philippians to attend to how Timothy places the interests of others ahead of his own when he visits them (2:19–24). That is, Timothy himself models the self-effacing Jesus. We learn from this a key part of Paul's mission strategy: Christian leaders are to model Jesus's virtues in person so that the community can imitate them.[22]

[21] Philippians 2:5–11. Further discussion of the story of Jesus in Paul can be found in my essay "The Narrative Dimensions in Paul's Gospel," in *Narrative Dynamics in Paul: A Critical Assessment*, ed. Bruce W. Longenecker (Louisville, KY: Westminster John Knox, 2002), 97–124. See also Richard B. Hays, "The Story of God's Son: The Identity of Jesus in the Letters of Paul," in *Seeking the Identity of Jesus: A Pilgrimage*, eds. Richard B. Hays and Beverly R. Gaventa (Grand Rapids, MI: Eerdmans, 2008), 180–199.

[22] A seminal study describing much of this in conversation with neuroscience is Susan G. Eastman, *Paul and the Person: Reframing Paul's Anthropology* (Grand Rapids, MI: Eerdmans, 2017).

If the problem of toxic rivalry has (hopefully) been laid to rest, Paul is free to turn his attention in the rest of the letter to a secondary strategy designed to rebuff the external threats.

Self-effacement is not the right response to destructive interlopers. At the boundary of the community Paul wants the Philippians to stand firm, faithfully and courageously resisting their enemies like soldiers who hold the line in a long battle – an image that would have resonated strongly with the veterans in the congregation. It is the virtue of *faithfulness* that will enable the Philippians to withstand outside pressure, even as *humility* will repair their unity within.

Paul speaks of this steadfast faithfulness at least three times (in 1:25, 27, and 2:17), and an echo can be detected here of the important Roman virtue of *fides*, which soldiers especially esteemed.[23] But Paul couples faithfulness with the end of the story. Faithfulness will result, if it is maintained, in a marvelous reward. The battle will not go on forever but will result in victory. In terms of athletics rather than soldiering, a prize lies ahead for those who endure (3:12–16). For Paul, faithfulness must be combined with hope. Hope without faithfulness is aimless, and faithfulness without hope is weak. But together they bind into a formidable combination – one that can, from the most trying circumstances, even elicit joy, which is a repeated theme in the letter for these reasons (see esp. 3:1a; 4:4).

As we would by now expect, however, these virtues are not supposed to be ginned up from within by the Philippians' own zeal and commitment; Paul sees them flowing ultimately from Jesus. Jesus did not just humbly assume the awful fate of death by crucifixion: "he emptied himself, *becoming obedient* to the point of death" (v. 8). This obedience to an awful fate denotes the presence of a steely endurance in Jesus's life that can be spoken of as faithfulness. Hence, I would refer the double instance of faith language in 3:9 to Jesus's faithfulness as well rather than to the believing of the Philippians. The righteousness that comes from God is a righteousness made available through Jesus, and specifically through his faithfulness to the point of death, an event that was followed by his glorious resurrection.[24]

As was the case for humility, Jesus's heroic faithfulness and hope are again modeled concretely for the Philippians, although in this

[23] See esp. Teresa Morgan, *Roman Faith and Christian Faith:* Pistis *and* Fides *in the Early Roman Empire and Early Churches* (Oxford: Oxford University Press, 2015).

[24] For detailed arguments see my *Deliverance of God* (Grand Rapids, MI: Eerdmans, 2009), 897–911.

instance by Epaphroditus. In 2:25–30 Paul talks about how Epaphroditus has risked his life to bring aid to Paul during his imprisonment, and travel in the ancient world was always dangerous (2 Cor 11:25–28). To make matters worse, however, Epaphroditus fell ill on arrival and almost died. Fortunately, he survived, so Paul is sending him back, in part to relieve both him and the Philippians of their anxiety, but in part to reintroduce to them a model of steadfast courage to the point of death.

But Paul himself models this endurance as well, standing firm fearlessly and even joyfully in the face of his enemies, explicitly despising the threat of death. Such is its importance, he introduces this account of himself no less than three times. In 1:12–26 he describes the struggles of his current imprisonment, and they are considerable. He is shackled (vv. 13, 14, 17); he is being opposed legally, sadly, even by Christians (vv. 14–15, 17); and he is facing a death sentence (vv. 20, 21, 23). Yet, in the midst of all these travails, he is almost bizarrely positive. Then in 3:2–4:1 he races single-mindedly ahead, refusing to be distracted by other enticements. His eyes are on the prize! Finally, in 4:11–13 he is faithful irrespective of material resources. He can endure any conditions, whether sated or starving, overflowing with money or feeling the pinch. His strength comes from the one who strengthens him in everything (4:13) – and it is worth noting that we have a glimpse here of how the church later managed to survive frightful persecutions from the Roman emperor. That is, we are brought face to face here with *a theology of martyrdom*. Paul inherited much of this from Judaism, but the discourse has been translated here into a messianic (and ultimately into a Christian) key. The followers of the crucified and resurrected Jesus should be able to stand firm against *anything* that *any* outside force can throw against it, including the full weight of a hostile state.[25]

Paul's Strategy for Philemon

Turning to Colossae, we see that the situation is simpler, but not for that reason easier. Paul needs to repair the alienated relationship between Philemon and Handy as best he can, and so he has to alter the relating of these two figures toward one another. How does he do it?

If Colossians is any indication, Paul wants Handy to be a better slave to Philemon – to be a useful worker, as his name suggests (v. 11).

[25] Rodney J. Stark notes the helpfulness of martyrdom to the survival of a new religious movement in *The Rise of Christianity: A Sociologist Reconsiders History* (Princeton, NJ: Princeton University Press, 1996).

However, Paul has been working on Handy in person during his imprisonment. In his letter, we see Paul going to work on Philemon to try to change his posture toward his slave.

Paul's main goal for Philemon seems to have been for him to replace his authoritarian behavior toward Handy with *kindness*. Handy is to be received with any necessary forgiveness, and hopefully with more respect if not with affection, and not with punitive requests for damages and beatings. So here, just as in Philippians, relational dislocations are in view; unlike Philippians, however, the appropriate response to the particular dysfunction is not self-effacing humility and courageous fidelity but kindness, with all its component elements of forgiveness, welcome, and respect. But how does Paul foster kindness in Colossae? His tactics are a little different this time, although the basic strategy remains the same.

Paul inserts himself into this troubled relationship quite directly, thereby *triangulating* Philemon's relationship with Handy. Whereas previously a relationship was running directly between Philemon and Handy and functioning in a deeply alienated way, it now runs in relation to Paul. Three parties are involved. As a result of this, Philemon is to treat Handy mindful of his relationship with Paul – so he should do what Paul asks. *And* he is to treat Handy as Handy is treated *by* Paul, i.e., with affection – which is what Paul is asking Philemon for.

Paul makes it known that he expects Philemon to do what he asks in light of a number of considerations. First of all, Paul is suffering nobly for the gospel; he is "chained," detained in the usual horrible conditions of imprisonment in the Roman empire (vv. 1 and 9).[26] The mention of this situation, as every schoolchild in the Greco-Roman world would recognize, induces *pathos* or emotional empathy in the letter's audience.[27] But Paul goes on to emphasize that he is, in fact, an ambassador of Christ (v. 9). The claim to status is undeniable. In fact, Philemon owes his very life to Paul since the gospel has now been made available to Philemon through the Pauline orb of mission (v. 19). Nevertheless, Philemon is "beloved" and a co-worker, an equal to someone as important as Paul himself. Hence Paul remembers Philemon in his prayers with thanks, joy, and encouragement, knowing of his love and fidelity and the way in

[26] Fergus Millar, "Condemnation to Hard Labour in the Roman Empire, from the Julio-Claudians to Constantine," in *Rome, the Greek World, and the East: Government, Society, and Culture in the Roman Empire*, eds. Hannah M. Cotton and Guy M. Rogers (Chapel Hill, NC: University of North Carolina Press, 2004), 120–50.

[27] *Pathos* is usefully canvassed at https://en.wikipedia.org/wiki/Pathos.

which he refreshes the saints (vv. 4–7). In this vein, Paul then exhorts Philemon repeatedly to do the right thing as an equal (see vv. 8–9, 14). And adopting the right disposition toward Handy will be just one more instance of Philemon refreshing the saints (in this case saint Paul), thereby acting in the generous way for which he is well-known (vv. 7, 20).

However, an element of threat complements all these essentially positive and dignifying appeals. Paul could simply command Philemon to act in a certain way (vv. 8, 9, 14). Moreover, the obligation toward Paul that Philemon has incurred by entering into the apostle's saved community suggests that Philemon should waive any financial costs that Handy's departure may have caused, despite Paul's personal protestations that he will cover them all (vv. 18–19).

In short, Paul weaves together considerations from his present suffering, and from his superior status to place a great weight of obligation on Philemon. Philemon is under pressure from Paul! But to do what exactly?

It seems most likely that Paul is not asking Philemon to set Handy free, much as we wish that he was.[28] He is asking Philemon to receive Handy back without demanding recompense from him for his absence, treating him from now on as Paul treats him (v. 17). And Paul views Handy with *love*. Paul has apparently converted Handy during his visit (see vv. 10, 16), and he now loves him as a child (v. 10). He literally "begot" him during his imprisonment (v. 10), and so Handy is now "his very heart" (v. 12). The Greek used here, reflecting Hebrew idiom, is strong; Paul loves Handy "from his guts," which in the Jewish Scriptures are the seat of the emotions.

It is possible to doubt Paul's stated affections here somewhat cynically. Isn't he laying it on a bit thick? Is it really plausible that he, an apostle, did care about an absolute low-life in these strong terms? But the very differences between Paul and Handy (a vast social chasm) suggests that Paul's expressed posture is sincere. There is no reason for a person of Paul's stature to make these strongly affectionate claims on behalf of an AWOL, perfidious, barbarian slave. Hence, Paul's very insistence on his affection for Handy in a distinctly counter-cultural way, completely unnecessarily, suggests that he actually meant it. Paul

[28] Manumission is *implicit* in the command to treat Handy as a brother. People who are fundamentally equal in status, as Christian "brothers," should not own one another. But this implication was not realized by Christians for many centuries. See Willie J. Jennings, *The Christian Imagination: Theology and the Origins of Race* (New Haven, CT: Yale University Press, 2010).

does love a lazy, despised, pagan chancer like Handy – a posture of lowering and humbling that was so overtly stated in Philippians. Paul has lowered *himself* here to befriend Handy.

But again, as at Philippi, Paul does not leave his intervention to a letter alone. Drawing from Colossians, and recalling Philemon's named addressees, we see that Paul introduces someone called "Archippus" into the situation. It is possible that this veteran is the patron and consequent leader of the house church at Colossae. In this reconstruction of the situation, Philemon and Apphia are members of this community, along with their troubled slave. Moreover, by addressing Archippus in the prescript of his letter to Philemon (and by drawing attention to him explicitly in Colossians 4:17 as well, where Paul commands him "to complete the ministry that he has been entrusted with in the Lord"), Paul has involved him in the situation directly. The letter to Philemon must be read out to him, in front of the rest of the Christians meeting in his house. And from this moment he, Archippus, must carry out his ministerial duties. So here Paul, a religious superior (so perhaps think of the relevant bishop) is instructing the early equivalent of a local cleric to oversee and to resolve a problem in one of his congregation's homes – in this case, a toxic domestic relationship between a master and his servant (and this will not be the last time that this scenario unfolds in the church).

In addition, however, and somewhat predictably, Paul, inserts himself into the situation as well, although in this instance not as a model. He wants Philemon to prepare a guest room for him (v. 22) because he is anticipating being released quite shortly (and this is one significant indicator why the imprisonment Paul is currently enduring must be close by where Philemon lives). Then he will visit, to be "refreshed" by Philemon, and also to check up and see how Handy is getting on. Moreover, he will stay with Philemon, not Archippus. The great ambassador of Christ will grace Philemon with his very presence, thereby continuing to dignify him as an equal, although doubtless not failing to command him if things are not working out to his liking.

In sum, Paul's letter to Philemon, although compact, is a masterpiece of coordinated influence. It is different in its specifics from his letter to the Philippians: the presenting problem is different, and the virtues Paul enjoins to fix it are different as well. The problem at Colossae is a broken owner-slave relationship. So Paul urges kindness, forgiveness, and affection in the owner, in place of retribution and despisement, and a more conscientious and honest disposition in the slave. But the basic strategy is the same as at Philippi: a set of appeals to

Christ-like virtues, intertwined with personal visits modeling them directly (e.g., Timothy and Epaphroditus who will come to Philippi, and Paul who will come to Colossae). Moreover, although the story of Jesus is not articulated overtly, the kindness of Jesus presupposed by Paul's song in Philippians 2:5–11 is everywhere apparent in this short letter. And the humility of the incarnate and executed Jesus maps precisely Paul's relation to Handy, as he stoops down, crossing the vast social space between them, to befriend, to convert, and to love the disaffected and indolent slave. We might say in closing then that the specific contextualized instantiation of Jesus-like relationships in Colossae is clearly different from its instantiation in Philippi; but the underlying strategy of mobilizing a story of Jesus both conceptually by letter, as well as directly and personally through a disciple or envoy, remains the same. Paul clearly believes that Jesus, rightly understood and rightly followed, makes a difference to the basic issue that tends to concern all communities, namely, how people relate to one another.

Further Reading

Barclay, John M. G. *Colossians and Philemon*. New Testament Guides. Sheffield: Sheffield Academic Press, 1997.

Bauckham, Richard. "Paul's Christology of Divine Identity." In *Jesus and the God of Israel*, 182–232. Grand Rapids, MI: Eerdmans, 2008.

Campbell, Douglas. *Framing Paul: An Epistolary Biography*. Grand Rapids, MI: Eerdmans, 2014.

Campbell, Douglas. *Paul: An Apostle's Journey*. Grand Rapids, MI: Eerdmans, 2018.

Glancy, Jennifer A. *Slavery in Early Christianity*. New York: Oxford University Press, 2002; Philadelphia: Fortress Press, 2006.

Gordley, Matthew E. *New Testament Christological Hymn: Exploring Texts, Contexts, and Significance*. Downers Grove, IL: InterVarsity Press, 2018.

Graves, David E. "What Is the Madder with Lydia's Purple? A Re-examination of the Purpurarii in Thyatira and Philippi." *Near East Archaeological Society Bulletin* 62 (2017): 3–28.

Hays, Richard B. "The Story of God's Son: The Identity of Jesus in the Letters of Paul." In *Seeking the Identity of Jesus: A Pilgrimage*, edited by Richard B. Hays and Beverly Roberts Gaventa, 180–199. Grand Rapids, MI: Eerdmans, 2008.

Lampe, Peter. "Keine 'Sklavenflucht' des Onesimus," *Zeitschrift für die Neutestamentliche Wissenschaft* 76 (1985): 135–137.

Malina, Bruce J. *The New Testament World: Insights from Cultural Anthropology*. 3rd ed. Louisville, KY: Westminster John Knox, 2001.

Millar, Fergus. "Condemnation to Hard Labour in the Roman Empire, from the Julio-Claudians to Constantine." In *Rome, the Greek World, and the East: Government, Society, and Culture in the Roman Empire*, edited by Hannah

M. Cotton and Guy M. Rogers, 120–150. Chapel Hill, NC: University of North Carolina Press, 2004.

Petersen, Norman. *Rediscovering Paul: Philemon and the Sociology of Paul's Narrative World*. Philadelphia: Fortress Press, 1985.

Richards, E. Randolph. *Paul and First-Century Letter Writing: Secretaries, Composition and Collection*. Downers Grove, IL: IVP Academic, 2004.

Scott, James C. *Domination and the Arts of Resistance: Hidden Transcripts*. New Haven, CT: Yale University Press, 1990.

Wright, N. T. "Jesus Christ Is Lord: Philippians 2.5–11." In *Climax of the Covenant: Christ and the Law in Pauline Theology*, 56–98. Minneapolis, MN: Fortress Press, 1992.

7 Colossians and Ephesians

SYLVIA C. KEESMAAT

A long time ago, in the Greek provinces of the Roman empire, two similar letters were sent to assemblies of people who were followers of Jesus, a Jewish messiah – letters authored in the name of Paul. The people who received these two letters lived in Colossae and perhaps Ephesus, which is why the letters are called "Paul's Epistle to the Colossians," and "Paul's Epistle to the Ephesians."[1] Because the earliest manuscripts of the letter we call Ephesians do not contain the phrase "to the Ephesians" in the greetings of the letter itself (1:1), there is some question about the intended destination of that particular letter, even though it is clear that the earliest church fathers thought the letter was written by Paul to the Ephesians. However, since we know that Colossians was intended to be shared with a similar community in Laodicea, a town 15 km downstream from Colossae (see Col 4:16), it is possible that Ephesians was also likely written with the intent of being read aloud in various cities and villages within active communities of Jesus-followers. As we shall see, the subject matter suggests that the prominent and influential city of Ephesus was one of those cities.

For those of us who read Ephesians and Colossians today, the fact that these letters were supposedly written by Paul seems puzzling: they seem different from his other letters in style, in vocabulary, and in theological emphasis.[2] For those who received these letters, however, these would not have been issues. For instance, where we see stylistic *difference*, they would have seen stylistic *similarity*. These assemblies in Asia Minor did not have experience with Paul's other letters, written to communities that were more Roman in character. In their ears, the

[1] Ancient Colossae and Ephesus are in modern-day Turkey.

[2] See Stephen Fowl, *Ephesians: A Commentary* (Louisville, KY: Westminster John Knox, 2012), 9–28, and Jerry L. Sumney, *Colossians: A Commentary* (Louisville, KY: Westminster John Knox, 2008), 1–21, for more detailed descriptions of the arguments for and against Pauline authorship.

wordy, stylistically dense sentences at the start of both Colossians and Ephesians (piling clause upon clause without pause and in a flamboyant manner in Col 1:3–8 and Eph 1:3–14) bore a close resemblance to the honorific inscriptions and even the occasional letter from the Greek east.[3] Rather than suggesting that this letter was not written by Paul because of such stylistic differences, it is entirely possible that Paul was suiting his writing to his audience in Asia Minor, who would have appreciated this wordy verbose style.

Similarly, the different theological emphases in these letters reflects the way in which the religious and political context differed in the Greek east in comparison to the western part of the empire. As we shall see, the way that imperial power was configured in Asia Minor in relation to the popular gods and goddesses such as Artemis, Aphrodite, and Zeus seems to have shaped Paul's argument, necessitating theological arguments that differ from those found in his other letters. I will be assuming in this chapter that Paul wrote these letters, and that the different vocabulary, style, and emphases reflect the specific context of the recipients. That said, my exegesis does not depend upon Pauline authorship, focused as it is primarily on the recipients of the letter.

Right from the outset, the honorific style of the introductions would have signaled to those who heard this letter that Paul was talking about matters of great religious, political, and social importance: Which god controls history so as to bring salvation and blessing? What kind of political body does this god shape? And how could this community live in such a way that this god could be seen in their midst?

These are cosmic questions about the shape of the world, its origin, and its goal. In the ancient world, the answers to such questions were not just religious; they were also political and social. And because the religious and the political were not separable but occupied a space together, we shall see that these two letters also move within this shared discourse.

PAUL IN CHAINS

The different context of the recipients was not the only influence on these letters. They were also shaped by the fact that Paul was in prison when he wrote them, providing time for both theological reflection and

[3] Frederick J. Long, "Ephesians: Paul's Political Theology in Greco-Roman Context," in *Christian Origins and Greco-Roman Culture: Social and Literary Contexts for the New Testament*, eds. Stanley E. Porter and Andrew W. Pitts (Leiden: Brill, 2012), 273.

the conditions for deepening his pondering on the meaning and cause of his suffering.

The letter to the Colossians ends with the graphic picture of Paul writing the concluding sentences with shackled hands (Col 4:18). This image of tied hands was common in Asia Minor, where the victory statues that celebrated Roman conquest often included a woman (symbolizing a conquered people) crouching at the feet of Caesar with her hands bound in chains. This image of Paul in chains would have evoked this image of someone defeated and humiliated by the empire. For Paul, however, any humiliation he has experienced parallels the humiliation of Christ on the cross, where peace is made (Col 1:20) and where Christ made a public example of rulers and authorities (Col 2:15). In fact, Paul sees his suffering as completing what is lacking in Christ's afflictions for the sake of the body, the church (Col 1:24). While this statement has raised questions for some regarding the sufficiency of Christ's crucifixion, Paul seems to be emphasizing how his humiliation, like Christ's, continues the work of bringing an end to hostility, creating reconciliation and peace throughout the cosmos (Col 1:20) and between Jews and Gentiles (Eph 1:15).

Moreover, Paul indicates in both letters that his suffering is for the sake of those Jesus-followers to whom he is writing (Eph 3:1, 13; Col 1:24). Rather than being defeated, Paul's imprisonment is the result of the success of his proclamation of the mystery of the gospel and of Christ (Eph 6:19, 20; Col 4:3). It will be helpful to briefly explore this "mystery" that, as Paul sees it, has resulted in his imprisonment.

THE MYSTERY

For most inhabitants of Ephesus or Colossae, or indeed any other city in Asia Minor, the language of "mystery" was closely aligned to a number of religious cults dedicated to the worship of such deities as Demeter, Dionysius, Aphrodite, and Artemis, and even to the Roman emperors. During the celebration of "the mysteries," a cultic official would "reveal" a sacred object. In many cases we don't know what this object would have been, although in the mysteries of Demeter and Kore it was a reaped ear of grain – a fitting symbol for the goddess associated with agriculture and fertility.[4] In the imperial cult, the mystery revealed was

[4] Guy MacLean Rogers, "An Ephesian Tale: Mystery Cults, Reverse Theological Engineering, and the Triumph of Christianity in Ephesus," in *The First Urban*

a symbol of the empire, likely an imperial image or bust.[5] When Paul says in Colossians, therefore, that the mystery that had been hidden throughout the ages and generations has now been "revealed" to God's saints (Col 1:26), the recipients of this letter would have heard overtones of these other cultic and religious festivals. A similar theme is found in Ephesians, where Paul indicates that the mystery was made known to him by revelation (Eph 3:3), a mystery that, as in Colossians, was hidden for ages (3:9). Given that the mysteries of the Artemis cult permeated Ephesian life, it is no wonder that Paul uses the language of mystery more in his letter to the Ephesians than the letter to the Colossians.

Paul's hearers were being asked to do more, however, than simply notice similar language and motifs between his gospel and the mystery rituals of other gods and powers. Instead, when Paul talks about the mystery that has been revealed to the saints and to the holy apostles and prophets by the Spirit (Eph 3:5), he is referencing an entire narrative in which "the Gentiles have become fellow heirs, members of the same body, and sharers in the promise of Jesus Christ" (Eph 3:6). The Gentiles are now the ones who have the hope of glory that comes from Christ dwelling within the body (Col 1:27).

This story challenged the narrative that surrounded the believers of Colossae, Ephesus, and almost every other city in Asia minor. For instance, in the city of Aphrodisias, just over the hill from Colossae, we have evidence of a great causeway, filled with images three stories high. On one side of the causeway are images of the gods and the emperors; on the other side are images of the *ethnē*, the peoples (translated as "the Gentiles" in Eph 3:6 and Col 1:27). Representing a wide spectrum of peoples, the images embedded within the causeway of Aphrodisias advertise that Rome is now ruler of all the peoples of the earth. Similar to images of the various nations that were found in porticoes, in temples, and on coins, these images are rooted in the narrative of Roman conquest. Even the clothing on the women demonstrates how these peoples have become progressively "Romanized." In contrast, Paul does not narrate a story in which the various nations of the world are defeated or dominated, but rather one where the nations are fellow heirs, reconciled in healthy relationship with each other.

Churches 3: Ephesus, eds. James R. Harrison and L. L. Welborn (Atlanta, GA: Society of Biblical Literature, 2018), 85–86.

[5] S. R. F. Price, *Rituals and Power: The Roman Imperial Cult in Asia Minor* (Cambridge: Cambridge University Press, 1984), 190.

It is important to note that Paul's language here would have been heard differently by the Jewish and non-Jewish people in his audience. Gentiles would have heard the word *ethnē* as referring to many different peoples and nations, all of whom are now equal heirs of the promises of the God of Israel. Those in his audience who were Jewish, however, would have heard the word *ethnē* as referring to a homogenous group of people, the Gentiles – that is, those who are not Jewish, who are being welcomed as heirs into the promises of the God of Israel. Paul's characterization of the Gentiles as strangers and aliens, together with his references to one new humanity in which two groups are reconciled in the cross into one body (Eph 2:11–21), unmistakably demonstrates his Jewish view of the world.

ALIENS AND STRANGERS

As we shall see, Paul draws on and alludes to the story and scriptures of Israel throughout these letters. However, it is also clear that he is writing to an audience of Gentiles. This is only suggested in Colossians, where Paul says that before being reconciled in Jesus, the members of the community were "estranged and hostile in mind, doing evil deeds" (Col 1:21). In Ephesians Paul is much more explicit, describing those in the Ephesian community as previously having followed "the ruler of the power of the air, the spirit that is now at work among those who are disobedient" (Eph 2:1–3) – perhaps a reference to Jupiter (known as Zeus in the Greek pantheon), the patron god of Rome who was also the god of the skies (or the air).[6] Paul is addressing the Ephesian community as if they were Gentiles who formerly participated in the worship of pagan gods. As a result, these Gentiles (or "the uncircumcision") were aliens from the commonwealth of Israel, and strangers to the covenant of promise, having no hope and being without God in the world (Eph 2:12). Because Jesus has reconciled both groups into one, the hearers of the letter are no longer "strangers and aliens, but citizens with the saints" (Eph 2:19).

In fact, Paul has suffered (Eph 3:13) so that these very Gentiles might experience the glory and riches of Jesus. As a result, he says that

[6] Frederick J. Long, "Roman Imperial Rule under the Authority of Jupiter-Zeus: Political-Religious Contexts and the Interpretation of 'The Ruler of the Authority of the Air' in Ephesians 2:2," in *The Language of the New Testament: Context, History, Development*, ed. Stanley E. Porter (Leiden: Brill, 2013), 113–154, esp. 137–142. The eagle used on Roman coins and the Roman standard was also associated with Jupiter.

he bows his "knees before the Father, from whom every family in heaven and on earth takes its name" (Eph 3:14–15). Literally this could be translated, "I bow my knees before the *Father*, from whom every *fatherland* in heaven and on earth takes its name." In a world where the Roman emperor was known as "Father of the Fatherland" (*Patria Patriae*), Paul's assertion is a challenge both to the realm of the gods (in heaven) and the realm of Roman empire (on earth) – all are subject to God as Father. If one were to picture that long three-story high colonnade in Aphrodisias once more, with images of the gods and the emperors on one side and the nations of the world on the other, it is as if Paul has swept his arms along the whole lot and said that they are all – nations, gods, and rulers alike – subject to the one God and Father of Jesus Christ (see also Eph 1:20–21).

Paul has previously described this God as having great power (Eph 1:19). But, unlike the power that is exercised by imperial rulers, God used his power not to inflict violent death on his enemies, but rather to raise Jesus from the dead (1:20), a challenge to all other authorities and powers, as we shall see below.

INHERITANCE

Since God is the Father of all peoples, it is no surprise that both Colossians and Ephesians describe redemption and forgiveness in terms of obtaining and sharing in an inheritance (Col 1:12; Eph 1:11, 14, 18). Such language had powerful resonance for both Gentile and Jewish hearers of these letters. Those who were welcomed into an inheritance by adoption in the first century received the legal rights of the family (along with land grants and, if necessary, citizenship) and, moreover, for security a pillar or statue was engraved with the honor and placed in the temple.[7] In this context, Paul's description of believers as growing into a temple, a dwelling place for God, is quite evocative.[8]

While these resonances might have been present for Gentile hearers of the letters, for those Jewish followers of Jesus in Colossae and Ephesus, there would have been another layer of meaning arising out of the story of Israel, a story Paul is alluding to throughout both letters. In the

[7] Long, "Ephesians," 278.

[8] Long, "Ephesians," 279, makes the point this way (with reference to the linking of citizenship, household, and temple motifs in Eph 2:19–22): "the letter's recipients might understand, in addition to their official adoption with full inheritance rights, that they themselves are likened to the inscribed pillars and statues that testified to the transaction, especially as they themselves are built into a temple of God."

story of Israel, the language of adoption and being welcomed into an inheritance is rooted in the exodus tradition, where Israel is adopted by God and redeemed in order to inherit the land. In other Jewish writings of the time, the inheritance of land is extended to encompass the whole of creation. For Paul, this latter development in the tradition is prominent in Romans 4:13, where he describes the promise to Abraham as "the promise that he would inherit the earth." Later in Romans this promise is deepened, as Paul describes the restoration of creation (Rom 8:18–23). Such creation themes are also present in Colossians and Ephesians.

A CHALLENGE TO IMPERIAL AUTHORITY

The creational restoration that Paul later describes in Romans 8 for those who will be restored in the resurrection is also found in Col 1:15–20 – a passage that is rich in allusion to the scriptures of Israel. The passage begins with a reference to Jesus as the image of the invisible God. That claim seems designed as a direct challenge to not only the images of the emperor that were found on coins or on statues in city squares and temples, but also the images of the gods and goddesses that were similarly widespread in Colossae, Ephesus, and the surrounding cities. Alluding to the Jewish wisdom tradition, where wisdom was the firstborn of creation (Prov 8:22–31), Paul not only describes Jesus as the firstborn of all creation but also as the one through whom "all things on heaven and earth were created, things visible and invisible, whether thrones (*thronoi*), or dominions (*kuriotētes*), or rulers (*archai*), or powers (*exousiai*)" (Col 1:16). Such language would clearly have challenged the throne on which the emperor sat, the dominion he held over the whole land and sea, and the local civic rulers in which his authority rested.

But the powers of the gods would also have been challenged – those invisible powers (*exousiai*) that supported the authorities of rulers. This challenge in Col 1:16 clearly parallels that of Eph 1:20–21, where Paul describes the great might of God "which he accomplished in Christ when he raised him from the dead and made him sit at his right hand in the heavenly places, far above all rule (*archē*) and (heavenly) power (*exousia*) and (earthly) power (*dunamis*) and dominion (*kuriotēs*), and above every name that is named not only in this age but in that which is to come." The context of these challenges is different in each letter, however. In Colossians, this challenge to imperial and cultic power is rooted in the creation: Jesus is the one through whom and in whom all things have been created (1:16); Jesus is the one in whom all things hold together (1:17). And all of creation, all things on earth and in heaven, are reconciled by Jesus, who makes peace through the blood of the cross (1:20). This creational theme is emphasized in Col 1:22, where Paul describes the gospel as having been proclaimed to every creature under heaven, a further emphasis on the wide creational scope of Paul's vision here.

In Ephesians, however, rather than being rooted in creation, Jesus's authority over imperial powers and rulers is rooted in his resurrection and ascension into the heavenly places, where he sits at the right hand of God (Eph 1:20). The allusion works two ways. For those familiar with the Psalms, this verse evokes Ps 110:1: "The LORD says to my lord, 'Sit at my right hand until I make your enemies my footstool.'" The allusion is strengthened in Eph 1:23. There, after asserting that Jesus is far above all rule and authority and power and dominion, and above every name that is named, not only in this age but in the age to come, Paul continues: "and he has put all things under his feet." While this sounds like a continued allusion to Ps 110:1 and the subjection of enemies, it actually employs the words of Ps 8:6. The effect of this double allusion is striking. On the one hand, Psalm 8 is a celebration of humanity as those to whom God has given glory and honor and dominion over all of creation, so that all of creation is under their feet – that is, under their rule. The echo then suggests that the Messiah (the Christ of Eph 1:20) is the one whose dominion over all things fulfills what it is to be truly human in the world (linking in with Col 1:15 and 3:10)

For those unfamiliar with the scriptures of Israel, however, Paul's assertion that Jesus is now seated at God's right hand would have evoked the *apotheosis* of the emperors, who were deified after death and ascended to sit with the council of the gods. In Asia Minor, where the gods and the imperial rulers were intricately connected, devotion to Jesus would be seen as a challenge to both the gods and the empire.

The truly astounding challenge, however, occurs in the sequel to Paul's assertion of Jesus's exaltation. In Colossians, Paul's assertion that Christ is seated at the right hand of God occurs in the context of the calling of the Colossian community: "So if you have been raised with Christ, seek the things that are above, where Christ is, seated at the right hand of God" (Col 3:1). The community has been raised with Christ, and is now called to focus on the one who has ultimate authority. Ephesians is more radical still, for there Paul asserts that Christ "raised us up with him and seated us with him in the heavenly places in Christ Jesus" (Eph 2:6). Not only has the Messiah challenged the authority of the rulers of this age, but all believers themselves have a level of authority and exaltation previously only attained by the rulers of the empire. This is truly subversive to the hierarchies that kept the people in their place.

The different narrative grounding of the Messiah's authority in these letters reflects the contexts in which they were written. Colossians roots Jesus's authority in creation and emphasizes the reconciliation of all of creation; this is because some in the Colossians community have embraced creation-denying practices, saying things like, "Do not handle, do not taste, do not touch" (Col 2:21, discussed in 2:22–23). In such a context, the cosmic and creational aspects of Jesus's authority and reconciliation needed to be emphasized. The Ephesian community, however, was situated in a city dominated by the worship of Artemis, whose followers had come into conflict with Jesus-followers in the past (see Acts 19:23–41). In Ephesians, therefore, Paul roots the authority of Jesus in his exaltation to the status of the gods. This is a Messiah who challenges those gods on their own turf.

A STORY OF RECONCILIATION FOR THE ENTIRE WORLD

In spite of their different emphases, in both letters Jesus is the culmination of a story that is cosmic in scope. Paul's language is both deep and wide, telling the story through a lens that is temporally long and geographically expansive. In Colossians, Paul not only roots the story of Jesus in the very creation of the world itself (Col 1:15–17), but the gospel is bearing fruit and growing in the whole world (1:6). In Ephesians, Paul spends even more time describing the long historical sweep of God's plan: God "chose us in Christ before the foundation of the world" (Eph 1:4); God has a "plan for the fullness of time, to gather up all things in him, things in heaven and things on earth" (1:10). God's grace, lavish as it is, has been intended for all time not only for the human hearers of this letter but for the redemption of all creation, heavenly and earthly.

The Jesus-followers in Colossae and Ephesus, listening to the grand sweep of the story that Paul is telling, were intimately familiar with another grand story that sought to root their identity deep in the mists of time. For those who considered themselves to be Ephesian, the Artemis cult shaped all aspects of civic, economic, and religious life. By the first century, Artemis had been closely linked with the goddess Roma; her story came to its culmination in the establishment of the Roman empire. The architecture of Ephesus and the festivals that shaped the rhythm of the year were not only rooted in a past where Artemis provided stability for the social order, but also reflected a present where the blessing of Artemis was linked to the political power and blessing of Rome. Honor, glory, and hope for the future were all terms that evoked this blessing. But this was not a story that shaped only Ephesian civic life; the cosmic character of the story of Rome was found throughout Asia Minor, often linked with the story of Artemis, but not always.

How then does the story that Paul tells about the peoples of the world differ from the story of Artemis taken up into the narrative of Rome? The good news of the gospel that Paul proclaims is the reconciliation of all peoples; by contrast, the good news or gospel of Rome involves the victory over and subjection of all peoples. Although both Colossians and Ephesians emphasize the reconciliation of all things as the culmination of the story of Jesus and the world, this theme is treated only briefly in Colossians (1:20–22). Paul dwells on these themes at more length in Ephesians, where he focusses not only on the reconciliation of all things but specifically on the reconciliation of the *ethnē*, the peoples of the world who are welcomed into the Jewish story. As we saw above, Roman iconography portrayed imperial interaction with the nations in terms of violence and conquest. The power and rule of God (as seen in the rule of Jesus over all rulers, thrones, powers, and authorities; Eph 1:20–21; Col 1:16) is one where peace and reconciliation ensure that instead of enemies being destroyed, what is put to death is the *hostility* between peoples, not through subjugation, but by making home together and becoming the place where God dwells (Eph 2:13–21).

While Paul's Gentile hearers (the peoples who are welcomed into the story) would have heard these words as a contrast to the imperial story, those with roots in the scriptures of Israel would have heard allusions to a story that was deeply familiar. Ephesians 2:14–17 contains an allusion to Isaiah 57:19: "'Peace, peace, to the far and the near,' says the Lord." In Isaiah, these are words of comfort and healing for those who had engaged in idolatrous acts and wicked covetousness (Isa 57:1–13, 17). For the Ephesian Christians (whose former life is described by Paul as one of idolatry and covetousness, 4:17–23), this allusion places them in a different story line, one whose word of comfort becomes a word of reconciliation between people-groups.

Ephesians 2 is concerned with allegiance. In a world where allegiance to Rome was ultimate, Paul turns the categories on their head by describing a misplaced allegiance in terms of being aliens and strangers – not aliens and strangers to Rome but to the *politeias* (republic) of the people of *Israel*, through whom God's story has been working. However, whereas Rome severely judged those who were unfaithful to its *politeias* – and did so by subjecting them to death on a cross – Paul describes a Messiah who makes peace with those who are alien, and who does so by offering himself on such a cross (Eph 2:16; Col 1:20).

A NEW BODY WITH NEW PRACTICES

In both Ephesians and Colossians, Paul's description of the authority of Jesus culminates in a description of Jesus as the head of the body, the church (Eph 1:22; Col 1:18). It is in this body that the wisdom of God is being made known to the rulers and authorities (Eph 3:10). In this body, the divisive patterns of deceit, bitterness, and anger that tear apart the community (Eph 4:24–31; Col 3:8, 9) are replaced with humility, gentleness, compassion, and patience – all bound together in love (Eph 4:2; Col 3:12–15). It is this body that demonstrates what the reconciliation of all things looks like in community and relationships, for this is a community no longer under the sway of the rulers and authorities and cosmic powers of the present darkness or the spiritual forces of evil in the heavenly places (Eph 6:12). Those rulers and authorities have been disarmed in Jesus (Col 2:15).

What did the power of those rulers and authorities look like in the lives of the community? To address this, we need to identify these cosmic powers of the present darkness, or the spiritual forces of evil in the heavenly places (Eph 6:12). As intimated above, the language of authorities, rulers, and powers would have carried overtones of the imperial rule of law and the authority of the empire. In Ephesians, however, Paul also uses language that seems to refer to Jupiter, the god of the skies, the "ruler of the air," whose spirit is at work in the disobedient (Eph 2:2). Surely this is a spiritual force of evil in the heavenly places – the places where the gods live. It is the gods of Rome that provided legitimation for the violence and power of the empire, an empire that wielded cosmic power against which the Jesus-followers were resisting. And it is clear for Paul that such cosmic powers encourage precisely the destructive, evil living that he equates with the old self. Covetousness, sexual immorality, impurity, and greed are all practices of the violent sexual and economic consumption that characterized the Roman empire from top to bottom. Such destructive and greedy economic practices were perpetuated in religious practices cultivated by the Roman elite. In fact, the religious rituals connected to the celebration of the mysteries of Artemis, Dionysius, Aphrodite, and other gods in Asia Minor were contexts where those of high social status asserted and solidified their power and influence. In the communities to which

Paul wrote, politics and religion were both ways of constructing power, and such power was used relentlessly to support the lifestyle of the elites in ways that could only be interpreted in terms of greed, evil desire, and sexual exploitation. Such greed, says Paul in both Ephesians and Colossians, is idolatry (Eph 5:5; Col 3:5) and no one who participates in such practices has a share in the inheritance of the kingdom of God (Eph 5:5).

Both of these letters are remarkably homogenous in their description of the body of Christ (although Ephesians expands on these themes at greater length than Colossians). Their descriptions of the old nature and what it looks like to be clothed in the new self are remarkably similar: for the Ephesians, the new self is being created according to the likeness of God in true justice and holiness (Eph 4:23); for the Colossians, this new self is being renewed in knowledge according to the image of the creator (Col 3:10). Both communities are called to practice humility and patience, along with gentleness, kindness, meekness, and compassion – all rooted in love and grounded in peace (Eph 4:2; Col 3:12–15). Both communities are called to sing psalms, hymns, and spiritual songs (Eph 5:19; Col 3:16), perhaps in contrast to the drinking songs prevalent at Greco-Roman feasts. However only Colossians has an extensive emphasis on forgiveness. This is, I suggest, due to the specific nature and context of this letter – the pastoral issue that shaped its writing and the extensive section known as "the household codes," discussed below.

HUSBANDS & WIVES, FATHERS & CHILDREN, MASTERS & SLAVES

The letter of Paul to the believers in Colossae was carried by a man named Tychicus who was accompanied by another man who was also a part of the Colossian community: Onesimus (Col 4:7–9). Onesimus, of course, is known to us from the epistle to Philemon, where we find out that he was a slave who had for some reason left his master. Traditionally, scholars have thought that he was a runaway slave, but it is possible that he was simply an *erro* – that is, a vagrant slave who had intended all along to return to his master. Either way, the language used in Col 4:7–9 (where the free man Tychicus is called a fellow *slave* in the Lord and the errant slave Onesimus is called a faithful and beloved *brother*) indicates that Paul recognized a fraught situation in the community and intended to redefine the way this community thinks with regard to the slaves in their midst.

This is why Paul spends comparatively more time in Colossians on the master-slave relationship than he does on the other relationships in a section commonly called "the household codes" (Col 3:18–4:1). This passage is paralleled in Ephesians, where Paul also addresses household relationships (Eph 5:21–6:9). Unusually, in both letters Paul not only addresses those who are subordinate in the household – wives, children, and slaves – as if they are moral agents, he also addresses them first. Although he is telling them to submit to their husband, father, or master (who are all the same person), he also stipulates that these men should love their wives (Eph 5:25, 33; Col 3:19), not provoke their children (Eph 6:4; Col 3:21), do good to their slaves (Eph 5:8–9), and treat them with justice and with equality (Col 4:1) – all while remembering that they also have a Master in heaven who shows no partiality (Eph 6:9; Col 3:25–4:1). The overall effect in each letter is to undermine the absolute authority of the male-dominated household.

However, the passages have significant divergences. In Colossians (a letter that accompanied an errant slave and was quite possibly also sent at the same time as the letter to Philemon), Paul deliberately creates a tension between the earthly masters whom slaves serve and Jesus as their ultimate Master – a tension that is lost when the Greek word *kyrios* is translated in some cases as "master" and in others as "lord." A consistent translation of Col 3:22–4:1 reads:

> Slaves, obey your earthly masters in everything, not only while being watched and in order to please them, but wholeheartedly, fearing The Master. Whatever your task, put yourselves into it, as done for The Master and not for your masters, since you know that from The Master you will receive the inheritance as your reward; you serve the Messianic Master. For the wrongdoer will be paid back for whatever wrong has been done, and there is no partiality. Masters, treat your slaves justly and fairly, for you know that you also have a Master in heaven.

In these verses, the authority of earthly masters is relativized, especially when Paul uses the language of inheritance in relation to slaves. For those in his audience who were familiar with the story of Israel, slaves received an inheritance in the jubilee year, when they were set free and their land returned (Lev 25). Such an allusion would have provided a narrative basis that undermined the immutable character of the entrenched social system of the Roman world, with its utter dependence on slavery.

For those in the community who would not have heard these overtones of redemption, other hints in the letter indicate a liberative identification with the slave perspective. For instance, slaves who had been captured in war were paraded in the victory processions of the empire. Paul, however, claims that Jesus has made a public example of the *rulers and authorities*, over whom he triumphed in the cross (Col 2:15). The very powers that uphold the structures of slavery now suffer the humiliation of slaves. Similarly, later in the letter, Paul states that in the renewal found in Jesus "there is no longer Greek and Jew, circumcised and uncircumcised, barbarian, Scythian, slave and free" (3:11). And, it is possible that in the instruction to slaves to obey their masters "in everything," Paul is tacitly acknowledging that as owned bodies there are some actions that slaves have no control over, some of which are considered immoral. Under other circumstances these actions would result in their exclusion from the community; instead, given slaves' lack of agency, Paul is calling on masters to act with justice and equality.[9] Paul's instructions to Philemon concerning Onesimus dovetail well with this passage.

In Ephesians, however, Paul is not writing to a community that is wrestling with a pastoral problem concerning slaves. His section on slaves in Eph 6:5–9 does not have the same rhetorical elegance as the parallel passage in Colossians. However, there is a similar emphasis on working for God rather than their earthly master, as well as a warning to masters that they too have a Master in heaven, who shows no partiality (Eph 6:9). In the context of Rome, masters always received partiality over slaves; Paul's instructions to masters, then, have a deeply equalizing focus.

The extended section concerning husbands and wives in Ephesians contains some of the most puzzling material in the letters, moving back and forth as it does between relations between husbands and wives and the love of Christ for the church (Eph 5:21–33). Drawing together themes of Christ's sacrificial love for the church in comparison with the marriage relationship, Paul engages in a delicate dance of theological depth and imperial refutation. Throughout the empire, the emperor was thought to have a sacred marriage with Rome, depicted as the goddess Roma. This could be seen most clearly in the temple statues of Caesar and the goddess Roma.[10] This familial relationship at the top was

[9] This illuminating argument, which is far more complex than I have been able to indicate here, is made in detail by Margaret Y. MacDonald, "Slavery, Sexuality and House Churches: A Reassessment of Colossians 3.18–4.1 in Light of New Research on the Roman Family," *New Testament Studies* 53 (2007): 104.

[10] Long, "Ephesians," 302.

mirrored in relationships all the way down the social ladder, which faithfully reinforced the social structures of the empire. Paul, however, who has already described the Ephesian believers as being citizens with the saints and members of the household of God (2:19), now makes it clear that this political household has as its head Christ, who nourishes and cares for his body, the church, which consists of these citizen saints whom he has made holy (5:26–28).[11] In this way, Paul grounds those structures of relationality in a different savior and a Lord whose character is one of sacrificial love.

THE ARMOR OF GOD

This sacrificial Lord calls the community to a different sort of battle than the one advertised in Roman imperial propaganda and hinted at throughout both Colossians and Ephesians. Undermining the legitimacy of Roman violence, Paul describes the cross as the place where Jesus disarms the rulers and authorities, thereby making peace and reconciling all things in heaven and on earth (Col 1:20; 2:15; Eph 2:13–18; 6:11–17). As noted above, Paul sees the structures of the empire and the powers of the gods as phenomena over which Jesus has triumphed. In readying the community for the struggle, Paul draws on visual imagery that would have been unmistakable for the recipients of the letter. The Roman emperor was frequently depicted in armor with a belt, a breastplate, shoes, a shield, a sword, and a helmet. The goddess Roma was also frequently portrayed with weapons. The message of that imagery was unmistakable: Roman rule was grounded in military power and might.

Paul, however, speaks of weapons that themselves undermine enmity. In a list that is reminiscent of Isaiah, and using verb forms that indicate he is talking to the community as a whole and not to individuals, Paul echoes the baptismal language of "putting on" found earlier in the letter. Echoing the Greek form of Isa 11:5, he describes the belt of truth and the breastplate of justice.[12] In Isaiah, the shoot from the

[11] Paul's fluid movement between husbands and wives and Christ and the church begs the question of how the parallel works (which relationship illuminates which?) for in the first century the social structure of marriage mirrored the structure of the imperial house, and the latter depended upon a stable network of the former. They were mutually reinforcing and for Paul's audience his argument would not have seemed circular but rather descriptive of the structures that bound civil society together.

[12] On justice as a more faithful translation of *dikaiosunē*, see Sylvia C. Keesmaat and Brian J. Walsh, *Romans Disarmed: Resisting Empire, Demanding Justice* (Grand Rapids, MI: Brazos, 2019), 12.

stump of Jesse is the one who, wearing this truth and justice, will act for the poor and judge the wicked (Isa 11:3–4). His rule, like that of Jesus in Ephesians, will be a sign to other nations that god is glorious and has redeemed his people from their captivity (11:10–16). Such a hope is also found in another Isaiah passage that Paul alludes to in Eph 6:15:

> How beautiful on the mountains
> are the feet of those who announce peace,
> who brings good news,
> who announces salvation,
> who says to Zion, "Your God reigns."

For Isaiah, the gospel of peace is that, in spite of all appearances to the contrary, God is the one who reigns. This, of course, is the central message of hope in Ephesians.

Paul imagery of armor also echoes Isa 59:17. In a context that laments Israel's inability to practice justice or righteousness, that verse describes God's decision to intervene by putting on justice like a breastplate and the helmet of salvation on his head. However, Paul's language in Ephesians 6 is consistent with the rest of the epistle (and with Colossians). Whereas in Isaiah God also comes clothed not only in justice and salvation but also in vengeance and fury, the community in Ephesus is to foreground the peacemaking work of Christ on the cross. Their only weapon is God's word of restoration, nourishment, and forgiveness (see Isa 55:10–13). In short, it is a word that bears the fruit of good works, truth, and justice (Eph 5:9; Col 1:6, 10).

By the time Paul has come to the end of Ephesians, those listening to the letter would have realized that Paul is describing (1) an alternative Lord to the prevalent lordship of the Roman emperor and the gods, (2) an alternative community to the hierarchy that ordered Roman society at large, and (3) an alternative way of configuring relationships between peoples who had once been enemies.

Before Paul ends these epistles (mentioning only Tychicus in Ephesians and a number of other co-workers in addition to Tychicus in Colossians), he calls members of both communities to stay alert with prayer. Although Paul refers to his chains here, he does not ask for the communities to pray for his release. Rather, he asks believers to pray that he might be able to proclaim the mystery of the gospel for which he is an ambassador in chains (Eph 6:20), or the mystery of Christ for which he is in prison (Col 4:3). This mystery, that God's reconciliation is extended to the Gentiles who now become part of the household where God dwells, has led to his suffering. Paul ends both letters, therefore, with a somber reminder to the community: *this* good news, *this* gospel, *this* new community of peace and justice is deeply threatening to the powers that be and might well lead to suffering. Indeed, what else would be expected by those who follow a Messiah who brings cosmic reconciliation on a cross?

Further Reading

Ávila Arteaga, Mariano. *Efesios: Introducción y comentario. Tomos I y II.* Buenos Aires: Ediciones Kairós, 2018.

Fowl, Stephen. *Ephesians: A Commentary.* Louisville, KY: Westminster John Knox, 2012.

Harrison, James R., and L. L. Welborn, eds. *The First Urban Churches 3: Ephesus.* Atlanta, GA: Society of Biblical Literature, 2018.

Huttner, Ulrich. *Early Christianity in the Lycus Valley.* Translated by David Green. Leiden: Brill, 2013.

Long, Frederick J. "Ephesians: Paul's Political Theology in Greco-Roman Context." In *Christian Origins and Greco-Roman Culture: Social and Literary Contexts for the New Testament,* edited by Stanley E. Porter and Andrew W. Pitts, 255–309. Leiden: Brill, 2012.

Long, Frederick J. "Roman Imperial Rule under the Authority of Jupiter-Zeus: Political-Religious Contexts and the Interpretation of 'The Ruler of the Authority of the Air' in Ephesians 2:2." In *The Language of the New Testament: Context, History, Development,* edited by Stanley E. Porter, 113–154. Leiden: Brill, 2013.

MacDonald, Margaret Y. *Colossians and Ephesians.* Collegeville, MN: The Liturgical Press, 2000.

MacDonald, Margaret Y. "Slavery, Sexuality and House Churches: A Reassessment of Colossians 3.18–4.1 in Light of New Research on the Roman Family." *New Testament Studies* 53 (2007): 94–113.

Maier, Harry O. *Picturing Paul in Empire: Imperial Image, Text and Persuasion in Colossians, Ephesians and the Pastoral Epistles.* London: Bloomsbury T&T Clark, 2013.

Myers, Ched, and Elaine Enns. *Ambassadors of Reconciliation: Vol. I: New Testament Reflections on Restorative Justice and Peacemaking.* Maryknoll, NY: Orbis, 2009.

Price S. R. F. *Rituals and Power: The Roman Imperial Cult in Asia Minor.* Cambridge: Cambridge University Press, 1984.

Smith, R. R. R. "The Imperial Reliefs from the Sebasteion at Aphrodisias." *Journal of Roman Studies* 77 (1987): 88–138.

Smith, R. R. R. "*Simulacra Gentium*: The *Ethnē* from the Sebasteion at Aphrodisias." *Journal of Roman Studies* 78 (1988): 50–77.

Sumney, Jerry L. *Colossians: A Commentary.* Louisville, KY: Westminster John Knox, 2008.

Walsh, Brian J., and Sylvia C. Keesmaat. *Colossians Remixed: Subverting the Empire.* Downers Grove, IL: InterVarsity Press, 2004.

8 The Pastoral Epistles

JAMES W. AAGESON

Few readers of the thirteen New Testament epistles attributed to Paul are apt to think of 1 Timothy, 2 Timothy, and Titus as representing the beating heart of Pauline theology. These texts approach neither the theological loftiness of Romans and Galatians nor the ecclesiastical and ministerial depth of 1 and 2 Corinthians. Addressed to Timothy and Titus (two of Paul's younger co-workers), these letters seem preoccupied with exhortation and instruction rather than forging new theological and ethical insights in the context of an apostolic mission to the Gentiles.

To the extent this assessment is warranted, it may also obscure from us the significance of these documents for the development of early Christianity and Paul's legacy in the second and third centuries. The Pastoral Epistles, read individually or together, give us glimpses into the way the church was developing institutionally and the way the Christian message was to be understood and handled in the period beyond Paul's death. They represent a particular way of thinking about the church and exercising leadership in a church that was moving from a charismatic movement to an institutional reality prepared for life in the Greco-Roman imperial world. In short, the Pastoral letters represent an important hinge point in the development of early Christianity and, as such, they are fascinating both historically and theologically and deserve attention in their own right.

Since the nineteenth century, many scholars have raised questions about the authorship of the Pastorals, despite the fact that the texts themselves claim to be letters from Paul. The conclusion is often drawn that these letters are pseudonymous, written in the name of Paul by a disciple of Paul sometime after the apostle's death, perhaps well into the second century. For the past two centuries, this question has preoccupied a great deal of scholarship on the Pastorals and more broadly on the history and legacy of Paul. Whatever the merits of these debates, they have often diverted attention away from the more important issues of the Pastorals and their place in the development of early Christianity.

Does early Christian usage of the Pastoral Epistles help us decide whether these texts were written by Paul or by someone seeking to extend his voice into later situations? The Pastoral Epistles appear in the list of canonical texts assembled in the Muratorian Canon (usually dated between 170–200 CE), but they are conspicuously absent from Papyrus 46, the earliest codex manuscript of Paul's letters (dating from as early as 200) and from Codex Vaticanus (in the fourth century). However, Irenaeus later in the first century (born sometime toward the middle of the second century and becoming bishop of Lyon in perhaps 177 or 178) opened the preface to Book 1 of his magisterial work *Adversus haereses* with a reference to 1 Tim 1:4. Likewise, Tertullian (who lived in Carthage during the second half of the second century and first quarter of the third century) and Clement of Alexandria (who wrote during the last two decades of the second century and the beginning of the third) cite or echo material from the Pastorals. What this indicates is that the earliest manuscript traditions and canonical lists are divided regarding the inclusion of the Pastorals, but that by the end of the second century references to the Pastorals appear in writings by many of the great thinkers of the church. This raises not only the question of when these epistles were written but how these epistles might have been viewed and what authority they were given in different corners of the church.

The absence of the Pastoral Epistles from some canonical sources does not necessarily suggest their pseudonymity. More telling, perhaps, is the fact that many terms and expressions found in the epistles that Paul unquestionably wrote do not appear in the Pastorals, and vice versa. Likewise, certain theological concepts and expressions found in the major Pauline epistles are absent from or used differently in the three Pastoral letters. (For further discussion of these issues, see below.) In 1 Timothy and Titus, the instructions to church leaders (overseers, elders, and deacons) appear to many scholars to represent a later period in the church, when discrete leadership roles had likely developed, perhaps as late as the first half of the second century. Finally, it is difficult to fit the Pastorals into the chronology of Paul's life and ministry as we see it in his other letters and in Luke's account of Paul in Acts. For many scholars, when all these factors are considered, the preponderance of the evidence suggests that the Apostle Paul did not actually write these three letters.[1] They were written by someone in the Pauline tradition at a later date and then gradually over the second century incorporated into the Pauline tradition and eventually into the New Testament as we know it today. It is fair to say that this view predominates among modern scholars, though it is by no means unanimous.

Other scholars have sought to refute this view or have tried to find some other way of thinking about the issue of authorship. Regarding the issues of terminology and style, they often point to the changed audience, circumstance, purpose, and function of the Pastoral letters in order to account for their apparent differences from the other Pauline letters. Likewise, some of these scholars think that proponents of the majority view often engage in a circular form of argumentation. Assuming the letters are later and written by someone other than Paul, the texts are then forced into that mold.[2] It is the case, however, that circular forms of argumentation can run in both directions. While it is important to understand the basic contours of these debates, it is unfortunate if they divert the reader of these letters from their larger place in early Christian tradition and obscure their fundamental importance in the development of Paul's legacy.[3]

OVERVIEW OF THE LETTERS

The Pastoral letters can be fruitfully explored through selected themes and issues: God and Christ; godliness, truth, knowledge, and faith; qualifications and instructions for Leadership in the church; other groups identified; opponents and their opposition; and the purpose and nature of scripture.

God and Christ

Three features display important characteristics of the Pastorals' theology and their Christology, as well as how the Pauline tradition ever so subtly expanded and adopted new ways of describing and imagining

[1] For more detailed analyses of these differences, see any scholarly commentary on the Pastoral Epistles. For example, Raymond F. Collins, *I & II Timothy and Titus: A Commentary* (Louisville, KY: Westminster John Knox, 2002), 1–5; Arland J. Hultgren, "The Pastoral Epistles," in *The Cambridge Companion to Paul* , ed. James D. G. Dunn (Cambridge: Cambridge University Press, 2003), 141–144; Philip H. Towner, *The Letters to Timothy and Titus* (Grand Rapids, MI: Eerdmans, 2006), 15–20.

[2] See Luke Timothy Johnson, *Letters to Paul's Delegates: 1 Timothy, 2 Timothy, Titus* (Valley Forge, PA: Trinity Press International, 1996), 1–36.

[3] For my own way of dealing with these issues, see Aageson, *Paul, the Pastoral Epistles, and the Early Church* (Peabody MA: Hendrickson, 2008), 3–5, 10–17, 86–102.

divine activity. First, in the other ten Pauline epistles, the term "savior" is used only twice (Phil 3:20 and Eph 5:23), though the verbal form of the word is common. The term "savior," however, appears in all three of the Pastoral letters, and rather extensively in 1 Timothy and Titus (1 Tim 1:1, 2:3, 4:10; 2 Tim 1:10; Tit 1:3, 4, 2:10, 13, 3:4, 6). Moreover, it is interesting to note that whereas God alone is referred to as savior in 1 Timothy, in Titus the term is applied both to God and Christ. In 2 Timothy the designation is used solely in relation to Christ. This suggests that Paul's theological and Christological language is being pressed more firmly into savior imagery and symbolism in the Pastorals.

Second, in 1 Tim 2:5 Christ is referred to as the mediator between God and human beings. Elsewhere in the New Testament, the term "mediator" is used only in Gal 3:19–20 and in Heb 8:6, 9:15, and 12:24, where Christ is portrayed as the mediator of a new covenant. In short, we see in 1 Timothy the beginning of a new way of speaking about Christ, imagery that depicts Christ as the intermediary between God and humans.[4]

Third, most of the writings in the New Testament (Paul's letters included) describe the return of Christ as a "coming," but in the Pastorals the terminology used to describe Christ's coming both past and future shifts to "appearance" terminology. The Pastorals prefer this epiphany language, emphasizing that something previously hidden is now revealed.

Godliness, Truth, Knowledge, and Faith

One of the most prominent features of 1 Timothy is the emphasis on godliness as the proper way of life for those in the household of God, the church (1 Tim 2:2, 3:15, 4:7, 8, 6:3, 5, 6, 11; cf. also 5:4). According to 1 Timothy, godliness describes and represents the manner of life that conforms to faithfulness in the divinely ordered world of God's household (1 Tim 1:4). But even more, the theology represented by 1 Timothy interweaves notions of godliness, faith, truth, and knowledge, which are said to govern how those in the church ought to live. This is not true of 2 Timothy or Titus in the same way, even though they also use forms of the word "godliness" (2 Tim 3:5, 12; Titus 1:1, 2:12; the word "ungodliness" also appears in these letters, as in 2 Tim 2:16 and Titus 2:12). 2 Timothy and Titus certainly share the theology of godliness found in 1 Timothy, but in these epistles they do not rise to the same theological level as in 1 Timothy. However, both 1 Timothy and Titus also convey

[4] This is imagery that is picked up later by Irenaeus, *Against Heresies*, 3:18:7 and 5:17:1.

the notion of training in godliness (1 Tim 4:7) or training to reject ungodliness (Titus 2:11–12). Conditioning and training are to be part of life in the household of God. In Titus, the grace of God is said to be the agent of the training, whereas in 1 Timothy the appeal is to train oneself. This kind of exhortation is absent from 2 Timothy and on the face of it seems to give way to the appeal to suffer as Paul (or Christ?) has suffered (see 2 Tim 1:12, 2:3, 9, 3:11–12, 4:5).

The three epistles consistently represent the connection between knowledge, truth, and faith. These verbal and conceptual associations represent one of the most conspicuous features of the Pastoral letters. For example, the expression "knowledge of truth" (1 Tim 2:4; 2 Tim 2:25, 3:7; Titus 1:1; cf. also 1Tim 3:15, 4:3; 2 Tim 2:15) designates knowledge of the true faith or the true doctrine that Paul proclaims to Timothy, Titus, and their congregations. Faith, too, is closely linked to knowledge, sound teaching, and truth (1 Tim 1:4–5, 16, 4:3, 6, 10, 6:10; 2 Tim 1:13, 3:10, 15; Titus 1:4, 9, 11, 13, 2:2). Faith in the Pastorals cannot be reduced only to correct teaching, but clearly that is one of its implications. Each of the letters makes reference to sound teaching, which is considered to be a feature of the household of God, and the content of sound teaching is said to correspond to the truth and to genuine faith. In the communities represented by these texts, teaching is considered an important activity, but the doctrinal content of the teaching is also critically important. Those who stray need to be resisted.

In 6:20, the writer of 1 Timothy says: "O Timothy, guard the *good deposit* that has been entrusted to you and turn away from the profane chatter and contradictions of what is falsely called knowledge." Similarly, in 2 Tim 1:12–14 the reference to sound teaching in 1:13 links two appearances of the term which is often translated "good deposit" or "good treasure":

> I am sure that he is able to guard the good deposit that I have entrusted to him [or "that has been entrusted to me"] until that day. Hold to the standard of sound teaching that you have heard from me, in faith and love that are in Christ Jesus. Guard the good deposit entrusted to you through the Holy Spirit which dwells in us.

Despite certain ambiguous translation issues, the substance of these references is clear enough to indicate that the sound teaching passed on by Paul and held in trust by the people of God is likened to a treasure or a good deposit. In the theological worlds of 1 and 2 Timothy, the implication is that the good and proper teaching that Paul taught is to be preserved by Timothy and all those charged with leadership in the church. Although the Pastorals do not elaborate to any great extent the precise character of the correct doctrine that must be preserved, it is now clearly part of the early church's vocabulary and will reappear in the way later thinkers in emerging normative Christianity express themselves. For example, Irenaeus writing in *Adversus haereses* late in the second century compares the apostles to a rich man who deposits his money in a bank account from which all those who desire can withdraw the water of life (3:4:1). Irenaeus links this imagery to the apostolic tradition in new ways for new purposes, but he still echoes the idea of 1 and 2 Timothy that the church is the caretaker of a good deposit of truth that derives from the teaching of the apostles and is now passed on and preserved by those charged with leadership in the household of God. Hence, it is not an overstatement to say that in the Pastorals we see for the first time sound Christian teaching represented as a body of Christian truth under the safekeeping of the church. If so, we witness in the Pastoral Epistles a notable intensification of a concept of Christian orthodoxy, although the precise content of that orthodoxy is not spelled out in much detail.

Qualifications and Instructions for Leadership in the Church

1 Timothy and Titus (but not 2 Timothy) state the personal qualifications appropriate for "overseers" (bishops) "deacons," and "elders." They do not offer lists of duties or job descriptions for the respective positions, but instead highlight the personal qualities and behaviors required for those who hold those positions. In 1 Tim 3:1–7, those who wish to be overseers are said to desire a noble task, a statement that is followed immediately by a series of qualities that these people are to exhibit: They are to be above reproach; to have married only once; to be temperate, sensible, respectable, and hospitable; to be apt teachers and good managers of their own households; to keep their children submissive and respectful; not to be recent converts; and to be thought well of by others. Some of these qualities for overseers are also echoed in Titus 1:7–9. There it is said that they should be blameless and not be arrogant, quick tempered, a drunkard, violent, or greedy; they are to be hospitable, lovers of goodness, prudent, upright, devout, self-controlled, and having a firm grasp of the word in accordance with sound doctrine. Apart from Phil 1:1, these are the only references to overseers in the corpus of Pauline letters, and they indicate that reflection on issues of leadership in the church is moving to a new level. In later years, those reflections will develop into claims about the nature and authority of church leadership positions

themselves, not just the qualities considered necessary for those who hold the positions. These reflections and arguments will mark new and important developments in the nature and authority of the church with its more formal structures and leadership roles. 1 Timothy and Titus represent an important stage on the way to a church structured around episcopal authority, a stage that will come to fuller expression later in Christian writings from the second and third centuries.

Similarly, 1 Timothy (though not Titus or 2 Timothy) also lists a series of qualities appropriate for deacons (3:8–13). As with the overseers, the qualities identified are largely behavioral, and they pertain to those designated as servers in the church. Both 1 Timothy and Titus also address matters pertaining to elders. Whether addressing men as a group (as in 1 Tim 2:8) or specifically addressing older men (as in Titus 2:2) or younger men (as in Titus 2:6), these letters consistently delegitimize anger as a legitimate form of Christian identity for men, substituting temperance and self-control in its place. In 1 Timothy 5:17–21, Timothy is instructed to give double honor to elders who preach and teach, not to accept any evidence against an elder without the evidence of two or three witnesses, and to rebuke those who persist in sin. In Titus 1:5–6, Titus (who is on the island of Crete off of the mainland of Greece) is instructed to appoint elders in every town who are blameless, who have married only once, whose children are believers, who are not accused of debauchery or rebelliousness. Once again, we see instructions, ostensibly from Paul, reflecting concerns about church leadership and procedures that suggest a community in the early stages of maturation and institutional development within the Greco-Roman world.

Other Groups Identified

1 Timothy and Titus also address other groups of individuals. Both epistles counsel believing slaves to submit to their masters in order to avoid blaspheming the name of God and the teaching of the church (1 Tim 6:1) and to ensure that their obedience adorns the church's teaching (Titus 2:10). In contrast to the ideal expressed in Gal 3:28 (where Paul writes that "in Christ there is no longer Jew or Greek, slave or free, male and female"), these two Pastoral letters deal with the concrete reality of slavery in churches embedded within the Roman Empire (perhaps more along the lines of the epistle to Philemon). 1 Timothy, too, raises directly the issue of a believing master, a believing slave, and the challenges this might present in the household of God. This is less an abstract theological issue and more a matter of pastoral advice and how those in the household of God will be perceived by the

larger imperial society. In this way, the Pastorals seek to accommodate to larger societal expectations in order to give the church a stronger foothold for mission within that society. There seems to be no willingness to resist or challenge the institution of slavery theologically or pastorally, and it is precisely this kind of text that those Christians who later sought to abolish slavery had to address.

Equally as jarring to modern sensibilities is the statement about women in 1 Tim 2:9–15, which needs to be quoted at length:

> Women should dress themselves modestly and decently in suitable clothing, not with their hair braided, or with gold, pearls, or expensive clothes, but with good works, as is proper for women who profess reverence for God. Let a woman learn in silence with full submission. I permit no woman to teach or to have authority over a man; she is to keep silent. For Adam was formed first, then Eve; and Adam was not deceived, but the woman was deceived and became a transgressor. Yet she will be saved through childbearing, provided they continue in faith and love and holiness, with modesty. [NRSV]

In addition to what is proper for women in the household of God to wear, women are to learn in silence and submission. And no woman is to teach or have authority over a man. The stated justification for this is that Adam was created before Eve, and Eve was deceived by the serpent but Adam was not. She was the transgressor, not Adam. The statement concludes with the peculiar assertion that women will be saved through childbearing provided they continue in faith, love, holiness, and modesty. Once again, this statement seems to contrast with the implications of what Paul said in Gal 3:28. It is easy to understand the pernicious consequences this statement in 1 Timothy has had for women through the centuries in Christianity and far beyond as well. In the text's historical context, it seems that the household of God is being instructed to conform to certain Roman societal norms and not to deviate from them. Should the church deviate and hence threaten Roman social stability, it would open itself to the charge that it is subversive, thereby bringing disrepute upon the entire community. It is also the case that overseers and elders in the church are spoken of in terms of being male, which is likely a reflection of the role of the *paterfamilias* (the male head in the Roman household) making itself felt on the household of God.[5] In the case of both slavery and of women,

[5] The presence of female deacons might be suggested in 1 Tim 3:11, depending on how we translate and interpret that verse. Does it refer to (1) women deacons or (2) women

both 1 Timothy and Titus unmistakably adopt positions that resonate with cultural perceptions of the day, precisely as the church was struggling to develop institutionally within its historical context.

First Timothy includes instructions for two other groups of people. Widows are singled out as a group in 1 Tim 5:9–16, which deals with who is to be listed among the widows, how they are to be treated, and how they ought to behave. It is difficult to know whether these comments pertain to specific circumstances in Ephesus or are more general instructions. However, it seems clear there is concern over how widows should behave and be treated in the community (cf. also Titus 2:3–5). Another group of people identified in 1 Timothy are those who want to be rich. They are warned of the temptations that may befall them, including harmful desires, ruin, pain, straying from the faith, and destruction (1 Tim 6:9–11). This instruction, perhaps most notably, includes the famous statement that "money is the root of all kinds of evil" (6:10). Later (6:17–19) the rich are instructed to avoid arrogance and display their dependency on God by taking initiatives toward those who are needy.

These instructions in 1 Timothy and Titus deal primarily with matters of communal concern rather than abstract theological concepts – except for the notion of maintaining the good deposit of sound teaching and the true faith. But even this notion undoubtedly required a concrete application in the life of a community trying to define and organize itself in new circumstances. In most of the matters related to church leadership and instructions concerning particular groups of people, 2 Timothy stands apart from 1 Timothy and Titus. Most conspicuously, the writer of 2 Timothy calls on Timothy to follow the path of suffering and in that sense to go the way of Paul. This theme is largely absent from 1 Timothy and Titus.

Opponents and Their Opposition

It has often been thought that a type of "gnostic" or "proto-gnostic" teaching within Christian groups facilitated the need for the instructions of the Pastoral letters (see e.g., 1 Tim 1:4, 4:3–5). In this view, at the heart of the opponents' viewpoint lay a gnostic tendency to diminish the goodness of creation and to interpret redemption as pertaining only to the spirit as it is released from the shackles of the human body. We cannot be sure of this reconstruction of the opponents' view,

who are the wives of male deacons? Either way, the character of church leadership reflected in the Pastorals appears highly patriarchal.

however. In fact, some hints about who the various opponents might have been and what they taught may suggest that they prioritized certain readings of the Hebrew Bible and understandings of Torah, which the author refers to as "the law" (*nomos*). In 1 Tim 1:6–7, we hear about those who engage in meaningless talk and desire to be teachers of the law but have no understanding about what they are saying or about what they claim to teach. Here the opponents are those who are ignorant and teach things that deviate from the faith. Immediately following in 1:8–11, the text makes the claim that the law is good if it is used properly, namely, with the understanding that the law is not given for the innocent but for the lawless and disobedient. Presumably, the law spoken about here is the Jewish law given originally to Israel; and, if that is correct, those who the author depicts as false teachers are those who, in his view, misunderstand and misuse the law. Later in 1 Timothy (in particular 4:1–5), the writer makes the further claim that in later times some people will turn from the faith and follow deceitful spirits and the teachings of demons. The error of these people is that they forbid marriage and require abstinence from foods that God created. While some scholars have argued that this is evidence of some type of gnostic opposition between the created order and the world of the "spirit," the more likely explanation (taking account of 1:6–7) seems to be that the author's opponents were deviating from the faith by misapplying the scriptures. As a consequence, the goodness of creation was being diminished in favor of abstinence from marriage and the avoidance of certain foods.

If the author's opponents were Jewish believers in Jesus Christ, this would cohere well with the author's comments in Titus 1:10–11 and 13–14:

> There are also many rebellious people, idle talkers and deceivers, *especially those of the circumcision*; they must be silenced, since they are upsetting whole families by teaching for sordid gain what it is not right to teach.
>
> That testimony is true. For this reason rebuke them sharply, so that they may become sound in the faith, not paying attention to *Jewish myths or to commandments of those who reject the truth.* [NRSV]

In the eyes of the author, "those of the circumcision" are to be silenced because their views were luring others from the truth by means of certain "Jewish myths" and commandments. The discussion continues in Titus 1:15 with the statement that to those who are pure, everything is pure, but to the unbelievers, everything is impure. This claim resonates with Jewish concerns about purity and appears to echo the statement in 1 Tim 4:3 about refraining from marriage and certain foods. In 3:9, Titus is warned among other things about senseless disputes about the law, and in 3:5 the writer of the epistle makes clear that salvation does not come by doing works of righteousness but according to divine mercy. To what extent these statements reflect specific controversies is perhaps unclear, but they do suggest that certain people identified as faithless are misusing the scriptures and commandments originally given to Israel. Once again, 2 Timothy stands apart from the other two Pastoral letters, since Jewish identity is not mentioned with regard to those the author opposes. Instead, the issues of controversy in 2 Timothy are largely about people of wicked passions, persecutions leading to suffering, and some people who falsely claim that the resurrection has already taken place.

The Purpose and Nature of Scripture

The most explicit and detailed account of the purpose and nature of Scripture in the New Testament appears in 2 Tim 3:14–16:

> But as for you, continue in what you have learned and firmly believed, knowing from whom you learned it, and how from childhood you have known the *sacred writings* that are able *to instruct* you for salvation through faith in Christ Jesus. All *scripture* is *inspired by God* and is useful for teaching, for reproof, for correction, and for training in righteousness. [NRSV]

Beyond the scriptures of Israel, it is unclear what other early Christian writings, if any, might be included among the sacred writings here identified. We know that authoritative writings, Paul's letters included, emerged quite early and were considered important to various church communities, but it would seem anachronistic to think that by the time of the Pastoral Epistles these had achieved anything approaching formal canonical status. This is not to suggest that some of them did not have importance and exercise considerable authority. Whether they were yet considered sacred writings or God-inspired Scripture is unclear. What is clear is that the utility of the sacred writings is explicit. They are useful for teaching, reproof, correction, and training. The household of God reflected in 2 Timothy is a community of "God-breathed," "God-inspired" writings. However, beyond these general assertions about these writings and their utility, what this actually means about the precise character of the texts themselves is not clear.

THE PASTORALS AND PAUL

The Pastoral letters represent an important hinge point in the development of early Christianity generally and the Pauline tradition specifically. It is important to think about them in relation to what has come before them (earlier Pauline letters) and to developments in the second century church (Ignatius, Polycarp, 1 Clement). In this section, we will look comparatively at the Pastoral letters in relation to three topics found respectively in Philippians, Galatians, and 1 Corinthians (friendship and suffering, "the law," and the church). This will illustrate from a different perspective other features of these three letters, as well as suggest directions for further study.

Philippians and the Pastorals

In scholarship on Philippians, one feature often noted is its connection to ancient friendship letters.[6] In the ancient world, friendship letters functioned as stand-ins when friends were absent from one another; as a result, expressions of affection were commonly part of these kinds of letters. Another feature often present is a sense of opposition accompanied with pleas to stand firm in the face of suffering perpetrated by one's enemies. In the case of Philippians, the members of the church are exhorted by Paul (as friends in Christ) to live together in a manner worthy of the gospel (see Phil 1:27–2:11) and to prevail against hardship (1:7, 12–14, 22–23, 2:17, 3:8). In the letter to the Philippians, there is clearly a sense of affection and intimacy expressed by Paul to his fellow partners in Christ.

Despite the apparent differences between Philippians and 2 Timothy, the issues of friendship and suffering most conspicuously connect them. Both letters contain a retrospective orientation, autobiographical references, a concern about opponents, and a sense of partnership and reciprocity between Paul and the letters' recipients. Especially noteworthy is the theme of imprisonment and the call to suffer that appears in both Philippians and 2 Timothy (see 2 Tim 1:8, 12, 29; 2:3, 9; 3:11, 17; 4:5). This is not the case for 1 Timothy or Titus, neither of which

[6] See e.g., Stanley K. Stowers, "Friends and Enemies in the Politics of Heaven: Reading Theology in Philippians," in *Pauline Theology*, vol. 1 (Minneapolis, MN: Fortress Press, 1991), 105–121.

emphasize Paul's suffering. In fact, we might say that the point where 2 Timothy is most like Philippians is the point where it is least like the other two Pastorals, and vice versa.[7]

Galatians and the Pastorals

The arguments in Galatians over "the law" and faith are well known, involving the rejection of the idea that circumcision was necessary for Gentile inclusion in the Christ-community. In Paul's day, this was clearly a contentious issue and one that threatened to tear apart early church communities. What we see in 1 Timothy and Titus regarding the law is of a quite different order. As we have seen, Titus 1:10–16 identifies "those of the circumcision" as upsetting whole families for shameful gain. The author admonishes Christians to be sound in their faith and not be led astray by Jewish myths and the commandments of those who deny the truth. Although "deceivers" of this kind claim to know God, they deny God by what they do. The issue at stake in Titus is related to matters of purity: "To the pure all things are pure, but to the corrupt and unbelieving nothing is pure." Even though issues related to "the law" appear in both Galatians and Titus, the underlying concerns of each letter seem largely unrelated. The arguments in Galatians are against the necessity of circumcision for Gentile inclusion, since faith in Christ is the sole mark of Christian identity. In Titus, the "Judaizing" opposition seems to argue for certain notions of purity that the author says should be rejected, but these notions are no longer framed primarily by the issue of Gentile inclusion. "The law" is at issue in 1 Tim 1:7–8 as well, where it is declared to be good but misused by the false teachers. This is also related in 1 Timothy to the problem of forbidding marriage and not eating certain foods. Once again, the problem here is about the misuse of scripture in ethical decision-making. Perhaps the closest connection to Galatians in the Pastorals is the statement in Titus 3:5 that we are saved not by works of righteousness but according to the mercy of God. In short, the Pauline notion of righteousness according to faith and "not by works of law," which was intended to undermine the prioritization of ethnic Israel over against the gentiles, has largely given way in the Pastorals to the misapplication of the scriptures in the face of certain purity and ascetic practices.[8]

[7] For a fuller discussion see my argument in *Paul, the Pastoral Epistles, and the Early Church*, 73–78.

[8] Aageson, *Paul, the Pastoral Epistles, and the Early Church*, 78–82.

1 Corinthians and the Pastorals

Writing in 1 Cor 12:4–29, Paul likens the church, as the body of Christ, to the human body with its mutually interdependent members. It is a beautiful image and in Paul's hands has important social consequences for the life and ministry of the church. In the Pauline church, there is to be unity in the Spirit (just as there is always the threat of disunity). The ruling image for the church in 1 Timothy, however, is the household of God with its notions of order and godliness that correspond to the divine order in faith and truth (1 Tim 3:15).[9] The vision of the church as an organic body with its many members making various contributions is somewhat different from the image of the structured household of God in 1 Timothy. These two images of the church are certainly not incompatible, but they do appear to come from two quite distinct patterns of thought and experiences of the church. In the case of 1 Timothy, the imagery of "the household of God" seems to derive from an experience of institutional development and the challenges of church leadership, which were requiring the establishment of more formal structures. The issue of the preservation of the truth is clearly in view in the Pastorals. By contrast, the imagery of "the body of Christ" emphasizes unity and interdependence, a vision of the church that is seemingly less hierarchical and more inter-relational. It is certainly not surprising that over time the hard realities of institutional development would place demands on the church that needed to be addressed in new and more formal ways.[10]

THE PASTORALS AND THE POST-PAULINE CHURCH

Ignatius, Polycarp, and 1 Clement represent three early church leaders and writers who provide glimpses into the way the church and the Pauline tradition were developing. Each of them speaks of Paul with great esteem. While under arrest early in the second century and anticipating his martyrdom, Ignatius, the bishop of Antioch, wrote a series of letters to local churches on his way to Rome. He presumed Paul's apostolic status and authority, a status he will only approach as a true disciple through his martyrdom, much as Paul was martyred (Ign. *Rom* 4:3). This echoes the plea in 2 Timothy to suffer as Paul had suffered. But even more, Ignatius also had an elevated notion of church leaders'

[9] Cf. also the references to the household of faith in Gal 6:10 and the household of God in Eph 2:19.

[10] Aageson, *Paul, the Pastoral Epistles, and the Early Church*, 82–84.

authority and the role they play in the church and its worship. He wrote: "I exhort you: be eager to do all things in harmony with God, with the bishop set over you in the place of God, and the presbyters in the place of the council of apostles, and the deacons, most dear to me, entrusted with the service of Jesus Christ" (Ign. *Magn.* 6:1, cf. Ign. *Smyrn.* 8:1–2, Ign. *Trall.* 3:1). In this way, Ignatius represents a much loftier view of church leaders and their roles than 1 Timothy and Titus. Between Paul and Ignatius, a generational shift has taken place in the church, and 1 Timothy and Titus clearly stand in that line of development. Conceptually, they are somewhere between the two.[11]

Polycarp, the bishop of Smyrna in Asia Minor, wrote to the Philippian church prior to his martyrdom in the mid-second century. Knowing Paul's connection to the church in Philippi, Polycarp wrote in glowing terms about the apostle (Pol. *Phil.* 3:2):

> For neither am I, nor any other like me, able to follow the wisdom of the blessed and glorious Paul, who when he was among you formerly face-to-face taught accurately and steadfastly the word concerning truth (word of truth), who also when he was absent wrote epistles to you, from the study of which you will be able to build yourselves up into the faith which was given to you.

As bishop, he reminded Christians of the word of truth Paul taught and how he wrote to build them up when he was absent from them. As a bishop of the church, Polycarp depicted himself as also writing to build up the churches under his authority, but he declared that in no way can he live up to the wisdom of the blessed and glorious Paul. In the case of both Polycarp and Ignatius, these two bishops sought to extend the authority of Paul's voice and example, but they wrote in their own names and from their own positions as authority figures in the emerging church. Regardless of who actually wrote the Pastorals, they purport to represent the voice of Paul directly, whereas Polycarp and Ignatius claim to stand historically in the line of Paul, both in the line of his memory and his authority.

The ancient church historian Eusebius claimed that Clement was the third successor of Peter in overseeing the Christian churches. Upon hearing about a dispute in the Corinthian church, Clement wrote a letter instructing them what they should do to resolve their differences (the letter we call 1 Clement). In the course of that discussion, Clement

[11] Aageson, *Paul, the Pastoral Epistles, and the Early Church*, 123–140.

wrote this to the Corinthians: "Take up the epistle of the blessed Paul the apostle. What did he first write to you in the beginning of his preaching the gospel?" (47:1–2). Assuming the authority to intervene in the Corinthian conflict, Clement reinforced his argument with a reminder of Paul's memory and of what he first wrote to them. Here again, we see the legacy of Paul's words being brought to bear on the life of one of the early Pauline churches.[12]

While the Pastorals were written to two individuals, the known writings of Ignatius, Polycarp, and the author of 1 Clement were written to churches (with one exception). That does not mean, however, that the three Pastoral letters were not in some sense also intended for church communities. They undoubtedly were, foreshadowing new developments the church will undergo and challenges the church will face later in the second and third centuries. Among these issues are: the nature of the true faith and how to preserve it; the relationship of the church to Judaism and to some interpretations of the Jewish scriptures; church unity and the threat of disunity; the purpose and function of Scripture; the place of women; Christian asceticism; and the character and roles of authorized leaders in the church. In each of these areas, the Pastoral Epistles provide glimpses into the development of the early church and what was increasingly at stake for it.

Further Reading

Aageson, James W. "The Pastoral Epistles and the Acts of Paul: A Multiplex Approach to Authority in Paul's Legacy." *Lexington Quarterly Review* 40 (2005): 237–248.

Aageson, James W. *Paul, the Pastoral Epistles, and the Early Church*. Peabody, MA: Hendrickson, 2008.

Beker, J. Christiaan. *Heirs of Paul: Paul's Legacy in the New Testament and in the Church Today*. Minneapolis, MN: Fortress Press, 1991.

Collins, Raymond F. "The Image of Paul in the Pastorals." *Laval Theologique et Philosophique* 31 (1975): 147–173.

Collins, Raymond F. *I & II Timothy and Titus: A Commentary*. Louisville, KY: Westminster John Knox, 2002.

Hultgren, Arland J. "The Pastoral Epistles." In *The Cambridge Companion to St Paul*, edited by James D. G. Dunn, 141–157. Cambridge: Cambridge University Press, 2003.

Johnson, Luke Timothy. *Letters to Paul's Delegates: 1 Timothy, 2 Timothy, Titus*. Valley Forge, PA: Trinity Press International, 1996.

[12] Aageson, *Paul, the Pastoral Epistles, and the Early Church*, 148–156.

Johnson, Luke Timothy. *The First and Second Letters to Timothy*. New York: Doubleday, 2001.

Marshall, I. Howard. "Recent Study of the Pastoral Epistles." *Themelios* 23 (1997): 3–21.

MacDonald, Dennis R. *The Legend and the Apostle: The Battle for Paul in Story and Canon*. Louisville, KY: Westminster John Knox, 1983.

MacDonald, Margaret Y. *The Pauline Churches: A Socio-Historical Study of Institutionalization in Pauline and Deutero-Pauline Writings*. Cambridge: Cambridge University Press, 1988.

Maier, Harry O. *Picturing Paul in Empire: Imperial Image, Text and Persuasion in Colossians, Ephesians and the Pastoral Epistles*. London: Bloomsbury T&T Clark, 2013.

Schröter, Jens. "Paul the Founder of the Church: Reflections on the Reception of Paul in the Acts of the Apostles and the Pastoral Epistles." In *Paul and the Heritage of Israel: Paul's Claim upon Israel's Legacy in Luke and Acts in light of the Pauline Letters*, edited by David Moessner, Daniel Marguerat, Mikeal Parsons, and Michael Wolter, 195–219. New York: T&T Clark, 2012.

Torjesen, Karen Jo. *When Women Were Priests: Women's Leadership in the Early Church & the Scandal of Their Subordination in the Rise of Christianity*. San Francisco, CA: Harper San Francisco, 1993.

Towner, Philip H. *The Letters to Timothy and Titus*. Grand Rapids, MI: Eerdmans, 2006.

Part III

Paul's Theological Discourse

9 What Did Paul Think Is Wrong in God's World?

BRUCE W. LONGENECKER

When Paul gave consideration to the issue of what is wrong within God's good creation, he saw a consistently repeating pattern all around him – from the lowest to the highest levels of created existence. No matter where he looked, Paul observed relationships distorted by the ongoing and ever-present quest for self-preservation in combination with a consequent unjust abuse of power. Paul saw this same pattern of distorted relationality repeated in every area of life.

In this essay, we will tease out the character of the relational distortion that Paul found lying at the heart of the problem that required God's salvific intervention. Profitable advances into understanding Paul's view of "the problem" can be achieved if we place our focus on a single motif: power. That motif includes within itself at least two separate but interrelated phenomena that, for Paul, lie at the root of all that had gone wrong within God's good creation. Those two phenomena are: (1) the abusive application of power within patterns of dysfunctional relationship, and (2) human inability (or the lack of power) to offset those abusive applications of power. These phenomena and their interrelatedness provide a stark backdrop against which to perceive what Paul thought God had done and was doing in Christ. But even as we explore these two phenomena, we will also see more than them as well, as things get progressively complicated in Paul's portrait of what is wrong in God's world.

SUPRAHUMAN POWERS THREATEN THE SOVEREIGNTY OF GOD

In Paul's day, it was common to imagine the material world (the world of concrete reality, we might say) as being closely related to supramaterial forces – forces that influenced the course of the material world for better or for worse. Invisible to the human eye, these "spiritual" realities exercised their power within human affairs, having intentionality and purpose to effect outcomes.

This way of perceiving the world had a long and widespread history for millennia prior to the first century. Its longevity testifies to the fact that ancient people found it useful as a way of interpreting the twists and turns of human experience. This worldview captured the sense that the course of everyone's life was vulnerable to forces that lay beyond one's own control. And this was true not just of individuals but of people-groups as well – whether that be families, neighborhoods, towns, cities, regions, nations, or even the whole of the created order. No matter how many controls they tried to implement, people usually found themselves unable to determine the course of their lives. There was a sense that dynamic forces beyond human control could shape the flow of life. Cause-and-effect relations could not always be explained in relation to the input and output of human energies. As a consequence, it was believed that a cadre of suprahuman agencies had a part to play in the running of the world.

In the ancient world, people sought to harness the goodwill of those spiritual forces. The primary means for accessing beneficial forms of spiritual power was sacrifice – making offerings to spiritual entities in order to earn their favor and increase the chances of success in life. In Paul's world, the conglomerate of these spiritual entities included, first and foremost, the deities of the Greco-Roman world – the almost incalculable number of deities who were thought by many to oversee human society. Other spiritual entities that could be harnessed included (but were not restricted to) spirits of the deceased and the spirit of the locale (a concept largely foreign to contemporary Western society).

Against this backdrop, when we ask what Paul saw wrong with the world, one answer falls naturally into place: the common practice of worshipping the deities of the Greco-Roman world. Like most Judeans of his day, Paul had been taught that worship was only legitimate if it was directed toward the one who had brought the whole of the created order to life. This creator was the deity of the Judean people and, for the early Jesus-followers, the deity who had brought life to the crucified messiah and Lord. If devotion is directed away from the creator to other realities, the whole of one's relational matrix is skewed.

This probably explains the flow of Paul's discourse in the second half of Romans 1. Paul highlighted improper forms of worship as lying at the heart of the desperate situation of humanity (e.g., 1:21–23, 25, 28). Moreover, he connected that fundamental relational abuse to what he perceived to be other forms of relational abuses that emerge as a consequence – abuses played out in human relationships (e.g., 1:24, 26–32). For Paul, if worship is misdirected, a whole gamut of further relational abuses emerge in its wake.

Although Paul placed improper worship at the heart of relational misfires (as outlined in Romans 1), it is also important to note what he does later in Romans to add depth to his analysis. Paul wanted Jesus-followers to be able to interpret that complex of relational dysfunction not simply as an indictment against humans who go wrong by errors in their own judgment. Later in Romans, Paul placed another interpretative layer onto that whole complex of distorted relationality. In that regard, Paul recognized human relational dysfunction as a by-product of the influence of cosmic forces that run contrary to the will of the creator.

The first place where this is evident is Rom 3:9, where Paul speaks of "both Jew and gentile" as "being under the power of Sin." The first letter of the last word in that phrase has been capitalized (i.e., "Sin") in order to capture what becomes clearer later in Romans. That is, in Rom 3:9 Paul is thinking not about the transgressions that individuals commit on an everyday basis (i.e., "sin"); instead, he is articulating the sense that an ominous entity that stands over the whole of humanity ("both Jew and gentile"), an entity with a sense of purpose and the ability to act on its intention – the cosmic power of Sin, which Paul foregrounds in much of Romans 5 through 7 in particular.

It is notable that Paul prefaces this charge (that all are "under the power of Sin") with the claim that he has "already made the charge" earlier in his letter. Since he never made the point explicitly, it seems that Paul is intimating that what he was constructing earlier in his letter was, in fact, a situation that itself testifies to the influence of the cosmic power of Sin. Fractured forms of relationality (both "vertical" in relation to God and "horizontal" in relation to others) are all to be seen as being intricately intertwined with the cosmic power of Sin. The scenarios he recounted in Romans 1 turn out to be scenarios in which God's good creation is under attack by suprahuman forces intent on undermining the will of God.

At stake, then, is ultimately the reputation of the creator God. There is opposition to that deity, and the opposition might be thought to be superior to the creator God, having conscripted all of humanity to participate in its goal of immersing God's good creation in relational chaos of every kind. There is a sense, then, in which the world's problems force the question, "What is God doing to restore the honor of the divine name?" If we only knew this much about Paul's theological discourse, we might say that what is wrong with the world is that suprahuman forces have taken over God's good creation. What will God do about that threat to divine sovereignty?

SUPRAHUMAN POWERS IN KEY PAULINE TEXTS

This way of looking at the situation permeates a number of significant passages within the Pauline letter collection. In Galatians (probably one of his earliest letters, perhaps written in 51), Paul contrasted (1) being children of God in Christ and (2) being enslaved to "the fundamental elements of the cosmos" (*ta stoicheia tou kosmou*; see 4:1–11). Determining the interpretative options for understanding this phrase would take an inordinate amount of space for our purposes, and even then it would not render certain results. For our purposes, it is enough to note how Paul seems to give the intriguing phrase "the fundamental elements of the cosmos" something of an ominous tone. In Galatians, human beings are placed in the scenario of becoming subjugated and exploited by these "fundamental elements" in a master–slave relationship. In Paul's theological worldview, when those who "receive adoption" in Christ become children of God, the chains of enslavement to these "elemental" forces are broken. In contrast, if the Galatians were ever to compromise their status as children of God, they would be returning to the time when they were exploited by "the weak and impoverished fundamental elements" (weak and impoverished only in comparison to the power of God in Christ). The Galatians were, in Paul's estimate, flirting with the prospect of becoming "enslaved" all over again "to beings that by nature are not gods" (4:8).

A particular cosmic power is highlighted in 1 Corinthians 15 (probably dated to 54 or 55) – a chapter dedicated to setting the record straight about the resurrection of Jesus Christ and its implications for Jesus-followers and for the whole of the cosmos. Paul's discourse there does not simply offer theological nuances regarding resurrection bodies and the like; those nuances play out against a broad backdrop about what's wrong within God's world – a backdrop that features the all-encompassing grip of cosmic powers. In Paul's words (15:24–28), the story of God's sovereignty results in the subjugation of "every ruler and every authority and power" – forces that are "enemies" of the sovereign deity. In this chapter's depiction of the problem, the most entrenched enemy is "death" – or better, "the power of Death." God will place even this adversarial tyrant "in subjection" under Christ. This is nothing short of the triumph of God in denying the "victory" to this cosmic power, Death (15:54–56).

This strand of theological discourse carries over from 1 Corinthians 15 into Romans (probably dated to 57). In Rom 5:12–21, the cosmic power of Death is said to have "reigned as sovereign" over the course of human history in the wake of Adam's "trespass/sin" (5:14, 17).[1] The sovereignty of that suprahuman power is evidenced in the deaths of every human being (e.g., 5:12). It is little wonder, then, that at the climax of Romans 8 Paul includes "powers" in his list of things that cannot separate us from the love of God (8:38–39).

Romans 5 links the cosmic power of Death to another cosmic power – the power of Sin, which Paul had already mentioned in 3:9 (as noted above; the same power is referenced in Gal 3:22). Like the power of Death, so too the power of Sin is said to have "reigned as sovereign" (5:21; cf. 6:12, 14) prior to the time of God's acting in Christ Jesus. Paul makes extensive use of this notion of Sin as a power throughout Romans 6 and 7. There, the power of Sin is likened to a tyrannical overlord who dictates the life of his subjugated slaves, making them captive to serving his purposes.[2] "I am sold as a slave to the lordship of the power of Sin" (7:14), cries the speaker of 7:7–25.[3] Even the Torah given by God (itself "holy" and "spiritual"; 7:12, 14) is conscripted by this all-encompassing power. If God's own initiatives (i.e., the giving of the Torah) are used by the power of Sin to fortify its own interests, the question "who will deliver me" (7:24) contains within it an outcry against the way that Sin has embedded itself so deeply within the structures of the world that even the sovereignty of God seems to be in question (a situation that Paul finds resolved only in Christ Jesus).

A full catalog of cosmic powers in the Pauline corpus lies beyond the scope of this essay (and would need to consider passages like Col 1:16; 2:15; Eph 1:20–21; 3:10; possibly 1 Cor 2:6–8). Our survey of cosmic powers in Paul's letters might best be summarized in the words of Eph 6:12, where these powers are insightfully described as "cosmos grabbers" (*kosmokratoras*). This brief term captures how Paul seems to have imagined them – powerful forces intent on subjecting humanity in their program of inserting chaos into God's good creation. The verse

[1] The Greek verb is *basileuô*. A good English equivalent might be "reign." In Greek, nouns such as "king" and "queen" derive from this verb.

[2] See for instance Rom 6:6–7, 16–18, 20, 22; 7:14; other depictions of Sin as a cosmic power include Rom 6:2, 11, 13; 7:11, 13, 17, 20.

[3] On the issue of the voicing in Rom 7:25a and 7:25b, see Bruce W. Longenecker, *Rhetoric at the Boundaries: The Art and Theology of New Testament Chain-Link Transitions* (Waco, TX: Baylor University Press, 2005), 88–93.

vividly captures what Paul thought to be wrong in God's world: "Our struggle is not against enemies of blood and flesh, but against the rulers, against the authorities, against the cosmos grabbers of this present darkness, against the spiritual forces of evil in the heavenly places."

HUMAN SINFULNESS IN KEY PAULINE TEXTS

We have seen that suprahuman forces are often at the forefront of Paul's thought when depicting what is wrong within God's world. While this aspect of Paul's thought is critical to understanding his worldview, his analysis of what has gone wrong also includes a focus on human wrongdoing, or sin. We will need to consider how these two aspects relate to each other, but before doing that, some of the data regarding human sinfulness needs to be registered.

Writing to the Corinthians in the mid-50s, Paul reminds them of the message he originally brought to them. In that regard, the phrase "Christ died for our sins" (1 Cor 15:3) stands toward the start of a chapter where Paul ultimately foregrounds the cosmic power of Death (chapter 15, as we have already seen). This intertwining of cosmic forces with human wrongdoing is evident in almost all the letters where cosmic forces are at the forefront of Paul's discussion.

Let's take Romans as an example. We have already seen how the cosmic powers of Sin and Death take center stage in much of his discussion in that letter, and at key parts of it. But human beings are also said to be "sinners for whom Christ died" (Rom 5:8). Whereas those cosmic powers have a foothold in Rom 5:12–21, human transgression and sinfulness do as well: "all sinned" (5:12, with participle forms of this verb appearing in 5:14 and 5:16), and human "trespass" increased (5:20). At times it isn't quite clear from Rom 5:12–21 whether the Greek word *hamartia* references the cosmic power of Sin or human sinfulness.[4] Paul's focus seems to shift from one kind to the other, keeping them both in play in this section of Romans.

In this regard, we might also think back to Romans 1–3, headed as it is by the notion that the wrath of God is revealed from heaven against the "ungodliness and wickedness of those who by their wickedness suppress the truth" (Rom 1:18). Of course, we might want to say that this wickedness is simply a perverse consequence of being enslaved to the cosmic power of Sin – just as Paul (as already noted) thinks his

[4] Perhaps he even has both in mind simultaneously; see, for instance the first two clauses of Rom 5:12, and also 5:20.

account of human depravity in Romans 1–3 ultimately testifies to the overwhelming influence of the cosmic power of Sin (as in 3:9). But there is too much in Romans to allow us to lay all the blame solely at the feet of the cosmic power of Sin. Paul said that those who commit "ungodliness and wickedness" are "without excuse" (1:20); he did not say they are excused – not even that they are excused because of their unfortunate enslavement to the inexcusable cosmic power of Sin. It would have made good sense to say that God's wrath is stirred up solely by the cosmic power of Sin creeping around within God's good creation, but Paul's discourse does not follow that route; instead, the wrath of God is directed against the one with a "hard and impenitent heart" (2:5).[5] This is evidently what Paul has in mind when he claims that "those who live according to the flesh set their minds on the things of the flesh" (Rom 8:5; cf. 8:7–8; Gal 5:16–17, 24; 6:8).

Evidently, the cosmic power of Sin is not the only problem to be resolved when the sovereign creator takes decisive action to rectify the created order. If the narrative of God's sovereignty cannot be successfully resolved without the dethronement of the powers, human sinfulness seems also to be a part of that cosmic story. When that full story is in view, human sinfulness might be seen as playing only a minor role; after all, Paul does not depict human sinfulness itself as threatening to dethrone the sovereignty of the creator God; only the powers of Sin and Death are in that position (together, perhaps, with the Satan figure, who enters the frame only at Rom 16:20, albeit in a highly suggestive fashion). But even if human sinfulness is not the leading antagonist, it is still an important feature that requires attention if the story of God's cosmic sovereignty in Christ is truly to find its ultimate resolution. Paul might even say that failure to recognize that the human heart is prone to sinfulness is itself a trick of the power of Sin.

CONCEPTUALIZING THE PROBLEM

It is sometimes difficult for people in the twenty-first-century Western world to conceptualize the suprahuman powers of Paul's discourse. Could the powers simply be personifications of aspects of the human condition – say, human sinfulness and human death simply projected

[5] Compare also 2:9 (with its intriguing link to 3:8), "there will be anguish and distress for everyone who does evil"; cf. 3:5–8, where God's wrath is discussed in relation to human "falsehood" and the status of "sinner" (*hamartôlos*).

onto the screen of the heavens?[6] We might want to interpret them as such, but Paul seems to have imagined them as having both intentionality and independent existence to an extent that characterizing them as personifications seems to misrepresent his own view of things (as, for example, Eph 6:12 suggests, as noted above). In fact, Paul's discourse regarding Christ's resurrection in 1 Corinthians 15 would crumble into dust if "death" in that context were simply an anthropological personification rather than a cosmic power. In that chapter Paul argued against the Corinthian tendency to spiritualize theological concepts so as to anthropomorphize them (as in the Corinthian view that since Jesus-followers are already resurrected in their souls, who needs to be resurrected bodily in the future); to understand the cosmic power of Death as a collective personification of human death would simply reinforce the theological deficiencies of some Corinthian Jesus-followers. Evidently, then, Paul did not understand these cosmic powers to simply be personifications of human conditions. They were objective entities in Paul's mental universe – the sort of thing that came easily to Jewish and non-Jewish minds of the Greco-Roman world. *We* might want to imagine these powers to be projections of human psychological and anthropological phenomena onto the heavenly screen, but Paul seems to have imagined them as objective realities that transcended the human realm and act with intentionality upon that realm.

Could the power of Sin be a way of expressing the sense that human sinfulness has accumulated to such an extent that it has simply taken on an objective life of its own, evidenced now in sinful social structures and transgressive cultural forces that hawkishly predetermine the predisposition of each and every person born into this world?[7] Is it the case that each human being becomes socialized into the snowballing sinfulness of the human race, and that is what Paul meant by "the power of Sin"? There is much to commend this view, since it rightly recognizes that cosmic power to be an entity above and beyond any particular individual (even though its origins lie in a human phenomenon). Nonetheless, it is hard to replicate the same pattern of interpretation for the power of Death that Paul conceptualizes as "the final enemy" (1 Cor 15:26); whatever interpretive measures we might apply to one of these

[6] This would be congruent with the fact that Paul can at times speak of "grace" and "righteousness" as if they too are personified suprahuman forces; for grace, see Rom 6:14–15; for righteousness, see Rom 6:18–19.

[7] See for instance Matthew Croasmun, *The Emergence of Sin: The Cosmic Tyrant in Romans* (Oxford: Oxford University Press, 2017).

cosmic powers should be applicable to the other, since Paul can at times speak of them in much the same terms (as in Rom 5). And again, the author of Ephesians (whether Paul or someone articulating his theology in fresh discourse) leaves little room for seeing the cosmic powers as operating as anything other than independent and forceful entities at the cosmic level.

Perhaps, then, it is best to leave the matter as it generally appears from a cross section of Pauline texts – that is, Paul seems to have imagined human sinfulness to have some relationship to external suprahuman cosmic powers. However we are to conceptualize that analysis today, we should at least appreciate the way that Paul has captured a sense that there is more trouble in God's world than can be accounted for by individual acts of human sinfulness. Beyond human sinfulness lies something else, something ominously threatening, which God must ultimately deal with.

Can we press further into conceptualizing the relationship between the cosmic powers and human sinfulness? Various analogies might be suggested to shed light on the complexity of Paul's analysis. Of course, analogies are never perfect, but they are sometimes helpful. Two of the most productive analogies will be explored here.[8]

The analogy of "a rescue operation" goes some way in capturing aspects of Paul's discourse about the problem that God must deal with. Since Paul presents a situation in which humans are enslaved to suprahuman cosmic powers, the solution will ultimately have some semblance to a rescue operation. A pious posture of remorse and repentance, for instance, will do nothing to release those who are held hostage (and in this regard, it is noticeable just how infrequently Paul speaks of things like guilt, repentance, and forgiveness). Some form of rescue is ultimately needed. This is why Paul speaks of Jesus Christ delivering us from the present evil age (Gal 1:4), using a Greek verb (*exelêtai*) that denotes deliverance of those enslaved or imprisoned (e.g., Acts 7:10, 34; 12:11; 23:27).

Nonetheless, since there is more to Paul's analysis of the situation than suprahuman powers, a rescue operation alone is not enough to deal with the full extent of the problem. Humans are not simply enslaved to

[8] These otherwise helpful analogies amplify only Paul's discourse in relation to all of humanity apart from Adam, without doing justice to Adam's situation itself, which is another matter altogether. See further Bruce W. Longenecker, "Sin and the Sovereignty of God in Romans," in *Sin and Its Remedy in Paul*, eds. John K. Goodrich and Nijay K. Gupta (Eugene, OR: Cascade), forthcoming.

cosmic powers; Paul also saw humans as complicit with those powers – even if he can sometimes depict this as a conflicted form of complicity (or so Rom 7:12–25 would suggest). Because Paul can depict humans as being "without excuse" for their relational dysfunction, it cannot be that humans are simply unfortunate hostages, even though they are also that. If the full scope of the problem is to be resolved, a rescue operation, while wholly necessary, is not wholly sufficient.

In that regard, the most helpful analogy to shed light on the complexity of Paul's analysis is the curious phenomenon popularly referred to as "Stockholm syndrome," in which someone who is abducted against her/his will becomes sympathetic to the cause of the abductors. The most famous case of this in recent history was the 1974 abduction of Patty Hearst who was kidnapped for more than a year and a half, her kidnappers hoping to extract money from her rich father. Just over two months after her abduction, however, Hearst surprisingly joined with her captors in a bank robbery, evidently standing alongside them in their cause. If this was willingly done (and interpretations vary on that point), it would be a classic case of a kidnapped person becoming complicit with her kidnappers. In this interpretation of events, Patty Hearst needed to be rescued from her captors as well as needing to be reformed, because her captivity had fundamentally altered her volitional commitments. She was, in a sense, held captive "under the power of" her kidnappers but she had also become involved in complicit "sins" of her own.

In much the same way, Paul foregrounds both the enslaving power of Sin and human sinfulness in a matrix of interlocking coalition. If Paul is to present God's action in Christ as the solution to a problem, we can see just how complex that solution will need to be, involving the unravelling of this intertwined nexus of structural and personal dysfunction.

WHAT RELATIONAL DYSFUNCTION LOOKS LIKE

As we have seen (especially in section 1 above), Paul imagined the effect of the cosmic powers to be most evident in forms of relational dysfunction – dysfunction in human relationships with God and with others. Here we note a particular form of relational dysfunction that emerges frequently in Paul's writings.

Paul's letter to Jesus-followers in Rome creates a clear view of the moral world that is created under the influence of suprahuman powers. In a word, that moral world is characterized by and engulfed in "covetousness." Paul uses different Greek words to highlight this phenomenon (e.g., *pleonexia* in 1:29, and *epithymia* in 7:8), but both words reference the covetousness that drives the world as Paul looked out on it from his viewpoint "in Christ." This posture of covetousness captures Paul's sense that the world is characterized by a form of "social Darwinism" – a competition of the survival of the fittest through the acquisition of status and the accumulation of power over others.[9] In that world of abusive relationality, people (whether individuals or people-groups) inevitably seek their own advantage over the wellbeing others. The moral posture of this dysfunctional world involves hawkishly being set to pounce on any others who might show a moment of weakness, and doing so in order to appropriate whatever resources they might have, thereby bolstering one's status storehouse.

This is what Paul calls "covetousness," and it is induced in the hearts of human beings who are under the cosmic power of Sin. The best game plan of this suprahuman power involves harnessing the good things of God's created order (and even the good people, as in the case of the person who speaks in Romans 7) and drafting them into the agonistic program of social Darwinism (as in the drama of Romans 7).

It is little wonder that, after declaring all humanity to be "under the power of Sin" (in 3:9), Paul strings together a collection of verses from scripture (3:10–20) that culminate toward the end in the words heavily drawn from Isa 59:7–8 (in Rom 3:15–17): "Swift are their feet for shedding blood; destruction and wretchedness are in their paths, and the way of peace they have not known." This extreme moral dysfunction is probably to be thought of as the goal of the program of the cosmic power of Sin. It testifies to the fact that "There is no fear of God before their eyes" (from Ps 36:1, cited in Rom 3:18) – which perhaps suggests that the ultimate ploy of the power of Sin is to eradicate the fear of God within complicit humanity. Moreover, in contrast to the sovereign God who produces life and the conditions for its flourishing, the cosmic power of Sin seems able to produce only one thing: death and the conditions for its flourishing (cf. 5:12). Death is the arena of Sin's dominion (cf. 5:21). In moral terms, the cosmic power of Sin holds dominion over all that leads to death in the competitive realm of interpersonal relationships and the inequities and injustices that are so obviously evident within those relationships.

[9] This is called "the system of Domination" by Walter Wink; see especially his *Engaging the Powers: Discernment and Resistance in an Age of Domination* (Minneapolis, MN: Fortress Press, 1992), 13–31, 93–112.

Paul's letter to Jesus-followers in Galatia tells much the same story. When Paul saw the Galatians taking initiatives that left them precariously close to stepping outside of those "in Christ," he depicted them as participating in that world orchestrated by the suprahuman powers other than God, in which they are in danger of "biting and devouring each other" to the extent that they will ultimately "be destroyed by each other" (5:15). Paul even offered a list of what that world looks like, including not only traditional Jewish depictions of sexual immorality, drunkenness, and idolatry, but also various entries that seem to target aggressively antagonistic attitudes and activities between people and people-groups (5:20–21). These include the following:

(1) acts that induce hatred between people,
(2) competitive strife between people,
(3) envious jealousy between people,
(4) acts that are motivated by and incite anger between people,
(5) acts that promote rivalry between people,
(6) acts that promote division between people,
(7) acts that induce schisms between people, and
(8) acts of selfish envy.[10]

In Galatians Paul captured all this in the word "conceit," which he amplified as "provoking and envying each other" (5:26). For Paul, a cutthroat competitiveness and warlike hostility demarcates the moral world apart from what God has done in Christ. A cancer of unbridled self-interest has spread into every sector of human life – whether individual, corporate, cultural, societal, national, or international.

One form of cultural antagonism that Paul frequently addressed pertained to Jews (or Judeans) and gentiles. As a case study in connecting the dots between antagonism of this kind and suprahuman powers, the letter to the Ephesians highlights "the dividing wall of hostility" between Jews and gentiles (2:14) and sees the solution (the unity that God brings in Christ) as being a testimony against "the rulers and authorities in the heavenly places" (3:10). For Paul, hostility among people and people-groups is likely to testify to the lordship of the suprahuman powers. The triumph of God in Christ involves the reconciliation of hostile groups "in one body through the cross, thus putting to death that hostility through it [the cross]" (2:16). When Paul looks to

[10] These entries are translated in a way that diverges from common translations in order to bring out the sense of the plurals that Paul uses, which correspond to the word "acts" in this translation.

the body of Christ, he sees the opposite to the relational dysfunction that he sees everywhere beyond the "in Christ" groups. This conclusion goes beyond the scope of this essay, of course, but it illustrates the ease with which toxic relationships can be traced to suprahuman influences in the Pauline worldview.

DETHRONING A COUNTERFEIT GOSPEL

One important verse of the Pauline corpus captures yet another aspect of Paul's discourse regarding what he thought is wrong within God's world. This single verse adds an additional dimension to our understanding of Paul's analysis, highlighting a complexity that requires consideration, helping to illustrate something further about Paul's theological imagination – it's tendency to analyze and unmask cultural forms of power. To catch a glimpse of this important feature of Paul's theologizing, a brief contextual overview is first required.

In Paul's day, urban centers were enthralled by the promise of the Roman imperial order, aroused about the promises of its ideology. A wave of enthusiasm had spread throughout the Mediterranean basin that heralded the coming of Roman imperial reign as the beginning of a new era, in which order and justice was becoming established throughout the world (or "the world-that-mattered" anyway). According to common propaganda, this era had been promised beforehand by the deities of Rome, who now oversaw Roman imperial reign as the instrument of divine beneficence, with the nations now being harmoniously united under Rome's auspices and benefitting from the marvelous and unprecedented riches of Rome's divine reign. Roman imperial rule was advertised as a splendid new era of synergistic concord for the human race, with human civilization rising to its full potential under the oversight of the deities of Rome, through the emperor enthroned in the glorious city of Rome. This narrative was consolidated and proclaimed in the temples of the imperial cult, temples that civic officials throughout the Mediterranean basin were eagerly and actively building in their urban centers, fully expecting their cities and towns to benefit from the blessing of the deities in return for aligning civic piety in relation to the emperor.[11]

[11] For instance, the relatively small town of Pompeii (with roughly 12,000 residents) had two or perhaps three temples dedicated to the emperor, his family, and the fortune of Rome at the time of its destruction in the eruption of Mount Vesuvius in 79 CE.

Space does not permit a full overview of this phenomenon deeply entrenched in Paul's world.[12] It will be helpful, however, to foreground one Roman inscription that captures something of the ideology that had spread like wildfire throughout the cities in which Paul undertook his mission. In the year 9 BCE in the city of Priene (in the country now known as Turkey), civic officials set up an inscription declaring that the annual calendar should be reordered in relation to the birthday of the divine emperor Augustus (*Supplementum Epigraphicum Graecum* 4.490). Components of that declaration include the following assertions:

- divine Providence "has divinely ordered our existence ... and has brought to life the most perfect good in Augustus, whom she [Providence] filled with virtues for the benefit of humanity"
- the emperor has been "bestowed upon us and our descendants as a savior"
- this savior has "put an end to war" and "will order peace"
- "by his divine epiphany" the emperor has "exceeded the hopes of those who prophesied the good news [or gospel]"
- therefore, the calendar should be reordered around his birthday, "the birthday of the god who first brought to the world the good news [or gospel] that rested in him."

Paul would have known of this widespread Roman "gospel," and so would those in the Jesus-groups that he founded. In fact, this gospel is probably what Paul is referencing in what seems to be his earliest (surviving) letter, 1 Thessalonians (probably written in 50 CE). Toward the end of that letter, Paul warned the newly-converted Jesus-followers of Thessalonica to be on guard against those who announce, "There is peace and security" (1 Thess 5:3). Paul made it clear that this "good news" is not the solution that the world is waiting for; instead, those who extol this Roman gospel are said to dwell in the world of darkness (5:4–5) and will ironically meet "sudden destruction" (5:3).

The warning is probably so sharply worded because this gospel of "civil religion" was both so powerfully embedded in the surrounding culture and so dangerously at odds with Paul's gospel. Of course, Paul saw a place for the proper functioning of political authorities in the ordinary running of an orderly society (as he takes pains to point out

[12] For more on this, see Bruce W. Longenecker, "Peace, Security, and Propaganda: Advertisement and Reality in the Early Roman Empire," in *An Introduction to Empire in the New Testament*, ed. Adam Winn (Atlanta, GA: Society of Biblical Literature, 2015), 15–46.

in Rom 13:1–7). But because a cultural conglomeration of power had begun to adopt the appearance of the divine, Paul saw this as an affront to the only true deity and, in particular, a form of idolatry (e.g., 1 Thess 1:9–10) – precisely the kind of thing that the cosmic powers themselves prop up and propel (as we've seen from our study of Romans above).

Notice where these observations have taken us – into the heart of a first-century political gospel that preached the blessedness of peaceful and secure unity in the salvation that is in abundance and in accordance with the divine will. In some ways this form of theological discourse parallels the pattern of discourse that Paul articulated in his own gospel. The Roman gospel of peaceful unity and abundance was attractive within Paul's world, but in at least one instance of theological reflection Paul protested against thinking of it as the antidote to the deeply embedded problems within God's world. As evidenced in 1 Thess 5:3, Paul was not averse to speaking truth to power-gone-wrong; in his world and in his worldview, to do otherwise would be to acquiesce with idolatrous ideologies that had embedded themselves within God's good creation.

CONCLUSION

Paul's most pronounced assessments of what is wrong in God's world cohere around the word "power."

(1) Paul often highlighted suprahuman forces as wielding enslaving power that ensnares human beings within discordant relationships, both vertically in relation to God (i.e., idolatry) and horizontally in relation to others (i.e., covetous injustice).
(2) On at least one occasion he decried a particular form of cultural power as a counterfeit gospel, with people desperately clamoring after its proclamation of unity and security.
(3) Frequently, Paul spotlighted human beings as fully immersed in the problem, being sinners who are without power to pull themselves out of the mire of their desperate dysfunctional state. Even if they have been taken captive by forces greater than themselves, they nonetheless have shown themselves to be complicit with the program of those greater forces.

Paul's analysis of this conglomeration of power (and the lack of power) places humanity within a bleak and perilous situation. Making things even more desperate is Paul's view that the Torah (or "law"), given by God, was itself "powerless … because it was weakened by the flesh" (Rom 8:3; cf. Gal 3:21). If that glorious divine initiative cannot disentangle the multilayered cords of intertwined sin/Sin, what can? What can God do about it? Is God up to the job of being sovereign, or have the cosmic powers proved to be too powerful, overwhelming the divine initiatives and sinking God's good creation into a perpetual downward spiral of moral and relational chaos? What can God do about all this?

Further Reading

Beker, J. Christiann. "The Dilemma of Sin and Death: Equivalent or Disparate Powers?" In *Paul the Apostle: The Triumph of God in Life and Thought*, 213–234. Minneapolis, MN: Fortress Press, 1980.

Brand, M. T. *Evil Within and Without: The Source of Sin and Its Nature as Portrayed in Second Temple Literature*. Göttingen: Vandenhoeck & Ruprecht, 2013.

Croasmun, Matthew. *The Emergence of Sin: The Cosmic Tyrant in Romans*. Oxford: Oxford University Press, 2017.

Dunn, James D. G. Chapter 3 in *The Theology of Paul the Apostle*. Edinburgh: T&T Clark, 1998.

Gathercole, Simon. "'Sins' in Paul." *New Testament Studies* 64, no. 2 (2018): 143–161.

Gaventa, Beverly Roberts. "The Cosmic Power of Sin in Paul's Letter to the Romans: Toward a Widescreen Edition." *Interpretation* 58 (2004): 229–240.

Harding, Sarah. *Paul's Eschatological Anthropology: The Dynamics of Human Transformation*. Minneapolis, MN: Fortress Press, 2016.

Keener, Craig S. Chapters 1 and 3 in *The Mind of the Spirit: Paul's Approach to Transformed Thinking*. Grand Rapids, MI: Baker Academic, 2016.

Longenecker, Bruce W. "Peace, Security, and Propaganda: Advertisement and Reality in the Early Roman Empire." In *An Introduction to Empire in the New Testament*, edited by Adam Winn, 15–46. Atlanta, GA: Society of Biblical Literature, 2016.

Longenecker, Bruce W. "Sin and the Sovereignty of God in Romans." In *Sin and Its Remedy in Paul*, edited by John K. Goodrich and Nijay K. Gupta, forthcoming.

Wink, Walter. *Engaging the Powers: Discernment and Engagement in a World of Domination*. Minneapolis, MN: Augsburg Fortress, 1992.

Wright, N. T. "The Dark Side of Revised Monotheism: The New Vision of Evil." In *Paul and the Faithfulness of God*, 737–772. Minneapolis, MN: Fortress Press, 2013.

10 What Did Paul Think God Is Doing about What's Wrong?

MICHAEL J. GORMAN

One of the most unforgettable songs in the musical *Fiddler on the Roof* is entitled "To Life," or (in Hebrew and Yiddish) "L'Chaim." It joyfully expresses our deep longing for human flourishing. This desire for life is not far from the biblical notion of shalom. Often translated as "peace," the Hebrew word *shalom* also signifies life in its fullness, including right relations with God, with others, and with the entire creation.

Such fullness of life, however, often escapes us in this fractured world. The apostle Paul, looking back on his own story before being transformed by Christ, and scrutinizing both the wider world and his own people, sensed the need for such life: life in its fullness; a world restored to wholeness.

The previous chapter considered different aspects of the human predicament. Understanding Paul's perspective on the human condition is vital to appreciating what he sees as the divine solution to the human problem. In traditional language, this chapter will consider Paul's understanding of "salvation" – God's rescuing people, and eventually the entire cosmos, from the reign of the powers of Sin and Death, thereby offering the gift of new life through Jesus Christ. This means that the present chapter flows inevitably and inseparably out of the preceding chapter and into the next (which will focus specifically on what God is doing within Christian communities).

FRAMING THE SUBJECT

Paul makes use of various metaphors or images to explain his underlying understanding of salvation. These metaphors or images express his highly complex solution to a highly complex problem. The diverse images he uses are not just various expressions of one simple reality called "salvation" but are, instead, interrelated images of the diverse dimensions of this complex solution. Paul probes the breadth and depth of the problem's "fix" as fully as he explores the problem itself, and the various metaphors and images are themselves essential components of Paul's multifaceted articulation of what God is doing in Christ.

Paul's various images of salvation are frequently interpreted in an individualistic and private way, reflecting the ethos of Western society, where (historically) most interpretations of Paul have occurred. Paul, in contrast, understands salvation and life to be corporate as well as individual, social and even political as well as "spiritual," and cosmic as well as human.

Because Paul was a Jew, his description of the multifaceted and multilayered resolution of the human condition is very Jewish in character. Images like new creation, new exodus, and new covenant are central to his discourse, and his understanding of salvation involves the rescue and renewing of a people – a corporate body, not just individuals. At the same time, Paul revised all of these images in light of the peculiar character of the story of Jesus, especially his death and resurrection.

So what does Paul's complex, corporate Jewish understanding of salvation look like? In brief, we may characterize what Paul thought God is doing as follows:

> God is creating a forgiven, liberated, and reconciled people who are being renewed together in the image of God, found in the crucified and resurrected Messiah Jesus, so that they, by the power of the indwelling Spirit, will lead lives of faithfulness, hope, and love as the body of the Messiah in the world – the people of the new covenant and new creation inaugurated by Christ's coming, death, and resurrection, all in anticipation of the restoration of the entire cosmos.

More briefly, we may say that, for Paul, God is now enabling transformative participation in the life of God the Father, Jesus the Son, and the Holy Spirit. This can all be captured in a single word: life.

DIVINE INITIATIVE: GOD'S GRACE

In Paul's view, human beings cannot simply extricate themselves from the mess that engulfs them. Neither can the Jewish law save people, whether Jewish or gentile. Although it is holy and good (Rom 7:12–13), the law cannot give life (Gal 3:21); it is impotent in the face of the human predicament (Rom 8:3). In fact, the situation is so dire that it is beyond human making; there are malevolent powers at work, especially what Paul calls the powers of Sin and Death. If the Jewish law cannot give life and fix the problem, neither can human effort. Nor can political entities save humanity, as they are often corporate incarnations of the problems present in individuals and even instruments of the powers of Sin and Death; after all, "the rulers of this age ... crucified the Lord of glory" (1 Cor 2:8). Humanity is in a "dead end" situation that requires an intervention – a benevolent, divine intervention.

According to Paul, that is precisely what has taken place in what is sometimes referred to as the "Christ-event." More insightfully, some label it the divine *apocalypse* – an earth-shattering event of divine revelation. Note the following texts (drawn from across the Pauline letters) that stress God's initiative, paying special attention to the way some highlight the stark contrast between the human predicament and divine action:

- In Christ God was reconciling the world to himself, not counting their trespasses against them. (2 Cor 5:19)
- For God has done what the law, weakened by the flesh, could not do: by sending his own Son in the likeness of sinful flesh, and to deal with sin, he condemned sin in the flesh, so that the just requirement of the law might be fulfilled in us, who walk not according to the flesh but according to the Spirit. (Rom 8:3–4)
- [The Lord Jesus] was handed over to death for our trespasses and was raised for our justification. (Rom 4:25)
- For the grace of God has appeared, bringing salvation to all. (Titus 2:11)
- For you know the generous act [lit. "grace"] of our Lord Jesus Christ, that though he was rich, yet for your sakes he became poor, so that by his poverty you might become rich. (2 Cor 8:9)
- God proves his love for us in that while we still were sinners Christ died for us. (Rom 5:8)
- God, who is rich in mercy, out of the great love with which he loved us even when we were dead through our trespasses, made us alive together with Christ – by grace you have been saved. (Eph 2:4–5)
- When the fullness of time had come, God sent his Son, born of a woman, born under the law, in order to redeem those who were under the law, so that we might receive adoption as children. And because you are children, God has sent the Spirit of his Son into our hearts, crying, "Abba! Father!" (Gal 4:4–6)
- Now in Christ Jesus you who once were far off [gentiles] have been brought near by the blood of Christ. (Eph 2:13)

Several observations about this brief collection of texts (which could easily be expanded) are in order:

(1) They testify to the inability of humans to engage in self-rescue, highlighting the merciful action of God to rectify the human condition. The key Pauline word for this is *grace*.
(2) They indicate that both gentiles and Jews (that is, all people) need saving.
(3) They inform us that the primary reality that needs to be addressed is sin, whether that be Sin (singular) or sins/trespasses (plural).
(4) They reveal that the divine intervention involves three parties acting in concert: (1) God (i.e., God the Father); (2) God's own Son; and (3) the Spirit, who is identified as both the Spirit of the Son (Gal 4:6 above; cf. Rom 8:9; Phil 1:19) and the Spirit of God (e.g., Rom 8:11, 14).
(5) They state or imply that this divine rescue occurs through both the death and the resurrection of Jesus, and through our participating in that two-part event.
(6) They suggest that the result of this rescue operation will be the reparation of relationships, both "vertical" (people to God) and "horizontal" (people to people, especially between gentiles and Jews).
(7) They demonstrate that salvation includes new life under the direction of the Spirit. For Paul, what God has done in Christ impacts the ethical life of believers. People are not just saved *from* something; they are saved *for* something.

We will consider each of these observations more or less in sequence, though there will inevitably be some reshuffling and overlap. Moreover, we will focus our attention on various aspects of the fourth, fifth, and sixth observations, since the first three and the last are discussed in the previous and subsequent chapters of this book, respectively.

THE GOSPEL OF ISRAEL'S FAITHFUL AND GRACIOUS GOD: POWERFUL GOOD NEWS FOR ALL

In the first chapter of his majestic letter to the Romans, Paul describes his message of salvation as "good news" – that is, as the "gospel." It is the gospel of God concerning his Son (1:1, 3, 9), which Paul proclaims like a trumpeting herald without shame (1:15–16). This last remark raises the question, "Why might the gospel cause shame?" The answer: Paul's gospel centers on a crucified Messiah, "a stumbling block to Jews and foolishness to gentiles" (1 Cor 1:23). Crucifixion was a horrific form of death and deterrence; it was a topic to be avoided in polite conversation. For Paul, however, the crucifixion of Jesus revealed, paradoxically, "the power and wisdom of God" (1 Cor 1:24). He captures this paradox in 1 Corinthians 1:18: "The message about the cross is foolishness to those who are perishing, but to us who are being saved it is the power of God." The saving power of the cross is not self-evident, but for those who have believed the gospel and are in the process of being transformed by its power, the cross is in fact the event of God's saving activity.

Of course the *cross* of Jesus has no saving power apart from the *resurrection* of Jesus, as Paul makes clear at length in 1 Corinthians 15 and in brief at the start of Romans: Jesus "was declared to be Son of God with power according to the spirit of holiness by resurrection from the dead" (Rom 1:4). Accordingly, as we will see in more detail below, the saving event (and thus the good news) is constituted by both the death and the resurrection of Jesus. For now, however, we return to Paul's summary of the gospel in Romans 1, offering two further observations.

First, Paul indicates that the gospel was "promised beforehand through his [God's] prophets in the holy scriptures," and that Jesus (God's "Son" and the gospel's fundamental content) "was descended from David according to the flesh" (Rom 1:2–4). Paul's gospel recounts the promised saving activity of Israel's God through the royal Davidic Messiah, Jesus.

Second, echoing 1 Corinthians, Paul says this gospel "is the power of God for salvation to everyone who has faith, to the Jew first and also to the Greek [gentile]" (Rom 1:16). This salvation from the God of Israel is for all people because this God is the only God, the God of all (Rom 3:29). The phrase "Jew and gentile/Greek" becomes a refrain throughout Romans (1:16; 2:9–10; 3:9; 9:24; 10:12; 15:7–12).

The gospel, then, is power. It *affects* people. It *effects* transformation. It engenders life. As a "performative utterance," the gospel is a declaration that causes something to happen, like the performative utterances "I now pronounce you husband and wife" and "Let there be light." Paul summarizes the content of this transformative good news in Rom 1:17: "For in it the righteousness [or justice] of God is revealed through faith for faith; as it is written [in the prophet Habakkuk], 'The one who is righteous will live by faith'" – or perhaps "'the one who is righteous by faith (or faithfulness) will live!'"

This sentence has received significant scholarly scrutiny. My own interpretation is one shared by many, though not all: "In the gospel,

God's justice (that is, the transformative saving power of God that makes things right again) is revealed through the faithful death of Jesus for the purpose of creating a faithful people who share in the faithfulness of Jesus displayed on the cross and thereby share also in his resurrection life." This interpretation depends on both an analysis of Romans as a whole and a close reading of Rom 3:21–26 (discussed below), which is often understood as an expansion of the succinct summary of Paul's gospel in Rom 1:16–17.

THE (APOCALYPTIC) NEW COVENANT: THE SOLUTION TO THE PROBLEM

To say that the saving power of God is intended to create a people goes against the grain of much Western thinking about religion, and even much Christian thinking about "salvation." But if the gospel is grounded in Israel's Scriptures, then it will be about a people, and not merely about individuals. As Israel's Scriptures attest, the people of Israel had been chosen to be in a faithful and loving relationship with their God and to live righteously and justly in relationship with others, giving special attention to the weak, the immigrant, the widow, and the orphan. As such, this people would be a light to the gentiles/nations (Isa 42:6–7).

The two tables of the Mosaic law (Exod 20:1–20; cf. Deut 5:5–21) represented the fundamental obligations of this binding relationship, or covenant. These obligations were frequently summarized by Jews as love for God and love for neighbor, as we see even in the words of Jesus (Mark 12:28–34 and parallels) According to Paul, these basic obligations to God and others were not restricted to Jews but were expected of all people. However, human beings are covenantally dysfunctional – unwilling and unable to fulfill even the most basic obligations to God and to others. Instead, idolatry, immorality, injustice, and violence reign among humans (Rom 1:18–32).

Jewish prophets long before Paul had recognized Israel's failure to keep the covenant, both its "vertical" and its "horizontal" dimensions. They promised a day when a "dead" Israel would be revivified, a day in which the law and the Spirit of God would be internalized, with the law placed in the human heart (Jer 31:31–34; Ezek 11:17–20; 36:23–28; 37; Deut 30:1–8). At that time, the covenant would be renewed and the people would live faithfully as originally set out by God: "I will be your God, and you will be my people" (a scriptural refrain known as the covenant formula). In other texts, certain prophetic voices expected the gentiles to be included in the scope of God's future blessings, an expectation that became central to Paul's theology. This renewed covenant involves such a transformation of the people and their relationship with God that Jeremiah calls it a *new* covenant (Jer 31:31), and Paul, echoing both Jeremiah and Jesus, uses the same language (1 Cor 11:25; 2 Cor 3:6; cf. Luke 22:20).

Although some scholars doubt the importance of "covenant" for Paul, it seems clear that Paul believes the death of Jesus and the gift of the Spirit have inaugurated this new covenant. As illustrated by Gal 4:4–6 (quoted above), the death of Jesus and the gift of the Spirit belong hand in hand and must not be separated. This two-part divine intervention has created a people that is not marked by physical circumcision but is open to all: "real circumcision is a matter of the heart – it is spiritual and not literal" (Rom 2:29a). This spiritual heart surgery is what Paul calls becoming part of a "new creation" (Gal 6:15). That is, the new covenant also means new creation, and hence new life (see also 2 Cor 5:17, discussed below).

The influential scholar E. P. Sanders coined the term "covenantal nomism" (from Greek *nomos*, "law") to describe the essence of Second Temple Judaism. This term summarizes Sanders's answer to two basic questions: (1) how did Jews *get into* the covenant, and (2) how did they *stay in*? Sanders proposed that they *got in* by grace and *stayed in* by faithful obedience, that is, by observance of the law. They did not get in, or "earn" salvation, by good works (as many Christians have thought over the years). Whatever the fate of Sanders's proposals, his questions are important, and are taken up by Paul. How do we "get in"? Paul's answer is, "By the grace of God demonstrated in the death of Jesus." How do we "stay in" and keep covenant? Paul's answer is, "By the power of God made available by the indwelling Spirit."

This new covenant is, however, *radically and unexpectedly* new; hence the label "apocalyptic" new covenant. God's act was a shocking revelation. No prophet foresaw the odd way God would intervene. No prophet imagined that the shameful death of a crucified Messiah would inaugurate the new covenant.

We turn now to consider Jesus' strange but saving death, though this cannot be considered in isolation from either his coming ("incarnation") or his resurrection. Indeed, we will start with the inseparability of these major aspects of what God has done in Jesus for the salvation of the world, before looking in some depth at the significance of the cross in Paul's theology.

THE *MEANS* OF SALVATION: THE MESSIAH'S COMING, DEATH, AND RESURRECTION/EXALTATION

In this and the following sections of the chapter, I will distinguish between the *means* and the *mode* of salvation: that is, the *objective* act of God and the *subjective* human response to that act.

The Unity of God's Action in Christ

Although it is sometimes thought that Christ's death is *the* saving event for Paul, this perspective underestimates Christ's initial coming (what Christians would later call "the incarnation") and especially his resurrection. Together, Christ's coming, his death, and his resurrection/exaltation are sometimes designated "the Christ-event." It is perhaps best to replace this rather cold term with "the Christ-story," as long as we remember that the story refers to real events, or one dramatic event in three movements, not to some pious fiction.

Regarding the initial coming of Jesus, several texts suggest that this is an important part of Paul's vision of the Messiah's activity. Galatians 4 speaks of God's sending the Son, born of a woman "under the [Jewish] law" (Gal 4:4). Second Corinthians 8:9 characterizes the "grace" (or "gift") of Jesus as his self-impoverishment for our enrichment. This text probably refers to the entirety of Jesus' mission, including his incarnation and death, while emphasizing the incarnation in particular. Similarly, the Christ-poem in Philippians (which some call Paul's "master story") portrays "the mind of Christ": Jesus Christ first voluntarily "emptied himself" (figuratively speaking) in becoming human and then, similarly, humbled himself in an obedience that led to crucifixion:

> Though he [Christ Jesus] was in the form of God, [he] did not regard equality with God as something to be exploited, but emptied himself, taking the form of a slave, being born in human likeness. And being found in human form, he humbled himself and became obedient to the point of death – even death on a cross. (Phil 2:6–8)

But this, of course, is not the end of the story. The Philippian poem ends not in death, but in exaltation:

> Therefore God also highly exalted him and gave him the name that is above every name, so that at the name of Jesus every knee should bend, in heaven and on earth and under the earth, and every tongue

should confess that Jesus Christ is Lord, to the glory of God the Father. (Phil 2:9–11)

This inseparable connection between Christ's death and his resurrection is consistently depicted throughout Paul's writings, including the following texts:

- [Jesus our Lord] was handed over to death for our trespasses and was raised for our justification. (Rom 4:25)
- Christ Jesus, who died, yes, who was raised, who is at the right hand of God, who indeed intercedes for us. (Rom 8:34)
- For to this end Christ died and lived again, so that he might be Lord of both the dead and the living. (Rom 14:9)
- And he died for all, so that those who live might live no longer for themselves, but for him who died and was raised for them. (2 Cor 5:15)
- [Paul's apostleship is] through Jesus Christ and God the Father, who raised him from the dead. (Gal 1:1)
- For since we believe that Jesus died and rose again, even so, through Jesus, God will bring with him those who have died. (1 Thess 4:14)

This pattern of humiliation/suffering/death leading to exaltation/vindication/life is common in Israel's Scriptures, reaching a climax in Isaiah's fourth servant poem (Isa 52:13–53:12): "Therefore I [YHWH] will allot him [my servant] a portion with the great, and he shall divide the spoil with the strong; because he poured out himself to death, and was numbered with the transgressors; yet he bore the sin of many, and made intercession for the transgressors" (53:12; cf. 52:13).

A critical text connecting Christ's death and resurrection appears in another gospel summary, one that Paul received and passed on to the Corinthians. This summary contends

> that Christ died for our sins in accordance with the scriptures, and that he was buried, and that he was raised on the third day in accordance with the scriptures, and that he appeared to Cephas, then to the twelve. (1 Cor 15:3b–5)

Here we see the two-part saving event of (1) Christ's death for sins and (2) his being raised (by God) on the third day, each according to Scripture (recall Rom 1:2). The reality of each component is demonstrated, respectively, by reference to (1) Christ's burial and (2) his appearances. As we will discuss below, people benefit from this two-part saving act by not only believing that it occurred (and occurred for their benefit) but also by participating in it.

New Exodus and New Covenant: Christ's Death for Sin, for Sins, for Us

According to Paul's account of the Lord's Supper (in which he again passes on a tradition he has received), Jesus said this on the eve of his crucifixion: "This [broken loaf of bread] is my body that is for you. Do this in remembrance of me .... This cup is the new covenant in my blood. Do this, as often as you drink it, in remembrance of me" (1 Cor 11:24–25; cf. Luke 22:14–20). Jesus' imminent death would be the inauguration of the new covenant, just as covenant renewal in Israel came by sacrifice (Exod 24:1–8).

The gospel summary in 1 Corinthians 15 says Jesus died "for our sins" (1 Cor 15:3). Israel's covenant relationship with God required the forgiveness of sins, and this was accomplished by sacrifice. Closely related to the claim that Jesus died "for our sins" is the claim that he died "for us" (Rom 5:6, 8; 2 Cor 5:14–15; 1 Thess 5:10). There is significant debate about the precise meaning of "for us." It is most likely, however, that both phrases ("for our sins" and "for us") are drawing on Isaiah's description of the suffering servant:

> Surely he has borne our infirmities and carried our diseases; yet we accounted him stricken, struck down by God, and afflicted. But he was wounded for our transgressions, crushed for our iniquities; upon him was the punishment that made us whole, and by his bruises we are healed. All we like sheep have gone astray; we have all turned to our own way, and the Lord has laid on him the iniquity of us all .... They made his grave with the wicked and his tomb with the rich, although he had done no violence, and there was no deceit in his mouth. Yet it was the will of the Lord to crush him with pain. When you make his life an offering for sin, he shall see his offspring, and shall prolong his days; through him the will of the Lord shall prosper. Out of his anguish he shall see light; he shall find satisfaction through his knowledge. The righteous one, my servant, shall make many righteous, and he shall bear their iniquities. (Isa 53:4–6, 9–11)

It is the suffering, dying Messiah who is the source of salvation, of forgiveness for sins. Jesus, as the fulfillment of Isaiah 53, inaugurates the new covenant by his act of self-giving love and service, dying for others and their sins, not his own. For this reason, Paul stresses the sinlessness of Jesus: "For our sake he [God] made him [Christ] to be sin who knew no sin" (2 Cor 5:21). This is almost certainly an allusion to Isaiah 53, especially vv. 10–11.

But Christ's sacrificial, covenant-renewing death for sins did not occur on just any night; in Paul's presentation, as in the gospels, it happened at Passover, the time when Jews remembered their exodus from Egyptian slavery: "Our paschal lamb, Christ, has been sacrificed" (1 Cor 5:7b). The inauguration of the new covenant is, therefore, also the event of a new exodus: a liberation. The tyrant now is not the enslaving Egyptian pharaoh, but Sin. This is not sins (plural) but Sin (singular and capitalized) – the power that enslaves (Rom 3:9), that renders people incapable of doing what they know they should do or want to do (Rom 7:14–23).

Both kinds of sin need to be dealt with: sins (plural), meaning "trespasses" or violations of the commandments, and Sin (singular), the force that is beyond and behind those various sins. Sin is a power that both surrounds and overwhelms people from without (Rom 7:14), and indwells and manipulates them from within (Rom 7:17, 20). This insidious force needs to be defeated and replaced with a beneficent and more powerful force. *The death and resurrection of Jesus as a second exodus, God's liberating act of deliverance, accomplishes the defeat; the gift of the Spirit, God's empowering act of indwelling presence, is Sin's replacement.*

Romans 3:21–26 offers a case study in this way of thinking about what God has done in Christ. Although this passage is fraught with interpretative challenges, it presents Christ's death as dealing simultaneously with both sins and Sin. Here is my translation, with important alternatives from the NRSV appearing in brackets:

> But now, apart from law, the saving justice ["righteousness"] of God has been disclosed, and is attested by the law and the prophets, the justice ["righteousness"] of God through the faithfulness of Jesus Christ ["faith in Jesus Christ"] for all who have faith ["believe"]. For there is no distinction, since all have sinned and lack ["fall short of"] the glory of God; they are now justified by his grace as a gift, through the redemption that is in Christ Jesus, whom God put forward as a means of expiation ["sacrifice of atonement"] by his blood, effective through Christ's faithfulness ["through faith"]. He did this to show his justice ["righteousness"], because in his divine forbearance he had passed over the sins previously committed; it was to prove at the present time that he himself is just ["righteous"]

in that ["and that"] he justifies the one who shares in the faithfulness of Jesus ["has faith in Jesus"].

This passage is the initial substantive account in Romans explaining the divine solution to the human predicament. Although we will return to it later in this essay, for now we need to note two main images used in reference to Christ's death: (1) "redemption" (3:24) and (2) "means of expiation" by his blood (3:25, sometimes translated as "sacrifice of atonement" or "mercy seat").

The word "redemption" refers to the liberation of slaves, alluding both to the ancient practice in general and to the liberation of enslaved Israel in particular. Christ's death effects liberation from the power of Sin. The image of expiation, sacrifice of atonement, and/or mercy seat (in the holy of holies of the Jewish temple, where the priest made sacrifice for sins) refers to the removal of sins; Christ's death also takes care of trespasses. In other words, this text recognizes both Sin and sins, claiming that Christ's death deals with both, effecting both forgiveness (expiation) and liberation (redemption). The human condition has been addressed in its totality with one saving act. Notice how both aspects are captured by Paul at the start of his letter to the Galatians: Jesus Christ "gave himself for our sins to set us free from the present evil age" (Gal 1:4).

In a nearby text echoing Gal 1:4, Paul describes this saving, liberating divine act as one motivated by Jesus' self-giving love: he "loved me and gave himself for me" (Gal 2:20). This is partly why Paul can say that God's justice (Rom 3:21–22) and love (Rom 5:1–11, treated below) are manifested in Christ's death; the Father and Son are working in concert. Similarly, Paul says both that the Son handed himself over to death (as in Gal 1:4; 2:20) and that God, for our sake, delivered him up to that death (e.g., Rom 4:25; 8:32). What one does, the other does.

Justification and Reconciliation

It is the combination of forgiveness for sins and liberation from Sin (as expressed in Rom 3:21–26) that brings people into right covenant relation with God. That, I would suggest, is the basic meaning of "justification." Justification, then, is more than a forensic or juridical transaction carried out in a divine courtroom ("I, the righteous divine judge, declare you, the guilty human, innocent"), and it is certainly not a legal fiction ("I declare you innocent even though you are actually guilty"). If justification is in any sense a pronouncement, it is a performative utterance; it effects transformation, the restoration of covenantal and intimate status: "I will be your God, and you will be my people." Because justification has this personal and relational character, Paul can easily pair it with reconciliation:

> Therefore, since we are justified by faith, we have peace with God through our Lord Jesus Christ .... For if while we were enemies, we were reconciled to God through the death of his Son, much more surely, having been reconciled, will we be saved by his life. But more than that, we even boast in God through our Lord Jesus Christ, through whom we have now received reconciliation. (Rom 5:1, 10–11)

Before exploring this passage in more detail, we should first note how it combines the past, present, and future dimensions of salvation. This threefold reality is celebrated in the Lord's Supper (see 1 Cor 11:17–34), in which (1) Christ's death is remembered and re-experienced, (2) his presence and love are known in the way others are treated (especially the least and the last), and (3) his future coming (*parousia*) is anticipated. In relation to this threefold saving act of God, Paul envisions a community characterized by the triad of faith, love, and hope (1 Cor 13:13; Gal 5:5–6; 1 Thess 1:3; 5:8).

The shocking aspect of the divine reconciliation narrated in Romans 5 (cited above) is that God, in love, has taken the initiative while we were *enemies* (v. 10). In Rom 5:6–8 Paul describes humanity as "ungodly" and "sinners," not as "righteous" (or "just") or "good" people who deserve God's love. The normal way of effecting reconciliation in antiquity required the offending party to take the initiative to seek reconciliation with the offended party; by contrast, Paul highlights how the offended party (God) lovingly initiated the reconciliation: Christ died "for us" (Rom 5:8). That same love was then "poured into our hearts through the Holy Spirit that has been given to us" (Rom 5:5).

As in Galatians 4, the saving activity of God entails the gift of both the Son and the Spirit. Paul offers an extraordinary portrait of three actors in the drama of salvation in intricate, intimate relationship, with the death of the Son and the gift of the Spirit constituting the demonstration of the Father's love.

The identity overlap between the Father and the Son appears explicitly in 2 Corinthians 5, where Paul states that "God was in Christ, reconciling the world to himself" (5:19, author's translation). Here we see once again that God takes the initiative; and the object of reconciliation is not merely Israel but the world. We also witness another example of the connection between justification and reconciliation. Within the wider context of this verse we also see an explicit emphasis on the transformative character that results from God's reconciling initiative – a radical transformation that is described as proof of the inbreaking of the new creation: "If anyone is in Christ, there is a new creation: everything old has passed away; see, everything has become new!" (5:17).

In this context, Paul probes the reconciling, new-creation-inaugurating event of Christ's death and resurrection, noting various dimensions of transformation:

- an *existential* transformation that radically alters a person's identity and orientation to life: "For the love of Christ urges us on, because we are convinced that one has died for all; therefore all have died. And he died for all, so that those who live might live no longer for themselves, but for him who died and was raised for them" (2 Cor 5:14–15).
- an *epistemological* transformation that completely rearranges a person's "intellectual furniture": "From now on, therefore, we regard no one from a human point of view; even though we once knew Christ from a human point of view, we know him no longer in that way" (2 Cor 5:16).
- an *ethical* transformation that immerses a person within a new moral world: "For our sake he made him to be sin who knew no sin, so that in him we might become the righteousness [or "justice"] of God" (2 Cor 5:21).

This last point merits further comment. Although neither "justify" nor "justification" appears in 2 Cor 5:21, the verse has generally, and rightly, been understood as a text about justification. Justification, then, must be understood as both participatory (we participate in Christ) and transformative (we are transformed in Christ). Paul expresses this in what some have called an "interchange" formula: there is an interchange between the sinless one who "became" sin (that is, became fully identified with sin in his role as sacrifice) and sinners who can become like the sinless one.

The purpose of this exchange was so that *in Christ* (and this location is critical) people who were sinful might become righteous, or just. Justification produces just people – people who exist in and are shaped by the living, resurrected Messiah who embodies the justifying, justice-making activity of God. Paul does not say that the gospel entails merely *believing in* the saving justice of God but *being transformed into* that justice, embodying it corporately and individually. This is because Christ was and is the location of God's justice. Those who are in Christ are, literally, in the center of God's dynamic, saving, transformative justice.

Similar interchange texts exist, including 2 Cor 8:9 (quoted above) and Gal 3:13–14: "Christ redeemed us from the curse of the law by becoming a curse for us ... in order that in Christ Jesus the blessing of Abraham might come to the Gentiles, so that we might receive the promise of the Spirit through faith." As in 2 Corinthians 5, this passage in Galatians 3 also implicitly expresses the purpose of the interchange in terms of transformation: the Spirit is the divine provision, promised by the prophets, for the moral and missional life expected of God's people (an aspect that Paul unpacks at length in Gal 5–6).

All of this takes us back to Rom 3:21–26 to offer two additional (somewhat more controversial) observations. First, we should probably understand its subject to be the "justice" of God understood as *the saving activity of God that makes things right and brings about justice.* This means that the liberation and forgiveness offered in Christ are transformative, making people right with God and therefore also righteous/just. As with the exodus, those released from bondage are delivered into a new bonded relationship with God the deliverer – a new covenant of such radical fidelity that Paul can refer to it as a re-enslavement. This new slavery is not to the power of Sin, of course, but to righteousness/justice – that is, ultimately to God (a subject that Paul examines at length in Rom 6, expanding the discussion further in Rom 12–15).

Second, we should probably also understand the manifestation of God's justice to be the *faithfulness of Jesus.* This claim reveals my conclusion about a huge debate in Pauline studies: does Paul refer to faith *in* Jesus or the faith (faithfulness) *of* Jesus when he uses a particular Greek phrase (*pistis Christou* and its variations in Rom 3:22, 26; Gal 2:16, 20; Phil 3:9; see also Rom 1:16–17)? In my view, the evidence best aligns in favor of "the faithfulness of Jesus" (compare *pistis Abraam*, the "faith [or faithfulness] of Abraham" in Rom 4:16). Thus Rom 3:26 conveys the idea that justification comes by "participating in the faithfulness of Jesus," that is, by participating in his death and, consequently, his resurrection.

We turn now to Paul's understanding of salvation as participation in Christ's death and resurrection.

THE *MODE* OF SALVATION: PARTICIPATING IN THE MESSIAH'S DEATH AND RESURRECTION

How does a person benefit from, or appropriate, the salvation offered by God in Christ? People often imagine that Paul's answer to this question is simply "faith" (e.g., Rom 10:9–10) or "faith and baptism" (see 1 Cor 6:11).

Such a view is true enough, but only if both faith and baptism are understood as modes of *participation* in Christ.

To see the point, we can place side by side two passages that focus on Christ and on believers respectively. In 1 Cor 15:3–9, Paul reminds the Corinthians that the gospel is summarized in a sort of mini-creed that narrates four main acts in a dramatic salvation story: (1) Christ's death, (2) his burial, (3) his resurrection, and (4) his post-resurrection appearances. In Romans 6, this drama reappears as a narrative of believers' experience, as they enter into the story, participating in each of its four acts:

Dramatic Act	*The Story of Christ (1 Corinthians 15)*	*The Story of Believers (Romans 6)*
Death	Christ died for our sins in accordance with the scriptures (15:3)	died to Sin ... baptized into his death (6:2–3); united with him in a death like his (6:5); our old self was crucified with him (6:6); died with Christ (6:8); dead to sin (6:11)
Burial	he was buried (15:4a)	buried with him by baptism into death (6:4)
Resurrection	he was raised on the third day in accordance with the scriptures (15:4b)	*Present (resurrection to new life):* just as Christ was raised from the dead ... so we too might walk in newness of life (6:4); alive to God in Christ Jesus (6:11; cf. 6:13) *Future (bodily resurrection):* we will certainly be united with him in a resurrection like his (6:5); we will also live with him (6:8)
Appearance	he appeared to Cephas ... the twelve ... others (15:5–9)	present yourselves to God as those who have been brought from death to life (6:13)

In other words, believing the gospel (or affirming the creed) is not merely assenting to its truths; it also involves participating in its story or, more precisely, participating in the reality that the story narrates. Being baptized means being immersed into water, which signifies being immersed into Christ and his story – an image of full participation and transformation. To be baptized is to be *transferred* from *outside* Christ *into*

Christ and his story. From then on, the immersed (baptized) person is "in" Christ, which means both being in covenant relationship to Christ as Lord and being part of his body, the "church" or "assembly" (Greek *ekklēsia*). As individuals and as a community, "the immersed" live life "*in* Christ" and "*with* Christ" – phrases we find repeatedly in Paul's letters.

To believe and be baptized is also to be transformed (through sharing in Christ's death and resurrection) into something altogether new – becoming part of the new creation. And in becoming immersed and transformed, the immersed begin enacting the Christ-story, step by step, as a living embodiment of it. This starts at baptism, is reaffirmed at the Lord's Supper, is performed in daily life, and continues until death or the second coming of Christ (the *parousia*). Paul's vision of new life in Christ, therefore, is one of resurrection *in* the body now (a life of holiness and justice; Rom 6:4, 11–19), followed by resurrection *of* the body later (eternal life; Rom 6:8, 20–23).

This helps to shed light on the motif of "justification by faith" in Paul's thinking. Justification by faith is a significant aspect of Galatians and Romans, and it is present or assumed in other letters too. But as we have already seen, justification needs to be understood in covenantal and relational terms, and not merely legal or forensic categories. We will see as well that faith also needs to be understood in Paul as something more than assent to truth or even trust in a person.

But first, it is important to note that there is disagreement among Pauline scholars about the place of justification in Paul's thought. Some would say justification by faith (or, more precisely, justification by grace through faith) is the distinctive and central mark of Paul's theology. Others contend that it is of secondary importance to his notion of participation in Christ. Still others think that these two themes are both important in Paul but are fundamentally independent of each other (though not necessarily incompatible) – one is forensic (or legal) in character, involving a divine verdict of "not guilty," while the other is participatory, involving union with Christ.

One way of considering these issues, in conjunction with the question of the meaning of faith for Paul, is to look closely at Gal 2:15–21. (Along the way, we will note its similarities to baptism by co-crucifixion and co-resurrection with Christ in Romans 6.) The opening and closing of the passage are particularly important. Here is how the NRSV translates the passage:

> We ourselves are Jews by birth and not Gentile sinners; yet we know that a person is justified not by the works of the law but

> through faith in Jesus Christ. And we have come to believe in Christ Jesus, so that we might be justified by faith in Christ, and not by doing the works of the law, because no one will be justified by the works of the law . . .
>
> For through the law I died to the law, so that I might live to God. I have been crucified with Christ; and it is no longer I who live, but it is Christ who lives in me. And the life I now live in the flesh I live by faith in the Son of God, who loved me and gave himself for me. I do not nullify the grace of God; for if justification comes through the law, then Christ died for nothing. (Gal 2:15–16, 19–21)

This passage is a critical part of Paul's response to the question of whether and why Jewish and gentile believers belong at the same table. It is often described as an exposition of the meaning of justification by faith, which it is. But it is also a passage that both includes the explicit language of *co-crucifixion* with Christ and strongly implies *co-resurrection* to new life. It is therefore often described as an exposition of participation in Christ and his story, which (again) it is. Rather than an either-or, justification and participation are a both-and. Unfortunately, however, these two characterizations of the passage (justification, participation) are often seen as sequential (whether in this text or more generally in Paul's theology). That is, justification by faith is thought to precede, or at least be distinguishable from, co-crucifixion and its resulting new life with Christ dwelling within.

But the structure of this passage (which begins and ends on the subject of justification) will not permit such a separation or sequence. Rather, Paul is defining justification by faith in terms of participation: co-crucifixion and co-resurrection. Justification is inseparable from union with Christ. As in baptism, the old self dies and a new self is born (esp. 2:20). In other words, for Paul the internal act of faith and the external act of baptism are inseparable and (together) effect new life. It is a life of allegiance to and participation in a new lord, an existence focused not on oneself but on the indwelling crucified and resurrected Messiah Jesus (cf. Rom 14:7–9; 2 Cor 5:15).

To further complicate matters, however, this passage also contains some crucially important language like that of Romans 3, possibly referring to Christ's faithfulness in three places. Here is the alternative reading supplied by the NRSV of Gal 2:16 and 20 (note the italicized texts):

> yet we know that a person is justified not by the works of the law but through *the faithfulness of* Jesus Christ. And we have come to

> believe in Christ Jesus, so that we might be justified by *the faithfulness of* Christ, and not by doing the works of the law, because no one will be justified by the works of the law . . . and it is no longer I who live, but it is Christ who lives in me. And the life I now live in the flesh I live by *the faithfulness of* the Son of God, who loved me and gave himself for me.

If this rendering is correct, then Paul says that justification, while requiring belief/faith (the *mode* of justification), is nonetheless grounded in Christ's act of faithfulness (the *means* of justification), and even the believer's new life is grounded in the ongoing reality of that faithfulness. Faith is a sharing in Christ's faithfulness, his obedience to the Father (cf. Rom 5:19), and specifically his death. Thus, faith as participation is as much *allegiance* as it is *trust*, which is why Paul can speak of the "obedience of faith" (Rom 1:5; 16:26).

Faith, then, by God's grace and the working of the Spirit, actualizes all the intended outcomes of Christ's death and resurrection. This grace-and-Spirit-enabled faith both liberates and enslaves; it incorporates and inaugurates. It liberates people from the interlocking directorate of hostile and enslaving powers in order to re-enslave those same people as God's beloved and obedient children; it incorporates people into Christ; and it inaugurates in them a new life of faithfulness and love.

The faithful, self-giving love that Paul sees in Christ's cross is the antithesis of the idolatry, self-centeredness, will to power, domination, greed, hatred, and violence that Paul documents especially in Romans 1–3. The new life of the new covenant and new creation will (or at least should) embody this antithesis of the surrounding culture's practices that are idolatrous and/or unjust and immoral. The ecclesial body of Christ is an alternative culture that (paradoxically) is intimately involved in the world, like Christ himself (just as the poem about Christ's self-giving in Phil 2:6–11 is presented in Phil 2:1–5 as the pattern for those in Christ). But this way of life is possible only by the working of the Spirit.

EMBODYING THE NEW COVENANT: THE MUTUAL INDWELLING OF CHRIST/THE SPIRIT AND BELIEVERS

The Gift of the Spirit

We have seen from Gal 4:4–6 and Rom 5:1–11 how Paul reveals the divine work of salvation to consist of a double gift: the gift of the Son and the gift of the Spirit. The experience of salvation is also a partaking of this double reality (1 Cor 6:11). Both individuals in Christ (1 Cor 6:19) and communities in Christ (1 Cor 3:16) are temples of the Holy Spirit, manifestations of the God revealed in the Messiah Jesus for the sake of the world:

> Do you not know that you [all] are God's temple and that God's Spirit dwells in you [or "among you all"]? (1 Cor 3:16)
>
> Do you not know that your body is a temple of the Holy Spirit within you, which you have from God, and that you are not your own? (1 Cor 6:19)

This indwelling Spirit ensures the empowerment and transformation of those who participate in Christ's death and resurrection.

The Shape of the Spirit-Filled Life

As the people of the new covenant and new creation, the Spirit-filled body of Christ is called to be the revivified people of God that was promised in Israel's prophetic literature. They are to be a community of shalom, of anticipatory participation in the coming eschatological kingdom of peace: "the kingdom of God is ... righteousness [or justice] and peace and joy in the Holy Spirit" (Rom 14:17). The next chapter of this book will have much more to say about the shape of life in Christ by the Spirit. For now, we will make two observations.

First, the amazing grace, or divine gift, displayed in Christ is (in the words of John Barclay) *unconditioned* but not *unconditional*. God's wholly unmerited gift comes with the expectation of an appropriate response. This is due both to the reciprocal character of gift-giving in the ancient world (so Barclay) and to the similar mutuality of the covenant between God and God's people in the Bible. The covenant formula, "I shall be your God and you shall be my people," is not merely a statement about election by God or even intimacy with God. It is, like the declaration of justification discussed above, more like a performative utterance. It brings about a mutuality of commitment and thus action on the part of both parties in the covenant.

Second, because Paul refers to the new-covenant gift of God's Spirit as the *Holy* Spirit (e.g., Rom 5:5; 1 Cor 6:19; Eph 1:13) and the Spirit *of the Son* (e.g., Gal 4:6), a primary activity of the Spirit is to make believers holy (both individually and corporately) by transforming them into Christlike people. Practically speaking, God's act of salvation means the creation of a community of Jews and gentiles with a new heart, by virtue of internal rather than external circumcision (Rom

2:25–29), who, enabled by the Spirit, live faithfully toward God and lovingly toward others, thus fulfilling the "just requirement of the law" (Rom 8:3–4). The very purpose of Christ's incarnation and death was to create such a multicultural community of transformed people (Gal 5:6, 13–14; Rom 8:3–4; 15:1–12; 2 Cor 5:21; Eph 2:11–22), in collective worship of the one true God (Rom 15:1–13).

This transformation is nothing other than ongoing participation in the death and resurrection of Jesus. The narrative shape and pattern of the Christ-story becomes the shape and pattern of believers: a life story of sacrificial faithfulness to God and self-giving love for others. In other words, believers fulfill the covenant's "vertical" requirement (to love God) and the "horizontal" requirement (to love neighbor) in a Christlike way, the way of Christ seen in his self-emptying incarnation and self-humbling death for others. This cross-shaped life-pattern is sometimes called cruciformity, or conformity to the crucified Messiah. It does not mean primarily suffering, but faithfulness and love, which (nonetheless) often results in suffering. Thus, the ecclesial body of Christ is cross-shaped.

At the same time, however, because believers participate in Christ's resurrection as well as his crucifixion, cruciformity is suffused with the life and power of the resurrection. It is life-giving, both for those who embody the cross-shaped love of Christ and for those who receive it. It is *resurrectional* cruciformity: "For while we live, we are always being given up to death for Jesus' sake, so that the life of Jesus may be made visible in our mortal flesh" (2 Cor 4:11). This is not a spirituality or story of triumphalism, or of pursuing individualistic self-fulfillment; instead, it is a story of self-giving love that, paradoxically, is full of joy and life: the life of God the Father, Christ the Son, and the Spirit of the Father and the Son.

CONCLUSION: THE FUTURE OF SALVATION

We have already noted that, for Paul, salvation is a reality with past, present, and future dimensions. While much has already been said about the future of salvation, there is still more to be registered here, even if only briefly, and as a way to conclude our reflections on Paul's view of what God is doing in the world.

The reality of God's new creation has begun in Christ by the power of the Spirit, who is the down payment on, and guarantee of, final glory (2 Cor 1:22; 5:5; Eph 1:14). But the new creation is not yet complete. Human beings, even those in Christ, do not experience the fullness of

God's presence, God's glory, in their lives. The powers of Sin and Death obviously still exist, and often seem victorious. Salvation, the kingdom of God, is both "already" and "not yet." The "blessed hope" (Titus 2:13) is Paul's answer to the "not yet" dimension of God's rescue project. This hope is focused on the "day of the Lord": the "appearance" (*epiphaneia*) or "(second) coming" (*parousia*) of Jesus, and the glorious aftermath of that event (see, for instance, 1 Cor 15:23–28; 1 Thess 4:13–18; 2 Tim 4:1–8).

The notion of "the day of the Lord" comes from Israel's prophets. In the hands of Paul, it maintains the twofold character of the prophetic tradition: wrath and judgment on the one hand, and salvation and human flourishing on the other. Paul's emphasis is on the latter. He believes the coming of Jesus will result in the transformation of those who are alive in Christ and the bodily resurrection of those who have died in Christ. This will lead to eternal, incorruptible life in the presence of God as "adopted" children of God and heirs of Christ (Rom 8:10–30; cf. Gal 4:5). Suffering will give way to the fullness of glory (2 Cor 4:17–18) as the process of conformity to Christ in his humiliation and exaltation reaches its glorious climax (Rom 8:17, 29–30).

Paul further claims that "all Israel will be saved" (Rom 11:26, a claim that has generated various interpretations). He also believes that this final salvation of humans will trigger the liberation of all creation, which (like humanity itself) has been subject to pain and suffering (Rom 8:18–25). God's rescue project extends to all of creation – "all things" will be reconciled in Christ (Col 1:19–20; Eph 1:9–10). Finally, Paul believes that the cosmic powers of Sin and Death that have ravaged God's good creation will be fully and finally defeated (1 Cor 15:20–28, 54–57).

Paul sometimes refers to this saving activity of God as a "mystery" – something that is revealed but is also somewhat inscrutable. Its goal, however, is clear: the undoing of Sin and Death and all their consequences in order to bring about that which God has intended from the beginning for humanity and for all creation. In the words of the song from "Fiddler on the Roof," the saving justice of God is a rescue project that is truly summarized in the refrain "l'chaim, l'chaim, to life!"

Further Reading

Barclay, John M. G. *Paul and the Gift*. Grand Rapids, MI: Eerdmans, 2015.

Bates, Matthew W. *Salvation by Allegiance Alone: Rethinking Faith, Works, and the Gospel of Jesus the King*. Grand Rapids, MI: Baker Academic, 2017.

Blackwell, Ben C. *Christosis: Pauline Soteriology in light of Deification in Irenaeus and Cyril of Alexandria*. Rev. ed. Grand Rapids, MI: Eerdmans, 2016.

Campbell, Douglas A. *The Deliverance of God: An Apocalyptic Rereading of Justification in Paul*. Grand Rapids, MI: Eerdmans, 2009.

Colijn, Brenda B. *Images of Salvation in the New Testament*. Downers Grove, IL: IVP Academic, 2010.

Dunn, James D. G. Chapters 5 and 6 in *The Theology of the Apostle Paul*. Grand Rapids, MI: Eerdmans, 1998.

Gathercole, Simon J. *Defending Substitution: An Essay on Atonement in Paul*. Grand Rapids, MI: Baker Academic, 2015.

Gaventa, Beverly Roberts, ed. *Apocalyptic Paul: Cosmos and Anthropos in Romans 5–8*. Waco, TX: Baylor University Press, 2013.

Gorman, Michael J. *Inhabiting the Cruciform God: Kenosis, Justification, and Theosis in Paul's Narrative Soteriology*. Grand Rapids, MI: Eerdmans, 2009.

Gorman, Michael J. *Participating in Christ: Explorations in Paul's Theology and Spirituality*. Grand Rapids, MI: Baker Academic, 2019.

Hooker, Morna D. "Interchange in Christ." *Journal of Theological Studies*, 32, no. 2 (1971): 349–361. Reprint, *From Adam to Christ: Essays on Paul*, 13–69. Cambridge: Cambridge University Press, 1990. Reprint, Eugene, OR: Wipf and Stock, 2008.

Longenecker, Bruce W. "Faith, Works, and Worship: Torah Observance in Paul's Theological Perspective." In *The Apostle Paul and the Christian Life*, edited by Scot McKnight and Joe Modica, 47–70. Grand Rapids, MI: Baker Academic, 2016.

Pitre, Brant, Michael P. Barber, and John A. Kincaid. *Paul, a New Covenant Jew: Rethinking Pauline Theology*. Grand Rapids, MI: Eerdmans, 2019.

Tamez, Elsa. *The Amnesty of Grace: Justification by Faith from a Latin American Perspective*. Translated by Sharon H. Ringe. Nashville, TN: Abingdon, 1993.

van der Watt, Jan G., ed. *Salvation in the New Testament: Perspectives on Soteriology*, 163–358. Leiden: Brill, 2005.

11 What Did Paul Think God Is Doing in Christian Communities?

SUSAN GROVE EASTMAN

Writing to the Christians in Rome, Paul addresses them as "all God's beloved, who are called saints" (Rom 1:7).[1] If we ask what God is doing in Christian communities, the first answer is this: God is loving the saints. Paul picks up on this theme of love in Rom 5:5: "The love of God has been poured out into our hearts through the Holy Spirit who has been given to us." This could mean that human love *for* God has been given through the outpouring of the Spirit, but in the immediate context Paul's emphasis is on God's preemptive, undeserved self-giving on behalf of all humanity in the midst of its weakness, sinfulness, and even enmity towards God (Rom 5:8–11). In Rom 8:35–39 Paul extols the constancy and power of this divine love; he is confident that the recipients of such love will in turn love God (Rom 8:28) and one another (12:9; 13:8). God is loving and creating a fellowship of mutual love extended not only to friends, but also to enemies, without regard to their moral or social status.

As recipients of God's love, these early believers are also "called saints"; that is, they have been summoned by God, and together *all* of them have been sanctified for God's service, despite any social identities that might otherwise separate them. The little word "all" figures largely in Paul's conception of Christian fellowship (Rom 7:7, 8, 16, 18; 3:23; 4:16; 5:18; 11:32); the scope of God's salvation is inclusive and global. Similarly, Paul addresses the Corinthians as those who are "called saints" – again, not in an exclusive way, but "together with *all* those who in *every* place call on the name of our Lord Jesus Christ" (1 Cor 1:2). He simply names the Philippians "*all* the saints in Christ Jesus" (Phil 1:1). Loving, calling, sanctifying – this is what God is doing in communities of believers. Paul's ethical exhortations make no sense apart from the dynamic, indwelling, transforming presence of God in and among

[1] All translations are mine unless otherwise noted.

gathered believers. Paul's frequent use of "all" emphasizes the inclusiveness of that divine activity, both across social, economic, and ethnic divisions within local gatherings, and across geographical distances between scattered communities "in Christ."

Although the language of a "universal church" is not yet in place, Paul certainly wants his listeners to see themselves as part of a larger network of believers around the Roman empire. He often calls the specific congregations to whom he writes, "the church" or "churches": "the church of God" (Gal 1:13; 1 Cor 1:2; 2 Cor 1:1), "the churches of Galatia" (Gal 1:2), and "the church of the Thessalonians in God the Father and the Lord Jesus Christ" (1 Thess 1:1). The word translated church (*ekklēsia*) means "assembly" or gathering, in this case the gathering of those summoned by God in Christ. The language draws on both common Greek notions of the assembly of citizens in the *polis*, and on Israel's identity as the "assembly of the Lord." In the case of Israel, as of the church, God is the one who chooses or elects the members of the community, and this divine election has nothing to do with their prior behavior. Those summoned by God are not self-selecting; they are not simply an association of volunteers; together they belong to the God who called them, and in and through belonging to God, they belong to one another.

Such congregations are characterized by a double location: they are "in Christ," and they live out their calling in their specific social locations. The Philippian saints, for example, are both "in Christ Jesus" and "in Philippi" (Phil 1:1).[2] Their way of life, shaped by belonging to Christ, does not take them out of the concrete circumstances of their enmeshment in the world, but rather stands as a public sign of the reality of salvation (Phil 1:27–28). Indeed, Paul joyfully tells the Roman believers: "I thank my God through Jesus Christ for all of you, because your faith is proclaimed in all the world" (Rom 1:8). What is their "faith" (*pistis*) that is so publicly proclaimed? Is it their trust in Christ? Is it their faithful manifestation of new life in Christ? The two cannot be separated; "proclaimed in all the world," their faith has an element of public testimony to the gospel as "the power of God for salvation to all who believe" (Rom 1:16). The community's double location in Christ and in the world thus highlights two intertwined aspects of God's action in and among Christian communities: the sustenance and transformation of believers in and through their shared life in Christ, and the

[2] See, for example, the discussion of Phil 2:1 by Stephen E. Fowl, *Philippians* (Grand Rapids, MI: Eerdmans, 2005), 17–19.

manifestation of Jesus in and for the world. We will discuss these themes somewhat sequentially, but in practice they cannot be separated.

THE SUSTENANCE AND TRANSFORMATION OF BELIEVERS

Indwelling and Transformation

Located and finding their most basic identity "in Christ," Christian communities are indwelt by the Spirit. This metaphorical language of being indwelt by the Spirit, while also living "in Christ," conveys both an interpersonal matrix and a divine presence active in the midst of interpersonal connections. Paul can speak of the metaphorical space where Christians belong as "this grace in which we stand" (Rom 5:2), suggesting it is a relational network funded and sustained by unmerited divine gift rather than human achievement.[3]

Such a gift-based relational matrix conflicts with worldly systems of worth and identity, which Paul links with "the flesh" (*sarx*) as an opposing systemic social and spiritual reality. Hence, he later tells the Roman Christians,

> You (plural) are not in the flesh, you are in the Spirit, since in fact the Spirit of God dwells in and among you. Anyone who does not have the Spirit of Christ does not belong to him. But if Christ is in and among you, although your bodies are dead because of sin, the Spirit is [the source of] life because of righteousness. If the Spirit of him who raised Jesus from the dead dwells among you, he who raised Christ Jesus from the dead will vivify your mortal bodies also through his Spirit which dwells in and among you. (Rom 8:9–11)

Paul identifies the Spirit interchangeably as "the Spirit of God," "the Spirit of Christ," simply "Christ," and finally "the Spirit of the one who raised Jesus from the dead." Dwelling in the midst of the community, this multifaceted divine presence acts through human interactions and promises life to mortal bodies. I have rendered the preposition "in" as "in and among," in order to get across the sense of the plural pronoun "you" (i.e., "in and among you"). Paul is not talking here about the Spirit living separately in isolated individuals, but rather, the Spirit

[3] On the theme of gift in Paul's letters, particularly as the gift of God in Christ subverts human systems of worth, see John M. G. Barclay, *Paul and the Gift* (Grand Rapids, MI: Eerdmans, 2015).

moving in and among and between the members of Christ, in their worship and their common life.[4] The Spirit also draws believers into a new family system in which they belong to Christ, and join in calling on God as Abba, father (Rom 8:9, 15; cf. Gal 4:6). The language of indwelling and kinship suggests that Paul envisions Spirit-indwelt communities as places where God is reconstituting the identities of their members from the ground up, in a renewal that is so profound as to transplant them into a new family system. This new family is the place of transformation, through the power of God's freely gifted, non-condemning love.[5]

Body and Mind

Romans 12 gives a picture of what such transformation looks like:

> I encourage (*parakalō*) you therefore, brothers and sisters, by the mercies of God, present your bodies as a living sacrifice, holy and acceptable to God, which is your reasonable (*logikēn*) worship. And do not be conformed to this age, but be transformed by the renewing of the mind, so you may prove what is the will of God, what is good and acceptable and perfect. (Rom 12:1–2)

Paul here amplifies his appeal for mutual encouragement (*sumparaklēthēnai*) in Rom 1:12. Each phrase of these tightly packed verses illuminates his understanding of God's transforming movement in and through Christian fellowship. First is the little word, "therefore," which links Paul's appeal to what has preceded it, both immediately in Rom 9–11, and in the letter as a whole up to this point. Paul makes the connections even clearer with the phrase, "by the mercies of God." He has just been talking about God's mercy toward both Jews and Gentiles, leading up to the climactic and startling claim, "God has imprisoned all in disobedience, in order that he might have mercy on all" (Rom 11:32; see Rom 9:15–18; Exod 33:19). The abiding power of this divine mercy is demonstrated by the love of God shown in Christ's death for the ungodly, the weak, the sinners, even God's enemies (Rom 5:6–10). Thus, when Paul bases his appeal to the Roman Christians on

[4] For the theme of participation in Christ, see Robert Tannehill, "Participation in Christ: A Central Theme in Pauline Soteriology," in *The Shape of the Gospel: New Testament Essays* (Eugene, OR: Cascade, 2007): 223–237.

[5] See Joseph H. Hellerman, *The Ancient Church as Family* (Minneapolis, MN: Fortress Press, 2001), 92–126 for discussion of this familial imagery in Paul in its first century context.

"the mercies of God," he grounds it in the character of God as one of abundant generosity. In the larger context of Romans 1–8, Paul has explicated the transforming power of the gospel (Rom 1:16–17) in terms of the "free gift" of God's abounding grace through the death and resurrection of Christ (Rom 5:15–21), which alone has power to liberate humanity from the deceptive and lethal power of Sin (Rom 5:21; 6:14, 23; 8:1–4). Unmerited grace, unmerited mercy, acting through Christ's solidarity to the death with and for humanity in bondage to Sin – this is the leverage that pries Paul's converts free from systemic, ingrained sin, and establishes them in a new community under the banner of "no condemnation."

Therefore, based on the revelation of God's merciful generosity, Paul appeals to his listeners to take certain actions. It is worth pausing to emphasize this appeal. One possible deduction from Paul's emphasis on God's unmerited, freely given grace and mercy would be to render human beings simply as passive recipients, as if God's action canceled out human action. Paul, to the contrary, has a noncompetitive account of divine and human agency, because he sees God's mercy and grace as impelling its recipients toward a holistic transformation that is both embodied and cognitive. He tells his listeners, "present your *bodies* as a living sacrifice, holy and acceptable to God, which is your reasonable worship" and in the next breath he tells them to "be transformed by the renewal of your *mind*" (Rom 12:1–2). Paul is referring to physical bodies here (see Rom 6:12–13, 19; 7:5, 23; 8:11–13), and he clearly thinks bodily actions cannot be disconnected from mental states. The mind and the body are intricately intertwined[6].

Furthermore, bodily actions have consequences in the metaphorical social "body." Bodies are participatory entities; they connect persons to their environments and to each other, whether in harmful or healthful ways. Paul has warned against presenting body parts (*melē*) to sin as weapons of unrighteousness (Rom 6:12–13, 19); now he begins to talk in depth about life-giving uses of the body. There is nothing otherworldly or ineffable about this command; bodies are concrete, limited, visible, and connective, and through bodily existence we are enmeshed in larger social realities. In Rom 12:5 Paul calls the larger social reality of the church "the body of Christ," thereby making explicit the participatory aspects of embodiment; in their individual bodies believers are

[6] For this link between body and mind in Paul, see Susan Eastman, *Paul and the Person: Reframing Paul's Anthropology* (Grand Rapids, MI: Eerdmans, 2017), 85–105.

connected to one another in the metaphorical, but nonetheless real, body of Christ.[7]

This bodily self-giving to God is an act of worship. The imagery of sacrifice recalls Israel's system of sacrifice; in continuity with that system, but also in contrast to it, believers are to offer their own bodies as a *living* sacrifice, in union with Christ's own self-giving on the cross. Such an offering is not for God's sake and not transactional, because God is beyond all bargaining or all transactions of giving and receiving: "who has given a gift to him, that he might be repaid?" (Rom 11:35 / Job 41:3). Rather, the living sacrifice of which Paul speaks is part and parcel of the holistic transformation that God is accomplishing among believers, in and through their embodied participation in the body of Christ. Offering their bodies to God, believers engage in an intentional response to the gift of Christ, a response that mirrors Christ's self-giving.

Thus, fusing bodily practice and mental states, Paul immediately commands a cognitive transformation that sets believers at odds with the status quo, which Paul here calls "this age," and elsewhere calls "the present evil age" (Gal 1:4). "Do not be conformed (*suschēmatizesthe*)" and "be transformed (*metamorphousthe*)" are passive imperatives, which are difficult to translate into English. The passive suggests that Paul sees other agents at work exerting pressure on his listeners: on the one hand, the influence of the present age dominated by systemic sin, which is to be resisted; on the other hand, the transforming power of God, which is to be welcomed. A paraphrase might run like this: "Do not let your whole way of thinking, acting, and being be fashioned in line with the *modus operandi* of this age, but be transformed by God as your whole way of thinking, acting, and being is made new. In this way, together you may publicly demonstrate (*dokimazein*) the will of God, which is good and acceptable and perfect" (Rom 12:2). Paul addresses his listeners as those who are communally indwelt by the Spirit of God and thus never acting on their own power or initiative, but made responsible agents by the power of God. He encourages a process of corporate discernment and decision-making, in which their whole life, including attitudes and practices toward one another and toward unbelievers, is resourced by the Holy Spirit and restructured in line with God's new

[7] For the understanding of the body as a mode of communication and connection, see Ernst Käsemann, "On Paul's Anthropology," in *Perspectives on Paul,* trans. J. Kohl (Mifflintown, PA: Sigler, 1996 [1969]), 1–31.

creation through Christ (see, e.g., Gal 6:15), and thereby exhibits God's will in action.

THE MANIFESTATION OF JESUS IN AND FOR THE WORLD

Crossing Boundaries: Unity and Diversity

As the visible outworking of God's loving and sanctifying presence, the renewal of common life takes public, concrete shape in the particular communities to which Paul writes. Like metal filings moved by a magnet hidden underneath the surface of a table, the members of those communities are to find themselves moved in harmony with the shape of Christ's own self-giving love. The first thing to note about this homology between Christ's love and the character of Christian community is that it crosses social boundaries, and therefore encompasses dissimilarities. Differences between people, and the ensuing potential for misunderstanding and conflict, are built into Christian fellowship.

Central to Paul's gospel is the crucifixion of the incarnate Lord as the enactment of God's boundary-crossing love for all humanity. This divine displacement is most vividly displayed in the Christ hymn (Phil 2:5–11): Christ did not exploit equality with God, but made himself null, crossing the immense chasm between God and humanity in its most wretched and culpable state, in order to take on human likeness and be executed as a criminal. Paul sums up the message more succinctly in 2 Cor 5:21: "For our sake he made him to be sin who knew no sin, so that in him we might become the righteousness of God." This interchange has economic impact: "you know the grace of our Lord Jesus Christ, that though he was rich, yet for your sake he became poor, so that by his poverty you might become rich" (2 Cor 8:9). This shocking divine dislocation, this movement into the sphere of impoverished humanity, under the power of Sin and the sentence of death, catalyzes a reverse movement into the sphere of righteousness and abundance. It is the interchange at the heart of the good news, and it underlies Paul's vision for Christian communities.[8]

Paul's mission illustrates the practical implications of such a vision: following a dislocated Lord, he lives a dislocated life. He is indifferent toward the practices and marks of identity that once gave him standing in his former social and religious circles, sometimes embracing his Jewish

[8] See Morna Hooker, "Interchange in Christ," *Journal of Theological Studies* 32, no. 2 (1971): 349–361.

credentials (Rom 11:1), and sometimes setting them at naught (Phil 3:4–8; 1 Cor 9:20–21). He knows God as the God and Father of our Lord Jesus Christ, and through that knowledge, he affirms God's embrace of both Jew and Gentile in one new fellowship in Christ. In terms of the social realities dividing Jews and Gentiles in Paul's context, such an affirmation casts a global vision of all humanity, including former enemies, together worshipping God in mutual welcome (Rom 15:7–13). The sweep of Paul's vision is breathtaking; the consequences for daily life are radical, complex, and difficult. We can see the issues for Jewish and Gentile believers displayed in Galatians and Romans. How is food to be prepared for common meals, and what food is acceptable (Rom 14:2–3)? What about Sabbath observation? (Rom 14:5–6)? Should male converts be circumcised (Gal 5:2; 1 Cor 7:17–19)? Who eats with whom (Gal 2:12–13)?

Paul's letters also reveal socioeconomic tensions running through some of his churches, such as the congregations in Corinth. Is it acceptable to eat meat put up for sale in the market if it came from a pagan sacrifice (1 Cor 10:25–28)? What about eating a meal *in* a pagan temple (1 Cor 8:10)? Are there limits and guidelines for sexual behavior in the new communities of freedom in Christ (1 Cor 5:1–2; 6:15–18)? And what about the travesty of some believers going hungry, while others eat and drink to excess (1 Cor 11:21–22)? How is worship to be conducted (1 Cor 14)? And how are these fledgling communities to conduct themselves in the challenging social environments in which they find themselves (1 Cor 14:23–25; Phil 1:27–28; 1 Thess 4:11–12)?

The complexity and diversity of the issues Paul addresses in his letters implies an equal complexity and diversity in the socioeconomic makeup of his churches. Paul may frequently remind them of their unity in Christ because they need such reminding; clearly unity did not preclude struggle. Rather, the global reach of the good news ensured the existence of different social practices within Christian fellowships, arising from the different social backgrounds of his converts. And just as Paul himself experienced a rupture with his former life, so he expects the members of the churches he founded to experience a dislocation from their former sources of identity and practice, and to be transformed through their relocation into a new community of faith and practice.[9]

[9] That such transformation necessarily involves conflict is a word of hope to Christian communities today when they struggle to maintain unity in the midst of deep differences; conversely, it may be a word of warning to communities that experience no such struggles, because they have become so homogenous as to exclude others not like themselves.

Paul does not envision a unity made possible by enforced conformity, but one based on the encompassing scope of God's self-giving in Christ.

If believers come into the fellowship from diverse religious, social, and economic locations, they also find themselves differentiated within the community through a variety of gifts and callings from God. Paul's primary image for such gifted difference is the metaphor of the body of Christ: "For as in one body we have many members, and all the members do not have the same function, so we, though many, are one body in Christ, and individually members one of another" (Rom 12:4–5; cf. 1 Cor 12:27). Paul's language is vividly physical; he expands the metaphor of connective tissue in 1 Cor 12:14–26, such that each member of the fellowship is connected to all others as intimately as a finger is to a hand: hands, fingers, arms, feet, toes, noses, ears, eyes, all are members in the sense that all radically need one another in order to sit, rest, eat, touch, smell, see, taste, grasp, walk, run – that is, to perceive and act in the world. Paul's imagery undercuts the social hierarchies of the Roman empire, because the differences between the members are essential to the health of the whole body.

Such individuation arises from God's varied gifts, not from any prior social markers or skills or attainments; it is not to be confused with identity markers stemming from social location or ethnic background, and indeed destabilizes such distinctions. For example, Paul strongly entreats Philemon to receive the runaway slave Onesimus "no longer as a slave but more than a slave, as a beloved brother" (Phlm 16).[10] We do not know how Philemon responded to Paul's appeal, but it seems likely that the same Onesimus appears in Col 4:9 as the "faithful and beloved brother," now traveling with Tychicus as a worker for the Gospel. If so, now as a "beloved brother," Onesimus has a new calling and source of worth that transcends and potentially conflicts with his social location as a slave. Paul does not call for a cultural revolution; indeed, elsewhere he advises slaves not to worry about their bondage, although they should obtain their freedom if possible (1 Cor 7:21, in one interpretation of that difficult verse). Nonetheless, the radically countercultural proclamation of a savior who became a slave has the power to generate new social realities. The fact that the church has so often fallen short of these new realities does not lessen the radical implications of Paul's gospel. Rather, the gospel continues to call the church to account.

[10] For theological commentary on Philemon, see Daniel Migliore, *Philippians and Philemon* (Louisville, KY: Westminster John Knox, 2014).

Practical Wisdom for Life Together

Paul's practical vision of God's transforming power at work in Christian fellowship may be discussed under four headings: (1) navigating different cultural and religious practices, (2) mutual discernment grounded in love, (3) eschatological reservation, and (4) the radical redistribution of resources. The last two headings have particular implications for Paul's view of the manifestation of Christ in the world.

First, we already have discussed the existence of varied practices among Christians in Paul's communities, but how did he think believers should navigate such differences? His answer can be summed up very briefly: through mutual welcome that flows out of God's welcome of each person. The clearest guidance comes in Romans 14, where Paul tackles diverse views of religious customs such as food laws and the liturgical calendar. The basic principle is this: "Who are you to judge the servant of another? It is before his own master that he stands or falls. And he will be upheld, for the Master is able to make him stand" (Rom 14:4). In deference to God's sole authority to judge, then, members of the community are not to judge one another's eating habits or liturgical customs, for each person acts in service of the one Lord, who is the final judge (Rom 14:10–12). Taken by itself, however, such an injunction against judging one another could simply lead to a tolerant laissez-faire attitude, in which each individual is free to do what he or she wants without regard to the good of the whole. Paul does not allow this. Rather, he gives further guidance that entails curtailing one's own freedom for the good of one's neighbor: "Let us no more judge one another, but rather exercise judgment in this way: not to put a stumbling block or hindrance before a brother or sister" (Rom 14:13). This is a social ethos of freedom exercised for the sake of the other: "Let us then pursue what makes for peace and for mutual up-building" (Rom 14:19; see also Gal 5:13).

Second, then, while the Christian community is to embrace great diversity in backgrounds, gifts, and practices, it also is to develop a capacity for group decision-making grounded in the self-giving love of Christ. Paul's goal is the formation of shared moral agency through the interpersonal bonds of love in the body of Christ.[11] The theme of mutual discernment grounded in love runs through 1 Corinthians, as Paul exhorts his fractious congregations to grow up into maturity in

[11] See Margaret M. Mitchell, *Paul and the Rhetoric of Reconciliation: An Exegetical Investigation of the Language and Composition of 1 Corinthians* (Louisville, KY: Westminster John Knox, 1991), 168–169.

Christ: "Brothers and sisters, do not be children in your thinking; be babes in evil, but in your thinking be mature" (1 Cor 14:20). He repeatedly warns the Corinthians against a kind of knowledge or cognition that "puffs up" (1 Cor 8:1), which is the domain of those who are "puffed up in favor of one against another" (1 Cor 4:6). Such presumed knowledge is an expression of arrogance, sometimes disguised as a kind of pseudo-spirituality (1 Cor 4:18–19; 5:2). The problem with such knowledge is that it is ignorant of the needs of others in the fellowship, concerned only with self-aggrandizement. That is why Paul contrasts it with love that "builds up" by seeking the good of the other, and of the community as a whole (1 Cor 8:1–2). And how can the Corinthians practice such discernment and love if they do not have the kind of interpersonal knowledge necessary for discerning what their brothers and sisters need –that is, if they do not know their neighbor? Paul is describing and seeking to inculcate in his listeners a kind of mutual discernment that arises out of attentive, loving attunement to one another: "Make love your aim" is, in effect, what he tells the Corinthians. This love is not in alignment with worldly wisdom but with the wisdom of the cross, which leads to an ethic of interpersonal knowledge and attunement to the work of God in one another. Rather than setting down formulaic guidelines for behavior, Paul thinks God is transforming fellowships of believers into communities of shared moral agency – a moral agency that is both grounded in Christ's other-regarding love and sourced continually by the movement of the Spirit in their midst.

Third, Paul thinks God is not yet finished with the church or its members, and neither the church nor its members have arrived at perfection. To the contrary, "Now we see in a mirror dimly, but then face to face. Now I know in part; then I shall understand fully, even as I have been fully understood" (1 Cor 13:12). Paul hopes to attain the resurrection of the dead, but he adds, "Not that I have already obtained this or am already perfect; but I press on to make it my own, because Christ Jesus has made me his own" (Phil 3:12). In each case, Paul articulates both present limitation and a future hope of full understanding and completion, grounded in what God already has done. God, that is, is setting God's people on the way to triumph, to a victory already accomplished in Christ. But this future hope accompanies a present realism about the failures of the community of faith. The church is not yet complete, its doors must be open to the stranger, and its imagination must be open to a future yet to arrive. Such eschatological reservation generates a kind of epistemic humility in the present alongside a glorious vision of the future. What does Paul think God is doing in Christian communities? More than we can ask or imagine (2 Cor 4:17)!

Believers learn patience as they wait for God's full redemption of themselves, their neighbors, and the world. Such patience is not passivity, but recognition of the limitations of their own perception and transformation, and of the imaginative shortcomings of every manifestation of the church. It is also a frank acknowledgement that the status quo is far from the revelation of God's glory and grace. So he writes in Romans:

> For I consider that the sufferings of this present time are not worth comparing with the glory that is to be revealed (*apokaluphthēnai*) to us. For the creation waits with eager longing for the apocalypse of the sons of God .... We know that the whole creation has been groaning in labor pains until now; and not only the creation, but we ourselves, who have the first fruits of the Spirit, groan inwardly as we wait for adoption as sons, the redemption of our body. For in this hope we were saved. Now hope that is seen is not hope. For who hopes for what he sees? But if we hope for what we do not see, we wait for it with patience. (Rom 8:18–19, 22–25)

The final in-breaking of God's glory is still in the future. In the meantime, both all creation and the community indwelt by the Spirit long for full redemption, with a hope for what is not yet seen. God is teaching the church humility and hope, and along with that, patient solidarity with a suffering world.

Such solidarity and shared hope is striking, running precisely counter to some eschatological visions in which the righteous are snatched out the world, leaving the rest of humanity and the environment to judgment and destruction. For Paul, however, just as the well-being of individual believers cannot be separated from the health of the whole community (1 Cor 12:26), so also the well-being and ultimate salvation of the church cannot be separated from the redemption of all creation. But naming such a hope, along with the fact that it is not yet seen, also names the present dire straits of the creation, including all humanity. In light of this disjunction between present status quo and final hope, the church's witness includes solidarity with human longing, and the expression of the pain of an unredeemed world.[12] In this sense, as in

[12] Ernst Käsemann, "The Cry for Liberty in the Worship of the Church," in *Perspectives on Paul*, trans. M. Kohl (Mifflintown, PA: Sigler, 1996 [1969]), 122–137.

others, the church's witness extends beyond the boundaries of the community, just as Christ's action broke through all boundaries between God and humanity.

Paul comes to this understanding of God's redemptive activity through his own experience of Christ's presence in the midst of suffering. His display of Christ's victory over sin and death is counter-intuitive, to say the least. Yes, he cries out, "Thanks be to God, who in Christ always leads us in triumph, and through us spreads the fragrance of the knowledge of him everywhere" (2 Cor 2:14). But the image is of a public victory parade accompanied by incense, leading prisoners of war destined for execution. Elsewhere Paul uses similar imagery describing himself and his fellow missionaries as the spoils of war, or as criminals condemned to death in the arena: "For I think that God has exhibited us apostles as last of all, like those sentenced to death; because we have become a spectacle (*theatron*) to the world, to angels, and to human beings" (1 Cor 4:9). The word translated "spectacle" implies "a place of seeing." Paul and his fellow missionaries are the place where the world, angels, and other people "see" Christ, and what they see is Christ on the cross. This paradoxical witness threads throughout Paul's letters. On the one hand, "it is the God who said, 'Let light shine out of darkness,' who has shone in our hearts to give the light of the knowledge of the glory of God in the face of Christ" (2 Cor 4:6). On the other hand, "we have this treasure in earthen vessels . . . always carrying in the body the death of Jesus, so that the life of Jesus may also be manifested in our bodies" (2 Cor 4:7, 10). Paul sees his own tortured body as a billboard for Jesus, a public manifestation of the Lord who loves to the death. Again, this is an ethic of solidarity, enacting God's union with suffering creation, and witnessing thereby to God's boundary-crossing love for all humanity.

Fourth, Paul expects Christian fellowship to be shaped in material, monetary ways by Christ's participation in the regime of human destitution and injustice: "For you know the grace (gift) of our Lord Jesus Christ, that though he was rich, yet for your sake he made himself poor, that by his poverty you might become rich" (2 Cor 8:9). It would be a mistake to read "made himself poor" simply as a metaphor for spiritual lack; Jesus of Nazareth was poor, homeless, and outcast, and Paul (himself homeless and outcast) surely knew this. The Lord who took the form of a slave (Phil 2:7), and impoverished himself on behalf of destitute humanity (2 Cor 8:9), cannot very well be proclaimed by believers who hoard their possessions and ignore their neighbors in need.

2 Corinthians 8–9 comprises two "sermons" in which Paul encourages the Corinthians to make good on their promise to contribute to the collection of funds for the destitute saints in Jerusalem.[13] In these chapters we find Paul's fullest exposition of this very practical matter – the fair distribution of resources so that no part of the church is in need. As is typical of Paul, he bases his instructions on the prior gift of God in Christ, and he gives a practical human example. Here, he describes the churches of Macedonia, whose "abundance of joy and extreme poverty overflowed in a wealth of liberality" (2 Cor 8:1–2), which in turn was a spillover from their self-giving "to the Lord and to us" (8:5). The three-way relational bond between the Lord, the Macedonians, and Paul and his fellow missionaries, catalyzes and guides their generosity, so that both givers and receivers are, in effect, recipients of the overflowing grace of God.

The goal of such giving is not impoverishment of the giver, but a reciprocal exchange of resources over time, "so that there may be equity" (*isotēs*)" (2 Cor 8:14). The theme of divine generosity and abundance flows through both chapters, as the gift results in thanksgiving to God, and in prayers on behalf of the givers, who in turn may become receivers. The way Paul describes such generosity is noteworthy: "Through the testing of this ministry you glorify God by your obedience to the confession of the gospel of Christ, and by the generosity of your sharing (*koinōnias*) with them and with all others" (2 Cor 9:13). This is a present, concrete manifestation of God's glory, through joyful sharing of material possessions. Such sharing is a matter of obedience to the confession of the gospel, precisely because it mirrors the generosity of Christ and thereby witnesses to the truth of the gospel. That is, it is a way of life that publicly confesses the good news of Christ. More than a financial transaction, it a matter of fellowship, indeed mutual participation in Christ, yet such generous sharing extends not only to the intended recipients in Jerusalem, but to "all." The economics of Christian communities are, in Paul's view, manifestations of the divine economy, which is one of overwhelming abundance and therefore confident liberality. Paul's immediate concern is the contribution for the saints in Jerusalem, but the ethics of abundance potentially overflows beyond the bounds of the community of faith. In this, too, Paul sees God transforming both givers and receivers, who indeed exchange places in a

[13] See Bruce W. Longenecker, *Remember the Poor: Paul, Poverty, and the Greco–Roman World* (Grand Rapids, MI: Eerdmans, 2010); Robert Moses, "Discerning the Body of Christ: Paul, Poverty, and the Powers," *Journal for the Study of the New Testament* 40, no. 4 (2018): 473–493.

fluid expression of God's destabilizing grace. But he also sees a witness to the self-giving of Christ on behalf of "all" – not just present believers, but all humanity.

CONCLUSION

For Paul, the social ethos of Christian communities grows directly out of Christ's movement into the sphere of sin and death, there to rescue derelict humanity through the radical solidarity of the cross and the power of the resurrection. This movement reverses hierarchies and destabilizes social norms, in visible, counterintuitive ways: the inclusion of socially incompatible members, the redistribution of resources, solidarity with all humanity in its most desperate cry for liberation, and the creation of a fellowship in which diverse people with divergent backgrounds and different gifts grow together into moral agents shaped by Christ's self-giving love.

Further Reading

Barclay, John M. G. *Paul and the Gift*. Grand Rapids, MI: Eerdmans, 2015.

Eastman, Susan Grove. *Paul and the Person: Reframing Paul's Anthropology*. Grand Rapids, MI: Eerdmans, 2017.

Fowl, Stephen E. *Philippians*. Grand Rapids, MI: Eerdmans, 2005.

Hellerman, Joseph H. *The Ancient Church as Family*. Minneapolis, MN: Fortress Press, 2001.

Hooker, Morna. "Interchange in Christ." *Journal of Theological Studies*, 32, no. 2 (1971): 349–361.

Käsemann, Ernst. "On Paul's Anthropology." In *Perspectives on Paul*. Translated by J. Kohl, 1–31. Mifflintown, PA: Sigler, 1996 (1969).

Käsemann, Ernst. "The Cry for Liberty in the Worship of the Church." In *Perspectives on Paul*. Translated by M. Kohl, 122–137. Mifflintown, PA: Sigler, 1996 (1969).

Longenecker, Bruce W. *Remember the Poor: Paul, Poverty, and the Greco-Roman World*. Grand Rapids, MI: Eerdmans, 2010.

Migliore, Daniel. *Philippians and Philemon*. Louisville, KY: Westminster John Knox, 2014.

Mitchell, Margaret M. *Paul and the Rhetoric of Reconciliation: An Exegetical Investigation of the Language and Composition of 1 Corinthians*. Louisville, KY: Westminster John Knox, 1991.

Moses, Robert. "Discerning the Body of Christ: Paul, Poverty, and the Powers." *Journal for the Study of the New Testament* 40, no. 4 (2018): 473–493.

Tannehill, Robert. "Participation in Christ: A Central Theme in Pauline Soteriology." In *The Shape of the Gospel: New Testament Essays*, 223–227. Eugene, OR: Cascade, 2007.

12 How Did Paul Read Scripture?

DAVID LINCICUM

Approaching Paul's letters for the first time, one might naturally be concerned with coming to grips with Paul as an author, a writer of pastoral and theological missives. But close attention to his activity as a writer inevitably leads to a distinct but related observation: that Paul is not simply an author creatively pulling his ideas out of thin air, or even from oral tradition, but rather that his letters give profound evidence of his activity as a *reader*. He constantly points back to predecessor texts, appealing to their authority to ground or illustrate his claims. And those texts are not drawn willy-nilly from a wide selection of ancient literature, from, say, Homer to Cicero, but rather come overwhelmingly, with only minor exceptions, from the ancient library of Jewish scriptures.[1]

Why does the self-described Apostle to the gentiles (Rom 11:13) make constant recourse to the sacred texts of Israel? If Paul is fairly described as a reader of scripture, what kind of reader might he be? And why does he refrain from explicitly citing scripture in some of his letters altogether? To answer those questions fully one would need to offer an account of virtually the entirety of Pauline thought. This essay does not attempt that grand synthesis, but rather offers an introductory account of Paul's reading of scripture and of some of the questions his reading poses for our attempts to understand the apostle's corpus today.

SCRIPTURAL SOURCES AND CITATION TECHNIQUE

By Paul's own testimony, he was "a Hebrew born of Hebrews" (Phil 3:5) who was "zealous for the traditions of [his] ancestors" (Gal 1:14). This zeal certainly contributed to his deep knowledge of the scriptural traditions of Israel. The precise contours of Paul's own education remain

[1] Exception: 1 Cor 15:33 (Menander); cf. also Titus 1:12 (Epimenides) and the citation of Aratus in Paul's Areopagus speech in Acts (17:28).

hazy at important points, but whether he undertook his primary education in Tarsus or in Jerusalem, he clearly developed an intimate acquaintance with Israel's scriptures in their Greek form, habituated no doubt through long years of liturgical exposure and study.

It is important to guard against anachronism at this point. While scholars sometimes imprecisely speak of Paul's "Bible,"[2] there was no single book that contained all the authoritative scriptural traditions of Israel in Paul's day. Not only was such a feat technologically impossible before the invention and diffusion of the codex,[3] but it might also require a universal, or at least widespread, agreement as to which books counted as scripture – that is, agreement regarding a closed canon. Such a fixed canon does not seem to have predominated in Paul's day (as the evidence of the Dead Sea Scrolls from Qumran suggests), even if there was broad agreement about the scriptural status of many of the scriptural texts. Rather than thinking of a closely bounded Bible or its virtual equivalent, it does better justice to the historical evidence to imagine Paul (like other Jews of his day) accessing a collection of scrolls containing authoritative scriptural texts. There was widespread agreement among Jews about the status and importance of the Pentateuch (Genesis through Deuteronomy), and only slightly less agreement about the prophets and some of the writings (in particular, the Psalms). We can detect no anxiety in Paul's letters about the extent of the canon, but the distributions and frequency of his citations of texts are fairly standard for Jewish practices of his day. Although the numbers vary slightly depending on the criteria by which one distinguishes a citation, Paul (like some of his Jewish contemporaries) seems to have favored Isaiah, Psalms, Genesis, and Deuteronomy.[4]

Close comparison of Paul's quotations with modern editions of the Hebrew Bible and the Septuagint (the Hebrew Bible in Greek translation) indicates that, on the whole, Paul draws his citations from

[2] Note the classic study by Otto Michel, *Paulus und seine Bibel* (Darmstadt: Wissenschaftliche Buchgesellschaft, 1972 [1929]).

[3] See, among others, L. Hurtado and C. Keith, "Writing and Book Production in the Hellenistic and Roman Periods," in *The New Cambridge History of the Bible, Volume 1: From the Beginnings to 600*, eds. James Carleton Paget and Joachim Schaper (Cambridge: Cambridge University Press, 2013), 63–80; H. Y. Gamble, *Books and Readers in the Early Church: A History of Early Christian Texts* (New Haven, CT: Yale University Press, 1995), 42–81, 264–279.

[4] George J. Brooke, "'The Canon within the Canon' at Qumran and in the New Testament," in *The Scrolls and the Scriptures: Qumran Fifty Years After*, eds. Stanley E. Porter and Craig A. Evans (Sheffield: Sheffield Academic Press, 1997), 242–266.

Septuagintal texts (though even those texts are often not identical to the initial text of the Greek Old Testament as modern critical editions reconstruct it). What explains this variation? An answer to this puzzle must be sought in two places: first, in the state of the Septuagint's text in Paul's day, and second, in Paul's own citation technique.

We can deduce (from the apologetic *Letter of Aristeas* and other evidence) that after the Pentateuch was initially translated into Greek, certain detractors immediately began to criticize the translation and improve upon it. These alterations would eventually culminate in the three revisions to the Septuagint – we know these as the work of Aquila, Symmachus, and Theodotion. The discovery of the Dead Sea Scrolls proved decisively that this process of revision was well under way by the first century BCE.[5] These revisions often involved "hebraizing" the translation – that is, attempting to ensure the Greek text adheres more closely to the Hebrew original.[6]

If we carefully analyze the textual form of Paul's quotations, we see that on the whole his citations are drawn from texts that are distinctively Septuagintal in nature. Several of Paul's citations seem to come from Septuagintal texts that show some degree of revision. For example, in 1 Cor 15:54 Paul cites Isa 25:8: "death has been swallowed up in victory." This citation deviates from both the Hebrew and the original Greek of Isaiah, but agrees precisely with a rendering that the Theodotionic revision later adopts. Paul seems to have drawn on a contemporary tradition of revision that eventually became formalized in Theodotion. In other words, Paul often cited Greek texts as they circulated in his day.

The second major source of textual variation is Paul's own citation technique. We must remember that Paul is not writing studied philological treatises with an emphasis on precision and exactitude, with fully lemmatized citations that are only subsequently analyzed in detached commentary. Rather, he is quoting scripture *in scribendo*, on his way to making a point, and so he needs to contextualize his

[5] This is illustrated particularly well in texts like the Greek Minor Prophets scroll from Naḥal Ḥever (8ḤevXIIgr). Note the classic study by Dominique Barthélemy, *Devancies d'Aquila: Première publication intégrale du texte des fragments du Dodécaprophéton* (Leiden: Brill, 1963); for the edition of 8ḤevXIIgr, see Emanuel Tov, Robert A. Kraft, and P. J. Parsons, *The Greek Minor Prophets Scroll from Naḥal Ḥever (8ḤevXIIgr)* (Oxford: Clarendon, 1989).

[6] See the helpful treatment in Natalio Fernández Marcos, *The Septuagint in Context: Introduction to the Greek Versions of the Bible*, trans. Wilfred G. E. Watson (Leiden: Brill, 2001).

quotations to fit their epistolary context. This may at times appear to the modern reader as a certain freedom or looseness in his citations, but this is only to be expected. At times he omits introductory particles, employs a limited selection from a verse, changes the word order, alters grammatical features, substitutes words or phrases, or adds to the text.[7] Moreover, it would be an anachronism to imagine Paul owning his own Bible, which would entail carting around the Mediterranean an unwieldy and expensive basket of scrolls from which to cite (although the author of 2 Timothy does imagine Paul requesting "the books, and above all the parchments," [4:13], which might refer to rolls of scripture). Paul thus probably had recourse to citations from memory,[8] and may well also have kept a set of notes with choice scriptural quotations to employ in his argument, which may go some way toward understanding the types of variation we see in his citations.

DESCRIBING PAUL'S SCRIPTURAL ENGAGEMENT

Paul's letters are replete with scriptural reminiscences, but not all of these can be accurately characterized as citations. Rather, Paul (like most authors who repay careful study) has used a variety of intertextual techniques to weave in references to predecessor texts. These range across a sliding scale of explicitness, and have been described with a bewildering array of terminology.[9] If we imagine these references laid out along a spectrum, at one end are verbatim quotations of scripture that are marked for the reader by an introductory formula, such as "It is written" or "For Moses says."[10] At the other end are echoes of scriptural

[7] For a careful study that isolates such adaptations systematically, see Christopher D. Stanley, *Paul and the Language of Scripture: Citation Technique in the Pauline Epistles and Contemporary Literature* (Cambridge: Cambridge University Press, 1992).

[8] See the argument in D. Lincicum, "Intertextuality, Effective History, and Memory: Conceptualizing Paul's Use of Scripture," in *Paulinische Schriftrezeption: Grundlagen – Ausprägungen – Wirkungen – Wertungen*, eds. Florian Wilk and Markus Öhler (Göttingen: Vandenhoeck & Ruprecht, 2017), 9–22.

[9] Cf. Stanley E. Porter, "Pauline Techniques of Interweaving Scripture into His Letters," in *Paulinische Schriftrezeption*, eds. Florian Wilk and Markus Öhler (Göttingen: Vandenhoeck & Ruprecht, 2017), 23–55; Porter, "The Use of the Old Testament in the New: A Brief Comment on Method and Terminology," in *Early Christian Interpretation of the Scriptures of Israel: Investigations and Proposals*, eds. C. A. Evans and J. A. Sanders (Sheffield: Sheffield Academic Press, 1997), 79–96.

[10] On citation formulae, see Dietrich-Alex Koch, *Die Schrift als Zeuge des Evangeliums: Untersuchungen zur Verwendung und zum Verständnis der Schrift bei Paulus*, BHT 69 (Tübingen: Mohr Siebeck, 1986), 25–32.

texts, and it is not always possible to decide whether Paul intended the echo or whether it simply slipped in as an unconscious reflection of one who had long soaked in Israel's scriptural traditions. Between these two poles we find unmarked citations and intentional allusions. The former are verbatim repetitions of substantial predecessor texts but without any quotation formula to signal to the reader that a predecessor text has been quoted. The latter are briefer but significant recollections of scripture that bear some assertorial weight in context. We also find Paul referring to narratives or concepts derived from scripture, even if not always in the form of an identifiable allusion to a particular text. Naturally it is not always possible or necessary to distinguish among these various categories, even if paying some attention to them helps us to grasp the range of Paul's scriptural engagements.

In his groundbreaking book, *Echoes of Scripture in the Letters of Paul* (1989), Richard Hays roused Pauline scholars from their literary slumber and introduced them to the rich benefits of paying careful attention to the ways in which allusions can draw into the text something of the original context of the predecessor text.[11] As Hays put it (drawing on the sensibilities of John Hollander and others), echoes can activate the metaleptically suppressed original and resound in the cave of resonant signification, creating a complex poetics of intertextual significance for the reader who can appreciate the subtlety of "the hermeneutical event." For example, in Paul's letter to the Philippians, he urges them to "Do all things without murmuring and arguing, so that you may be blameless and innocent, children of God without blemish in the midst of a crooked and perverse generation, in which you shine like stars in the world" (2:14–15). The descriptive phrase, "a crooked and perverse generation", echoes Deut 32:4–5:

> God – his works are genuine,
> And all his ways are justice.
> A faithful god, and there is no injustice,
> A righteous and holy Lord;
> Blemished children, not his, have sinned,
> A generation, crooked and perverse.
> (NETS)

Deuteronomy 32, which Paul cites numerous times throughout his letters, tells a story about God's people rebelling and growing faithless,

[11] Richard B. Hays, *Echoes of Scripture in the Letters of Paul* (New Haven, CT: Yale University Press, 1989).

before being restored by God's showing of favor to a foreign people. In Romans, Paul seems to read this as a prophetic foretelling of God's intention to provoke Israel to jealousy by showing favor to the gentiles (more on this below). Does Paul's allusion here indicate that he wants the gentile Philippians to bear witness to an Israel that has become "crooked and perverse"? Or is it simply a turn of phrase that can be adroitly adapted to speak of the "pagan" world more broadly? In the nature of the case, it is difficult to make an argument with certainty, but the intertextual sensibilities Hays's book has inculcated in scholarship have sparked questions like this for a generation of readers, and sensitivity to such allusions heightens the reader's appreciation for Paul's literary achievements.

The invocation of a concept like "intertextuality" might, however, offer some readers pause. Initially stemming from the literary critic Julia Kristeva and post-structuralist literary circles in the 1960s, intertextuality was originally not a method of reading per se, but rather a theory about the nature of language as such.[12] The domestication of a theory into a method (a knack for which biblical scholarship has become well-known) might entail risks of distortion. In particular, for those with some concern to grasp Paul's meaning within the horizon of the first century, one might wonder whether a method that considers the interplay between two texts in a direct sense (Paul's letter and the scriptural text to which he cites or alludes) could lead to an unintentional collapsing of the distance between the original scripture and Paul's own day. But of course, that distance between Paul and the scriptural text was peopled with other interpreters who also read, say, Genesis or Isaiah or Psalms, and so helped to fashion a trajectory of interpretation through which Paul approaches the text. Paul might accede to or resist this trajectory, but without some grasp of the long history of reading scripture that the Second Temple literature preserves for us, do we risk the possibility of distorting what is either novel or commonplace in the apostle's interpretation of scripture? Is Paul's way of reading scripture comparable to other Jewish reading strategies in antiquity, or is he somehow unique?[13] Questions like these about the most productive

[12] For a helpful introduction to these issues, see John Barton, "Déjà Lu: Intertextuality, Method or Theory?" in *Reading Job Intertextually*, eds. Katharine Dell and Will Kynes (London: Bloomsbury, 2013), 1–16.

[13] For the argument that Paul does make good sense in the spectrum of Second Temple biblical interpretation, see D. Lincicum, *Paul and the Early Jewish Encounter with Deuteronomy* (Tübingen: Mohr Siebeck, 2010; repr., Grand Rapids, MI: Baker Academic, 2013).

sensibilities for understanding Paul's engagement with scripture will no doubt continue to animate scholarship.

PAUL AS A READER OF SCRIPTURE

If we turn now to consider Paul's letters as a record of his reading, what do we find? The apostle's letters do not intend to offer a disinterested commentary on scripture that attempts to respect the historical distance between the original text and Paul's contemporary situation. Rather, Paul operates under the profound conviction that "whatever was written in former days was written for our instruction" (Rom 15:4) and that the events in scripture "were written down to instruct us, on whom the ends of the ages have come" (1 Cor 10:11).[14] This conviction imbues his scriptural interpretation with a tone of immediacy. Coupled with a deep certainty that whatever scripture says God also says (cf. Rom 9:17; Gal 3:8), this sense of scriptural immediacy enables Paul to bring scripture to bear on a broad array of theological, ethical, and practical questions in his foundling communities. In the givenness of the scriptural texts (expressed most tersely in Paul's invocation of what "is written," *gegraptai*), Paul finds a pluripotent fund on which to draw for his varied purposes. We see this in play as Paul invokes the concept of "accordance": just as God has acted for Israel in her past and this action has been memorialized in her scripture, so also in the history of Jesus we find a pattern of God's action that "accords" with scripture. Paul surprisingly suggests, perhaps following early Christian tradition, that even the death of Christ for sin and his resurrection on the third day happened with such accordance (1 Cor 15:3–4).

All of this indicates that Paul operates with a contemporizing sense of scripture as divine address to the present. As Paul says when he reflects on Deut 25:4: "Is it for oxen that God is concerned? Or does he not speak entirely for our sake?" (1 Cor 9:9–10; cf. Rom 4:23–24). In certain respects, Paul preaches a radical novelty – a message about a crucified Messiah that confounds the wisdom of the world. But even as he presents his gospel as being "apart from the law," in the same breath he alleges it is "attested by the law and the prophets" (Rom 3:21). Thus, a certain productive tension exists in Paul's understanding of history. On the one hand, he can read the long history of Israel as a story of

[14] Cf. Koch, *Die Schrift als Zeuge des Evangeliums*, 322–353.

preparation for the Messiah's coming, full of foreshadowing, promise, and expectation. At other times, he can place stress on the unexpected nature of the proclamation, its character as a disruption or invasion of history-as-routine. Scripture can be marshalled to serve either end, and this suggests that for the apostle, scripture and gospel are mutually interpretive.

Paul's letters, moreover, attest the fundamental importance of narratives in Paul's theological vision. Intriguingly, Paul does not pause to insert clarifying comments: "Adam, who, as you might not know, is the first-formed of all God's created people," or "Now David was an important king of Israel about whom you should know." Rather, he assumes the basic contours of the major structuring narratives of Israel's history: the creation account, the Abraham story, the exodus, the Sinai covenant. This may indicate that Paul took such knowledge for granted because he had taught these stories to those communities he had founded, or, in the case of the letter to the Romans, assumed that the early Christ-followers would have been catechized along such lines.[15] Scripture's narrative quality seeps into Paul's own vision, and he orients his basic thinking by means of Israel's founding stories.

But if the narratives are foundational for Paul's vision, it is to the prophets that he turns again and again (and above all to Isaiah) to make sense of the mission to the gentiles and his own vocation as an apostle.[16] In Isaiah's call to preach to a hardened Israel, Paul finds foreshadowed his own apostolic imperative to hold out the gospel to his contemporary coreligionists, many of whom did not receive it. In fact, much of Paul's explicit engagement with scripture (above all in Romans and Galatians) could be subsumed under the rubric of reflection on and defense of the gentile mission.

[15] For an attempt at a large-scale reconstruction of Paul's narrative sensibilities, see Francis Watson, *Paul and the Hermeneutics of Faith*, 2nd ed. (London: T&T Clark, 2015); and note the important essays in Bruce W. Longenecker, ed., *Narrative Dynamics in Paul: A Critical Assessment* (Louisville, KY: Westminster John Knox, 2002).

[16] For Paul's reading of Isaiah, see Shiu-Lun Shum, *Paul's Use of Isaiah in Romans: A Comparative Study of Paul's Letter to the Romans and the Sibylline and Qumran Sectarian Texts* (Tübingen: Mohr Siebeck, 2002); J. Ross Wagner, *Heralds of the Good News: Isaiah and Paul in Concert in the Letter to the Romans* (Leiden: Brill, 2002); Florian Wilk, *Die Bedeutung des Jesajabuches für Paulus* (Göttingen: Vandenhoeck & Ruprecht, 1998); for the minor prophets, see Barbara Fuß, *"Dies ist die Zeit, von der geschrieben ist ..." Die expliziten Zitate aus dem Buch Hosea in den Handschriften von Qumran und im Neuen Testament* (Münster: Aschendorff, 2000), esp. 156–192.

Roughly 25 percent of all quotations in the *corpus Paulinum* are clustered in Romans 9–11, and accordingly it is worth examining this section in a bit more detail, since it allows us to see Paul's scriptural sensibilities in action. In light of tensions in the Roman churches between Jewish and gentile Christians, and in order to address a potentially defeating objection to faith in the fidelity of God, Paul offers an intensive engagement with the scriptures of Israel as he advances his argument. In 9:1–5, Paul enumerates the advantages Israel has historically enjoyed, and laments the lack of response among contemporary Jews to his message. This leads to the posing of a question about the fidelity of God to his word: has God revoked his election, and so made false promises in scripture? No, Paul replies, "it is not as though the word of God had failed" (9:6). Paul then re-reads the Pentateuchal narratives to discover a pattern of election by which only some from Israel are in fact Israel: Isaac is preferred over Ishmael, Jacob over Esau. The reversal of primogeniture authorizes Paul to make a generalizing deduction about God's electing activity, which he confirms by appealing to the example of God's raising up of Pharaoh to serve the purposes of his own glory. Paul goes on to find in Hosea's rhetoric of reversal a precedent for including the gentiles in the bounds of the people of God: "those who were not my people I will call my people." At the same time, Paul sees in Isaiah a remnant theology that also helps to make sense of the weak response to his message. All this is the first major movement in his argument, in 9:6–29.

A second major movement in Paul's argument turns from God's election to Israel's responsibility (9:30–10:21). Israel has stumbled on Isaiah's stone (9:33), since they sought to establish their own righteousness, according to Paul, rather than pursuing the righteousness from faith that comes by the Messiah. Rather than conceding that Israel has an excuse for not believing that Jesus is God's promised agent, Paul marshals a series of scriptural witnesses to accuse Israel of having clear access to the message of the gospel but failing to believe. The second movement, then, is accusation, supported by scriptural witnesses. Third, Paul poses the logical question: "Has God rejected his people?" (11:1). The answer in reply is emphatic: By no means! Paul first appeals to the presence of a remnant, grounding his appeal in the example of the seven thousand righteous ones in Elijah's day. But then he goes beyond this to argue from especially Isaiah, Psalms, and Deuteronomy, that God had partially hardened Israel in order to show favor to the gentiles, but this favor, in turn, was calculated to provoke Israel to jealousy and so ultimately to salvation – all Israel being saved once the full number of gentiles has come in. Arguably the language of provocation to jealousy is rooted in Deut 32:21 (cited in 10:19) and the broader context of the Song of Moses, which Paul conceives of as a "mystery" – that is, a hidden truth that God's eschatological action has brought to light. This mystery ultimately pertains to the salvation of both Jew and gentile, and so to the fulfilment of Paul's apostolic vocation.

Thus, in these three dense, quotation-laden chapters, Paul evinces a deep and wide-ranging reading of scripture in pursuit of a solution to the vexing problem of Jewish unbelief. The scriptural material is addressed to the specific situation of the Christian audience in Rome by means of Paul's exhortation that gentiles should not boast over the stumbling of the Jews (cf. 11:20). But the response is much more than sufficient to answer a niggling problem in Rome, and indeed gives us our fullest picture of Paul's scriptural imagination at work. Throughout, Paul weaves quotation, allusion, and analysis with his own argumentation, offering eloquent testimony to the ways in which every word of scripture can resource the urgent task of Paul's missionary endeavors.[17]

The engagement with scripture is most intensive in Paul's letters to the Galatians and to the Romans – precisely where we might imagine it would be, as he wrestles with the terms of the gentile mission and the boundaries of the covenant. But paying careful attention to Paul's aims in citing scripture also sheds some light on those places where he refrains from citing it. Calling attention to the relative paucity of scripture in the Pauline letters beyond the *Hauptbriefe* (or "main letters" of Paul), Adolf von Harnack famously suggested that Paul himself turned to scripture as a source of "edifying power," but that he "did not give the Old Testament to the young churches as the book of Christian sources for edification."[18] This striking judgment is usefully provocative, but most interpreters of Paul have rather preferred to see Paul's relative reticence to introduce quotations of scripture in his shorter letters as due to the pressing questions he adjudicates and the epistolary constraints of brevity and focus. After all, even if these shorter letters do

[17] Indeed, sometimes, it must be admitted, Paul's appeals to scripture are downright alarming. For example, in the context of Romans 9–11, Paul seems to juxtapose Lev 18:5 with Deut 30:11–14, and to do so to Leviticus's detriment; see further Preston Sprinkle, *Law and Life: The Interpretation of Leviticus 18:5 in Early Judaism and Paul* (Tübingen: Mohr Siebeck, 2008).

[18] Adolf von Harnack, "The Old Testament in the Pauline Letters and in the Pauline Churches," in *Understanding Paul's Ethics: Twentieth Century Approaches*, ed. Brian Rosner (Grand Rapids, MI: Eerdmans, 1995), 28, 44 (this essay originally appeared in 1928 in German).

not contain the same density of quotation, they are full of allusion and scriptural turns of phrase, not to mention basic concepts that came to Paul by means of a reading of scripture.

It would, moreover, be possible to point to a certain process of "scripturalization" in the deutero-Pauline tradition. If one were to compare Colossians and Ephesians in detail, and argue, with the majority of Pauline interpreters, for the use of Colossians as a literary source by the author of Ephesians, then one of the most significant changes that Ephesians has introduced to its Colossian *Vorlage* is the introduction of explicit scriptural citations and implicit allusions. Or again, the Pastoral Epistles do not feature citations of scripture prominently, but where scripture is cited it seems to be largely "lifted" from the undisputed Pauline epistles, even as the author reflects on the nature of scripture more programmatically than Paul does in his own letters: "All scripture is inspired by God and is useful for teaching, for reproof, for correction, and for training in righteousness" (2 Tim 3:16).[19] This statement could be read without difficulty as a synthetic judgment about the nature of the scriptures arrived at by careful reflection on how the apostle himself had put them to use in his letters.

HOW TO DO THINGS WITH SCRIPTURE

Those interested in reconstructing Paul's own reading of scripture from the evidence of his letters quickly come up against a complication: we do not have a raw, unprocessed record of the apostle's engagement with scripture, but rather a highly rhetorical series of quotations and allusions designed to elicit some response from his audience. We see Paul citing his ancestral texts on the way toward some other point. He is attempting, for example, to dissuade the gentile Galatian churches not to adopt Jewish ritual practices, while at the same time outmaneuvering rival teachers and their arguments for the necessity of adopting those very practices. Or again, he is constructing an account of the enduring election of Israel that is directed to the practical problem of gentile boasting in Rome. Precisely because the extant literary output that survives from Paul is a corpus of letters that are "situational" in nature, every engagement with scripture bears the marks of specific rhetorical purposes occasioned by problems or concerns that arose in local communities.

[19] See Gerd Häfner, *'Nützlich zur Belehrung' (2 Tim 3,16): Die Rolle der Schrift in den Pastoralbriefen im Rahmen der Paulusrezeption* (Freiburg: Herder, 2000).

This is not to say that Paul's reading of scripture is *merely* rhetorical, as though he were somehow dishonestly representing his views or crassly attempting to associate his own advice with God's voice for the purpose of exercising power.[20] But it is the case that any adequate grasp of Paul's engagement with scripture will have to pay careful attention to the ways in which he marshals it for effect.[21] Paul's own rhetorical purposes vary, and thus the interpreter will need to attend to the particular epistolary context into which each quotation is placed, rather than focusing exclusively on the context of the cited original. Given that the scriptures are charged with authority, to appeal to them is to draw on that authority, and so in some sense to join one's own discourse to the discourse of God.

We see this sensibility in action as Paul allows the words of scripture to do the talking for him. For example, in Galatians 4 Paul constructs an elaborate allegory about Abraham's two sons, Isaac and Ishmael. Isaac is the son of a free woman and stands, in Paul's reading, for the promise, while Ishmael is the son of a slave woman, Hagar, who corresponds to the Sinai covenant (4:21–31). At the end of Paul's subtle and complex set of identifications (which the Galatians themselves may or may not have been able to follow), Paul underscores the practical outcome of his exposition by asking: "what does the scripture say?" The answer allows scripture to urge what Paul himself wants: "Drive out the slave woman and her child; for the child of the slave will not share the inheritance with the child of the free woman" (4:30). Paul wants the Galatians to expel the judaizing agitators, and he employs scripture rhetorically to make the point for him.

Paul makes a very similar move in 1 Corinthians 5. After detailing his concerns that the community in Corinth is harboring a man living with the wife of his father, Paul argues from multiple sources that such action should not be condoned. But his practical urging comes to a head with a citation of a line repeated in Deuteronomy: "Drive out the wicked person from among you" (1 Cor 5:13; cf. Deut 13:5; 17:7; 19:19, etc.). Rather than relying on his own authority, Paul invokes the command of scripture to persuade the community in Corinth to act.

20 But cf. Christopher D. Stanley's *Arguing with Scripture: The Rhetoric of Quotations in the Letters of Paul* (London: T&T Clark, 2004).

21 See recently Katja Kujanpää, "From Eloquence to Evading Responsibility: The Rhetorical Functions of Quotations in Paul's Argumentation," *Journal of Biblical Literature* 136 (2017): 185–202; Kujanpää, *The Rhetorical Functions of Scriptural Quotations in Romans* (Leiden: Brill, 2019).

CONCLUSION

It is instructive to step back and imagine Paul's letters denuded of their scriptural citations and allusions (as perhaps someone inspired by Marcion, a second-century interpreter of Paul, might wish to see them). What would be left of Romans, or Galatians, or even large swathes of the Corinthian correspondence? All that might remain would be mere tissue of phrases untouched by scriptural idiom, or perhaps some practical words of guidance drawn from the moral koine of the ancient world. The influence of scripture is most in evidence when the argument of Paul's letters is most sustained, and this fact attests to the foundational importance of scripture for Paul's own theology and missionary praxis.

Although we have not dwelled on it here, it would be equally possible to illustrate the significance of scripture for Paul's ethical vision. While it is true that Paul does not always cite chapter and verse as motivating ground for his ethical teaching,[22] close examination of the paraenetic sections of his letters often discloses the deep scriptural roots of his teaching.[23] And of course Paul does sometimes cite scripture explicitly as moral guidance for his gentile communities (e.g., Rom 7:7; 12:19; 13:8–10, etc.).

Above all, Paul reads the scriptures of Israel as directed to the eschatological present, a gift of the God and Father of the Lord Jesus Christ to the communities of gentiles who seek to follow the Messiah. Paul walks a delicate line in balancing radical novelty and radical continuity, and he employs scripture to explain each side of that balance. At the distance of almost two thousand years, we have to work hard to reconstruct the factors that gave shape to Paul's reading, and scholars will continue to debate the precise form of Paul's textual exemplar (*Vorlage*) and citation technique, as well as to seek the most adequate conceptual frame to grasp Paul's letters as "hermeneutical events." But to grapple with Paul's reading and use of scripture is to come up against some of the deepest impulses in Paul's theology and practice, and so amply repays the reader for the effort.

[22] Urging this point with particular force is Christopher M. Tuckett, "Paul, Scripture and Ethics: Some Reflections," *New Testament Studies* 46 (2000): 403–424.

[23] Note, e.g., Peter J. Tomson, *Paul and the Jewish Law: Halakhah in the Letters of the Apostle to the Gentiles* (Minneapolis, MN: Fortress Press, 1990); Brian S. Rosner, *Paul, Scripture, and Ethics: A Study of 1 Corinthians 5–7* (Leiden: Brill, 1994; repr., Grand Rapids, MI: Baker, 1999).

Further Reading

Gamble, H. Y. *Books and Readers in the Early Church: A History of Early Christian Texts.* New Haven, CT: Yale University Press, 1995.

Hays, Richard B. *Echoes of Scripture in the Letters of Paul.* New Haven, CT: Yale University Press, 1989.

Kujanpää, Katja. *The Rhetorical Functions of Scriptural Quotations in Romans.* Leiden: Brill, 2019.

Lincicum, David. *Paul and the Early Jewish Encounter with Deuteronomy.* Tübingen: Mohr Siebeck, 2010. Reprint, Grand Rapids, MI: Baker Academic, 2013.

Marcos, Natalio Fernández. *The Septuagint in Context: Introduction to the Greek Versions of the Bible.* Translated by Wilfred G. E. Watson. Leiden: Brill, 2001.

Porter, Stanley E. "Pauline Techniques of Interweaving Scripture into His Letters." In *Paulinische Schriftrezeption: Grundlagen – Ausprägungen – Wirkungen – Wertungen,* edited by Florian Wilk and Markus Öhler, 23–55. Göttingen: Vandenhoeck & Ruprecht, 2017.

Porter, Stanley E. "The Use of the Old Testament in the New: A Brief Comment on Method and Terminology." In *Early Christian Interpretation of the Scriptures of Israel: Investigations and Proposals,* edited by C. A. Evans and J. A. Sanders, 79–96. Sheffield: Sheffield Academic Press, 1997.

Shum, Shiu-Lun. *Paul's Use of Isaiah in Romans: A Comparative Study of Paul's Letter to the Romans and the Sibylline and Qumran Sectarian Texts.* Tübingen: Mohr Siebeck, 2002.

Stanley, Christopher D. *Paul and the Language of Scripture: Citation Technique in the Pauline Epistles and Contemporary Literature.* Cambridge: Cambridge University Press, 1992.

Stanley, Christopher D. *Arguing with Scripture: The Rhetoric of Quotations in the Letters of Paul.* London: T&T Clark, 2004.

Wagner, J. Ross. *Heralds of the Good News: Isaiah and Paul in Concert in the Letter to the Romans.* Leiden: Brill, 2002.

Watson, Francis. *Paul and the Hermeneutics of Faith.* 2nd ed. London: T&T Clark, 2015.

13 Did Paul Abandon either Judaism or Monotheism?

MATTHEW V. NOVENSON

Did Socrates abandon Athenianness by propagating his controversial philosophy? Did the prophet Muhammad abandon Arabianness when he began to preach monotheism? We do not usually think about historical figures in this way, setting them over against their respective ancestral traditions. In the case of the apostle Paul, however, we do often think about him in this unusual way. The twofold question posed in this chapter (Did Paul abandon either Judaism or monotheism?) arises not so much from Paul's letters themselves as from his outsize place in subsequent religious history. Because historic Christianity is (a) trinitarian and (b) not Judaism, and because Paul has been widely understood as a, perhaps even *the*, founder of Christianity,[1] it has come to seem natural to ask whether these hallmarks of historic Christianity can be traced back to the apostle – that is, whether Paul himself abandoned either Judaism or monotheism in the course of his apostolic work. What is more, again because of his outsize place in subsequent religious history, although Paul never says in so many words that he renounces either Judaism or monotheism, some things that he does say in the letters have been taken by modern interpreters, both Jewish and Christian, to imply such a renunciation. In this chapter, we must look carefully at the passages that have been so taken and ask what they actually claim. Furthermore, we must interrogate what exactly is meant by 'Judaism' and 'monotheism', and what would count as a renunciation, deviation, departure, violation, compromise, or abandonment of either of these -isms. As in other aspects of the study of Paul, but even more so here, it is crucial to parse out what belongs to Paul and what belongs to his afterlives.[2]

[1] See, e.g., the classic statement of Adolf von Harnack, *What Is Christianity?*, trans. Thomas Bailey Saunders (New York: Harper, 1957 [1901]), 176–189.

[2] On this historical problem, see J. Albert Harrill, *Paul the Apostle: His Life and Legacy in Their Roman Context* (New York: Cambridge University Press, 2012).

DID PAUL ABANDON JUDAISM?

The modern commonplace according to which Paul is said to have abandoned Judaism is attested already in the first great modern critic of the Pauline letters, F. C. Baur. Writing in the early nineteenth century, Baur summarises Paul's gospel in this way: 'Christianity is the absolute religion, the religion of the spirit and of freedom, with regard to which Judaism belongs to an inferior standpoint, from which it must be classed with heathenism'.[3] According to Baur (himself a Christian), Paul abandoned Judaism, and this was a good thing. By contrast, the late nineteenth-century Jewish critic Kaufmann Kohler agrees with Baur that Paul abandoned Judaism, but he regards this to be a bad thing. Kohler writes, 'His [Paul's] conception of life was not Jewish. Nor can his unparalleled animosity and hostility to Judaism as voiced in the Epistles be accounted for except upon the assumption that, while born a Jew, he was never in sympathy or in touch with the doctrines of the rabbinical schools'.[4] As these examples illustrate, modern interpreters variously praise Paul or blame him for abandoning Judaism, but many agree that he did so.[5]

Their belief that he did so, however, is based on highly questionable assumptions about the supposed essences of Judaism and of Christianity and about how each came to be. In particular, it presupposes a sufficiently clear and simple concept of Judaism, from which Paul can then be shown to have deviated. For much of the modern history of research, this presupposition mostly went unchallenged, but recently it has met with some forceful objections.[6] In some recent research, it has been argued that ancient Jewish belief and practice were so diverse that we can only speak of Judaisms (plural), not Judaism (singular).[7] Meanwhile, and in an opposite direction, it has been argued that Judaism did not

[3] F. C. Baur, *Paul the Apostle of Jesus Christ*, vol. 1, trans. Eduard Zeller and rev. A. Menzies (London: Williams & Norgate, 1876 [1845]), 255.

[4] Kaufmann Kohler, "Saul of Tarsus," in *Jewish Encyclopedia*, vol. 11 (New York: Funk & Wagnalls, 1906), 80.

[5] See further Daniel R. Langton, *The Apostle Paul in the Jewish Imagination* (Cambridge: Cambridge University Press, 2010); Patrick Gray, *Paul as a Problem in History and Culture* (Grand Rapids, MI: Baker, 2016).

[6] Against cultural essentialism, see especially Kathy Ehrensperger, *Paul at the Crossroads of Cultures: Theologizing in the Space Between* (London: T&T Clark, 2013).

[7] See Jacob Neusner, "Preface," in *Judaisms and Their Messiahs at the Turn of the Christian Era*, eds. Jacob Neusner et al. (Cambridge: Cambridge University Press, 1987), ix–xiv.

exist at all in antiquity,[8] or, more ambitiously still, that not even religion existed in antiquity.[9] Now, in fact, such arguments pertain not to the social practices that we call 'Judaism' or 'religion', but to the concepts. That is to say, virtually no one denies that ancient Jews, for instance, worshiped the deity resident in the Jerusalem temple, but some historians argue that those ancient Jews lacked the concept 'Judaism' for what they were doing.[10] This lattermost possibility is potentially relevant to the case of Paul, because Christian theology has long looked to Paul for a reification of, and principled rejection of, Judaism. Let us consider the evidence of Paul's own letters, examining what he does and does not say about his ancestral religion.

The Greek word *Ioudaismos*, from which we get our English word 'Judaism', occurs only twice in the twenty-seven books of the New Testament, both instances in the same passage at the beginning of Paul's Letter to the Galatians. Explaining why his audience should trust that his message came from God, not humans, Paul writes, 'For you heard of my former occupation in *Ioudaismos*, that I was indicting the assembly of God severely, and was besieging it. And I was advancing in *Ioudaismos* beyond many of my contemporaries among my people, being exceedingly zealous for my ancestral traditions. But when God was pleased to reveal his son in me .... I went away into Arabia and then returned again to Damascus' (Gal 1:13–14). The point here is that Paul's well-known about-face confirms the divine origin of his message, showing that he was not just an understudy of the chief apostles in Jerusalem. But Paul characterises his former occupation (*anastrophe*) as being 'in *Ioudaismos*', from which we get (via a harmonization with the Damascus Road story in Acts 9) our centuries-long habit of thinking of Paul as a convert from Judaism to Christianity.[11] Contrary to this habit of thought, however, Paul himself never speaks of Christianity, or even of Christians.[12] What is more, Greek *Ioudaismos* does not mean, as 'Judaism' does in English, the religion of Jewish people. Paul calls the

[8] See Daniel Boyarin, *Judaism: The Genealogy of a Modern Notion* (New Brunswick, NJ: Rutgers University Press, 2018).

[9] See Brent Nongbri, *Before Religion: A History of a Modern Concept* (New Haven, CT: Yale University Press, 2013).

[10] For a lucid analysis of these arguments, see Seth Schwartz, "How Many Judaisms Were There?" *Journal of Ancient Judaism* 2 (2011): 208–238.

[11] For an interrogation of this habit, see Alan F. Segal, *Paul the Convert* (New Haven, CT: Yale University Press, 1990).

[12] The word "Christian" first occurs in 1 Pet 4:16; Acts 11:26; 26:28; Pliny, *Epistles* 10.96–97; Tacitus, *Annals* 15.44; and the word "Christianity" in the early second-century letters of Ignatius of Antioch.

religion of Jewish people 'the ancestral traditions' (Gal 1:14), which is what most ancient people called their respective religions, since they lacked specific names for those religions. *Ioudaismos*, by contrast, is what Paul calls his own exceptional activist program for the defence and promotion of those traditions (which is also what *Ioudaismos* means in its few other instances in 2 Macc 2:21; 8:1; 14:38; 4 Macc 4:26). When Paul met the risen Christ, he abandoned that activist program, *Ioudaismos*, but he did not abandon his ancestral traditions, which are what we call Judaism.[13]

Those ancestral traditions include, for instance, belief in the God of Abraham as the creator of all things (Rom 1:25; 1 Cor 8:6), reverence for the law of Moses as God's revelation to Israel (Rom 9:4, 31; Gal 3:19, 24), cultic worship of God in his temple in Jerusalem (Rom 9:4; 1 Cor 10:18), and belief in the future resurrection of the dead (Rom 1:4; 1 Cor 15:12) and the kingdom of God (1 Cor 6:9–10; Gal 5:21). All of these hallmarks, and many more beside, Paul has in spades.[14] Viewed from this angle, then, it is patently absurd to speak of Paul 'abandoning Judaism', since he shares virtually all of the essential features attested by other ancients whom we count as representing Judaism: the Qumran sect, Philo of Alexandria, Flavius Josephus, the sages of the Mishnah, and so on. The problem, if there is one, is not that Paul lacks any essential features of Judaism, but that, on top of these essential features, Paul also attests other features that later interpreters have thought put him beyond the pale. He attributes to the law of Moses a role in working wrath and effecting death (Rom 4:15; 7:5; 1 Cor 15:56). He calls all kinds of human beings, gentiles as well as Jews, sons of God (Rom 8:14; Gal 3:26). He can speak of the crucified and raised messiah Jesus as if he were divine (Phil 2:6–11; 2 Cor 4:4). That Paul makes these moves is basically undisputed; the crucial question is whether they do in fact put him beyond the pale. Imagine, for the sake of argument, that we had only the letters of Paul and other texts extant during Paul's lifetime (meaning, importantly, none of the other texts that are part of the New Testament, let alone later Christian writers). In that case, arguably, it

[13] See Matthew V. Novenson, "Paul's Former Occupation in *Ioudaismos*," in *Galatians and Christian Theology*, eds. Mark Elliott et al. (Grand Rapids, MI: Baker, 2014), 24–39.

[14] See Alan F. Segal, "Paul's Jewish Presuppositions," in *The Cambridge Companion to St Paul* , ed. James D. G. Dunn (Cambridge: Cambridge University Press, 2003), 159–172; Matthew V. Novenson, *Christ among the Messiahs: Christ Language in Paul and Messiah Language in Ancient Judaism* (New York: Oxford University Press, 2012).

would never occur to us to think that any of Paul's claims, even the more provocative ones, put him beyond, outside, or against Judaism. But of course, we do have the rest of the New Testament, and the works of Justin, Irenaeus, Tertullian, Origen, Chrysostom, Augustine, Jerome, and myriad other gentile Christian writers down to the present, almost all of whom count Paul's letters as Christian scripture and therefore cite Paul's words as representing Christianity. Under this tremendous weight of tradition, it becomes very difficult for any of us to read Paul's words as representing Paul's own religion as opposed to the religion of his later Christian tradents.[15]

Faced with this difficulty, one promising way forward is to ask whether Paul was in fact treated by others, during his own lifetime, as being beyond, outside, or against Judaism. From a social-scientific perspective, there is some evidence that Paul was regarded as deviant by other Jews who regarded themselves, and perhaps were regarded by others, as normal by comparison.[16] In a litany of traumas suffered in the course of his apostolic work, Paul writes, 'Five times I received from the Jews the forty lashes less one' (2 Cor 11:24), and a few lines later, 'in danger from my people, in danger from the gentiles' (2 Cor 11:26). The reference to 'danger from my people' could mean either unofficial hostility or official punishment, but the reference to 'the forty lashes less one' certainly points to formal synagogue discipline. Because the Torah had specified a maximum of forty lashes for corporal sentences (Deut 25:1–3), Jewish halakhah in the early Roman period allowed for discretionary punishments of up to thirty-nine lashes (*m. Makkot* 3). Diaspora synagogues will have made use of this provision in overseeing their internal affairs, of which the case of Paul is an example. For reasons he does not here detail but which had to do with the way his apostolic work was perceived by other Jews, Paul was subjected to synagogue discipline. This fact might seem to suggest a break between Paul and Judaism, but, as E. P. Sanders memorably put it, 'punishment implies inclusion'.[17] To submit oneself to discipline is to be still inside the fold. Diaspora synagogues had no police power. Paul could have avoided

[15] On this hermeneutical problem, see the essays collected in *Paul within Judaism: Restoring the First-Century Context to the Apostle*, eds. Mark D. Nanos and Magnus Zetterholm (Minneapolis, MN: Fortress Press, 2015); and *Paul the Jew: Rereading the Apostle as a Figure of Second Temple Judaism*, eds. Gabriele Boccaccini and Carlos A. Segovia (Minneapolis, MN: Fortress Press, 2016).

[16] See John M. G. Barclay, "Deviance and Apostasy: Some Applications of Deviance Theory to First-Century Judaism and Christianity," in *Pauline Churches and Diaspora Jews* (Grand Rapids, MI: Eerdmans, 2016), 123–139.

corporal punishment by absenting himself from the life of the synagogue. We know of other ancient Jews who took this step (see the famous case of Tiberius Julius Alexander in Josephus, *Antiquities* 20.100). Evidently, however, Paul did not do so. He stayed, and he was allowed to stay. Even in these episodes of severe social disapproval, then, Paul operated within Judaism rather than outside its bounds.

Why, though, this social disapproval? What did Paul do that would have warranted synagogue punishment? He himself does not say, so interpreters have had to fill in the gaps, which they have done with zeal. One passage often invoked in this connection is a part of 1 Corinthians 9 where Paul puts himself forward as a model of accommodation to the needs of others (1 Cor 9:19–22):

> Although I am free from all people, I have enslaved myself to them all, so that I may gain more. To the Jews I became as a Jew, that I might gain Jews. To those under the law, as one under the law (though I myself am not under the law), that I might gain those under the law. To the lawless, as a lawless person (though I am not lawless with God but am in the law of Christ), that I might gain the lawless. To the weak I became a weak person, that I might gain the weak. To all people I have become all things, so that by all means I might save some.

In the wider context of 1 Corinthians 8–10, Paul's point is to persuade his gentile auditors to adjust their dietary habits to accommodate the weaker consciences of other Christ-believers, lest anyone be tempted to commit idolatry. This is the context for his saying, 'I have enslaved myself to all people', and 'To all people I have become all things'.[18] It is striking, though, that one of the groups about whom he says that he became like them is the Jews. Striking because Paul is himself a Jew; hence it is hard to see why he would have to 'become as a Jew'. Perhaps Paul was usually in the habit, as he says Cephas was in Galatians 2, of 'living gentilishly' (Gal 2:14) – that is, of observing his Jewish diet and holy days in a manner that was workable in great gentile cities like Antioch or Tarsus (e.g., by eating in gentile homes even in the presence of household gods). Such practice was probably quite common among

[17] E. P. Sanders, *Paul, the Law, and the Jewish People* (Philadelphia: Fortress Press, 1983), 192.

[18] See Margaret M. Mitchell, "Pauline Accommodation and 'Condescension' (ΣΥΓΚΑΤΑΒΑΣΙΣ): 1 Cor 9:19–23 and the History of Influence," in *Paul beyond the Judaism/Hellenism Divide*, ed. Troels Engberg-Pedersen (Louisville, KY: Westminster John Knox, 2001), 197–214.

Jews in the Diaspora, even if some Jerusalemite Jews might have found it scandalous (e.g., Gal 2:12). If so, then 'to become as a Jew' might mean to set aside one's Diaspora halakhah and adopt a Judean halakhah when in the company of Judeans (which is precisely what Paul shames Cephas for doing in Galatians 2, though in that case because gentiles-in-Christ were watching).[19]

'Living gentilishly', then, is unlikely to have been the reason for Paul's punishment at the hands of synagogue authorities. A more plausible explanation, developed in particular by Martin Goodman, is that Paul was putting the already vulnerable Diaspora Jewish communities at risk from their gentile neighbours by recruiting gentiles into his Jewish movement and then teaching them to renounce their obligations to their civic and family gods.[20] This would have looked like Jewish promotion of impiety among gentiles, an understandable cause of outrage among the locals and a public relations nightmare for synagogue leaders, who would have used the means at their disposal to keep a self-authorised charismatic like Paul in line, for the health and safety of the community.

In social terms, then, Paul did not abandon Judaism, but what about in theological terms? In particular, what about the offence of the crucified Christ (1 Cor 1:23)? To be sure, Paul mourns that most of his co-ethnics do not recognise 'the glory of God in the face of Christ' (2 Cor 4:6) as he does. From his perspective, the majority of Jews 'have zeal for God, but not with recognition' (Rom 10:2), about which, Paul writes earnestly, he feels 'great pain and constant anguish' (Rom 9:2). Unlike the later Christian treatises *adversus Iudaeos*, 'against the Jews', however, Paul does not diagnose this as a symptom of some flaw inherent in Judaism itself. As noted above, unlike many later Christian thinkers, Paul does not reify and isolate Judaism as a thing at all; like most of his contemporaries, he only thinks in terms of 'ancestral traditions', whether Jewish, Greek, Roman, or what have you.

When he comments on majority Jewish 'distrust' or 'unbelief' (*apistia*), Paul either simply notes it without any attempt at explanation or he explains it with reference to a mysterious divine purpose. When he himself reads the law and the prophets, of course, Paul sees the messiah

[19] See further David J. Rudolph, *A Jew to the Jews: Jewish Contours of Pauline Flexibility in 1 Corinthians 9:19–23*, 2nd ed. (Eugene, OR: Pickwick, 2016).

[20] See Martin Goodman, "The Persecution of Paul by Diaspora Jews," in *The Beginnings of Christianity*, eds. Jack Pastor, and Menachem Mor (Jerusalem: Yad ben Zvi, 2005), 379–387; and similarly Paula Fredriksen, *Paul: The Pagans' Apostle* (New Haven, CT: Yale University Press, 2017), 77–93.

Jesus plainly attested there (Rom 3:21). But he is enough of a realist to admit that when most other Jews read the same scriptures, they do not see what he sees, and this because, he says, 'their thoughts were hardened' and 'a veil lies over their heart' (2 Cor 3:14–15). In the Letter to the Romans, Paul attributes this noetic hardening to the agency of God himself. Quoting Isaiah, Paul writes, 'God gave them a spirit of stupor, eyes not to see and ears not to hear' (Rom 11:8 citing Isa 29:10). Why would God do such a thing? Well, Paul reasons, it is an eschatological necessity that God should have mercy on all people. Gentiles had always been disobedient ('by nature', Gal 2:15), so now, quite straightforwardly, God can have mercy on them. Jews, however, had always been mostly obedient; hence God has *made* them temporarily disobedient now so that he can very soon have mercy on them, too (Rom 11:30–32). This explanation may seem strange, but then, the phenomenon Paul was trying to explain was itself strange: the Jewish messiah had appeared, but only gentiles, not Jews (for the most part), were bowing the knee to him. Desperate times call for desperate explanatory measures. None of this, however, amounts to abandoning Judaism. In fact, Romans 11 is nothing if not a manifesto against abandonment. 'The gifts and the call of God are irrevocable' (Rom 11:29). Paul can no more abandon Israel than God can.[21]

The grain of truth in the old saw that Paul abandoned Judaism is the fact that Paul does sometimes speak of abandoning, or being estranged from, the entire world as we know it. Through the cross of Christ, he says, 'the cosmos was crucified to me, and I to the cosmos' (Gal 6:14). Because of Christ, Paul abandons the cosmos, the universe, life itself, which technically does include (conventional, everyday) Judaism, although that is not Paul's point.[22] A similar logic is at work in another well-known passage in Philippians (3:4–9):

> If anyone else thinks that he has confidence in the flesh, I more so: an eighth-day circumcision, from the race of Israel, the tribe of Benjamin, a Hebrew born from Hebrews, in respect of the law a Pharisee, in respect of zeal indicting the assembly, in respect of righteousness in the law blameless. But whatever things were gains to me, these things I consider loss on account of Christ. What is more, I consider all things to be loss on account of the superiority of the knowledge of Christ Jesus my lord, on whose

[21] On this point, see the essays collected in *God and Israel: Providence and Purpose in Romans 9–11*, ed. Todd D. Still (Waco, TX: Baylor University Press, 2017).

[22] See Beverly Roberts Gaventa, "The Singularity of the Gospel," in *Our Mother Saint Paul* (Louisville, KY: Westminster John Knox, 2007), 101–112.

account I suffered the loss of all things, and I consider them excrement, that I may gain Christ and be found in him, not having my own righteousness from the law but that which is through Christ-faith, righteousness from God, upon faith.

Historians are grateful for these few, brief autobiographical details (e.g., Paul's Pharisaic affiliation), but Paul only includes them here because apparently some rival preachers have been touting their own credentials (Phil 3:2–4). Paul one-ups these rivals by citing his own superior credentials but then undermines the whole contest by declaring all such things worthless in comparison to Christ. To be sure, this is an emphatic devaluation of certain aspects of Paul's Jewishness, but, crucially, it is a devaluation relative to other aspects of Paul's Jewishness. The comparison is not between Judaism and Christianity (the latter concept being not yet available to Paul), but between Jewish piety in the present evil age and Jewish mythology about the perfect age to come, or in other words, between everyday Judaism and eschatological Judaism. If, in the new creation, Jews and gentiles alike are all sons and heirs of God, then Benjaminite ancestry is effectively superfluous. If, in the new creation, everyone is perfectly righteous all the time, then conventional law observance, repentance, atonement, etc. are likewise effectively superfluous. And so on.

Which brings us to one final passage that has been widely taken to be a direct renunciation of Judaism: 'Through the law, I died to the law, that I might live to God. I have been crucified together with Christ; I am no longer alive, but Christ is alive in me' (Gal 2:19–20). Many interpreters have assumed that no good Jew could write the sentence, 'I died to the law'; hence many Jewish interpreters have scolded Paul for writing it, even as many Christian interpreters have praised him for writing it (e.g., Kohler and Baur, respectively, both cited above). But their shared assumption about what a Jew would or would not say is simply false. Jews can express and have expressed sentiments like this not infrequently in the long history of Judaism.[23] In particular, apocalyptic Jews (Jews who thought they were actually living at the end of the present age and the dawn of the age to come) have expressed, and indeed acted upon, sentiments like this.[24] Such people do of course sound strange relative

[23] See Joshua Garroway, "Paul: Within Judaism, without Law," in *Law and Lawlessness in Early Judaism and Christianity*, eds. David Lincicum et al. (Tübingen: Mohr Siebeck, 2019).

[24] See the examples documented in Gershom Scholem, *Major Trends in Jewish Mysticism* (New York: Schocken, 1995 [1946]); Gershom Scholem, *The Messianic*

to conventional, majority piety, but they are an important part of the history of Judaism, not to mention the history of religions more generally. Paul's point about 'dying to the law' is not that the law makes for a bad kind of religion, but that the entire age of sin and death (over which the law exercised benevolent jurisdiction) is now over. 'Living to God' here refers not to Christianity (which Paul did not live to see), but to the immortal, pneumatic life of the age to come. Or, to put it another way: Had Paul known of such a thing as Christianity, he would have said that he had died to that, too.

DID PAUL ABANDON MONOTHEISM?

We can think of our second question (Did Paul abandon monotheism?) as a subset of the first (Did Paul abandon Judaism?). We can think of it in this way because, in much modern discussion of the issue, monotheism has been thought to be a defining characteristic of Judaism, upon which Paul's Christology (i.e., his understanding of Jesus) supposedly infringed in one way or another. In fact, as we shall see, there are problems with both halves of this assumption, but its basic logic is clear enough. Thus, for instance, Kaufmann Kohler (cited above in connection with Paul and Judaism) writes about Paul and monotheism as follows: 'To a Jewish mind trained by rabbinical acumen, this [viz. Paul's argument in Romans 5–8] is not pure monotheistic, but mythological, thinking. Paul's "Son of God" is, far more than the Logos of Philo, an infringement of the absolute unity of God'.[25] While historic Judaism does not have and does not need anything quite like the ancient Christian creeds (e.g., the Nicene Creed), it has long been noted that the Shema (the confession of the oneness of God from the Torah) has at least a broadly analogous kind of status: 'Hear, O Israel, the Lord our God, the Lord is one' (Deut 6:4). Making this confession is among the most fundamental acts of Jewish piety, still performed morning and evening by Jews everywhere, down to the present. Its symbolic power is attested, for instance, by the famous story of the martyr Rabbi Akiba, who endured Roman torture and died with the Shema on his lips (*b. Ber.* 61b). To balk at confessing the Shema would be to put a question mark to one's Jewishness.

Idea in Judaism and Other Essays on Jewish Spirituality (New York: Schocken, 1995 [1971]); and the example *par excellence* detailed in Gershom Scholem, *Sabbatai Zevi: Mystical Messiah, 1626–1676*, trans. R. J. Zwi Werblowsky (Princeton, NJ: Princeton University Press, 1973).

[25] Kohler, "Saul of Tarsus," 83.

Does Paul balk at confessing the Shema? On the face of it, certainly not. Several times, in fact, he confesses it explicitly. In Galatians 3, Paul appeals to the oneness of God to explain the priority of God's promise to Abraham over God's giving of the law to Israel at Mount Sinai. He writes (Gal 3:19–20):

> Why then the law? It was added on account of transgressions – until such time as the seed should come to whom the promise was made – arranged through angels, in the hand of a mediator. The mediator is not of one, but God is one.

There are several puzzling aspects to this passage, but the central claim is clear. The oneness of God, which Paul takes as axiomatic, corresponds to God's very ancient promise to Abraham, which God made face to face and without the aid of a mediator.[26] In Romans 3, Paul again appeals to the oneness of God by way of establishing another theological point: the principle that God must justify gentiles in the same way that he justifies Jews. 'If God, who will justify the circumcision from faith, is one, [he will justify] also the foreskin through faith' (Rom 3:30). *Heis ho theos*, 'God is one'. Therefore, Paul reasons, God cannot have two different strategies for justification, one for Jews and another for gentiles.[27] Here again, Paul solves a theological problem by appealing to the axiom of the oneness of God.

As with the discussion of Judaism above, so with the Shema. The problem is not that Paul ever voices any doubts about the oneness of God; he does not. In fact, he pointedly affirms it. The problem, if there is one, is that Paul also says some things about Jesus that later interpreters have thought *should* have made Paul balk at confessing the Shema. According to these interpreters, Paul himself may not have recognised that he had abandoned monotheism, but he had in fact abandoned it. A key text here is Paul's third express citation of the Shema, where he is answering the question whether it is permissible for gentiles-in-Christ to eat meat that had previously been sacrificed to idols (1 Cor 8:4–6).[28]

[26] On this verse, see Francis Watson, *Paul and the Hermeneutics of Faith*, 2nd ed. (London: T&T Clark, 2016 [2004]), 256–258.

[27] On this verse, see Richard B. Hays, "Have We Found Abraham to Be Our Forefather according to the Flesh? A Reconsideration of Rom 4:1," *Novum Testamentum* 27 (1985): 83–85.

[28] On the occasion and the argument of this passage, see the discussion in Wayne A. Meeks, *The First Urban Christians: The Social World of the Apostle Paul*, 2nd ed. (New Haven, CT: Yale University Press, 2003 [1983]), 140–163.

> So then, concerning the eating of idol sacrifices: we know that an idol is nothing in the cosmos, and that there is no god but one. For if there are so-called gods, whether in heaven or on earth – as indeed there are many gods and many lords – nevertheless for us there is one god the father, from whom are all things, and we are for him, and one lord Jesus Christ, through whom are all things, and we are through him.

On the one hand, Paul here once again affirms Deuteronomic orthodoxy ('there is no god but one') but, on the other hand, he also concedes the existence of many other gods and lords ('so-called gods', perhaps, but gods nonetheless). According to Paul, idols, which are the cult statues of gentile deities, are nothing at all. But the deities themselves do exist, as Paul reaffirms at the end of his discourse on idol sacrifices: 'What [gentiles] sacrifice, they sacrifice to demons and not to God' (1 Cor 10:20). Unlike idols, Paul reckons, demons, gods, and lords are real things in the cosmos.

What is more, one of these other lords, namely Jesus, Paul also adds to his formulaic confession of divine oneness: 'For us there is one God the father *and* one lord Jesus Christ'.[29] Paul calls Christ a lord, not a god, which is interesting and perhaps significant (see further below), but God does at least now have a divine lieutenant, the messiah Jesus. The phrase 'for us' signifies that here Paul is talking about devotion, not ontology. The point, in other words, is not that no other divine beings exist except God and Christ, but rather that only God and Christ are worthy of devotion from Paul and his coreligionists.[30] Gentiles in their natural state may sacrifice to demons, but 'for us' there is only God and Christ. This is what is often called monolatry (as opposed to monotheism) in the secondary literature. If monotheism means belief in the existence of only one divine being and no others, monolatry means the reservation of worship for one divine being, even if other divine beings may exist. Monolatry is often (but need not be) coordinated with henotheism – that is, belief in the existence of a pyramid of divine beings with one higher than all the rest. These additional terms give us access to very helpful distinctions that we would lack if we only had the term monotheism, but unfortunately, many scholars (not to

[29] See N. T. Wright, *The Climax of the Covenant* (Minneapolis, MN: Fortress Press, 1992), 120–136.

[30] The usefulness of this devotion-versus-ontology distinction is illustrated on a large scale by Larry W. Hurtado, *Lord Jesus Christ: Devotion to Jesus in Earliest Christianity* (Grand Rapids, MI: Eerdmans, 2003).

mention lay people) do not avail themselves of these distinctions. Many persist in using just the one word 'monotheism' for a number of quite different phenomena. Or they create their own bespoke distinctions, such as William Horbury's distinction between exclusive monotheism (which denies the existence of all gods but one) and inclusive monotheism (which allows that other gods exist but ranks them below the high god),[31] or Angelos Chaniotis's distinction between monotheism and megatheism.[32] Ideally, when discussing these complicated matters, we should be maximally precise while also using terms that are intelligible to the largest possible number of people. Along these lines, we might say that, in 1 Corinthians 8, Paul starts by striking an apparently monotheistic note ('there is no god but one'), but as he goes on it emerges that his position is perhaps better described as henotheistic and monolatrous (or, perhaps better, duolatrous): There are many gods and lords in the cosmos, but one father God is above them all, and only he and his son the messiah are worthy of devotion in Paul's assemblies.

This passage fits with a pattern whereby Paul often speaks of Christ in ways that ancients would recognise as ways one would speak of a god (invoking him, acclaiming him, delivering oracles from him, celebrating him in a ritual meal, etc.)[33] but does not actually call Christ a god, or God. Paul overwhelmingly speaks of God as the father of Jesus (Rom 15:6; 2 Cor 1:3; 11:31), not as Jesus. And, correspondingly, he speaks of Jesus as the son of God, not as God. Admittedly, Titus 2:13 arguably does call Jesus a god: 'the appearing of the glory of our great god and savior Jesus Christ.' But Titus is (rightly) regarded by many scholars as a pseudepigraphon – that is, a letter attributed to Paul but actually written by someone else. In the undisputedly authentic Pauline letters, there is only one passage that might conceivably call Jesus God, and it probably does not do so. The passage is Rom 9:5, and the problem for translators is how to punctuate the sentence. It reads in one of two ways: either 'From the Israelites comes the messiah, according to the flesh, *who is* God over all, blessed forever, amen' or 'From the Israelites

[31] William Horbury, "Jewish and Christian Monotheism in the Herodian Age," in *Herodian Judaism and New Testament Study* (Tübingen: Mohr Siebeck, 2006), 2–33.

[32] Angelos Chaniotis, "Megatheism: The Search for the Almighty God and the Competition of Cults," in *One God: Pagan Monotheism in the Roman Empire*, eds. Stephen Mitchell and Peter van Nuffelen (Cambridge: Cambridge University Press, 2010), 112–140.

[33] On this issue, see M. David Litwa, *Iesus Deus: The Early Christian Depiction of Jesus as a Mediterrean God* (Minneapolis, MN: Fortress Press, 2014).

comes the messiah, according to the flesh. God who is over all be blessed forever, amen'. Either punctuation is technically possible. But the second rendering, where we have not one sentence but two, is arguably the more likely. It would be more consistent both with Paul's usual way of writing benedictions (Rom 1:25; 2 Cor 1:3; 11:31) and with his usage of the names 'God' and 'Christ' elsewhere.[34]

If Paul's Christ is not identical with God the father, then what kind of divine being is he? Where, exactly, does Christ fit in Paul's cosmology? This turns out to be a rather difficult question, and it has generated a number of different, even conflicting, answers. Bart Ehrman has argued, for instance, that Paul thinks that Christ is an angel.[35] He points to Gal 4:14: 'You [Galatians] received me [Paul] as an angel of God, as Christ Jesus'. Ehrman takes the two parallel phrases as synonymous, but that is neither necessary nor (arguably) likely. Like an angel, Christ is a divine being who is not God the father, but there are things other than angels that fit these criteria. Elsewhere, Paul speaks of Christ much more like one would speak of a deified human being. Christ was born of a woman (Gal 4:4), from the bloodline of king David (Rom 1:3), but having died and then been raised by God, he is now immortal (Rom 6:9). These passages would seem to suggest a kind of deified king or hero (e.g., Hercules, Alexander the Great, Julius Caesar).[36] But here, too, there is more to it than that.

Paul's Christ is not identical with God, but he stands in a closer relation to God than any other divine being does. In the letters of Paul, angels and demons are called angels and demons, not 'sons of God', as they often are in the Hebrew Bible (e.g., Ps 29:1; 89:7; Job 38:7). For Paul, only Christ is the son of God, with the rule-proving exception of people who get joined to Christ and thereby become sons of God themselves (Rom 8:14, 19; 9:26; Gal 3:26; 4:6–7). Christ is, moreover, 'the image of God' (2 Cor 4:4), the visible representation of the invisible God (analogous to the measure of the heavenly body of God [*shiʿur qomah*] in late antique Jewish mysticism). God's glory (that is, his *kavod* or bodily

[34] This is how I, with many other interpreters, understand Romans 9:5. But for an exhaustive argument that Paul *does* in fact call Jesus God in this verse, see George Carraway, *Christ Is God Over All: Romans 9:5 in the Context of Romans 9–11* (London: T&T Clark, 2013).

[35] Bart D. Ehrman, *How Jesus Became God: The Exaltation of a Jewish Preacher from Galilee* (San Francisco, CA: HarperOne, 2014), 251–254.

[36] On this pattern, see in particular Michael Peppard, *The Son of God in the Roman World: Divine Sonship in Its Social and Political Context* (New York: Oxford University Press, 2011).

presence) has always been hidden in his sanctuary in Jerusalem (Rom 9:4), but in the new creation, all human beings (not only priests but also laypeople, not only Jews but also gentiles) can attain 'knowledge of the glory of God in the face of Christ' (2 Cor 4:6). The divine *pneuma* (usually translated 'spirit') that people receive in the new creation is, at the same time, the *pneuma* of God and the *pneuma* of Christ (Rom 8:9). Paul's Christ is the son of God, the image of God, the face of God. These descriptions are tantalizingly brief, but in one passage Paul supplies a narrative within which their sense becomes a bit clearer (Phil 2:5–11):

> Christ Jesus, who, although he was in the form of God, did not consider it as spoils to be equal with God, but he emptied himself, taking the form of a slave, being in the likeness of humans; and being found as a human in regard to figure, he humbled himself, becoming obedient to the point of death, the death of a cross. Therefore indeed God highly exalted him and gave him the name higher than every name, so that at the name of Jesus every knee should bow, of beings in heaven and on earth and in the underworld, and every tongue confess that Jesus Christ is lord to the glory of God the father.

In this fascinating passage, Christ is neither God nor human, exactly. He exists in the heavenly form of God, but his likeness and figure are human. He undergoes the quintessentially human experience of death (and thus is a mortal, strictly speaking), but he receives obeisance from human and superhuman beings like a high god would.[37] Like Metatron in the Jewish mystical text *3 Enoch*, Christ in Philippians 2 is both a deified human being and the archangelic form of God.[38] If we recall that 'Christ' means messiah, then this is not as strange as it might at first seem. There were a number of types of messiahs in ancient Jewish imagination: priest, king, warrior, angel, and more. Nor is it at all uncommon to find features of different types mixed up in the sources, as we find in Philippians 2.

[37] Here, however, when *Christ* receives obeisance from human and superhuman beings, glory redounds to *God the father*, on which see further Hurtado, *Lord Jesus Christ*, 151–153.

[38] See Gedaliahu G. Stroumsa, "Form(s) of God: Some Notes on Metatron and Christ," *Harvard Theological Review* 76 (1983): 269–288; Markus Bockmuehl, "'The Form of God' (Phil 2:6): Variations on a Theme of Jewish Mysticism," *Journal of Theological Studies* 48 (1997): 1–23.

Does any of this, though, put Paul in contravention of a Jewish doctrine of God? Paul himself certainly does not think so. Strenuously to the contrary, he thinks that his gospel calls gentiles away from idolatry to the worship of the one true God, just as other Jewish Greek texts like *Letter of Aristeas* or *Wisdom of Solomon* do. 'You turned to God from idols, to serve a living and true God, and to await his son from heaven, whom he raised from the dead, Jesus who delivers us from the coming wrath' (1 Thess 1:9). Of course, Paul speaks not only of 'the living and true God' but also of 'his son from heaven', which *Letter of Aristeas* and *Wisdom of Solomon* do not do. But as we have seen, the idea of a heavenly lieutenant (God's son, or messenger, or chosen one, or anointed one) who will execute judgement on God's behalf is not at all unusual in Jewish texts that speculate about such things.

The conventional way of putting the question, 'Did Paul abandon Jewish monotheism?' assumes that we know where Paul's Jewish contemporaries stood vis-à-vis monotheism, that they were all good, traditional monotheists, and the only question is whether Paul parted ways with them on this issue. But do we know that? We have a concept of monotheism, and we plausibly associate it with ancient Jews and their scriptures, but we often overlook the actual evidence for what Paul's contemporaries believed about God and other superhuman beings. As Paula Fredriksen has perceptively put it, in antiquity, even the monotheists were polytheists.[39] With a very few exceptions, mostly philosophers, in the ancient world virtually everyone (Jews, Greeks, Romans, Egyptians, Arabians, Gauls, Britons, and the rest) believed that the heavens teemed with superhuman beings: angels, demons, spirits, gods, demigods, stars, heroes, ancestors, and so on. Such beings existed and therefore merited due attention from humans, just as very powerful human beings (e.g., emperors, kings, patrons) would. So if 'monotheism' means denying the very existence of any superhuman beings save one, then there were almost no monotheists in antiquity. Certainly, most Jews were not monotheists in this sense. Our ancient Jewish texts are full of references to superhuman beings, many of them even having proper names such as Michael, Gabriel, Uriel, Raphael, Metatron, Samael, Azazel, Semihazah, Satan, Belial, Beelzebub, Asmodeus, Mastema, and many more. If we approach the question from this angle, then when we find Paul speaking not only of God and Christ but also of Satan, Belial, the god of this age, angels, demons, elements, spirits,

[39] Fredriksen, *Paul*, 12.

rulers, authorities, powers, and more,[40] Paul suddenly looks much more like his Jewish contemporaries (and his non-Jewish contemporaries, too, for that matter), 'monotheist' or not.[41]

In other words, although in the history of interpretation readers have been most anxious about whether Paul's view of Christ compromised monotheism, they might have done just as well to direct their anxiety towards Paul's view of other divine beings. Older scholarship often rushed to demythologise, metaphorise, or explain away these other beings, but recent scholarship has taken them more seriously and more realistically. The so-called apocalyptic school of Pauline interpretation has emphasised both the threat posed by 'anti-God powers' (especially sin and death) and God's conquest over those powers in the death of Christ as features of Paul's gospel.[42] Meanwhile, from a history-of-religions perspective, other interpreters have asked whether Paul actually thinks of sin and death as demons, rulers, or authorities (see Rom 5:12–21) – that is, as particular named beings analogous to the Greek gods Planē, Thanatos, or Hades. In short, there is nowadays a greater interest in and patience with Paul's frankly rather mythological cosmology, with all its many-colored divine beings.[43]

It should be noted that Paul specifically classifies many of these divine beings as created things: 'Neither death, nor life, nor angels, nor rulers, nor things that are, nor things that shall be, nor powers, nor height, nor depth, nor any other creature [*ktisis*] shall be able to part us from the love of God that is in Christ Jesus our lord' (Rom 8:38–39). So death, angels, powers, and rulers, at least, are created things, even if they are also superhuman (and thus divine in this latter sense). This illustrates once again a key point of confusion in the secondary literature: what exactly is meant by 'god' and 'divine'. Some interpreters urge that these terms should only be used of the highest god, while others allow them for other superhuman, celestial beings, too. Both groups of interpreters can claim warrant from Paul, who, as we have seen, gives a complicated account. For Paul, 'There is no god but one' – that is, no

40 See Rom 8:37–39; 16:20; 1 Cor 4:9; 5:5; 6:3; 7:5; 10:20–21; 11:10; 12:10; 13:1; 14:12, 32; 2 Cor 2:11; 4:4; 6:15; 11:14; 12:7; Gal 1:8; 3:19; 4:14; 1 Thess 2:18.

41 See further Loren T. Stuckenbruck, "'Angels' and 'God': Exploring the Limits of Early Jewish Monotheism," in *Early Christian and Jewish Monotheism*, eds. Loren T. Stuckenbruck and Wendy E. S. North (London: T&T Clark, 2004), 45–70.

42 See, e.g., Beverly Roberts Gaventa, "The Cosmic Power of Sin in Paul's Letter to the Romans," *Interpretation* 58 (2004): 229–240.

43 On this mythological aspect, see Emma Wasserman, *Apocalypse as Holy War: Divine Politics and Polemics in the Letters of Paul* (New Haven, CT: Yale University Press, 2018).

creator but one. At the same time, however, 'there are many gods and many lords' – that is, many angels, demons, rulers, powers, etc., including Satan, Belial, the god of this age, and Christ. But Christ, as we have also seen, is a special case. He is one of the lords that exist in the cosmos, but he is the one lord 'for us', as Paul emphasises. He is not God, but he is, uniquely, the son of God and the image of God. All things are *from* God the father, but all things are *through* Christ, which might suggest that Christ is not a *ktisis*, a creature. This is what Richard Bauckham means by speaking of 'Paul's Christology of divine identity'.[44] Christ, death, angels, and archons may all be superhuman beings, but in respect of creation, Christ is different from all these others. They are called *ktiseis*, creatures; Christ is not. Nevertheless, Paul says, at the end of all things, even Christ will ultimately be subordinated to God the father (1 Cor 15:28).[45]

In sum, Paul was just as monotheistic as his Jewish contemporaries were, which is to say, moderately monotheistic by ancient standards, but not very monotheistic by medieval and modern standards. Like most ancient Jews, Paul differed from most ancient gentiles in regarding the deity resident in Jerusalem as the creator of all things, and in theoretically reserving cultic worship for him alone. Like almost everyone in antiquity, Jew or gentile, Paul also acknowledged the existence and agency of many other divine beings. Is this monotheistic? Perhaps it is, if we stretch the concept far enough to make it fit – for instance, by allowing an 'inclusive monotheism' in addition to the more familiar 'exclusive monotheism' (à la Horbury), or by stipulating that 'monotheism' means not belief in one god but belief in one creator (à la Bauckham). We are of course free to make moves like this, and there may be some good reasons (especially theological ones) for doing so. But we should also acknowledge that stretching the concept in this way makes it something other than what many people (e.g., modern Muslims, Jews, and nonreligious folk) recognise as monotheism. In any event, as the argument above has shown, it is not the case that the principle of monotheism was any kind of fault line separating Paul from other ancient Jews.

44 Richard Bauckham, "Paul's Christology of Divine Identity," in *Jesus and the God of Israel* (Grand Rapids, MI: Eerdmans, 2009), 182–232.

45 These subtle Pauline distinctions are part of the inheritance of the late ancient Christians who developed the doctrine of the trinity, on which see Wesley Hill, *Paul and the Trinity: Persons, Relations, and the Pauline Letters* (Grand Rapids, MI: Eerdmans, 2015).

CONCLUSION

For all of Socrates's conflict with the leadership of classical Athens, even to the point of his death at the hands of the state, we do not generally think of him as having abandoned Athenianness. Our intuition in the case of Socrates is right, and we should apply it also to the case of Paul. Did Paul abandon either Judaism or monotheism? We can take the latter part of the question first. Paul certainly did not abandon Judaism *by* abandoning monotheism, first because ancient Judaism itself was not monotheistic in the sense that most moderns mean that word, and second because Paul's cosmology actually agrees in most respects with the cosmologies of other ancient Jews. Like Deuteronomy, Ben Sira, Philo, and Josephus, Paul believes that the God of Abraham is the creator of the universe, but also that God is variously worshiped, assisted, and opposed by a host of lower deities. Like some (but not all) other ancient Jews, Paul believed that the messiah was one of these divine beings. So far, so conventional. The point on which most other ancient Jews disagreed with Paul (and with Peter, James, Barnabas, et al.) was the claim that the recently executed man Jesus was this messiah. That was an extreme minority opinion in ancient Judaism, but not because it was a different kind of thing from ancient Judaism.

But if not in respect of monotheism, did Paul nevertheless abandon Judaism in some other respect? Perhaps in respect of the law of Moses, since that is where modern interpreters have been most exercised? Again, at many points, what Paul says about the law agrees with what most other ancient Jews for whom we have evidence say about the law. God gave it to Moses on Mount Sinai. It is the patrimony of the Jews. It is altogether righteous. God has shown us how to fulfil it. And so on. In addition to these claims, however, Paul also makes some more controversial claims about the law. It works wrath. It effects death. It has jurisdiction over the present age but not over the age to come. It is powerless to bring about ultimate, eschatological righteousness. He, Paul, has died to it. It is in these claims that many modern interpreters have thought they have found Paul's supposed breach with Judaism and manifesto of Christianity. To be sure, late ancient, gentile Christianity found excellent grist for its mill in these latter sayings of Paul.[46] But when, say, Marcion and Augustine use

[46] See Matthew V. Novenson, "The Pauline Epistles in Tertullian's Bible," *Scottish Journal of Theology* 68 (2015): 471–483.

these words of Paul's, they mean quite different things from what the apostle meant when he said them.[47] In Paul's own context, even these more controversial claims about the law are recognizably, intelligibly, even familiarly Jewish. Admittedly, the closest parallel evidence comes not from everyday, conventional Jewish piety but from apocalyptic, millenarian Jewish circles, but it is no less Jewish for that. As we have learned from modern social theory of religion, ancient Judaism was whatever ancient Jews did. In short, then, Paul did not abandon Judaism. Over the course of late antiquity, Christianity abandoned Judaism, and it did so using Paul's words. But that is a very different thing.

Further Reading

Barclay, John M. G. *Pauline Churches and Diaspora Jews*. Grand Rapids, MI: Eerdmans, 2016.

Bauckham, Richard. "Paul's Christology of Divine Identity." In *Jesus and the God of Israel*, 182–232. Grand Rapids, MI: Eerdmans, 2009.

Boccaccini, Gabriele, and Carlos A. Segovia, eds. *Paul the Jew: Rereading the Apostle as a Figure of Second Temple Judaism*. Minneapolis, MN: Fortress Press, 2016.

Bockmuehl, Markus. "'The Form of God' (Phil 2:6): Variations on a Theme of Jewish Mysticism." *Journal of Theological Studies* 48 (1997): 1–23.

Ehrensperger, Kathy. *Paul at the Crossroads of Cultures: Theologizing in the Space Between*. London: T&T Clark, 2013.

Gaventa, Beverly Roberts. *Our Mother Saint Paul*. Louisville, KY: Westminster John Knox, 2007.

Fredriksen, Paula. *Paul: The Pagans' Apostle*. New Haven, CT: Yale University Press, 2017.

Hill, Wesley. *Paul and the Trinity: Persons, Relations, and the Pauline Letters*. Grand Rapids, MI: Eerdmans, 2015.

Nanos, Mark D., and Magnus Zetterholm, eds. *Paul within Judaism: Restoring the First-Century Context to the Apostle*. Minneapolis, MN: Fortress Press, 2015.

Novenson, Matthew V. *Christ among the Messiahs: Christ Language in Paul and Messiah Language in Ancient Judaism*. New York: Oxford University Press, 2012.

Novenson, Matthew V. "Paul's Former Occupation in *Ioudaismos*." In *Galatians and Christian Theology*, edited by Mark Elliott, Scott J. Hafemann, N. T. Wright, and John Frederick, 24–39. Grand Rapids, MI: Baker, 2014.

[47] On this point, see the classic essay of Krister Stendahl, "The Apostle Paul and the Introspective Conscience of the West," *Harvard Theological Review* 56 (1963): 199–215.

Sanders, E. P. *Paul, the Law, and the Jewish People*. Philadelphia: Fortress Press, 1983.

Segal, Alan F. *Paul the Convert: The Apostolate and Apostasy of Saul the Pharisee*. New Haven, CT: Yale University Press, 1990.

Wasserman, Emma. *Apocalypse as Holy War: Divine Politics and Polemics in the Letters of Paul*. New Haven, CT: Yale University Press, 2018.

14 Why Were People Attracted to Paul's Good News?

DAVID G. HORRELL

The question posed as the title for this chapter is an important one to ask, though it has been rather neglected in the voluminous discussions of Paul's mission, letter-writing, and theology. Perhaps such neglect owes something to the fact that it is, as we shall see, a question difficult to answer with confidence. It is also a question about which caution is required, not least because those who study the Pauline literature are often predisposed, by their own Christian commitment, to assume the uniqueness and attractiveness of Paul's message. I begin, then, by outlining some specific reasons why we should be cautious in approaching this question. Secondly, I offer some equally cautionary comments on comparison, as one key aspect of approaching this subject. Finally, in the longest section of this chapter, I offer a range of possible reasons why people might have been attracted to Paul's 'good news' (*euangelion*), though the cautionary remarks of the first two sections are an essential lens through which to view these more positive suggestions.

THE LIMITS OF OUR KNOWLEDGE

There are various respects in which we need to recognise that our attempts to answer the question under consideration are severely constrained by the limits of our evidence. Three particular aspects of these limitations are worth mentioning.

First, we do not have any first-hand accounts that record the motivations and reasons behind a conversion to the Christ-groups founded by Paul. Paul himself offers us something of a narrative concerning his own change (Gal 1:13–24), whether or not we label this change a 'conversion' (a matter of long-running debate), and he gives us various depictions of the kind of encounter with Christ he sees himself as having experienced (1 Cor 15:8–10; 2 Cor 12:1–10; Phil 3:4–11). Acts famously records the story of Paul's conversion three times, in slightly different forms (Acts 9:1–19; 22:3–21; 26:4–23), but none of these accounts, from Paul or from

Acts, gives us much sense of what we might call reasons or motivations for Paul to be convinced by the message about Christ. Rather, his own self-understanding is that this conviction came about by some kind of revelation (Gal 1:16; cf. 1 Cor 9:1; 15:8), and that he had little choice about his being 'seized' by Christ (Phil 3:12; cf. 1 Cor 9:16–17). More importantly, we do not have any indications as to how the converts to the groups established by Paul and his co-workers understood the nature of, or the reasons for, their own conversion. We have, unsurprisingly, no early accounts comparable to the introspective, autobiographical reflections famously offered in Augustine's *Confessions,* written in the fourth century.

Second, we do not know much about the size of the Christ-following groups to which Paul writes in places such as Corinth, Philippi, or Thessalonica. In other words, while we know that Paul was a sufficiently successful 'missionary' to have established (not single-handedly, but as part of a team; cf. 1 Thess 1:1; 2 Cor 1:19) groups of Christ-believers in various cities and regions across significant parts of the Roman Empire, we do not know *how* successful he was, in terms of the numbers convinced to accept his message. We should be wary of accepting a Lukan perspective, presented in Acts, that most likely exaggerates the scale of the positive response to the early Christian message – notably in the suggestion that 3,000 people accepted Peter's message on the Day of Pentecost (Acts 2:41) or in the depictions of Paul converting many and speaking in public places in various cities (e.g., Acts 14:1; 17:4, 21–34; contrast 1 Cor 2:1–5; 2 Cor 10:10). Given the number of names mentioned in connection with the assemblies in Corinth, for example, scholars have suggested that we might realistically think of around 40–50 people for a gathering of 'the whole assembly' at Corinth (Rom 16:23), and that this whole assembly is probably a coming together of various smaller groups, based in households (cf. 1 Cor 1:16) or workshops (cf. Acts 18:2–3; Rom 16:3–5).[1] Even these numbers are very rough guesses, based on the assumption that we can add to the seventeen names mentioned in connection with Corinth spouses, children, and a few slaves. But we have little idea how many people may have been among those unnamed by Paul but indicated in references to the majority who are not wise, powerful, or of noble birth (1 Cor 1:26) or to those who go hungry at the Lord's supper meal

[1] For the calculation of the rough size of the 'whole assembly' at Corinth as 40–50 persons, see Jerome Murphy-O'Connor, *St Paul's Corinth: Texts and Archaeology,* 3rd ed. (Collegeville, MN: Liturgical Press, 2002), 182.

(1 Cor 11:20–21). Romans 16, which is a comparatively rich source of insight into the composition of Christ-groups in Rome and in Corinth (from where the letter was sent), includes 35 personal names, and those related to Rome seem to indicate the existence of various house-groups or distinct clusters of Christ-followers.[2] But Paul himself did not found the congregations in Rome, nor had he even visited them at the time when he wrote the letter (Rom 1:8–15). This leads us to a third limitation of our evidence.

Third, then, it is difficult, not least given the severe limitations of our evidence, to assess the reasons why people were specifically attracted to *Paul's* message, in Paul's own time, as opposed to the early Christian message more generally in the first two or three centuries of the Christian movement. Indeed, most of the attempts to address the question concerning the appeal and success of the early Christian movement do so with a broader sweep across this longer time-period.[3] We cannot of course neatly distinguish Paul's own message or appeal from that of the broader movement of which he was a part: despite Paul's occasional (and polemical) insistence on his independence (e.g., Gal 1:16–17), he claims to proclaim a common message, which he received and shared with others (1 Cor 15:3–11). Presumably, he also learnt what he knew of Jesus's life and teaching from these others, not least on his first visit to Jerusalem, when he met Peter (Gal 1:18). Moreover, Paul worked with various others, and even these 'teams' of emissaries and missionaries were not neatly divided into 'Pauline' and non-Pauline groups (see, e.g., Acts 15:22–40 for Silas [=Silvanus], Barnabas, and Mark). Moreover, the earliest Christian assemblies, even those to which Paul wrote, cannot be distinguished into 'Pauline' and non–Pauline groups, despite a long-standing scholarly tendency to refer to 'Pauline churches', or 'Pauline assemblies'.[4] Rather, the communities in Corinth, Philippi, Galatia, Antioch, and elsewhere seem to have received and been influenced by

[2] See Peter Lampe, *From Paul to Valentinus: Christians at Rome in the First Two Centuries* (London: T&T Clark International, 2003), 359–360, and the detailed analysis of the names in Romans 16 on 153–183.

[3] See, e.g., the recent study of Larry W. Hurtado, *Why on Earth Did Anyone Become a Christian in the First Three Centuries* (Milwaukee, WI: Marquette University Press, 2016), though only the last ten pages (124–133) turn to the subject of Christianity's attractions. Also giving attention to this question, but focused on (roughly) the first century is Paul B. Duff, *Jesus Followers in the Roman Empire* (Grand Rapids, MI: Eerdmans, 2017).

[4] See David G. Horrell, "The Letters for All (Local) Christians: Were There Pauline Churches?", in *The Making of Christian Morality: Reading Paul in Ancient and Modern Contexts* (Grand Rapids, MI: Eerdmans, 2019), 15–26.

various travelling missionaries and leaders – much to Paul's displeasure, insofar as this sometimes left him needing to argue vehemently for these groups to accept *his* version of the Christ-story and remain loyal to him (see e.g., 2 Cor 11:1–6; Gal 1:6–9; Phil 3:2–3). So, it is hard to distinguish what made *Paul's* message attractive, even though it is this question in particular that is of primary relevance in the context of this book.

THE IMPORTANCE OF COMPARISONS

When considering the possible attractions of Paul's message, it is important to consider the *relative* success of Paul's mission (and the early Christian movement more generally) in comparison with other 'religious' affiliations available at the time. Was Paul's message particularly attractive compared with other options? Once again, even attempting this task is complex in many ways, not only due to limited evidence, but also, for example, due to the difficulty of distinguishing different kinds of groups and specifically 'religion' in the ancient world: many recent scholars have questioned the term's validity in this context and specifically in relation to Judaism (on which see below) and have argued that being a *Ioudaios* (Jew or Judean) is better seen as an ethnic identity than a religious one.[5] It is also worth noting that comparison, while often recognised as vital, has often been approached with questions about derivation and dependence in mind. If, for example, we see some similarities between a practice or idea evident in one of the ancient mystery cults and in Paul's theology, does this mean that Paul *derived* this idea from the mystery cults? Recent scholarship has generally warned against seeing such close connections, which risk distorting our understanding of both the ancient mystery cults (by viewing them through implicitly Christian categories) and the origins of early Christian theology. But genealogy and derivation may not be the best way to approach the task of comparison, which can be distorted by contemporary religious agendas, and are certainly not the only way to do so.[6]

[5] On the broader issue see Carlin Barton and Daniel Boyarin, *Imagine No Religion: How Modern Abstractions Hide Ancient Realities* (New York: Fordham University Press, 2016); on Jewish/Judean ethnic identity, see, e.g., Steve Mason, "Jews, Judaeans, Judaizing, Judaism: Problems of Categorization in Ancient History," *Journal for the Study of Judaism* 38 (2007): 457–512; Steve Mason, *Orientation to the History of Roman Judaea* (Eugene, OR: Cascade/Wipf and Stock, 2016), 97–112.

[6] See the classic study of Jonathan Z. Smith, *Drudgery Divine: On the Comparison of Early Christianities and the Religions of Late Antiquity* (Chicago, IL: University of Chicago Press, 1990).

Rather, what is vital is to set Paul's message in the context of other kinds of allegiance and religious affiliation that might also have proven attractive at the time, especially to guard against any tendency simply to assume that the early Christian message, and Paul's version in particular, was uniquely appealing or self-evidently superior.

We can hardly study the earliest Christian movement without considering the Judaism within which this movement arose. But when it comes to the appeal of Paul's message, the comparison has often been cast in terms of an ethnocentric or exclusive Judaism and a Pauline message that is open to all, and which therefore spread more widely. Paul's good news may be assumed to offer a more accessible and attractive form of the Jewish tradition, whose scriptures, theology, and ethics Paul largely continues to follow, but without requiring of gentile converts the demanding features of Jewish belonging: circumcision (for males), and observance of the Jewish law in regard to foods, Sabbath, and so on. It may well have been that some – perhaps many – of those attracted to Paul's message were people who already had some association with the Jewish community, such as those often described as 'god-fearers' or other kinds of sympathisers. But we need to be very cautious about any suggestion that Paul's good news offered a more attractive or appealing 'version' of Judaism, or an easier 'entry' into a kind of Jewish community (which is what the earliest Christ-following communities most likely appeared to be[7]).

First, we need to acknowledge the evidence that Judaism – specifically Jewish ethics and beliefs, based on its ancestral traditions and developed legal codes – was attractive to many people across the Roman Empire. The evidence comes both from sympathetic insiders, such as Josephus and Philo, who celebrated the widespread popularity and adoption of Jewish customs, and from hostile critics, such as Seneca and Horace, who lamented precisely the same trends (Seneca, cited by Augustine, *City of God* 6.11; Horace, *Satires* 1.4.142–43). Josephus may well exaggerate when he says, for example, that 'the masses have long ... shown a keen desire to adopt our religious observances' (*Against Apion* 2.282), as may Philo when he refers to the fact that 'almost every other people ... value and honour our laws' (*Life of Moses* 2.17). But for such claims to have had any plausibility, they must have reflected social reality to some degree, and this is confirmed by the hostile criticism of this spread of Jewish customs. Those attracted to Judaism sometimes took the step

[7] On this point, cf. Duff, *Jesus Followers*, 113–117.

of full 'conversion', becoming proselytes and (in the case of males) being circumcised. Others remained sympathisers, identifying with Jewish customs and the Jewish community to some degree, but without abandoning their other socio-religious affiliations.[8] One famous example is a wealthy woman by the name of Julia Severa, who funded the building of a synagogue (in the Phrygian city of Acmonia), but also functioned as priestess in a pagan cult.[9] Given the tendency to depict Paul's 'Christian' communities as more open, tolerant, and inclusive, compared with other 'Jewish' communities, it is worth stressing the extent to which this range of modes of affiliation with the Jewish community in various Diaspora locations offered, in some sense, a *more* tolerant and inclusive model, compared with Paul's insistence on exclusive devotion to the Christ-cult (e.g., 1 Cor 10:14–22; 1 Thess 1:9) – even if his converts may not always have followed his instruction in this regard. Recent scholarship has also largely agreed that the Judaism contemporary with Paul did not encourage deliberate missionary or proselytising activity intended to convince and win outsiders.[10] The appeal operated more by means of what some have referred to as 'passive attraction'. Paul, by comparison, along with other early Christ-followers, was clearly animated by an energetic drive to proclaim his message to all who would listen, and to win converts.

It is also worth noting that Paul's insistence that gentile converts could become Abraham's descendants and share in the blessing and salvation promised to those descendants without taking on a commitment to the whole Jewish law, and specifically the mark of circumcision (Rom 4:1–25; Gal 3:2–29), was not necessarily a more attractive option than full acceptance of Jewish practices and identity-markers. Some of the converts in Galatia, for example, seem to have wanted to undertake these signs of commitment and belonging, much to Paul's distress (Gal 1:6–9; 3:1–2; 5:2–6). One of the motivations, some have suggested, may have been to avoid censure for failing to participate in the imperial cult, by identifying as part of the Jewish community.[11] This does not seem to

[8] On these various modes of affiliation, see Terence L. Donaldson, *Judaism and the Gentiles: Jewish Patterns of Universalism (to 135 CE)* (Waco, TX: Baylor University Press, 2007).

[9] On this inscription, see Donaldson, *Judaism*, 463–466.

[10] An overview is provided by Michael F. Bird, *Crossing over Sea and Land: Jewish Missionary Activity in the Second Temple Period* (Peabody, MA: Hendrickson, 2010).

[11] See Bruce W. Winter, *Seek the Welfare of the City: Christians as Benefactors and Citizens* (Grand Rapids, MI: Eerdmans, 1994), 123–143.

have been an isolated local issue either, given the extent to which Paul warns about similar dangers elsewhere (e.g. Phil 3:2–3).

While Judaism was one ancestral, ethnic tradition from the east of the Roman Empire that was evidently appealing and attractive to outsiders, another cult from the East, the Egyptian cult of Isis, was also attractive to many at the time and, like Judaism, had spread widely into the western parts of the Empire, with temples to Isis commonly found, including in the cities visited by Paul. Indeed, one indication of both the popularity of Isis and the (limited) parallel with the appeal of Judaism may be found in the various bans on Jewish and Egyptian cults in Rome, when they were perceived to be a cause of trouble.[12] The cult in this period worshipped Isis as maternal giver of life, protector, saviour, ruler of the universe, and was one of the so-called mystery cults, which offered initiates entrance into what seems to have been perceived as an intimate encounter with the god, through a set of ritual and liturgical practices that were subject to strict secrecy. The account of an initiation in Apuleius' *Metamorphoses* (also known as *The Golden Ass*) book 11, 'the most detailed account of the Isis-liturgy that we possess from antiquity',[13] includes the initiate's emotional outburst of prayer and worship: 'O holy, perennial saviour of the human race, you are ever generous in your care for mortals, and you bestow a mother's sweet affection upon wretched people in misfortune' (11.25; trans. Walsh). Considering reasons for the attractiveness of the Isis cult in any depth is beyond the scope of this short essay, but we may briefly mention the potential appeal of the goddess's protection from fate, an intimate experience of encounter with the deity, heightened by the element of secrecy, and the prominence of women within the cult, which may have attracted women as well as men to participate.

Another mystery cult that was very popular, and had spread widely (though not through proactive missionary activity) by the mid-second century CE, was the Roman cult of Mithras. Often seen as another 'Eastern' cult, with possible Persian origins, this cult may, some have

[12] See Mary Beard, John North, and Simon Price, *Religions of Rome: Vol 1: A History* (Cambridge: Cambridge University Press, 1998), 230–231; Duff, *Jesus Followers*, 134.

[13] P.G. Walsh, *Apuleius, The Golden Ass* (Oxford: Oxford University Press, 1995), xxxvii. For a recent discussion of this initiation, see Jan Bremmer, *Initiation into the Mysteries of the Ancient World* (Berlin: De Gruyter, 2014), 114-25. For a valuable collection of primary sources on the mysteries, see Marvin W. Meyer (ed.), *The Ancient Mysteries: A Sourcebook* (San Francisco, CA: Harper and Row, 1987).

suggested, in fact have originated in or near Rome.[14] In contrast to our evidence for the Christ-movement at the time of Paul (a rich literary deposit but hardly anything directly from the archaeological record until rather later), the evidence for the Mithras cult is largely archaeological, meaning that literary records of liturgy and ritual are lacking. The central myth of the cult concerned the character Mithras killing a bull, some kind of sacrificial act that seems to effect salvation, at least for initiates. Mithras himself is acclaimed as *deus sol invictus Mithras* – 'the invincible sun god Mithras'.[15] Again, the cult involved an initiation ritual, which seems to have depicted a form of rebirth, and celebrated a ritual meal that symbolised the theme of life from death. Identification with the powerful and undefeated deity offers the hope of help and salvation. Unlike Isis, the cult of Mithras only allowed men to be initiates; it was especially popular among Roman soldiers, and recruited also among minor officials, including slaves. The focus on the deity being *invictus* ('unconquerable') most likely served as one obvious point of appeal to such people.

These comparisons are important in order to make clear that Paul's message, and the early Christian message more generally, was by no means uniquely or obviously an especially attractive option in this period. Judaism was evidently attractive and gaining adherents and sympathisers in many places, and other cults, notably Isis and (slightly later) Mithras spread widely and attracted many participants across the Empire. Furthermore, as we have already noted, we know so little about the size and growth of the earliest Christian groups that it is hard to conclude that Paul's message was especially convincing or appealing, although it clearly succeeded at least to the extent that Paul's visits to various cities and regions resulted in the formation of groups of Christ-followers with whom he remained in touch. Moreover, the scale and rate of growth in Christian numbers through the first, second, and third centuries is notoriously hard to determine, and depends largely on more or less informed speculation. It is hard – but important – not to view the question about the attractions of Paul's 'good news' from the perspective of later history, since we know that from the fourth century onwards Christianity, especially after the conversion of emperor

[14] See Manfred Clauss, *The Roman Cult of Mithras: The God and His Mysteries* (Edinburgh: Edinburgh University Press, 2000), 7. See also Bremmer, *Initiation*, 128–129, and the wider discussion of the cult of Mithras on 125–138.

[15] See Clauss, *Roman Cult of Mithras*, 25–26, 143; Simon Hornblower and Antony Spawforth, eds., *Oxford Classical Dictionary*, 3rd rev. ed. (Oxford: Oxford University Press, 2003), 991.

Constantine, did establish itself as the dominant religion of the Roman Empire. One result of that victory is that the shrines and temples of other cults, such as Isis and Mithras, were widely destroyed, due to what Manfred Clauss calls the 'fanatical intolerance' of the Christians.[16] Indeed, one key point of difference is that Paul's message called for complete and exclusive allegiance to one God (e.g. 1 Cor 10:14–22; 1 Thess 1:9), whereas other cults made no such exclusivist claims: they were hardly 'competing' for loyalty in the same way. Christianity's later victory, whether we regard it positively or negatively, can suggest that such success was somehow inevitable, or at least likely, due to the attractions of the movement from its earliest years. But these comparisons should at least caution us that at the time of Paul's missionary activity, there was little if anything to suggest that his message or the groups that accepted it would eventually come to succeed over their 'rivals', with all the profound consequences for the reconfiguration of the Empire's religious and sociocultural landscape that would eventually entail. Nonetheless, we can at least say that some people were attracted to Paul's 'good news' and formed the membership of the small groups to which he then wrote. Bearing in mind all the cautionary points already set out, both in terms of the limitations of our evidence and the important comparisons, we should at least attempt to consider what might have formed the basis for the attractions of Paul's message.

REASONS FOR ATTRACTION

As noted at the outset of this chapter, there has been comparatively little attention given to the reasons why people were attracted to Paul's good news, and the attention that has been given to this question has mostly considered the broader context of the early Christian movement in the first two or three centuries. The following set of factors, then, is offered as an attempt to set out some of the possibilities, by no means a comprehensive list, but potentially worthy of further consideration. I have ordered these potential factors in a way that moves from more 'theological' or 'religious' factors to more social ones. Of course, some combination of various factors is more likely to form a plausible answer to our question rather than any single factor alone. It is also worth reiterating that any suggestion that a certain factor made Paul's good news attractive does not imply that this factor was unique to Paul, or to

[16] Clauss, *Roman Cult of Mithras*, 170.

the early Christian movement. Other groups and allegiances may have offered comparable attractions in a more or less compelling way. There may, too, have been costs in practical and socioeconomic terms in joining Paul's Christ-groups, as the references to hostility and suffering in Paul's letters frequently imply (e.g., Rom 8:18–39; Phil 1:27–30; 1 Thess 2:14);[17] in some sense, then, the attractions or motivations to join, however they were perceived by converts, must have been stronger than these significant disincentives.

Rescue from Imminent Divine Wrath

In what is probably his earliest letter, 1 Thessalonians, Paul reminds the Thessalonians of their initial response to his message: 'how you turned to God from idols to serve the living and true God, and to wait for his Son from heaven, whom he raised from the dead, Jesus who delivers us from the wrath to come' (1 Thess 1:9–10).[18] Encapsulated within this brief summary are a number of indications about the core of Paul's 'good news'. It involves, for gentile converts, a turn from the many gods that, from a Jewish perspective, Paul labels as 'idols', to serve one God. This requirement for religious exclusivism was unusual in the ancient world, though the idea of there being one supreme God, what we have come to call monotheism, was arguably more evident in the period than has often been appreciated.[19] The popularity of Jewish custom and religious conviction, as we have noted above, may also have added plausibility and appeal to Paul's focus on the 'living and true God'. His message also conveys a sense of imminent eschatological expectation: Jesus will soon return to rescue these converts from 'the wrath to come'. This last motif may be significant. The idea that the gods could be pleased or displeased by human activity, and that they might thus show their wrath by bringing misfortune and calamity upon people (whether on an individual through tragedy or illness, or on a community through disaster or disease) was woven in various ways through the fabric of everyday belief. Indeed, later in the second century Tertullian famously remarks on how any disaster or misfortune could be blamed on the Christians (*Apology* 40), due to their refusal to worship the gods, which thus disrupted the fragile peace maintained by due obeisance to the gods

[17] On this broader issue, see Hurtado, *Why on Earth*, 11–15, 46–108.

[18] On this passage, and the broader reasons for the attractions of Paul's message, see Duff, *Jesus Followers*, 80–108.

[19] See Stephen Mitchell and Peter Van Nuffelen, eds., *One God: Pagan Monotheism in the Roman Empire* (Cambridge: Cambridge University Press, 2010).

(the so-called *pax deorum*) and brought manifestations of divine anger. Roman 'religion' pervaded everyday life, with numerous gods who needed to be given offerings, or placated, and from whom guidance might be sought.[20] It seems, then, entirely possible within that cultural milieu that Paul's message about the most supreme God, and the anger of that God that was very soon to be unleashed on human beings, due to their immorality (cf. Rom 1:18–32), could generate some response – albeit a response driven primarily by fear at the 'bad news' of what would otherwise come.

Mystical Experience: Union with the God

We have already noted above the popularity of the so-called mystery cults, in particular the cults of Isis and Mithras. There are various features of the practices and beliefs of these cults that find points of comparison with Pauline religion: ritual washing, the symbolism of blood, a shared meal, hopes for salvation and protection. But one particular and central idea we might explore is the notion of an intimate encounter with the deity. As Walter Burkert remarks, 'mysteries provide an immediate encounter with the divine'.[21] In Apuleius' famous account of an initiation into the Isis-cult, the centre of the rite is subject to strict secrecy but it evidently entailed an emotional and intimate experience of the deity, which left the initiate prostrate and in tears as he exclaims the kindness and greatness of Isis, conscious of the inadequacy of his praise (*Metamorphoses* 11.21–25). In the field of Pauline studies, Albert Schweitzer famously argued, long ago, that the centre of Paul's theology was not the established Lutheran theme of 'justification by faith' but rather the 'mystical' idea of union with Christ, an identification with Christ in his death and resurrection.[22] Many have followed Schweitzer at least to the extent of agreeing about the prominence of 'participation in Christ' within Paul's thought. Insofar as we can glimpse Paul's sense of his own 'conversion' experience, he seems to have perceived it to involve some kind of visionary encounter with the risen Christ. In Galatians, he strikingly speaks of God revealing his Son 'in' Paul (*en emoi*, Gal 1:16), and goes on to speak of this identification with Christ as involving nothing less than Paul's own death, such that

[20] See further Robert Turcan, *The Gods of Ancient Rome: Religion in Everyday Life from Archaic to Imperial Times* (Edinburgh: Edinburgh University Press, 2000).

[21] Walter Burkert, *Ancient Mystery Cults* (Cambridge, MA: Harvard University Press, 1987), 90.

[22] Albert Schweitzer, *The Mysticism of Paul the Apostle* (London: A & C Black, 1931).

the life he now lives is Christ's life 'in' him (Gal 2:20). In the initiation into the Isis cult, ritual washing (along with fasting) marked the period of preparation for the initiation, for which new robes were worn; in Pauline practice, the immersion into the water at baptism constituted the ritual act in which the identification of the convert with Christ took place, an identification that involved dying and beginning a new life, clothed anew with Christ (cf. Gal 3:27; Rom 6:3–11, 13:14; Col 2:12, 3:1–14). Moreover, just as initiates into the cults of Isis and Mithras seem to have experienced emotional, ecstatic, or psychically altered states, converts into the Pauline groups seem to have experienced such altered states and ecstatic speech during their meetings (1 Cor 14:22–23).[23] Would the promise of an intimate, mystical, and transformative encounter with the risen Christ, a quasi-divine saviour figure sent by the one supreme God, have been attractive, at least to some, perhaps for some of the same reasons that other mystery cults were attractive?

Salvation, Rescue, and Protection

Prominent in the Mithras cult appears to have been a focus on the 'help' the god could offer, the power of the omnipotent god to assist those who identified with him. Indeed, identification with the divinity, Clauss remarks, was believed to lead to salvation.[24] Likewise, in the Isis cult, the goddess is acclaimed as saviour, offering protection and governing the movements of the universe (Apuleius, *Metamorphoses* 11.25). The promise of rescue from coming wrath through identification with Jesus Christ may likewise have formed part of an offer of 'salvation' that proved attractive to some. This salvation may have been perceived to encompass both protection and help in the present (not least from curses or misfortunes brought by spiritual powers) and also hope beyond death, something less commonly found in other cults.[25] Allegiance to and identification with Christ may have been seen as one way to gain some kind of protection in a dangerous world. Of course, as Paul's letters reveal, in both his own case and that of his converts, this allegiance hardly guaranteed insulation against hardship and suffering, not least suffering caused by the hostile reaction of others. But, as Bruce

[23] See, e.g., Clauss, *Roman Cult of Mithras*, 107. In relation to the Pauline group at Corinth, see Dale B. Martin, *The Corinthian Body* (New Haven, CT: Yale University Press, 1995), 87–103.

[24] See Clauss, *Roman Cult of Mithras*, 14–15, 142–143.

[25] But see Beard, North, and Price, *Religions of Rome*, 289–291.

Longenecker and Natalie Webb argue, the symbol of the cross may have been seen by Paul and his converts as a powerful apotropaic device, comparable to other such devices and practices common in the ancient world: a means to ward off evil and misfortune in a world where hostile powers and enemies were seen as a constant threat.[26]

Missionary Zeal and the Charisma of Paul

Although it is not strictly one of the reasons that makes the message itself attractive or convincing, one factor that may be significant in understanding how Paul gained converts may be simply the missionary zeal with which he pursued his sense of calling to take the good news of Christ to the nations. As we have noted, recent scholarship has largely agreed that Judaism at the time, however open to welcoming sympathisers and converts, was not widely promoted through proactive missionizing activity. Neither did the mystery cults seek to attract new adherents in this way. For whatever reasons, by contrast, the first generation of Christ-followers, and Paul in particular, seem to have felt an imperative to spread the 'good news' about Christ. Paul is clear that this is a 'compulsion' laid upon him, about which he has no choice (1 Cor 9:16–17), and in one of his last letters he celebrates the fact 'that from Jerusalem and all the way around to Illyricum I have fulfilled the ministry of the gospel of Christ' (Rom 15:19). Paul was presumably successful, in some measure at least, in persuading people of the truth of his message, and that probably indicates some degree both of articulacy (as his letters well attest) and personal charisma. Also not to be underestimated is the apparent ability of Paul to 'work wonders', that is, to perform some kinds of deeds of healing or display of power (cf. 2 Cor 12:12). With his expertise in Jewish tradition and scripture, his labors and sufferings as an 'apostle' of Christ, his powerful deeds and 'wise' teachings, Heidi Wendt has suggested that Paul might well be seen in the category of 'freelance religious expert', like other such independent figures in the ancient world.[27] Indeed, as Wendt

[26] See Bruce W. Longenecker, *The Crosses of Pompeii: Jesus-Devotion in a Vesuvian Town* (Minneapolis, MN: Fortress Press, 2016), 261–262; Natalie R. Webb, "Powers and Protection in Pompeii and Paul: The Apotropaic Function of the Cross in the Letter to the Galatians," in *Early Christianity in Pompeian Light: People, Texts, Situations*, ed. Bruce W. Longenecker (Minneapolis, MN: Fortress Press, 2016), 93–121. For discussion of evidence in the second and third centuries, see Bruce W. Longenecker, *The Cross before Constantine: The Early Life of a Christian Symbol* (Minneapolis, MN: Fortress Press, 2015), 170–176.

[27] Heidi Wendt, *At the Temple Gates: The Religion of Freelance Experts in the Roman Empire* (Oxford: Oxford University Press, 2016), 146–189.

shows, there is plenty of evidence for such 'self-authorized religious experts' at the time, vigorously promoting their message and its promises, even though they are often caricatured as charlatans who deceive the gullible, as in Lucian's satirical portraits of the second-century figures of Alexander and Peregrinus.[28] Paul's impressive 'expertise' may well have formed part of the attraction of his message, though we need to remember that he operated as part of a team of collaborators, named as such in the activities of both mission and letter-writing (e.g., 1 Thess 1:1; 2 Cor 1:19). Even if Paul seems to have been the leading figure in his circle, he nonetheless undertook his activities as part of a group, such that any success of the message cannot be too heavily attributed to Paul's personal charisma or expertise alone. Indeed, he seems to indicate that his presence and speech were sometimes regarded as rather unimpressive, at least compared with his weighty letters (2 Cor 10:10; cf. 1 Cor 2:1–5). While such self-deprecation must be seen in context as part of a highly rhetorical appeal in which Paul threatens to be as powerful when he comes as he is by letter, it may nonetheless caution us against placing too much emphasis on Paul's own charisma as a basis for his success.

Community Meal and Group-Belonging

A common feature of Greco-Roman custom, central to the life of associations and cult-groups as well as the household, was the practice of gathering to eat a meal, specifically a ritualized meal in the form of a banquet – with a supper (*deipnon*) followed by drinking and entertainment (*symposion*). Ritual meals were central to the Mithraic cult and a banquet was part of the Isis-cult initiation depicted by Apuleius. The fact that the earliest Christ-group meetings centered around a meal thus made them typical rather than unusual in their cultural context. Of course, the Christian meal as Paul describes it had a particular focus and ritual meaning: it was an occasion to recall the story of Jesus's last meal and to await his return (1 Cor 11:23–25), and to reinforce the common identity and solidarity of the community, symbolized, for Paul, in the oneness of the shared bread and cup (1 Cor 10:16–17). But its broader structure, with the supper followed by the cup, and then a time of discussion, singing, prayer, prophecy, and so on after the meal (cf. 1 Cor 11:17–14:40) fits the common pattern.[29] The opportunity to join

[28] See Wendt, *At the Temple Gates*, 1–17 *et passim*.

[29] On this pattern, see Hal Taussig, *In the Beginning Was the Meal: Social Experimentation and Early Christian Identity* (Minneapolis, MN: Fortress Press, 2009), 67–85.

together in a communal meal, to be part of a close-knit group who saw one another as siblings (a prominent self-identification in Paul's letters), may thus have been another attraction, in concrete and social terms, of joining the Christ-groups. It should be clear, however, that this is by no means a unique attraction of Paul's message, but one that would also be pertinent to other groups, whether cultic, professional, or ethnic. It may be that part of the particular attraction of the groups for which Paul sought converts was the ways in which, not least through their communal meals, they embodied a charitable concern for the poor. As Longenecker has shown, this is a distinctive emphasis in the early Christian movement, and one to which Paul shows a commitment, not least through his 'collection' project (see 2 Cor 8–9). A general commitment to 'remember the poor', a commitment Paul shares with other early Christian leaders, may be signaled in Gal 2:10, even though this verse is often interpreted as a specific reference to Paul's collection for Jerusalem.[30] Paul's instructions concerning the meal at Corinth, however, may make a somewhat ambivalent contribution to this care for the poor. While Paul is concerned that the meeting should not be one in which 'some go hungry while others get drunk', or in which shame is brought on 'those who have nothing' (1 Cor 11:21–22), his instruction to 'eat at home' (1 Cor 11:34) seems at least to open the way to the eucharistic meal losing its character as a full meal, shared by all, and to legitimate 'private' eating at home instead. There may, then, have been attraction in joining a close-knit group that met for a shared meal, particularly, but by no means exclusively, for those who struggled to obtain enough to eat. This leads us to one final factor to consider.

Appeal to 'the Foolish, Slaves, Women, and Little Children'

Among the critical charges laid at the door of the early Christians was that their message was so unconvincing that it appealed only to 'the foolish, dishonourable and stupid, and only slaves, women and little children' (quoted in Origen, *Against Celsus* 3.44). Origen's response to this charge from his critic, Celsus, appeals to Paul's declaration that among the Corinthian community there were 'not many wise, powerful or of noble birth' (1 Cor 1:26). For Origen (and many modern scholars too), Paul's comment is significant in showing that there were *some* of higher social status within these Christ-groups. However, what is also clear, and has been emphasised in more recent studies, is that the

[30] See further Bruce W. Longenecker, *Remember the Poor: Paul, Poverty, and the Greco-Roman World* (Grand Rapids, MI: Eerdmans, 2010).

majority of these first Christian converts came from among the lower status groups, living in poverty close to subsistence level.[31] Paul's rhetoric in 1 Corinthians, while it is hardly a straightforward source of socioeconomic data, at least reveals Paul aligning himself with the foolish, weak, despised nobodies and insisting that these are precisely the people God has chosen (1 Cor 1:26–30; cf. 4:10–13). Such rhetoric may correspond to a certain appeal to those who are, as Celsus remarked, not among the supposedly wise and educated levels of society. Did Paul's message, then, appeal in particular to the poor, to slaves, and to women, and others who might resonate with a declaration that God had chosen the nobodies to shame the wise? There are certainly indications that women, some of whom may not have been particularly poor or low status, were not only to be found among the membership of these early Christ-groups but also that some of them held leading roles (see, e.g., Rom 16:1–7; Phil 4:2–3). There were clearly also slaves among the groups founded by Paul, including one, Onesimus, for whom Paul famously appeals to his owner (Philemon). However, we should not conclude that it was only the poorest or lowest status members of society to which Paul's message appealed. While recent scholarship has been sceptical of the idea, promoted as part of the so-called new consensus on the socioeconomic level of the Pauline Christians, that there were members of the wealthy upper class among the Christ-groups, most nonetheless conclude that there was a range of socioeconomic levels encompassed within them. What may have attracted people from more 'middling' social levels to join? Apart from the more theological or religious factors mentioned above, some have suggested specifically sociological considerations. In his now classic study, *The First Urban Christians*, Wayne Meeks suggested that the Pauline communities attracted a significant number of converts who experienced 'status inconsistency' in their wider society: their various status indicators (wealth, education, family background, etc.) did not consistently align but were mixed – such as in the case of an ex-slave (a freedperson) who acquired significant wealth. Meeks further proposed that Paul's message may have been particularly attractive to such people, 'who had experienced the hopes and fears of occupying an ambiguous position in

[31] Significant in establishing this view were Justin J. Meggitt, *Paul, Poverty and Survival* (Edinburgh: T&T Clark, 1998) and Steven J. Friesen, "Poverty in Pauline Studies: Beyond the So-called New Consensus," *Journal for the Study of the New Testament* 26 (2004): 323–361. See also Longenecker, *Remember the Poor*, 36–59, 317–332.

society', offering them a 'welcome refuge'.[32] One problem with Meeks' attractive suggestion is simply the lack of detailed or extensive information about the social or economic status of the earliest converts; we can hardly be confident about how many of them were 'status inconsistent' nor whether this proportion would be more or less than in society at large. Nonetheless, we may perhaps suggest that joining the early Christian groups offered some social advantages (as well as potential costs) that differed according to social level. For those who were from 'middling' social groups, the chance to support, sponsor, or host a congregation of Christ-followers may have offered the chance to feel significant and exercise leadership in the context of a small group. For women, these groups may have offered opportunities (though not uniquely, it should be stressed, given other evidence for their roles as benefactors, and so on) to exercise independent agency and leadership, especially if they followed Paul's advice that remaining unmarried to serve the Lord single-mindedly was the preferable course of action (1 Cor 7:8–9, 32–38). For slaves and the poor, the groups established by Paul and his co-workers may have offered material support and a certain dignity of status, famously expressed in the baptismal declaration that there is 'no longer slave or free' in Christ (Gal 3:28; cf. also 1 Cor 7:22–23).

CONCLUSION

This attempt to outline some of the possible reasons why at least some people were attracted to Paul's good news is sketchy and provisional, attempting to assemble at least some of the main factors that deserve consideration, though these also need to be set within the wider context of the Roman Empire, and specifically its expansion, civil war, localised revolts, and so on – all of which upheaval might have added to the attraction of turning to the deity Paul announced as the one true, just, benevolent, and all-powerful God. These various themes, and doubtless others too, are hopefully worthy of further study, especially given the relative neglect of our question in the field of Pauline studies. It is, however, worth stressing that any such studies must proceed with caution, for reasons outlined above, and must take care not to assume that any of these reasons for attraction are by any means unique to Paul's message. More likely, as we have seen above, is that at least some

[32] Wayne A. Meeks, *The First Urban Christians: The Social World of the Apostle Paul* (New Haven, CT: Yale University Press, 1983), 191; see further 22–23, 51–73.

of the reasons why people may have been attracted to Paul's good news – such as the hope of protection against evil and divine wrath, intimate encounter with the divine, communal bonds expressed through a shared meal, and so on – derive from shared cultural concerns, to which other groups and cults also offered their own answers and responses.[33]

Further Reading

Beard, Mary, John North, and Simon Price. *Religions of Rome: Vol 1: A History*. Cambridge: Cambridge University Press, 1998.

Bird, Michael F. *Crossing over Sea and Land: Jewish Missionary Activity in the Second Temple Period*. Peabody, MA: Hendrickson, 2010.

Bremmer, Jan. *Initiation into the Mysteries of the Ancient World*. Berlin: De Gruyter, 2014.

Burkert, Walter. *Ancient Mystery Cults*. Cambridge, MA: Harvard University Press, 1987.

Clauss, Manfred. *The Roman Cult of Mithras: The God and His Mysteries*. Edinburgh: Edinburgh University Press, 2000.

Donaldson, Terence L. *Judaism and the Gentiles: Jewish Patterns of Universalism (to 135 CE)*. Waco, TX: Baylor University Press, 2007.

Duff, Paul B. *Jesus Followers in the Roman Empire*. Grand Rapids, MI: Eerdmans, 2017.

Hurtado, Larry W. *Why on Earth Did Anyone Become a Christian in the First Three Centuries*. Milwaukee, WI: Marquette University Press, 2016.

Longenecker, Bruce W. *Remember the Poor: Paul, Poverty, and the Greco-Roman World*. Grand Rapids, MI: Eerdmans, 2010.

Meeks, Wayne A. *The First Urban Christians: The Social World of the Apostle Paul*. 2nd ed. New Haven, CT: Yale University Press, 2003.

Meyer Marvin W., ed. *The Ancient Mysteries: A Sourcebook*. San Francisco, CA: Harper and Row, 1987.

Mitchell, Stephen, and Peter Van Nuffelen, eds. *One God: Pagan Monotheism in the Roman Empire*. Cambridge: Cambridge University Press, 2010.

Turcan, Robert. *The Gods of Ancient Rome: Religion in Everyday Life from Archaic to Imperial Times*. Edinburgh: Edinburgh University Press, 2000.

Wendt, Heidi. *At the Temple Gates: The Religion of Freelance Experts in the Roman Empire*. Oxford: Oxford University Press, 2016.

[33] I am very grateful to Bruce Longenecker, Justin Meggitt, Teresa Morgan, and Tim Whitmarsh for sharing ideas and bibliographical suggestions when I first began to think about this essay. I would also like to thank Teresa Morgan for very helpful comments on a draft. Needless to say, aside from what constitutes reasonable editorial oversight (!), these people bear no responsibility for what I have ended up writing.

15 How Was the Reception of Paul Shaped in the Early Church?

MARGARET M. MITCHELL

THE MANY PAULS

A Greek-speaking Jew from the Diaspora with a common name, Paul (Greek: *Paulos*, Latin: *Paulus*) was a living, breathing, changing, urgent, fiery, meditative, and controversial human being who lived in the first century CE, and probably met his death in Rome in the 60s, during the reign of the emperor Nero (r. 54–68 CE). This figure is in many ways lost to us. But he did in fact exist, in all the complexities of any human life, built of deeds and words and relationships, identities, accidents, changes, and commitments. A living person, "Paul" (whom we may designate "P"), is a necessary, but not at all sufficient condition for how this figure will be remembered, refashioned, reanimated, and repurposed in the decades and centuries that followed. Beginning in his lifetime, and developing exponentially within the history of ancient Christ-believing communities in the next centuries around and beyond the Mediterranean ambit, "Paul" will multiply and proliferate. This variability is a crucial element in how the reception of Paul was shaped and animated in the early church.

It is the work of historical scholarship on Paul (as for any ancient person of note) to seek to reconstruct what we can know about that living person, based on the existing sources, both about himself and his broader historical contexts, and depending upon a series of analytical choices that must in every case be argued for and not just asserted. In what follows I shall give some basic facts about my reconstruction of the "historical Paul" ("HP," who is not identical with "Paul" but is one selective iteration of him), as a baseline for the discussion of the development of multiple Pauls in the early church. This reconstruction largely prioritizes the period in Paul's life about which we are best informed by primary sources, ca. 50–62 CE (i.e., during the reigns of Claudius and Nero), when he wrote his extant letters. Although the "HP" was not identical with the way Paul came to be known and reinterpreted, the seeds of some of the key features of "Pauline interpretation" were there from the beginning, as we can (only) retrospectively appreciate, and trace forward.

In his lifetime this obscure Greek-speaking Jewish provincial had journeyed around the Mediterranean in a "circle" (or, rather, semicircle), from Jerusalem to Illyricum (Rom 15:19), delivering what he termed the *euangelion*, or "good news missive," about his God, the God of Abraham, Isaac, and Jacob, and that God's son, "the Lord Jesus Messiah" (*kyrios Iēsous Christos*). Paul insistently claimed that his God had sent him as an envoy or emissary (that is what the term "*apostolos*" means) with an explicit invitation to Gentiles (i.e., non-Jews) to believe in this message of Jesus Messiah crucified, risen, and about to return as the final days of history were unfolding before his return. The *euangelion* Paul brought was an oral proclamation, an episodic narrative centered on Jesus Messiah's death on the cross and resurrection, but capable of being expanded to stretch all the way back to the creation of the world, and all the way forward to Jesus Messiah's imminent return (*parousia*) from heaven.[1]

Strikingly, the *euangelion* story as Paul related it during the time of his missionary work scooped up and incorporated into itself the events of its own reception, such that in 1 Cor 15:8–11 Paul had added his own experience of the resurrected Jesus to the *euangelion*-tradition he had received from those who were apostles before him (1 Cor 15:3–7; cf. 1 Cor 15:11; Gal 1:12 and 17). On this logic, he could refer to the start of his preaching activity in Macedonia as "the beginning of the *euangelion*" (Phil 4:15). As a result (as he claimed in his letters), Paul was not only the transmitter of the sacred story but one of the chief actors in the gospel story that he was telling in the very act of its unfolding. Indeed, in Rom 10:14–18 Paul insisted that he and his *euangelion*-mission to the Gentiles (who were formerly "not-God's-people"[2]) had been foretold centuries before by the prophet Isaiah and the psalmist.[3] Paul grandiosely insisted to the community of perhaps one hundred believers in the Romanized city of Corinth, to whom he had brought the *euangelion* a year or two prior (and who met in private homes and had no dedicated architecture), that he was a "master builder" (*tektōn*) who laid a

[1] On Paul's gospel as an "accordion," see Margaret M. Mitchell, *Paul and the Emergence of Christian Textuality: Early Christian Literary Culture in Context* (Tübingen: Mohr Siebeck, 2018), 111–132.

[2] Rom 9:25–26, quoting Hosea 2:1, 25.

[3] Isa 52:7; 53:1; Ps 18:5 LXX.

foundation (*themelion*) there on which others would build (1 Cor 3:10–17). Furthering the building theme, Paul insisted that these clusters of Corinthians who responded to his *euangelion* with the proclamation "Jesus is Lord" (1 Cor 12:3) and the ritual of baptism (1 Cor 10:1–4; 12:13) constituted the very temple of God (*naos tou theou*)[4] in which God's holy spirit dwells (1 Cor 3:16). One of the most astonishing things about the history of what would later become "Christianity" is that this outsized and metaphorical boast from the early 50s would in fact take concrete form in the decades and centuries to come.

Paul never wrote his *euangelion* down in full, even as he claimed to present it to those he met in these far-flung urban contexts in multimedia forms: in word, in acts of pneumatic power, and, most graphically, in his own diseased body, which he viewed as an epiphanic medium of Christ's death and resurrection.[5] Although he never composed a narrative *euangelion*, Paul did write increasingly long and complex letters back to communities he had founded (in Asia Minor, Macedonia, and Achaia) and forward to those that he had not yet visited (such as Rome). In these, he continually reinterpreted the significance and persuasive power of that *euangelion*, defended his apostolic commission to preach, despite vehement and powerful opposition that insisted he was a charlatan and not a true "apostle," and engaged in detailed arguments about the scriptures of Israel that, he insisted, were fulfilled in the *euangelion* story of God's surprising saving plan. Paul depicted himself in different guises in the letters – he was a former persecutor; an apostle called from his mother's womb; a calm and authoritative advisor; an angry spurned friend; a father or mother who gave birth to his converts; a dignified ambassador; a man of ignominious weakness; an unyielding defender of truth; a conciliatory force for unity; even (perhaps self-ironically) "all things to all people" (1 Cor 9:22). For all the singularity and particularity of each of these seven genuine letters[6] to diverse assemblies of believers in varied and specific circumstances (each distinct in topics, in tone and

[4] In order to recognize the outlandishness of this statement it is important to remember that the temple to the god of Abraham, Isaac, and Jacob was standing in Jerusalem, as the largest *temenos* (sacred sanctuary) in the Mediterranean world, when Paul wrote these words to groups of people meeting in Gaius' house or other rental spaces in Corinth.

[5] 1 Thess 1:5; 2 Cor 4:8–10; Gal 3:1; 4:13–14; 6:17. Fuller discussion in Mitchell, *Paul and the Emergence of Christian Textuality*, 111–132, 237–255.

[6] I cite the general (though not uncontested) consensus among scholars that 1 Thessalonians, Galatians, 1 and 2 Corinthians, Philemon, Romans, Philippians, are authentic.

temperament, in arguments, and in these memorable self-descriptions by their author), every one of these letters contains the term *euangelion*. And each begins with the word *Paulos*.

THE PAULINE LETTERS AS FOUNDATION

Some, but not all, of the letters (*epistolai*) that this figure Paul (together with members of his missionary team, such as Timothy) wrote and sent and delivered, were preserved to history as what we may term "the historical-epistolary Paul" (HEP), that is, *Paul as he became known through these texts he wrote during his lifetime.*[7] I use this designation (HEP) to ensure against any assumption that the extant genuine letters somehow equal either P (the human person), which, as a very partial and tendentious record, they cannot, or even HP ("the historical Paul"), since the historian cannot merely accept select and highly rhetorical documents as an accurate or in any sense complete record of the past in and of themselves. This construction also has the advantage of serving as a link with the history of Pauline influence to come, which, while not solely located in those seven letters, was always in profound ways, in whole or in part, generated by and in engagement with them. In his lifetime and after, these letters interacted closely with but were far more influential than the networks of human memories about the man himself that, absent the letters, might have dissipated within a single generation.[8] In fact, the Pauline letters had the opposite effect from disappearance in death. They created and maintained a captivating, living, portable,[9] memorable, flexible, and endlessly contestable

[7] I do not use the term "'real' Paul" even in scare quotes because no such thing exists (either then or now) and it just clouds the discussion (but cf. Benjamin L. White, *Remembering Paul: Ancient and Modern Contests over the Image of the Apostle* [Oxford: Oxford University Press, 2014], who employs the phrase throughout in order to contest it).

[8] This is not to deny ongoing oral traditions about Paul (or the relevance of social memory studies to Paul [see White, *Remembering Paul*, esp. 90–107]), but to insist on the importance of the letters in securing the legacy and (re)shaping of those memories. While one can try heuristically to separate out the letters, life, and theological teaching (see Daniel Marguerat, "Paul après Paul: une histoire de réception," *New Testament Studies* 54, no. 3 [2008]: 317–337), in practice these three things were thoroughly intertwined.

[9] As just two examples from the 180s, the "books and letters of Paul a just man" (*libri et epistolae Pauli uiri iusti*) are in a *kapsa* in a courtroom in Scilli where martyrs were convicted July 17, 180 CE (*Mart. Scil.* 12) and they accompanied Abercius of Hieropolis in Asia Minor in his carriage on his journey to Rome, Nisibis and back home (funerary inscription, line 12, also ca. 180).

trans-local and trans-temporal body of knowledge for the fledgling Gentile Christ-believing communities. And they set the standard that this body of knowledge was to be subject to ongoing reinterpretation given new contexts, new needs, and controversies old and new. We can see this emphatically in three references from perhaps as early as ca. 90–120,[10] which show that Paul's letters were viewed as foundational already across the Mediterranean ambit in the four main Roman provinces of Asia Minor, Macedonia, Achaia, and Italia.[11]

Ignatius of Antioch (in Syria), *Letter to the Ephesians* 12.1–2 (ca. 115 CE[12]):

> I know who I am and to whom I am writing. I am condemned (*katakritos*), you have been extended mercy (*ēleēmenoi*). I am under danger (*kindynos*), you stand firm (*estērigmenoi*). You are a way station for those being killed for God, co-initiates of Paul (*Paulos*) – Paul, who was sanctified (*hagiasmenos*), attested (*memartyrēmenos*), a man worthy of blessing (*axiomakarios*), who made mention of you (*mnēmoneuein*) in every letter (*epistolē*) in Christ Jesus (*en Christō Iēsou*). Oh, may I be found in his footsteps when I attain to God!

1 Clement (a letter from Rome to Corinth) 47.1–4 (90–100 CE?):

> Take up the epistle (*epistolē*) of the blessed Paul the apostle (*Paulos ho apostolos*) (i.e., 1 Corinthians). What first did he write to you "in the beginning of the gospel" (*en archē tou euangeliou*) (Phil 4:15)? In truth he wrote his letter (*epistellein*) to you in spiritual fashion (*pneumatikōs*) about himself and Cephas and Apollos (cf. 1 Cor 1:12; 3:22) because even then you made factions for yourselves!

[10] The boundary between "first" and "second" centuries did not exist in antiquity, but still has a profound (and problematic) influence on New Testament scholarship on a host of questions. We do better to stick with the regnal years of the emperors (hence, these texts were written sometime between the imperium of Domitian [d. 96 CE] and Hadrian [d. 138 CE] or Antoninus Pius [d. 161 CE]), in order to resist a temptation of placing the (presumably fixed) "historical Paul" in the first century and new and creative "Pauls" in the second.

[11] All translations mine; Greek text from Franz Xaver Funk, Karl Bihlmeyer, and Molly Whittaker, *Die Apostolischen Väter, Griechische-Deutsche Parallelausgabe* (Tübingen: Mohr Siebeck, 1992).

[12] I accept the traditional (Eusebian) dating for Ignatius within the reign of Trajan (with William R. Schoedel, *Ignatius of Antioch: A Commentary on the Seven Letters of Ignatius* [Philadelphia: Fortress Press, 1986]). This has been challenged by some scholars; see the collection of articles in *Journal of Ancient Christianity* 1 (1997), with further bibliography.

> But that factionalism brought a lesser sin (*hamartia*) on yourselves, since you were factionalized with reference to men who were attested to be apostles (*apostoloi memartyrēmenoi*) and a man who had been tested and found worthy among them (*anēr dedokimasmenos*).

Polycarp (of Smyrna, in western Asia Minor), *Letter to the Philippians* (in Macedonia) 3.1–3 (ca. 117–120 CE?):

> In writing these things to you about righteousness (*dikaiosynē*), sisters and brothers (*adelphoi*), I am not acting on my own initiative, but because you asked me yourselves. For neither I nor anyone else like me is able to follow closely the wisdom (*sophia*) of the blessed (*makarios*) and esteemed (*endoxos*) Paul (*Paulos*), who, when he was among you, face to face (*kata prosōpon*) with the people alive in those days, taught (*didaskein*) accurately (*akribōs*) and securely (*bebaiōs*) the word of truth (*logos alētheias*). This same Paul, when absent (*apōn*), wrote letters (*epistolai*) to you; if you look closely into them, you will be able to be built up (*oikodomeisthai*) into the faith (*pistis*) that has been given to you, which is the mother of us all, even as hope (*elpis*) follows, while love (*agapē*) for God and Christ and the neighbor leads the way. If anyone is within these, they have fulfilled (*peplēroun*) the commandment of righteousness (*entolē dikaiosynēs*).

These three passages offer attestation of a geographically widespread knowledge of Paul, *through letters*, within perhaps 50–60 years after his death.[13] In all three cases Paul, introduced by his proper name, *Paulos*, is assumed to be recognized and remembered by believers from a future beyond Paul's own imagining, as a *foundational* figure who had a "blessed" life and death in the past, a wise and esteemed teacher, whose influence they readily acknowledge. Paul's absence by geographic distance in his own lifetime was, as is emphasized by all three witnesses, mediated *by his letters*, which now after his death continue to convey his presence and fashion new memories of his ongoing significance.

[13] The idea in nineteenth and twentieth century scholarship that there was an extended period of silence about Paul in the half-century or more after his death, on the part of all, or at least the orthodox writers (out of concern he was the "apostle of the heretics" [*haereticorum apostolus*, as Tertullian, *Adv. Marc.* 3.5.4, famously put it]), has been pronounced dead in the last forty years. See the engaging discussion on this "Pauline captivity narrative" and its demise in White, *Remembering Paul*, 42–69.

At the same time, these passages enshrine the assumption that Paul's originally *particular* letters have a *universal relevance* across time, space, and generations. These later Ephesians are told by Ignatius that they are included (somehow) "in every letter"; the Philippians are told that Paul wrote "letters"[14] to them; and Corinthians likely unborn ca. 52 when Paul wrote the letter known to us as "1 Corinthians," are included in its intended addressees ("what did he first write *to you*?"). Moreover, these three authors show that Paul's letters are now being read in Antioch, Ephesus, Smyrna, Philippi, Corinth, and Rome, which means they are available in some material form in these different locales. The full works of these three authors (Ignatius, Polycarp, the writer of 1 Clement) indicate that they know more than one single letter[15] (as can also be inferred from these statements quoted above), which means they know Paul's letters in some form of an epistolary collection.

Furthermore, each of these three later authors themselves takes up the form of the letter, self-consciously imitating both the person and the letter writer Paul, generating a kind of echo chamber of Pauline effects. Each in his own way invokes some of the characteristic vocabulary by which the historical-epistolary Paul, a skilled wordsmith, gave linguistic shape to his emerging communities: "brothers and sisters," "sanctified ones," being "in Christ Jesus," leaders being "attested" and "tested and found worthy," and of the urgent need for steadfastness and for being "built up" (*oikodomeisthai*)[16] in the Pauline teaching and wisdom, which is referred to by the shorthand phrase, "the word of truth" (*logos alētheias*).[17] Polycarp incorporates Paul's own trademark

[14] Scholars debate whether this means (a) Paul wrote multiple letters to the Philippians of which only one (the canonical Philippians) survives; (b) the canonical Philippians is a composite from plural letters written by Paul; or (c) Polycarp is assuming a universalizing hermeneutic, such that Philippians read all of Pauline letters as including them.

[15] See the respective treatments in Andrew F. Gregory and Christopher Tuckett, eds., *The Reception of the New Testament in the Apostolic Fathers* (Oxford: Oxford University Press, 2005), including possible knowledge of Pauline pseudepigrapha (on which see below). Further evidence for knowledge of Paul's letters at Rome in this period is abundant, including Valentinus, Marcion, and, as is argued in Jonathan E. Soyars, *The* Shepherd *of Hermas and the Pauline Legacy* (Leiden: Brill, 2019), the tripartite work, *The Shepherd of Hermas*.

[16] Cf. 1 Thess 5:11; 1 Cor 8:1, 10; 14:3–5, 26; Eph 2:20.

[17] Cf. 2 Cor 6:7; Col 1:5; Eph 1:13. The appropriation and reuse of characteristic Pauline vocabulary unites all his devoted interpreters, those termed "proto-orthodox," like Ignatius, Polycarp, Irenaeus, Clement of Alexandria, and Origen, and their opponents, such as Valentinus, Marcion, and others.

triad of eschatological virtues, faith, hope, and love (*pistis*, *elpis*, *agapē*), recognizable and yet recast in yet another form by this Pauline admirer to fit a new argument, precisely as the historical-epistolary Paul himself was wont to do.[18] The letters of Paul in the hands of these three admiring readers and writers are able to be taken in some cases as a repository of words and keen phrases that can be picked out and used well beyond their original argumentative contexts. But this is not always the case, as we can see in *1 Clement*, where the overall rhetorical goal of Paul's long letter, 1 Corinthians, for unity in the *ekklēsia*, is important to the argument that Roman author sought to make in his new setting and in accord with his own rhetorical goals. These variable interpretive strategies for reading the variable "apostle" (the HEP), regarding whole and part, word and sense unit, apostolic intent and interpretative possibility for the present, will be found throughout ancient Christian interpretation, by "orthodox" and "heterodox" alike.[19]

In these three texts that date perhaps as early as ca. 90–120 CE, therefore, we can see that the letters of the historical-epistolary Paul have been transformed from the fragile papyrus of their autographs[20] (that were likely lost for decades by the time of Ignatius, *1 Clement* and Polycarp) into foundational building blocks of the Gentile Christ-believing communities around the Mediterranean.

FASHIONING A CULTURE OF PAULINE INFLUENCE

But how did this happen? And how would what had developed between Paul and these authors permanently shape the history that was to follow, in the next century and beyond? We can name at least five essential elements, which combine practical, technological,

[18] 1 Thess 1:3; Gal 5: 5–6; 1 Cor 13:13.

[19] While Irenaeus complained that Valentinians and others took the scriptures out of context and rearranged them to render their own, new meanings, in fact all early interpreters of Paul (including Irenaeus!) are capable of doing this (see, e.g., *Adv. Haer.* 1.8.1; 1.9.4; discussion in Frances M. Young, *Biblical Exegesis and the Formation of Christian Culture* [Cambridge: Cambridge University Press, 1997], 17–21). As a case in point, note how Polycarp in the quotation above uses Paul's characteristic term, *dikaiosynē* (righteousness), without either the forensic or the eschatological nuances it so importantly holds for Paul (e.g., Gal 2:16; 5:5).

[20] This term means the original text on papyrus written out and/or dictated by Paul. However, it is possible that some letters, like Galatians (having been a circular letter to multiple *ekklēsiai*), had multiple inaugural copies, and other letters may have existed in draft form. But, given that Paul's epistles were real letters to specific recipients, some actual version of each of them left him in the hands (and backpacks) of others, and was delivered and read.

bibliographic, and hermeneutical considerations, that went into the fashioning of a culture of Pauline influence in the half-century after his death.

Preservation and Preoccupation

Likely the original letters were preserved by some combination of Paul's own practice of retaining copies of his letters, and what would become local community archives of the recipients.[21] One of the reasons these epistles by Paul were retained is that they are not just everyday letters filled with occasional and immediately obsolete (and hence discardable) news and information. Instead, they contain complex and impassioned arguments about the meaning and implications of the *euangelion*, past, present, and future, which Paul audaciously regarded as the key to the meaning of all cosmic history and each human life. Indeed, Paul's genuine epistles were likely preserved and passed on in copies, and then copies of copies, precisely because of this complexity, and the empirical fact that their meaning is not always entirely clear, either on the first, or the fifth, or the twenty-fifth reading. These letters of Paul (HEP) invited, and were met by, continual rereading, debating, reinterpreting, and contesting, a process that began in his own lifetime as Paul himself engaged in continual self-interpretation of his words, his actions, and his own physical body, often in disputes with his own contemporaries about their meanings and significance.[22]

Collection and Circulation

In the decades after his death, some of the letters written by Paul were brought into early collections, perhaps initially in groups of four or seven letters,[23] and they were circulated beyond the city or person to whom they were originally addressed. In the early stages this likely involved various local collections,[24] which, as Colossians 4:16

[21] Harry Y. Gamble, *Books and Readers in the Early Church: A History of Early Christian Texts* (New Haven, CT: Yale University Press, 1997).

[22] We especially can see this unfold in the extensive Corinthian correspondence (fuller argument in Margaret M. Mitchell, *Paul, the Corinthians, and the Birth of Christian Hermeneutics* [Cambridge: Cambridge University Press, 2010]).

[23] For two hypotheses, see Gamble, *Books and Readers in the Early Church*, and David Trobisch, *Paul's Letter Collection: Tracing the Origins* (Philadelphia: Augsburg Fortress, 1994).

[24] So Brent Nongbri, "Pauline Letter Manuscripts," in *All Things to All Cultures: Paul among Jews, Greeks, and Romans*, eds. Mark Harding, and Alanna Nobbs (Grand Rapids, MI: Eerdmans, 2012), 84–102, who offers as a likely theory "a gradual accumulation of different [local] collections … [that] may then have eventually

envisions, may have been swapped with their neighbors near or far. Multiple editorial choices were involved in every such collection, and there was no uniformity for some time in the selection of letters (including in some cases the Letter to the Hebrews, which does not contain the word *Paulos*), the order in which they were arranged,[25] and the ways in which they were edited.[26] For example, what was eventually published as 2 Corinthians was likely formed from editing together parts of five originally separate letters, probably both to seek to mitigate some of the problematic relationship between Paul and the Corinthians that those letter fragments evidence, and to imitate the length and solemnity (and the success) of the earlier known 1 Corinthians.[27] Other editorial work concentrated on the beginnings and endings of letters, in an effort to add epistolary addressees where lacking,[28] or to remove material regarded as pedestrian, such as the long list of greetings in Romans 16 regarded as overly particular, since the shape of collected letters invited a more general readership. Paul himself at times envisioned a wider readership over the shoulder of his immediate addressees (e.g., 1 Cor 1:2; Philemon 2), but this occasional tendency within the historical-epistolary Paul takes on a much stronger character in the new hermeneutical setting of the collected letters being circulated, now destined for new audiences.

found their way to a scholarly center like Alexandria where higher quality, more comprehensive copies were produced" (100).

[25] See the table listing the order of letters in four major manuscripts in Nongbri, "Pauline Letter Manuscripts," 97–98, and discussion of Marcion's collection beginning with Galatians, perhaps due to his local collection, perhaps to its theological importance to his *Apostolikon* (Nonbgri, "Pauline Letter Manuscripts," 100–101; see also Judith M. Lieu, *Marcion and the Making of a Heretic: God and Scripture in the Second Century* [Cambridge: Cambridge University Press, 2015] 234–242). Further witnesses in Syriac and Latin to a collection beginning with Galatians add credence to the former hypothesis (see Jason D. BeDuhn, *The First New Testament: Marcion's Scriptural Canon* [Salem, OR; Polebridge, 2013] 207, 358).

[26] On the extant manuscript evidence for Paul's letters, none of which pre-dates the third century, see Nongbri, "Pauline Letter Manuscripts," 84–102. As Nongbri emphasizes (94–95), the work of modern textual criticism, due to the late nature of the evidence, is not to recover the "original" text (which is lost to history) but the "earliest recoverable text."

[27] See Mitchell, *Paul and the Emergence of Christian Textuality*, 141–158, for this, and alternative theories on the composition of 2 Corinthians.

[28] As in the famous example of Eph 1:1. See Richard I. Pervo, *The Making of Paul: Constructions of the Apostle in Early Christianity* (Minneapolis, MN: Fortress Press, 2010), 21, for assessments of the "integrity" of our current manuscript evidence in relation to the earlier forms of the letters.

Pseudepigraphy and Canon

The fact that Paul's letters were circulated in collections led also to the composition of new texts, pseudepigraphical letters, i.e., those written by others in Paul's name and even claiming his very signature (*Paulos*).[29] These newly composed letters (PsP, "Pseudepigraphical Paul") had the express purpose of joining the existing collection and "fixing" it, in both senses of the term: to *solidify* the teaching and memories about Paul into a firm and unambiguous deposit of teaching, and to *correct* errors in the existing letters or in readings of those letters that those later authors deemed deficient and dangerous.[30] A first wave of these Pauline pseudepigrapha was written perhaps before the reign of Trajan (2 Thessalonians, Colossians, Ephesians) and was included in what may have been the first attempt to fix a "canon"[31] of Pauline letters, by Marcion of Sinope in his sojourn in Rome, ca. 144 (though he termed the latter "the Letter to the Laodiceans," not Ephesians).[32] Marcion's "canon" did not include 1 and 2 Timothy and Titus, either because they had not yet been written, were not known to him if they had been written, or because they were regarded by him as illegitimate. These six letters (PsP) sought to steer the meanings of the HEP in their own directions.[33] In this goal they were, already by the end of the second century, wildly successful, as we can see in the writings of Irenaeus, where what will become the fourteen-letter "canon"[34] of Pauline

[29] E.g., 2 Thess 3:17, perhaps Col 4:18; cf. Gal 6:11; 1 Cor 16:21. Scholarly assessment of pseudepigraphical writing ranges from claims that this is a regular practice of either "biblical literature" or the students of great philosophers (such as the letters produced in the names of Plato, Socrates, Diogenes, and others) to a judgment of outright forgery (see Bart D. Ehrman, *Forgery and Counterforgery: The Use of Literary Deceit in Early Christian Polemics* [Oxford: Oxford University Press, 2012]).

[30] For this formulation about how the Pastoral Epistles seek to "fix" the corpus, see Mitchell, *Paul and the Emergence of Christian Textuality*, 302–322.

[31] I.e., an authoritative list. Scholars dispute whether Marcion initiated the delineation of a "canon," or if it is anachronistic to apply that later designation to him (contrast BeDuhn, *The First New Testament*, 60, and Lieu, *Marcion and the Making of a Heretic*, 432).

[32] So Tertullian, *Adv. Marc.* 5.11.12; 5.17.1. Marcion, spanning Asia Minor (Sinope, up on the Black Sea) and Rome, provides further evidence of the geographical spread of Paul's letters by ca. 140 CE.

[33] This ability to cross-reference meant that the self-conscious repetitions of the historical-epistolary Paul in the pseudepigrapha would (ironically) be taken as double attestation of the meaning of "Paul."

[34] But note that other pseudepigraphical letters, such as *3 Corinthians* and the *Epistle to the Laodiceans*, appear in some Armenian, Syriac, and Latin manuscripts or commentaries, treated as canonical (see Pervo, *The Making of Paul*, 96–104).

epistles may first be glimpsed (CanP, i.e., the thirteen epistles purporting to come from Paul, plus Hebrews, and the Acts of the Apostles).[35] In the history of reception of Paul, the PsP (regarded as authentic missives of Paul) had every bit as much influence as HEP.

Codex and Correction

Virtually all of the extant manuscripts and fragments in Greek of the Pauline epistles are in the form of a codex (a hinged book), rather than a scroll.[36] That material form of the circulated letters of Paul ensured the readiness of cross-reference and comparison among the different letters, which in turn will be an important hermeneutical move as early Christian interpreters engaged the legacy of the "canonical Paul" (CanP). Our earliest extant manuscripts containing gospels, epistles, and Acts date from the first half of the fourth century. But we know that already considerably earlier, although not bound together in a single codex, the Pauline letters were interpreted in relation to a Gospel (Marcion's *Euangelion*) or Gospels (Irenaeus's four-fold[37]), as well as with the Greek Bible (Septuagint), and other works, within the developing Christian bibliographic culture and its social practices.

At the same time, the medium of hand-copied texts, no matter how much scribes or readers might wish to preserve an earlier state of the text, is susceptible to multiple forms of variation. One is simple scribal error, produced perhaps by visual or aural similarity in the act of copying. For instance, did Paul write in 1 Cor 2:1 that he had proclaimed the *mysterion* of God or the *martyrion* of God? It depends only on a difference of three letters in the middle of two nine-letter Greek words that begin and end the same and have six letters in common; and yet the semantic difference is quite significant (either "mystery" or "testimony"). While this example may be due to accident, the textual tradition is also susceptible to intentional scribal emendation, to correct things that are deemed deficient, whether in orthography (spelling),

[35] The Pastoral Epistles play a conspicuous role in *Adv. Haer.* (see White, *Remembering Paul*, 135–158), in concert with Irenaeus' citations and allusions to all thirteen letters, and perhaps Hebrews (2.30.9).

[36] Nongbri, "Pauline Letter Manuscripts," 85–86. The well-known Christian preference for the codex over the scroll may be due to the bibliographic nature of the texts as collections of documents (letters, gospels, etc.).

[37] Significantly, in *Adv. Haer.* 3.1.1 Irenaeus explicitly links the composition of the four canonical gospels with the preaching of Paul and Peter. Such an argument encourages the reading of the gospel narratives alongside Paul's letters as a unified *euangelion* field.

grammar, or contents, such as theological, scriptural, or social claims. In ancient literary criticism this is called the practice of *diorthōsis,* or "correction"; but one person's "correction" may be another's "mutation" and even falsification of a received text in a new form.[38] For example, according to his critics (such as Irenaeus, Tertullian, and Origen), Marcion of Sinope "mutilated" the text of Paul's letters, such as by deleting "first" from Rom 1:16, "to Jew *first* and Greek,"[39] or excising chapters 15 and 16 from Romans. Marcion himself in turn questioned the authenticity of the versions of Paul's letters propounded by some of his own contemporaries, charging that he was not mutilating, but they were tampering with the text, interpolating into Paul's originals passages that did not belong there.[40]

In general, the textual traditions of Paul's letters in antiquity were in a contested but not completely random state, with enough fixity of wording that disputants could often cite the text and expect their opponents to agree to the textual reading (and then disagree about the meaning of those words), but with enough variance that those same disputants could also at times castigate others for promulgating an ostensible wording for a Pauline letter that is not found in their own copies (*antigrapha*).[41] "Paul" as he becomes texts has some definite outlines but varied details, not only in their original Greek language, but then as expanded into translations in Latin, Syriac, Coptic, and other languages in use within ancient Christian communities.

Acts, and More Acts

An inestimably important factor shaping the interpretation of Paul from the early second century forward and, once again, first indisputably attested in Irenaeus (ca. 180 CE), is the Acts of the Apostles. Acts fills

[38] As stated outright by Tertullian in *Adv. Marc.* 4.4.1: *ego Marcionis adfirmo adulteratum, Marcion meum,* "I maintain that Marcion's gospel is adulterated, and he that mine is."

[39] This reading is also lacking in the codices B (Greek, 4th c.) and G (Greek and Latin, 9th c.). Consequently, as is often the case with the reconstruction of Marcion's *Apostolikon,* it is hard to tell if this is due to his own editorial hand or the text he had received (ditto, for instance, with the case of Romans 15–16, which Marcion's text apparently lacked [see BeDuhn, *The First New Testament,* 221]).

[40] Tertullian presents Marcion as suspicious of the other, false apostles, as having contested the truth of Paul's gospel as he defends it especially in Galatians (such as Gal 1:7–9; 2:4; Tertullian, *Adv. Marc.* 4.3.2). For an attempt to show (in English translation) Marcion's possible wording of the letters of Paul (in Marcion's reconstructed order, beginning with Galatians), see BeDuhn, *The First New Testament,* 229–259.

[41] We see this principle at work in dialogues such as "Adamantius," *de recte in deum fide* (probably 4th century)

out in an extended narrative the impulse of the historical-epistolary Paul to include his mission within the *euangelion* itself. This lengthy work, which likely dates from ca. 115 CE,[42] is a non-epistolary attempt to steer the meaning of Paul and his letters, through a narrative in which the hero, Paul, is ironically not represented so much as a letter writer as a powerful orator, precisely the opposite of what the HEP had claimed (see 2 Cor 10:10; 11:6). The Acts of the Apostles seeks to demonstrate how the gospel message followed the very same half-circle outlined by the HEP in Romans 15:9, from Jerusalem to Rome, with Paul, the "vessel of election," carrying the gospel not only, as with the HEP, to Gentiles (Gal 1:15–16; Rom 11:13), but to "Gentiles and kings and the sons of Israel" (Acts 9:15; 26:17–20). Acts characterizes Paul as a cosmopolitan man who was "all things to all people" (bringing to life the HEP's incongruous boast in 1 Cor 9:22), a man who has both a Greek name and a Hebrew one (*Saulos*), speaks fluently and with rhetorical dexterity in both Greek and Hebrew, has the benefit of an outstanding education at the feet of the famous rabbi Gamaliel (Acts 22:3), and was, to boot, a Roman citizen[43] (22:25–29), who was viewed by Roman authorities as a curiosity, but no seditionist threat (24:24–27; 25:24–32). This depiction of Paul's cosmopolitan self is in service of several key theological and political themes: 1) Paul "converted" from his (Jewish) past to serve the *euangelion*;[44] 2) Paul brought the *euangelion* "first" to Jews and only after they rejected it did he turn to Gentiles;[45] 3) the Christian movement is an innocent philosophical "way" that supersedes the ordinary claims of the synagogue, the expectations of pagan cult and magic (whether of Lystra, Delphi, or elsewhere), and the wisdom of Greek philosophy as propounded in the very center of Athens; and 4) the conflicts one sees in Paul's letters (e.g., Galatians; 2 Cor 10–13) between missionaries and missions in the early decades have been sanded away through the retrojected recruitment of *all* of the

[42] Following Richard I. Pervo, *Dating Acts: Between the Evangelists and the Apologists* (Santa Rosa, CA: Polebridge Press, 2006), on both the dating and the conclusion that the author of Acts knew at least some of HEP (and perhaps PsP). Both claims are debated in contemporary scholarship.

[43] Something never mentioned in the letters and seemingly contradicted by Paul's statement that he had been beaten with rods (2 Cor 11:25), a punishment forbidden to be enacted on Roman citizens.

[44] The "conversion" story is told once by the narrator in Acts 9:1–9, and twice by Paul himself in speeches of self-defense (Acts 22:4–11; 26:12–23).

[45] Thus narrativizing Paul's theological claim in Rom 1:16–17 (with the textual reading "first"); see Acts 13:46–48; 28:23–31.

early apostles (Peter, James, Philip) to the Pauline position, unanimously on board the mission to the Gentiles.

The Acts of the Apostles was soon to be followed by the *Acts of Paul*, a work composed in Greek, probably in Asia Minor, that was already known to Tertullian in North Africa around 200 CE (*de baptismo* 17.5), who viewed it with disapproval for legitimizing women's ecclesial leadership. In the *Acts of Paul and Thecla* part of the fuller narrative, the hero, Paul, is provided with a physical description (short, bald, bow-legged, unibrowed, etc.) that had been lacking in existing Pauline lore until now.[46] The work casts Paul as a stringent and charismatic ascetic who attracts the strong devotion and ardor of, among others, the remarkable young woman of Iconium (in Asia Minor), Thecla.

In the decades and centuries that followed, Pauline acts and narratives grew more and more, filling the gaps left by the canonical Acts, most conspicuously about the circumstances around Paul's death,[47] and those left tantalizingly incomplete in the letters themselves, such as Paul's own reservation about describing his heavenly journey in 2 Cor 12:1–5, which various later authors, in multiple languages, were eager to remedy.[48] Even in death, Paul's literary life was extended, reshaped, and reanimated.

PAULINE INTERPRETERS AND THE ART OF PAULINE INTERPRETATION

The combination of these sources in these media offered a broad palette of Pauline possibilities. Each moment of Pauline interpretation in the first few centuries (as with modern interpretation) involved a selective

[46] See 3.2, and discussion and bibliography about this description and the work as a whole in Hans-Josef Klauck, *The Apocryphal Acts of the Apostles: An Introduction*, trans. Brian McNeil (Waco, TX: Baylor University Press, 2008), 52–53. In addition to *The Acts of Paul and Thecla*, extant portions of the larger work include *3 Corinthians* and the *Martyrdom of Paul*. This physical description of Paul will in various ways be taken up in artistic depictions of Paul, where, since Paul and Peter are often conjoined as the chiefs among the apostles, his baldness allows ready identification as contrasted with Peter, who gets a full head of hair. On portrayals of Paul in early Christian poetry and graphic arts, the earliest preserved being perhaps in the late third century, see the material collected by Roald Dijkstra, *The Apostles in Early Christian Art and Poetry* (Leiden: Brill, 2016), 324–329, 459–461.

[47] See David L. Eastman, *The Ancient Martyrdom Accounts of Peter and Paul* (Atlanta, GA: Society of Biblical Literature, 2015), for the texts, translations, and valuable overview.

[48] On the Greek, Latin, and Coptic versions, see Jan L. Bremmer and István Czachesz, eds., *The Visio Pauli and the Gnostic Apocalypse of Paul* (Leuven: Peeters, 2007).

reappropriation from among these tesserae into its own mosaic. In each case this depended upon the assumptions, the talents, the purposes, and requirements of the interpreter within the agonistic paradigm of interpretation[49] that early Christian interpreters shared with literate elites across the Mediterranean world, employing textual evidence to support their own arguments and refute those of their opponents. The historical-epistolary, pseudepigraphical and combined canonical Pauls attracted many fans of many stripes across the empire in the centuries after his death who engaged his words and legacy, from the Black Sea to Rome, from Alexandria to Lyons, and sought to rally him to their own causes. Keen and contentious minds in the first two centuries after his death, like Valentinus, Ignatius of Antioch, Marcion, Ptolemy, Justin,[50] the author of the *Acts of Paul*, Dionysius of Corinth, Athenagoras, Irenaeus, Theophilus of Antioch, Tertullian, Clement of Alexandria, Cyprian of Carthage, and Origen of Alexandria (the first we know of to have written commentaries on all the Pauline letters),[51] and others to follow, especially in the burgeoning of Pauline commentary and homiletics in the late fourth century (including in Greek John Chrysostom, Theodore of Mopsuestia, and Theodoret of Cyrrhus, among others, and in Latin Marius Victorinus, "Ambrosiaster," Jerome, Pelagius, and Augustine), found in Paul's letters building blocks for their own projects of theological exposition, apologetics, ethical instruction, invective against opponents, and community leadership and governance. Paul's invitation to "become imitators of me" (1 Cor 4:16; 11:1) extended beyond the letter writing and wordsmithing that we noted above, into painting Paul in their own image, and themselves in turn in his.[52] For example, the

[49] For an explanation of the term and how early Christian biblical interpretation was rooted in ancient rhetorical culture, see Mitchell, *Paul, the Corinthians, and the Birth of Christian Hermeneutics*, esp. 18–37; cf. Young, *Biblical Exegesis and the Formation of Christian Culture*.

[50] Probably; even though Justin does not ever quote from a Pauline letter, nor name Paul overtly, there are unmistakable echoes of Pauline arguments (see Pervo, *The Making of Paul*, 195–196).

[51] These are not extant in full, but fragments have come down in medieval "chain commentaries," and in many instances Origen's views on the Pauline letters have been taken over by Jerome (see Ronald F. Heine, *The Commentaries of Origen and Jerome on Saint Paul's Epistle to the Ephesians* [Oxford: Oxford University Press, 2002]).

[52] See Margaret M. Mitchell, *The Heavenly Trumpet: John Chrysostom and the Art of Pauline Interpretation* (Louisville, KY: Westminster John Knox, 2002), for the ways in which this dynamic of Pauline imitation worked with John Chrysostom, who boasted that it was his love for the apostle that powered his interpretation of the letters.

author of *1 Clement* finds in Paul an astute expositor of the rhetoric of reconciliation; Ignatius a saintly self-sacrificing martyr; Valentinus a wisdom teacher of profound philosophical and cosmological speculation; Marcion the singular, uncompromising apostolic voice and defender of truth; Irenaeus a keen exposer of heresies; Origen a philosophically-inclined biblical theologian; Chrysostom "the archetypal image" of how to imitate Christ; and Augustine a diagnostician of human sin and its need for redemption in the Christ event. And yet each of these great interpreters within their extensive oeuvres could also partake of many of the descriptions of Paul found among the others.

CONTROVERSIAL PAULS AND ANCIENT CHRISTIAN CONTROVERSIES

Every one of the multiple "Pauls" (P, HP, HEP, PsP, PACTS, CanP) is controversial. The Paul of the genuine letters (HEP) openly acknowledges direct challenges in his day to his legitimacy, to his personal ethics and actions, and to his theology, even as he seeks to confront them and defend himself. The Paul of the pseudepigraphical letters (PsP), in seeking to tamp down disputes about what Paul had really said during his lifetime (e.g., about imminent eschatology, women's leadership, prayers for imperial and other authorities, the governance of the *ekklēsia*), tacitly recognizes ongoing disputes after Paul's death, and the interpretive malleability of the extant letters. The Paul of the Acts of the Apostles (PACTS) is a heroic figure who at first murderously raged against the early Christ-believing communities (9:1), and, after his conversion, participated in discussions, disputations, and conflict with virtually everyone – the Jerusalem apostles (especially Peter and James), Pharisees and Sadducees, synagogue attendees and leaders, Greek philosophers, Roman procurators, king Agrippa II, members of the Jewish community at Rome. These multiple "Pauls" when read together as CanP also raised continual questions about inconsistencies, and whether it was possible to reconcile one "Paul" with another. How, for instance, was the Paul (HEP) who vehemently opposed circumcision of Gentile converts in Galatians and Phil 3:2–11 to be reconciled with the Paul (PACTS) who himself circumcised Timothy in Acts 16:3?

Some controversies from Paul's own day continued in the years beyond, but not always in the same form. The issue of whether male Gentile Christ-believers should become circumcised became less urgent in second and third generation Gentile-only communities (and beyond),[53] and HEP's arguments in Galatians (and elsewhere) were regarded as targeting Jews and the Torah itself, not a competing gospel of Christ-believing Judaizing missionaries.[54] With PACTS leading the way, and joined in the chorus by PsP (especially 1 Tim 1:12–14), the calling like the prophet Jeremiah that HEP had described in Gal 1:15–16 became understood as Paul's "conversion" out of "Judaism" (*Ioudaismos* in Gal 1:14) and to "the way" (Acts) or something that becomes "Christianity."[55] On this line of interpretation, which will dominate both in antiquity and into modernity, Paul was born a Jew, but later left his "Judaism" behind to become an apostle, an envoy of Christ, a "Christian."[56] It is impossible to pinpoint any single moment when this became a dominant reading, or how it was related to social facts on the ground within the Gentile Christ-believing and other communities, and the emergence of a distinctive "Christian" identity, because the processes were mutually dependent. But the division that becomes scripted within the life of Paul among ancient interpreters becomes emblematic for a division between "Judaism" and "Christianity."[57]

HEP shows ambivalence about the role of women in the early Christ-believing movements, since he knew and recognized women apostles, such as Junia (Rom 16:7), and deacons, like Phoebe (Rom 16:1–2), but also at times sought concord through compromise that

[53] But did not entirely disappear, as, e.g., Justin Martyr, *Dialogue with Trypho* 46–47; Irenaeus, *Adv. Haer.* 1.26.2; Pseudo-Clementine *Homilies* 7.8, show. On the complex issues surrounding "Jewish Christianity" (the category and the realities), see Annette Yoshiko Reed, *Jewish-Christianity and the History of Judaism* (Tübingen: Mohr Siebeck, 2018), and Matt Jackson-McCabe, ed., *Jewish Christianity Reconsidered: Rethinking Ancient Groups and Texts* (Minneapolis, MN: Fortress Press, 2007).

[54] On Paul as himself a "judaizer," see Paula Fredriksen, *Paul, The Pagans' Apostle* (New Haven, CT: Yale University Press, 2017), 94–130.

[55] This is something on which Marcion and Tertullian agree (see, e.g., *Adv. Marc.* 5.2.1, etc.; discussion in Lieu, *Marcion and the Making of a Heretic*, 72–75).

[56] Interpreters like John Chrysostom can affirm Paul's impeccable Jewish pedigree (e.g., Phil 3:2–6) in order to amplify the importance of his having left it (understood as "Judaism" entire) behind (see Mitchell, *Heavenly Trumpet*, 228–234, 257–259). Paul's activity as a persecutor of the *ekklēsia* becomes exemplary of the fault of "Judaism," as refracted through HEP's Rom 10:2: having "zeal for God but not with full understanding" (Mitchell, *Heavenly Trumpet*, 258).

[57] Among important modern voices questioning and overturning the self-evident or natural status of this reading, see Krister Stendahl, *Paul among Jews and Gentiles* (Philadelphia: Fortress Press, 1976); E. P. Sanders, *Paul and Palestinian Judaism: A Comparison of Patterns of Religion* (Philadelphia: Fortress Press, 1977); Pamela Eisenbaum, *Paul Was Not a Christian: the Original Message of a Misunderstood Apostle* (New York: HarperOne, 2009); Fredriksen, *Paul, the Pagans' Apostle.*

landed more harshly on the backs of women (e.g., 1 Cor 11:2–16; 14:33–36), as well as slaves (including women, as in 1 Cor 7:17–24). PsP will try to push this Pauline ambivalence into outright belligerence against women's teaching, or slaves' emancipation (e.g., 1 Tim 2:11–15; 6:1–2; Eph 5:22–6:9 and other "household codes"). Paul had also left an ambiguous legacy in Gal 3:28, as to whether it called for actual disintegration of existing forms of social status such as Jew/Greek, slave/free, and woman and man, or only a relativizing of those roles in light of the expectations that the end of days was near. The *Acts of Paul and Thecla* champion women's leadership, while Tertullian is disdainful of it. The extensive debates among Christians in the third and fourth centuries about gender roles, marriage, and celibacy frequently amounted to playing one "Paul" off against another, especially HEP's convoluted 1 Cor 7 against PsP's insistence on maintaining the order of the patriarchal household.[58]

The HEP engaged in complex and often fraught interpretations of his scriptures (the Torah, prophets, and writings), as read in Greek (the Septuagint), such as the claim that scripture itself "preached the gospel in advance" in the story of Abraham (Gen 12–24) in Gal 3:8.[59] Amazingly, the controversial interpreter was to become the model and mentor for all of Christian biblical interpretation in antiquity.[60] Paul's aphorism, "the letter kills, but the spirit gives life" (2 Cor 3:6), would be taken as the hermeneutical justification for "spiritual" interpretation of all of scripture, including Paul's letters. Paul's own example of reading beyond the surface meaning, as in 1 Cor 9:9 (the threshing ox) or 10:1–4 (the wilderness generation's "baptism," with Christ identified as "the spiritual rock that followed" them), also became part of how later interpreters could justify ways in which their own reading practices advanced a "deeper sense" of the texts they read. They also gained from Paul the terminology for this, of *typos* or *typikōs*, "figured" meaning (1 Cor 10:6, 11). This was of course crucial for Christological reading of the psalms and the prophets, which Christian interpreters continued to develop, filling in Paul's "empty footnote" of 1 Cor 15:3–4, that the events of Christ's death and resurrection were *kata tas graphas*,

[58] See Elizabeth A. Clark, *Reading Renunciation: Asceticism and Scripture in Early Christianity* (Princeton, NJ: Princeton University Press, 1999).

[59] Another passage lacking in Marcion's *Apostolikon* (see BeDuhn, *The First New Testament*, 218–219, 231).

[60] See the fuller treatment in Mitchell, *Paul, the Corinthians, and the Birth of Christian Hermeneutics*.

"in accordance with the Scriptures" (a passage that lists not a single scriptural verse!).

And yet no early Christian interpreter was solely an "allegorist" nor solely a "literalist," but they were (as was HEP) strategic and variable depending upon the text at hand and their own rhetorical, theological, or catechetical purposes. And there was keen debate among early Christian interpreters about whether or how their own use of "figurative" or "symbolic" reading of the scriptures was like and not like the "allegorical" readings that Greek philosophers like Plato or the Stoics applied to the myths of the Greeks. Within those disputes, some pointed to Paul's term *allēgoroumena* (meaning "allegorically rendered or interpreted" in Gal 4:24, used of the two covenants represented by Sarah and Hagar) as granting license for Christian allegorical reading. But others were more cautious, wanting to claim that their own non-literal readings of the Scriptures were not like those of outsiders (Greeks or Jews). For them (ingeniously) Paul had intentionally *misused* the term referring to "allegory" to emphasize his concern about exegesis that was too freewheeling, and perhaps due more to the inventiveness of the exegete than the sense of the text.[61] Paul is received in the early church not only as the source of texts that require hermeneutical ingenuity, but he becomes the master hermeneutician and exegetical mentor for many early Christian interpreters.

The most significant and revolutionary change from the historical Paul's own day is that the later "Pauls" were able to do decisively what he could only attempt in his lifetime: the embattled Paul of the letters within one hundred years becomes accepted not only as *an* apostle, but among many Christian authors[62] as "*the* apostle."[63] And in turn, if Paul is "*the* apostle," he can be treated, by Christians and non-Christians, by

[61] By their appeal to the Greek rhetorical term *katachrēsis* (deliberate misuse of a word), Chrysostom and Theodoret (following the Antiochene teacher Diodore of Tarsus) show their anxiety about Paul simply endorsing all "allegorical" reading in Gal 4:24.

[62] This is not to say that all agreed. On the history of "anti-Paulinism," including in the Pseudo-Clementine *Homilies* and *Recognitions*, see Patrick Gray, *Paul as a Problem in History and Culture: The Apostle and His Critics through the Centuries* (Grand Rapids, MI: Baker, 2016), 25–33, with further literature.

[63] See the convenient representation of this evidence in table 1.1 "Epithets for Paul in the Second Century," in White, *Remembering Paul*, 7–9 (but note that the second-century dating for some of these works is not certain). Paul was also called "the *divine* apostle" (by Clement of Alexandria, Origen, many others), and a host of other epithets, such as "the teacher of the world" or "the warm lover of Christ" (John Chrysostom alone employed over 65 different epithets for Paul [see Mitchell, *Heavenly Trumpet*, 69–93]).

"orthodox" and "heretics," as a metonymy for "Christianity." If he succeeds, they succeed. If he fails, they fail. And so the stakes of Pauline interpretation become exponentially higher than the mostly local skirmishes attested in the words left behind by the HEP in letters that are headed toward a history of effects that would have been unimaginable to the man, *P(aulos)*.

Further Reading

Fredriksen, Paula. *Paul, The Pagans' Apostle* (New Haven, CT: Yale University Press, 2017).

Fredriksen, Paula. "Paul and Augustine: Conversion Narratives, Orthodox Traditions, and the Retrospective Self." *Journal of Theological Studies* 37, no. 1 (1986): 3–34.

Gregory, Andrew F., and Christopher Tuckett, eds. *The Reception of the New Testament in the Apostolic Fathers*. Oxford: Oxford University Press, 2005.

Kovacs, Judith L. "Paul the Apostle." In *The Oxford Handbook of Early Christian Biblical Interpretation*, edited by Paul M. Blowers and Peter W. Martens, 614–625. Oxford: Oxford University Press, 2019.

Lieu, Judith M. *Marcion and the Making of a Heretic: God and Scripture in the Second Century*. Cambridge: Cambridge University Press, 2015.

Mitchell, Margaret M. *The Heavenly Trumpet: John Chrysostom and the Art of Pauline Interpretation*. Louisville, KY: Westminster John Knox, 2002.

Mitchell, Margaret M. *Paul and the Emergence of Christian Textuality: Early Christian Literary Culture in Context*. WUNT 393. Tübingen: Mohr Siebeck, 2018.

Mitchell, Margaret M. *Paul, the Corinthians, and the Birth of Christian Hermeneutics*. Cambridge: Cambridge University Press, 2010.

Nongbri, Brent. "Pauline Letter Manuscripts." In *All Things to All Cultures: Paul among Jews, Greeks, and Romans*, edited by Mark Harding and Alanna Nobbs, 84–102. Grand Rapids, MI: Eerdmans, 2012.

Pervo, Richard I. *The Making of Paul: Constructions of the Apostle in Early Christianity*. Minneapolis, MN: Fortress Press, 2010.

Roetzel, Calvin J. *Paul: The Man and the Myth*. Personalities of the New Testament. Philadelphia: Fortress Press, 1999.

Schröter, Jens, Simon Butticaz, and Andreas Dettwiler, eds. *Receptions of Paul in Early Christianity: The Person of Paul and His Writings through the Eyes of His Early Interpreters*. Berlin: De Gruyter, 2018.

White, Benjamin L. *Remembering Paul: Ancient and Modern Contests over the Image of the Apostle*. Oxford: Oxford University Press, 2014.

Wiles, Maurice. *The Divine Apostle: The Interpretation of St. Paul's Epistles in the Early Church*. Cambridge: Cambridge University Press, 1967.

Young, Frances M. *Biblical Exegesis and the Formation of Christian Culture*. Cambridge: Cambridge University Press, 1997.

16 What Makes Paul Challenging Today?

JOHN M. G. BARCLAY

Paul is a provocative figure, and always has been. Personally, he was often awkward to work with, and what we encounter in his letters sometimes seems to us, as to his first readers, authoritarian and overly concerned with himself (cf. 2 Cor 10:10). His arguments are sometimes difficult to follow, and his love of paradox leaves us scratching our heads in puzzlement (cf. 2 Pet 3:16). On some topics Paul's statements seem inconsistent, and their diversity is extended by the fact that the Pauline corpus of thirteen letters contains some letters written by Paul himself and some probably written in his name, adapting his legacy to later circumstances. Our primary focus will be the letters generally considered authentic, but we will note also some early developments in 'Pauline' thought, since the 'Paul' who has challenged his readers down the centuries has come to them already mediated through layers of interpretation, even within the New Testament (Acts and the deutero-pauline letters).

The challenges to be discussed here arise from the *content* of Paul's letters, their ideas and moral expectations. In his robust and polarising style, Paul makes a set of claims that have provoked his readers in numerous ways, at times spurring admirers to follow daring paths with radical implications for theology, church, and practice, but sometimes irritating his critics who have raised numerous objections on theological, philosophical, and moral grounds.[1] Paul is thus challenging in at least two senses: he stimulates his sympathisers to explore his angular perspectives, and he provokes his detractors to critique his views and their theological and social legacies. These two kinds of response can, of course, be mixed, but they can also polarise one another: the more that some hail Paul's statements on a controversial issue, the more others find reason to repudiate his views. Paul divides opinion as much today as he did in his own lifetime.

[1] See the survey in Patrick Gray, *Paul as a Problem in History and Culture: The Apostle and His Critics through the Centuries* (Grand Rapids, MI: Baker Academic, 2016).

We will discuss here five topics where Paul proves to be challenging in one or other of these two senses (sometimes in both). In each case, we will trace how Paul subverts some aspects of an ancient value system, not by a straightforward inversion of values but by his reconfiguration of what is good and necessary around the event of Christ crucified and risen. In many cases we will find that there is a partial, but *only partial*, match between Paul's Christological configuration of values and the liberal values espoused by the majority of intellectuals in the modern West, with respect to justice, equality, freedom, and human rights. On such topics there is just enough overlap between Paul and certain strands of thought in the modern and postmodern West to encourage the anachronistic expectation that Paul should think just like us. That false hope leads some to co-opt Paul for contemporary agendas without acknowledging deep elements of mismatch, while it leads others to voice severe disappointment that Paul's values do *not*, in the end, mirror the values embedded in the critical theories by which they measure his views. It should become clear through this analysis that the straight transfer of Paul's views to our own day is neither possible nor, perhaps, desirable. If Paul is to remain in any sense a constructive challenge, we will need to deploy, self-consciously, a creative theological hermeneutic, which attempts to recontextualise Paul's core insights in our own very different historical, intellectual, and social setting.

THE MESSAGE OF THE CROSS AND THE RECONFIGURATION OF WORTH

Paul's first letter to the Corinthians issues a challenge to the value systems of his contemporaries arising from the brutal truth at the centre of the 'good news': the message of 'Jesus Christ crucified' (1 Cor 1:18–2:5). Contrasting this story with the valuation of 'power' and 'wisdom' in Jewish and Greek cultures, Paul proclaims the event of salvation as operative in the degrading crucifixion of Jesus: 'we proclaim Christ crucified, a stumbling-block to Jews and foolishness to Gentiles, but to those who are called, both Jews and Greeks, Christ the power of God and the wisdom of God. For God's foolishness is wiser than human wisdom, and God's weakness is stronger than human strength' (1 Cor 1:23–25).[2] Paul here embraces the cruel semiotics of crucifixion – the slow, humiliating execution of a naked man, rendered powerless and

[2] Here and elsewhere, I use the NRSV translation, unless otherwise indicated.

degraded to the extreme – in order to challenge the automatic valuation of human power and what he calls 'wisdom', the supposed excellence of reason and communication taken to reside in any civilised culture.[3] In the crucifixion, Paul claims, God has not just ignored these normal criteria of worth, but has undermined them, and the composition of the church in Corinth reinforces his point: 'not many of you were wise, by human standards, not many were powerful, not many were of noble birth. But God chose what is foolish in the world to shame the wise' (1 Cor 1:26–27). Both the message and the community it creates embody a challenge to the normal hierarchies of value, by which social power, free birth, distinguished ancestry, and the skills of an 'educated' person constitute the symbolic capital or worth that was widely cherished in the Graeco-Roman world.

Paul does not simply invert these values, to give value to the weak over the strong, or the foolish over the wise, as if there were some inherent value in weakness or folly. His purpose is rather to dislodge the deep-rooted assumption that what counts as valuable in the 'highest' cultural systems reflects the natural, created, or divine scheme of things: no extrapolation can be made from the one to the other. The alternative value system he promotes is not just the old system turned on its head, but a system of worth created by the 'calling' of God, which he elsewhere associates with the grace or gift of God (Gal 1:6, 16; Rom 9:6–13, etc.). What is essential for Paul is that this gift is given *incongruously*, not matching the prior worth of its recipients – in status or achievement – but given without regard to worth as defined by ethnicity, gender, legal status, social level, or moral excellence. Such a gift, because it 'belongs' to no one, is applicable to everyone, and this conviction, as we see from Galatians and Romans, lies at the root of his radical Gentile mission, which took the good news of Jesus into the non-Jewish world, without requiring that its Spirit-gifted recipients adopt the cultural markers of Jewish identity (circumcision, food-laws, etc.). In this, as in other senses, Paul's good news is 'not according to human norms' (*ou kata anthrōpon*, Gal 1:11). There is enormous potential here for social creativity – for the formation of new communities that disregard social hierarchies and cross social boundaries. The experimental

[3] See L. Welborn, *Paul, the Fool of Christ: A Study of 1 Corinthians 1–4 in the Comic-Philosophic Tradition* (London: T&T Clark, 2005); John M. G. Barclay, "Crucifixion as Wisdom: Exploring the Ideology of a Disreputable Social Movement," in *The Wisdom and Foolishness of God*, eds. C. Chalamet, and H. C. Askani (Minneapolis, MN: Fortress Press, 2015) 1–20.

'assemblies' that Paul founded in various cities exemplify, at least in part, the radically new possibilities that his message evoked.[4]

This Pauline impetus has influenced many modern movements, from Methodism to Martin Luther King Jr., and the Pauline capacity to view social hierarchies with irony (regarding the 'so-called' wise and mighty) has contributed to many of the political movements that have undermined static systems of privilege and power. Indeed, 'the message of the cross' and the liberating theme of grace still retain their power to challenge social norms as merely human constructions of value. It spurs churches, for instance, to become communities where differences (in ethnicity, social class, or gender) are creatively deployed without hierarchical evaluation, and from which strong challenges can be issued to the political and intellectual elite who still look down on their social or educational 'inferiors' with contempt. Although, as we shall see, other elements of Paul's theology have been taken to validate a politically conservative vision, the shocking truth that God has chosen 'the low and despised' in order to shame the noble and strong (1 Cor 1:27–28) can support 'the preference for the poor' that has characterised Christian liberation theologies. More widely, the common cultural assumptions about the criteria for celebrity or (at a humbler level) the ingredients of worth that count on social media, can be challenged by a Pauline perspective in which worth is *given* by the grace of God, not measured by conventional criteria of happiness or success. In this sense, Paul's theology can be just as countercultural in our context as it was in his.

But it is important to be clear concerning the root of this challenge. This questioning of social norms is not grounded in a doctrine of human nature or universal human rights – even the theological motif of the creation of humanity in 'the image of God' is barely found in the letters of Paul. Paul's ironic distance from human systems of valuation comes from the *event* of Christ crucified, and the calling of God in Christ; in other words, it is irreducibly theological and Christological. Human dignity is, for Paul, not founded in human nature (as it was for Stoicism, in human rationality); what makes the weak count is that they are persons for whom Christ died (1 Cor 8:11). It is possible to put this Christological event on a universal map, as in Col 1:15–20, where it is said that Christ is the centre and head of all reality, and that the death of Christ reconciled 'all things' to God (Col 1:20). That in turn invites a broader theological mapping of reality, tracing the potential in 'creation'

[4] See further John M. G. Barclay, *Paul and the Gift* (Grand Rapids, MI: Eerdmans, 2015).

for 'new creation'. In any case, Paul will not fit well into a non-theological account of human rights, and he is apt to prove awkward for those who would deploy his language within a secular frame. If Paul is to be reclaimed as a social critic, we would have to begin with his unashamedly Christological account of truth, in which God has remade all things in Christ, including the systems of value by which we allocate honour and worth.

POWER AND POLITICS

Paul inhabits a paradox – that divine power operates within and despite human weakness. This is how he interprets the crucifixion of Jesus (1 Cor 1:18–25), and this paradox also shapes the way he figures his own experience – carrying about the dying of Jesus so that the life of Christ and the power of God might be operative in his life (2 Cor 4:7–15; 11:21–12:10). As we have seen, he does not validate weakness *per se*, as if frailty were somehow a better state than strength, or power inherently evil. Hence, Paul can claim that the good news is 'the power of God for salvation' (Rom 1:16), and can point to its effect in changed lives and new communities, while simultaneously noting his own weakness as an apostle (Gal 4:11–20). When he calls believers to imitate him, as he imitates Christ (1 Cor 11:1), it is because he reckons his own life to mirror this paradoxical effect of the good news, even as his authority derives from (and only from) the message he carries (Gal 1:6–10).[5]

For understandable reasons, many strands of Western intellectual culture have become deeply suspicious of power, and strongly opposed to manifestations of power inequalities. This suspicion, fostered by the legacies of Marx and Foucault, has been turned against Paul in his exercise of apostolic authority: his call to imitation can be represented as a self-interested play for power, while his instructions and appeals may appear to be manipulative forms of self-authorised control.[6] His mission itself, with its negative evaluation of Gentile religion, seems to some modern eyes a form of religious colonialism, while his rebukes of others' 'errors' can appear arbitrary, high-handed, and intolerant. There are, indeed, very considerable dangers in Paul's identification of his

[5] See John Howard Schütz, *Paul and the Anatomy of Apostolic Authority* (Cambridge: Cambridge University Press, 1975).

[6] See, e.g., Elizabeth Anne Castelli, *Imitating Paul: A Discourse of Power* (Louisville, KY: Westminster John Knox, 1991); for a more nuanced approach, see Kathy Ehrensperger, *Paul and the Dynamics of Power* (London: T&T Clark, 2009).

work with the operation of divine power, since religious authorisation can be used all too easily to legitimate and absolutise political power. If Paul's legacy is to be deployed at all in the complex sphere of religious authority, that may only be possible, theologically, by reiterating the submission of all, leaders and led, to the authority of Jesus and to the love-oriented power of God. Carefully deployed in political checks and balances, this may help to relativise and control forms of human religious authority, though the notion of submission to a higher authority clashes, at a deep level, with Western ideals of independence and autonomy. If Paul's central confession is 'Jesus is Lord (*kyrios*)' (1 Cor 12:3), and if the good news is predicated on the fact that God has made him such (Phil 2:11), Paul's theology will always be objectionable to those who consider any kind of hierarchical power in principle wrong.[7]

But if Paul was not against all forms of power, was he at least against the power of Rome? Paul's comments in Romans 13 are famous (or infamous): 'Let every person be subject to the governing authorities; for there is no authority except from God, and those authorities that exist have been instituted by God' (Rom 13:1). For centuries this text has been used by those in authority to legitimate the political status quo, including tyranny and apartheid, while Paul's critics have regarded such sentiments as naive, socially reactionary, or evidence of a disastrous disjunction between church and politics. In response, there have been several attempts in recent years to read Paul as a subtle, below-the-surface critic of the Roman empire (and by extension, of all empires and 'imperial' projects).[8] But the tendency in these attempts to over-read the evidence, or to offer unconvincing re-readings of Romans 13 and other awkward texts, has provoked in turn a counter-reaction, where Paul is found to be entangled in Roman systems of power even when he thinks he opposes them. Here post-colonial theory highlights the ambiguity in the position of those who are subject to an imperial power: even in resisting empire they mimic its language and its structures of thought,

[7] See Joseph A. Marchal, *The Politics of Heaven: Women, Gender, and Empire in the Study of Paul* (Minneapolis, MN: Fortress Press, 2008), drawing on Elizabeth Schüssler Fiorenza's critique of all forms of 'kyriarchy'.

[8] e.g. Richard A. Horsley, ed., *Paul and Empire: Religion and Power in Roman Imperial Society* (Harrisburg, PA: Trinity Press International, 1997); Richard A. Horsley, ed., *Paul and the Roman Imperial Order* (Harrisburg, PA: Trinity Press International, 2004); N. T. Wright, *Paul and the Faithfulness of God* (Minneapolis, MN: Fortress Press, 2013) 1271–1319. For analysis, see Christoph Heilig, *Hidden Criticism? The Methodology and Plausibility of the Search for a Counter-Imperial Subtext in Paul* (Minneapolis, MN: Fortress Press, 2017).

so that they are subtly co-opted by the hegemonic power even when they attempt to break free of its ideological entanglements. On this view, Paul was not a heroic anti-Roman rebel, and his ambivalence indicates how he unwittingly re-inscribed much of its 'imperial' ideology of power in the way he governed and controlled his assemblies.[9]

It is, indeed, difficult to identify Paul as the straightforward political rebel that some have imagined, and the danger of projecting our own political preferences onto his letters is as acute for those on the political left as for those on its right (as *we* construct that spectrum). Paul operates with a strong 'apocalyptic' conviction that 'this age' and its 'rulers' have become deeply opposed to God, but he sees this conflict operating both in political relations and on a level deeper than the visible, historical powers (1 Cor 2:6–8; 15:20–28). The credence that he gives to governing authorities in Romans 13 depends on their alignment with 'the good' (Rom 13:3–7), and he does not consider it impossible that a hierarchical structure will produce a socially beneficial result. At the same time, his allegiance to Jesus as universal 'Lord', and his deep suspicion of the corrupting powers of 'Sin' and 'Death' indicate a capacity to see through the pretensions of any governing power, or any idealised system of politics, and to look beyond claims to human finality in view of God's future restoration of the cosmos (Rom 8:18–25). Paul's letters do not develop a well-rounded vision of what social justice would look like on a general social scale, and those who find inspiration in Paul will need to supplement his resources with theological reflection from elsewhere in order to provide anything like a complete political vision.[10] Paul's ironic distance from human claims to power only partly matches the political agendas of our post-Enlightenment era, and it would be anachronistic in the extreme to measure him by modern definitions of democracy, justice, or equality. If there is a specifically political challenge worth hearing in Paul, it is less in foreshadowing modern political values, and more in the unsettling sense that all political claims to authority, and politics itself, are relativised by a superior allegiance to Christ, which has the capacity to supersede not only the Roman empire but also the best that 'advanced' Western

[9] See Christopher D. Stanley, ed., *The Colonized Apostle: Paul through Postcolonial Eyes* (Minneapolis, MN: Fortress Press, 2011).

[10] See, e.g., the nuanced conclusions of Dorothea H. Bertschmann, *Bowing before Christ – Nodding to the State? Reading Paul Politically with Oliver O'Donovan and John Howard Yoder* (London: T&T Clark, 2014).

politics will ever produce.[11] In other words, Paul's greatest political challenge may be to the way that we invest our hopes for salvation in politics; what he questions is the ultimate significance we accord to human behaviour that is inevitably flawed through its entanglement in 'the present evil age' (Gal 1:4).

OWNERSHIP BY CHRIST AND SLAVERY

The title *kyrios* that was applied to Jesus (1 Cor 12:3) means 'Master', in the sense of an owner of property, including slaves. Paul uses this metaphor frequently: believers were 'bought with a price' (1 Cor 6:20) and, as household slaves, they are expected to please their Master (Rom 14:1–9). Paul himself is a 'slave' of Christ (Gal 1:10), and he encourages his converts to think of themselves in similar terms (Rom 6:12–20). Whatever 'rights' he might be thought to have, they will be subordinated to the interests of the good news, for which he freely 'enslaves' himself to all (1 Cor 9:19). Such sentiments will clearly trouble those whose highest values are liberty, independence, and autonomy.

What does this mean in relation to legal freedom and slavery? In 1 Corinthians 7 Paul indicates how God's 'calling' (that is, God's drawing of the believer into Christ) is of higher value than any social condition, marital, ethnic, or legal (being enslaved or free).To those who were slaves when they were called by God, Paul has this to say (1 Cor 7:21–23):

> Were you a slave when called? Do not be concerned about it, but if you can gain your freedom, avail yourself of the opportunity.[12] For whoever was called in the Lord as a slave is a freed person belonging to the Lord, just as whoever was free when called is a slave of Christ. You were bought with a price; do not become slaves of human masters. In whatever condition you were called, brothers and sisters, there remain with God.

This passage offers the most programmatic discussion about slavery that Paul makes in the undisputed letters. Elsewhere, in his letter to Philemon, he re-presents the newly converted slave, Onesimus, to his owner, Philemon, and indicates that 'you may have him back for ever,

[11] See Douglas Harink, ed., *Paul, Philosophy, and the Theopolitical Vision* (Eugene, OR: Cascade, 2010).

[12] The Greek (*mallon chrēsai*) is notoriously ambiguous, but I here follow what is now the scholarly consensus (indicated as an option in the NRSV footnote).

no longer as a slave, but as more than a slave, a beloved brother – especially to me, but how much more to you, both in the flesh and in the Lord' (Philemon 15–16).

There is a measure of ambiguity in both texts, sufficient to allow some to hail Paul as the precursor of modern campaigns to emancipate all slaves, and others to regard Paul as condoning the general ancient assumption that slavery was, if not exactly natural, at least necessary for the successful functioning of society. But perhaps the most challenging aspect of these texts is that Paul appears to fit neither of these neat alternatives. The ancient Stoics distinguished between (1) what is ultimately and independently good, and (2) things they termed 'indistinguishable' (*adiaphora*, that is, of value only contingently, but inherently neither good nor bad). In a similar fashion, Paul seems to place 'belonging to Christ' as the only thing of ultimate value, while legal status (like other conditions of life) is not an equal, integral, or independent good.[13] Like the Stoics, he can judge some indistinguishable conditions *preferable*, if they are of instrumental value in serving the good (for Paul, serving Christ). Just as health, for the Stoics, is not integral to virtue (since one can be a healthy but bad person), but may, in many circumstances, enable one to deploy one's virtue well, so Paul can declare his preference for freedom ('avail yourself of the opportunity' for freedom; 'do not become slaves of human masters'), if that enables better service for Christ. But it appears that he does not insist on the emancipation of (even Christian) slaves, because he does not judge legal freedom to be a *necessary constituent* of the sole and only good – that is, belonging to Christ.

The implications of this position are challenging (in both senses of the term). If, for Philemon and Onesimus, their legal status is not integral to their only good (which is their new identity in Christ), this means several things:

(1) if necessary, for the sake of what counts (the progress of the good news), their legal status is disposable – i.e., each could act as if they were not slave or master, or they could change their legal status without change to their real worth;
(2) if they keep within their secondary roles, as slave or master, these are played out for a higher purpose (the service of Christ) and are useful only inasmuch as they serve that end; and

[13] See James L. Jaquette, *Discerning What Counts: The Function of the* Adiaphora *Topos in Paul's Letters* (Atlanta, GA: Scholars Press, 1995).

(3) the category 'slave' or 'master' is not salient on those occasions, or for those purposes, in which they are most truly themselves.[14] Their new status in Christ, and the goals to which that is orientated, have relativised their legal status (slave or free), such that that status is no longer the most important thing about them. It is not wholly irrelevant to their service of Christ, but it is important only as it constitutes the sphere in which their obedience to Christ may be more or less successfully enacted.

Paul's views here clash with the modern consensus that freedom is an intrinsic and independent good, and that slavery is wrong not only for the abuses associated with it, but because it deprives slaves of their fundamental human rights. Paul, we should acknowledge, does not hold to this modern conviction, even if there is some overlap in his language regarding the value of freedom. His complex position on the matter of slavery easily led to the full Christianization of master-slave relations, as in the household codes of Colossians 3–4, Ephesians 5, and 1 Timothy 6 (cf. 1 Pet 2:18–25), and even if these retain some relativisation of the slave owner's authority, they provided strong justification for the Christian continuation of slavery. As became clear in the British and American debates over the abolition of slavery, Paul's letters do not provide unambiguous support for the emancipation of slaves (they were used on *both* sides of the debate), and to that degree they stand at odds with core values that are largely (though not wholly) prevalent in the modern world.

A Christian theological reconfiguration of the Pauline legacy will want to take seriously his claim that belonging to Christ commandeers all other conditions in life, and that those in the most degraded circumstances are of equal worth in the sight of God with those who are socially and economically privileged. But it will also want to integrate the value of freedom into the concept of 'the ultimate good' more fully than was possible for Paul, while keeping his Christological vision of dignity or worth. Even if, with Paul, we consider equality and freedom to be *instrumental* goods, rather than ends in themselves, we may want to bring the instrument and the end into closer relation than he seemed able or willing to do. It would be easy to dismiss Paul's views on this topic out of hand, while, on the other side, he has been too easily

[14] See John M. G. Barclay, "ΚΟΙΝΩΝΙΑ and the Social Dynamics of the Letter to Philemon," in *La Lettre à Philémon et L'Ecclésiologie paulinienne/The Letter to Philemon and Pauline Ecclesiology*, ed. Daniel Marguerat (Leuven: Peeters, 2016) 151–169.

enlisted as a spokesman of modern egalitarianism. Both stances move swiftly across the chronological and ideological gap between then and now, between what was possible within Paul's social and political imagination and what is possible for us today. But even now he has the capacity to provoke us into a constructive theological interpretation, which thinks through afresh what it means to give prior and ultimate allegiance to Christ.

CELIBACY FOR CHRIST AND GENDER

Paul's judgement concerning slavery and freedom as 'indistinguishable' things is located within his discussion and radical relativisation of the state of marriage (1 Corinthians 7). The key purpose of marriage in the ancient world was not so much companionship as the lawful procreation of children as heirs, but Paul advocates radical disinvestment from such commitments and hopes, because of superior investment in the concerns of Christ. Counterculturally, throughout this chapter he regards celibacy as a superior state to marriage, except if celibacy were to lead to sexual immorality, in which case marriage would be better (1 Cor 7:1–11). The married person is distracted, with competing concerns for their spouse and for the Lord; the single person, by contrast, is single-minded (1 Cor 7:32–35). Strikingly, the concerns for the spouse are here described as anxiety for 'the things of the world' (1 Cor 7:33–35), and this reflects Paul's apocalyptic perspective, which places 'the world' into antithesis with Christ (cf. 1 Cor 2:6–16).[15] 'The world' or 'this age' are negatively tinged for Paul, insofar as they are unredeemed by the death and resurrection of Christ, and this fissure leads Paul to distance believers from the normal commitments of everyday life: 'the appointed time has grown very short: from now on, let those who have wives be as though they had none, and those who mourn as though they were not mourning, and those who rejoice as though they were not rejoicing, and those who buy as though they had no possessions, and those who deal with the world as though they had no dealings with it. For the present form of this world is passing away' (1 Cor 7:29–31). As the reference to the shortness of time suggests, Paul's chronological horizon is short (cf. 1 Thess 4:17; 1 Cor 15:51). But his stance is also, and more deeply, determined by the overriding demand of obligation to

[15] See Edward Adams, *Constructing the World: A Study in Paul's Cosmological Language* (Edinburgh: T&T Clark, 2000).

Christ, which does not sever entirely, but considerably weakens, the normal human ties to possessions and family.[16]

If we are apt to be disappointed that Paul is not more 'challenging' on other social issues, his evaluation of celibacy as preferable to marriage is an unambiguous challenge to almost every modern ideology of sex and marriage (including Christian 'family values'). Although the deutero-pauline Pastorals tone this down considerably (e.g., 1 Tim 5:3–16; Titus 2:3–5), the radical Pauline option reverberated throughout early Christianity as a symbol of Christian self-distancing from normal social commitments. This is not about 'asceticism' as an independent good, nor a negative evaluation of the body; it is precisely because the body is valuable that it is to be devoted wholly to the Lord (1 Cor 6:12–20). The celibate women who took this calling seriously were not necessarily more independent, unless they had their own means of support, and the call to celibacy was not, as is sometimes thought, a proto-feminist cause: celibate women were now financially dependent on the church rather than on the normal household structure. But their radical commitment to the Lord, and their freedom from family entanglements, made it possible to exercise roles that were usually closed off to married women and mothers, and in that sense Paul's policy could be 'liberating'.

As with slavery, Paul relativises gender distinctions not to erase them, but to render them no longer the most significant feature of a person's identity, and no longer ordered by a hierarchical system of worth. Galatians 3:28 ('there is no longer male and female') may have undercut, primarily, the presumption that marriage is the proper ordering of gender (cf. Gen 1:27: 'male and female he created them'). But it also, thereby, releases gendered identity to be rethought by reference to the believer's superseding commitment to Christ. Women are not rendered invisible as women, or treated as if they were honorary men, because precisely as women they can pray and prophesy in the 'assembly' (1 Cor 11:3–16), can function as a *diakonos* (Phoebe, Rom 16:1–2), can be counted as apostles (Junia, Rom 16:17), can be honoured for their work (Mary, Rom 16:7), and can host fellow believers in their homes (Prisca with Aquila, Rom 16:3–5). In exercising these prominent roles, Paul expects them still to look different from men, in their hair-arrangement or public attire, and in defending this difference old

[16] See John M. G. Barclay, "Apocalyptic Allegiance and Disinvestment in the World," in *Paul and the Apocalyptic Imagination*, eds. B. Blackwell, and J. Goodrich (Minneapolis, MN: Fortress Press, 2016) 257–274.

hierarchical assumptions creep into his text (1 Cor 11:3–16). It is notable that as soon as he harks back to Genesis 1–3, or appeals to 'nature', traditional assumptions about male superiority seem to re-emerge in his thought, and in the judgements of his followers (1 Cor 11:7–16; 14:33–36; 1 Tim 2:8–15); hints that things are different 'in the Lord' (1 Cor 11:11) are comparatively underdeveloped. The appeal to 'nature' in relation to homoerotic relations (Rom 1:26–27) is also atypical in Pauline ethics, and is not clearly related to Paul's central claim about the orientation of the body, first and foremost, to Christ.

It seems clear, once again, that whatever the partial overlaps with contemporary feminism, Paul is not straightforwardly an advocate of the equality of women. Indeed, equality is not, it seems, of central concern to Paul, as it is for many strands of modern thought. In the marriage relationship, the reorientation of both male and female to Christ is likely to find expression not in equality (and certainly not in autonomy) but in a reciprocal hierarchy of mutual 'ownership' (1 Cor 7:4). Paul's gender theology fits, it seems, neither simple equality nor static hierarchy, because his prior concern is not with human social structures but with putting every human resource into service for Christ. Unfortunately, Paul is still deployed in support of gender inequalities, by means of an over-simple transfer of Pauline statements to the modern world, and, in reaction, his gender remarks are obvious targets for hefty criticism. If he is to provide a constructive theological challenge to traditional constructions of gender, the solution is not to select those snippets that are more amenable to some modern agendas, nor to dance around those texts that say, to our ears, unacceptable things, but to apply a more thoroughgoing theological hermeneutic. Building on Paul's capacity to rethink and realign gender in relation to Christ, we may yet find Paul valuable as a critical resource in questioning both gender essentialism and gender hierarchies, both of which remain powerfully influential today. But a broader vision of embodied human flourishing, as integral to the good 'in Christ', would be needed to supplement Paul's remarks, and to provide criteria to judge why some of those remarks remain more relevant today than others, and more integral to the Christian good news.

IDENTITY IN CHRIST AND ETHNICITY

Current discussions of 'ethnicity' emphasise its malleability: it is a 'constructed' phenomenon that, even where it relates to ancestry and origin, always contains subjective elements dependent on political rhetoric and personal or cultural convenience.[17] When these contemporary discussions are brought in relation to Paul, the results can be very diverse. Does Paul erase ethnic identity (one reading of 'there is neither Jew nor Greek'), such that Christianity forms a monoculture whose 'universalism' is implicitly hegemonic? Or does he advocate an irreducible ethnic particularity, at least with regard to Jewish identity and the people of Israel (Romans 9–11)? Is ethnicity, for Paul, fixed by birth (Gal 2:15) or redefined in Christ (Rom 2:28–29)? Is it a precious characteristic (Rom 3:1–2) or a comparative 'loss' (Phil 3:8)? In fact, does Paul have a generalisable view on ethnicity, or is that expectation itself an imposition on his thought?[18]

As so often happens, Paul is tantalising and challenging precisely because he does *not* match our agendas or fit our contemporary categories. Although it might be considered extreme, his self-description in Phil 3:2–11 is perhaps the most revealing place to begin. Here Paul parades his impeccable ancestry and cultural excellence in a form that would fit ancient (and many modern) notions of ethnicity: 'If anyone has reason to be confident in the flesh, I have more: circumcised on the eighth day, a member of the people of Israel, of the tribe of Benjamin, a Hebrew born of Hebrews; as to the law, a Pharisee; as to zeal, a persecutor of the church; as to righteousness under the law, blameless' (Phil 3:4–6). Apart from persecution of the church, none of these credentials could be considered 'wrong' in Paul's eyes, but they are all eclipsed by something he goes on to describe: 'Yet, whatever gains I had, these I have come to regard as loss because of Christ. More than that, I regard everything as loss because of the surpassing value of knowing Christ Jesus my Lord. For his sake I have suffered the loss of all things, and I regard them as rubbish, in order that I might gain Christ and be found in him' (Phil 3:7–9).

Paul's former symbolic capital is here radically devalued compared to the one thing now of worth. It is not evil (he does not *disown* his ancestry), but it is comparatively worthless, since 'knowing Christ' has become the one good to which all other goods are secondary. It would be a mistake to read this (as has often been the case in Christian history)

[17] See Katherine M. Hockey and David G. Horrell, eds., *Ethnicity, Race, Religion: Identities and Ideologies in Early Jewish and Christian Texts, and in Modern Biblical Interpretation* (London: T&T Clark, 2018).

[18] For contrary views on such issues, see, e.g., Daniel Boyarin, *A Radical Jew: Paul and the Politics of Identity* (Berkeley, CA: University of California Press, 1994); Caroline E. Johnson Hodge, *If Sons, Then Heirs: A Study of Kinship and Ethnicity in the Letters of Paul* (Oxford: Oxford University Press, 2007).

either as a *negative* evaluation of Jewish identity, or as a 'spiritualising' of identity, such that all 'fleshly' and 'earthly' contingencies are rendered irrelevant in the light of a non-material and universal 'essence'. Paul embraces, as an alternative source of worth, his new identification with Christ, which does not erase his previous forms of identity, but subordinates, reorders, and realigns them. Now, for the sake of the good news, he can be 'as a Jew to the Jews', but 'to those outside the law' he can become 'as one outside the law (though I am not free from God's law but am under Christ's law)', in order to 'win' them all (1 Cor 9:20–21). This suggests not an abandonment of cultural difference, but its instrumentalisation for a higher end, in service of an identity and purpose that is superior to all forms of ethnic, national, and political belonging, not in metaphysical terms but in terms of allegiance. Again, there are some parallels with ancient Stoic 'cosmopolitanism', but Paul's confrontational claims could generate greater conflicts of interest. If, for Paul, the most essential identity, as a child of God, was *received* from God, in the gift of the Spirit (Gal 4:4–7), and if this new identity required placing no ultimate investment in earthly inheritance or territorial possession, then all secondary identities could be utilised or changed, as the strategy of Christ required. To this degree, Paul constitutes a radical challenge to modern nationalism and contemporary populism, since he refuses to grant ultimate allegiance to nations or ethnic groups. To the extent that contemporary churches identify politically with their ethnic or national tradition, or valorise national greatness at the expense of other peoples, they are apt to find Paul uncomfortably subversive.

There is, however, an important complication: Paul regards the *Jewish* people as in many senses special to God (Rom 9:1–5). This does not represent a generalisable commitment to ethnic 'particularity', since what Paul says here about 'Israelites' is quite different to his views about other nations, whom he regularly lumps together as 'the nations' without ethnic distinction, according no significance to their Greek or other characteristics. Neither is Paul's opinion on the Jews simply a residual privileging of his own ethnic identity, since he makes clear in Romans 9–11 that what is special about Israel is not something inherent in the nation, passed down by inheritance or held by right or achievement, but it is *given* by God and maintained by divine mercy.[19] In other words, Israel's unique status is a *theological* before it is an ethnic

[19] See Barclay, *Paul and the Gift*, 520–561.

phenomenon, but it is nonetheless powerful enough for Paul to insist that the future will entail the salvation of 'all Israel' (Rom 11:25–26). This stands as the strongest possible rebuke to anti-Semitism (Christian or other), which has sometimes, disastrously, traded on modern configurations of 'the universal' to characterise Judaism as inferior, unassimilable, and therefore to be eradicated or excluded. Paul's letters are available to be deployed by those who, on secular ethical and political grounds, deplore modern anti-Semitism, but again the overlap is only partial. Paul's reasons for holding to the preciousness of Israel (the people, not the state) are based on the fact that 'the gifts and the calling of God are irrevocable' (Rom 11:29) – a fact attested by the Scriptures, the 'oracles of God' (Rom 3:1–2). Shorn of this biblical and theological underpinning, Paul's arguments would have to be placed into a different, moral/political, register; arguably, in that process, they lose much of their power to subvert the arrogance of non-Jews.

CONCLUDING REFLECTIONS

It emerges from this analysis that Paul is challenging today for two different reasons, but these are so intertwined that it is difficult to disentangle them. The first reason is that he (inevitably) thinks in ancient terms, and within ancient horizons of the possible, such that his views on politics, gender, and slavery are at some distance from many modern expectations concerning liberal democracy, equality, and human rights. Paul's letters are products of the first century, and even if the church finds reason to grant them an authoritative voice in the task of contemporary theology, that does not (or need not) entail adopting his time-bound perspectives. The eschaton did not come, as he expected, in his lifetime, and when, for instance, he describes a married woman as (literally) a 'woman under man' (*hypandros gynē*, Rom 7:2), we are entitled to resist (on theological grounds) the patriarchal implications of such a description.

But the second reason for the challenge of Paul is that he approaches topics that matter to us from an unfamiliar, irreducibly Christological, basis, arguing from the Christ-event and its results. That is bound to stand at odds with many of the assumptions of modernity. As we have seen in each issue we have discussed, Paul's procedure is to reconfigure what counts in the light of Christ. The critical edge of that procedure is to expose as misguided (even idolatrous) the investments we place in politics, gender identity, ethnicity, or socially accorded worth, as if they were the means to the mending of our deepest human problems, or the canons of our ultimate value. Paul reads the human situation at a level deeper than these – not 'above' them in some ethereal, 'spiritual' dimension, but *within* them at a level beyond the capacity of our normal criteria of analysis. From a Pauline perspective, where the proper human allegiance to Christ is transferred to other goals or ideals, and where our ultimate hopes are placed in our capacity for progress, we will be sorely disappointed: to 'sow to the flesh' is to reap corruption (Gal 6:8). Since, for Paul, the human condition is at every point frustrated by suffering, sin, and mortality, to put our hopes in human utopias is bound to disappoint us, and to rest human worth on status, appearance, success, or popularity can only result in fragile egos, easily crushed. But if human worth is *given* in Christ, and given without regard to status or success, and if divine mercy is always greater than human disobedience and sin (Rom 11:32), there is good news that places all these agendas within their proper limits. In this sense, Paul's greatest challenge lies in his diagnosis of human failure and in his announcement of divine grace, compared to which every secular analysis reads reality only on its surface.

Since traces of its Christian heritage are still evident within Western culture, there is a common Western inclination – even among those who would otherwise repudiate Christianity – to adopt (or co-opt) Paul for our social and political causes, heroising him as, in some sense, a proto-feminist, an anti-imperial subversive, or an egalitarian. It is possible to do this because, for historical reasons (e.g., the Christian roots of the Enlightenment), many modern views on society and politics *partially overlap* with aspects of Paul's letters. Hence, with judicious selection and constructive interpretation, Paul can emerge, even in secular form, as a contemporary social critic.[20] The danger is that, in the absence of his theological vision, this brings to Paul quite unrealistic expectations, projecting onto him what *we* would want him to have said. And that, in turn, can lead to a subsequent backlash, where Paul proves, on further enquiry, out of line with modern critical sensibilities – not the antidote to our social problems, more the poison within them. In this backlash, framed by modern antitheses, the supposedly 'anti-imperial' Paul is now interpreted as the (naive or inadvertent) stooge of

[20] For examples of a consciously non-theological reading of Paul that still finds him politically useful, see, e.g., Alain Badiou, *Saint Paul: The Foundation of Universalism* (Berkeley, CA: University of California Press, 2003); Ward Blanton, *A Materialism for the Masses: Paul and the Philosophy of Undying Life* (New York: Columbia University Press, 2014).

Roman power; the 'liberationist' is flipped, and becomes the original architect of Christian oppression. Many complex dynamics, personal and political, enter into this fluctuating dynamic, but it is often insufficiently recognised that these varying reconstructions, however much they claim to be 'merely' historical readings, are inflected, if not determined, by certain modern measures of what we wanted Paul to say.

If Christian interpretation is to embrace the challenge of Paul, it needs to operate, self-consciously, with some form of theological *Sachkritik* – the critical *evaluation* of Paul's letters with regard to their central theological subject matter.[21] Although this will always be a subjective and provisional process, it recognises that Paul cannot be transferred, without critical sifting, straight from his own era to ours, given the time-bound elements in his thinking. Indeed, without some such critical sifting, Paul will cease to be challenging at all, since we will render him too remote to be of interest or relevance. To the extent that neither 'conservative' embrace of Paul nor 'liberal' engagement with his letters recognise the necessity of this constructive hermeneutical enterprise, their readings lack critical depth and intellectual credibility. A Christian engagement with Paul is committed to respond theologically to the challenge that issues from his articulation of the gospel. This, as we have seen, operates at a level deeper than simply modifying one item or another on our social agendas. In exposing ourselves to Paul's critical, Christological perspective, we will need to acknowledge that our own judgements may be deeply distorted by our cultural and social locations, and that our aims and goals are valuable only inasmuch as they correspond to the good news. Because of our human flaws, they will be provisional and limited, but they may nonetheless become meaningful insofar as they respond to the dynamic of divine mercy and grace.

Of course, in interpreting Paul, Christian theology is committed to read Paul within a wider frame of reference. Whatever the diversities of voice within the Pauline corpus, they will be heard, theologically, within the even more diverse chorus of voices within the biblical canon. How one hears Paul's distinctive voice well in that larger context is itself a difficult matter, but not even Lutheran theology takes Paul's to be the *only* voice in the canon, and there may be many places where gaps or silences in the letters that we have from Paul can be fruitfully filled from elsewhere in the canon. It is only in the modern era that 'the

[21] See Robert Morgan, "*Sachkritik* in Reception History," *Journal for the Study of the New Testament* 33 (2010): 175–190.

theology of Paul', in isolation, has been a subject of enquiry, and if his letters buckle under the weight of expectation that we have loaded upon them, that may be because they have been artificially removed from their larger biblical context. A responsible theological reading of these letters will want to remain in dialogue with contemporary critical theory, but it will not feel itself ultimately committed to its core critical values, unless these match the values central to its theological frame. Since it is mostly the theological and ecclesial tradition that sustains interest in Paul (even where contemporary scholarship is positioned in opposition to it), theological readings of Paul are entitled to use their own frames of reference in their engagement with him. And their default position is not to be ashamed of the good news (Rom 1:16), even, or especially, where it critically exposes the alternative narratives and substitute goals that replace Paul's story concerning the gracious reclamation of the world in Christ.

There is one final element of challenge. Paul's letters are arguably best heard not in the study (or the University), but in the complex challenges of everyday community life, especially the life of the church. Often what is challenging to a critically-trained academic is unproblematic for an 'ordinary' believer, and vice versa. There are many features of Paul's style and ethos that make him difficult for church hearers and readers, but the content of his letters continues to challenge the Christian imagination in the everyday sphere of social relations. In that sphere, for instance, Paul's description of love (1 Corinthians 13) is perhaps the most challenging text he ever wrote. What sounds academically uncomplicated turns out to be the hardest thing to put into practice. And since Paul wrote to shape not just minds, but whole lives, in their relation to Christ, perhaps the question of this chapter should be differently framed: what in Paul is *not* challenging today?

Further Reading

Badiou, A. *Saint Paul: The Foundation of Universalism*. Berkeley, CA: University of California Press, 2003.

Barclay, John M. G. "Crucifixion as Wisdom: Exploring the Ideology of a Disreputable Social Movement." In *The Wisdom and Foolishness of God*, edited by C. Chalamet and H. C. Askani, 1–20. Minneapolis, MN: Fortress Press, 2015.

Barclay, John M. G. *Paul and the Gift*. Grand Rapids, MI: Eerdmans, 2015.

Barclay, John M. G. "Apocalyptic Allegiance and Disinvestment in the World." In *Paul and the Apocalyptic Imagination*, edited by B. Blackwell and J. Goodrich, 257–274. Minneapolis, MN: Fortress Press, 2016.

Bertschmann, Dorothea H. *Bowing before Christ – Nodding to the State?: Reading Paul Politically with Oliver O'Donovan and John Howard Yoder*. London: T&T Clark, 2014.

Boyarin, Daniel. *A Radical Jew: Paul and the Politics of Identity*. Berkeley, CA: University of California Press, 1997.

Castelli, Elizabeth Anne. *Imitating Paul: A Discourse of Power*. Louisville, KY: Westminster John Knox, 1991.

Ehrensperger, Kathy. *Paul and the Dynamics of Power: Communication and Interaction in the Early Christ-Movement*. London: T&T Clark, 2009.

Harink, Douglas, ed. *Paul, Philosophy, and the Theopolitical Vision: Critical Engagements with Agamben, Badiou, Zizek, and Others*. Eugene, OR: Wipf & Stock, 2010.

Horsley, Richard A., ed. *Paul and the Roman Imperial Order*. Harrisburg, PA: Trinity Press International, 2004.

Johnson Hodge, Caroline E. *If Sons, Then Heirs: A Study of Kinship and Ethnicity in the Letters of Paul*. Oxford: Oxford University Press, 2007.

Marchal, Joseph A. *The Politics of Heaven: Women, Gender, and Empire in the Study of Paul*. Minneapolis, MN: Fortress Press, 2008.

Morgan, Robert. "Sachkritik in Reception History." *Journal for the Study of the New Testament* 33, no. 2 (2010): 175–190.

Stanley, Christopher D. *The Colonized Apostle: Paul in Postcolonial Eyes*. Minneapolis, MN: Fortress Press, 2011.

Welborn, L. L. *Paul, the Fool of Christ: A Study of 1 Corinthians 1–4 in the Comic-Philosophic Tradition*. London: A&C Black, 2005.

Bibliography

Aageson, James W. *Paul, the Pastoral Epistles, and the Early Church*. Grand Rapids, MI: Baker Academic, 2007.

Aageson, James W. "The Pastoral Epistles and the Acts of Paul: A Multiplex Approach to Authority in Paul's Legacy." *Lexington Quarterly Review* 40 (2005): 237–248.

Adams, Edward. *Constructing the World: A Study in Paul's Cosmological Language*. Edinburgh: T&T Clark, 2000.

Adams, Edward. *The Earliest Christian Meeting Places: Almost Exclusively Houses?* London: Bloomsbury T&T Clark, 2013.

Arnold, Clinton E. "Colossae." In *Anchor Bible Dictionary*. Vol. 1, edited by D. N. Freedman, 1089–1090. New York: Doubleday, 1992.

Ascough, Richard S. *Paul's Macedonian Associations: The Social Context of Philippians and 1 Thessalonians*. Tübingen: Mohr Siebeck, 2003.

Ascough, Richard S. "What Are They Now Saying about Christ Groups and Associations?" *Currents in Biblical Research* 13, no. 2 (2015): 207–244.

Ascough, Richard S. "Paul and Associations." In *Paul in the Greco-Roman World: A Handbook*. Vol. 1, edited by J. Paul Sampley, 68–89. London: Bloomsbury, 2016.

Ascough, Richard S. "Reimagining the Size of Pauline Christ Groups in light of Association Meeting Places." In *Scribal Practices and Social Structures among Jesus Adherents: Essays in Honour of John S. Kloppenborg*, edited by William E. Arnal, Richard S. Ascough, Robert A. Derrenbacker, Jr., and Philip A. Harland, 547–565. Leuven: Peeters, 2016.

Ascough, Richard S. *1 & 2 Thessalonians: Encountering the Christ Group at Thessalonike*. New York: Bloomsbury T&T Clark, 2017.

Ascough, Richard S., Philip A. Harland, and John S. Kloppenborg. *Associations in the Greco-Roman World: A Sourcebook*. Waco, TX: Baylor University Press, 2012.

Ávila Arteaga, Mariano. *Efesios: Introducción y comentario. Tomos I y II*. Buenos Aires: Ediciones Kairós, 2018.

Badiou, Alain. *Saint Paul: The Foundation of Universalism*. Translated by Ray Brassier. Stanford, CA: Stanford University Press, 2003.

Bailey, Jeremiah N. "Spheres and Trajectories: The Angels of the Churches (Revelation 1–3) in Context." In *Early Christianity in Pompeian Light: Texts, People, Situations*, edited by Bruce W. Longenecker, 167–192. Minneapolis, MN: Fortress Press, 2016.

Barclay, John M. G. *Obeying the Truth: A Study of Paul's Ethics in Galatians*. Edinburgh: T&T Clark, 1988.

Barclay, John M. G. "Thessalonica and Corinth: Social Contrasts in Pauline Christianity." *Journal for the Study of the New Testament* 47 (1992): 49–74.

Barclay, John M. G. *Paul and the Gift*. Grand Rapids, MI: Eerdmans, 2015.

Barclay, John M. G. "Crucifixion as Wisdom: Exploring the Ideology of a Disreputable Social Movement." In *The Wisdom and Foolishness of God*, edited by C. Chalamet and H. C. Askani, 1–20. Minneapolis, MN: Fortress Press, 2015.

Barclay, John M. G. "Apocalyptic Allegiance and Disinvestment in the World." In *Paul and the Apocalyptic Imagination*, edited by B. Blackwell and J. Goodrich, 257–274. Minneapolis, MN: Fortress Press, 2016.

Barclay, John M. G. "Deviance and Apostasy: Some Applications of Deviance Theory to First-Century Judaism and Christianity." In *Pauline Churches and Diaspora Jews*, 123–139. Grand Rapids, MI: Eerdmans, 2016.

Barclay, John M. G. "ΚΟΙΝΩΝΙΑ and the Social Dynamics of the Letter to Philemon." In *La Lettre à Philémon et L'Ecclésiologie Paulinienne*, edited by Daniel Marguerat, 151–169. Leuven: Peeters Publishers, 2016.

Barclay, John M. G. *Paul: A Very Brief History*. London: SPCK, 2018.

Bartchy, S. Scott. "Philemon." In *Anchor Bible Dictionary*. Vol. 5, edited by D. N. Freedman, 305–310. New York: Doubleday, 1992.

Barthélemy, Dominique. *Devancies d'Aquila: Première Publication Intégrale Du Texte Des Fragments Du Dodécaprophéton*. VTSup 10. Leiden: Brill, 1963.

Bates, Matthew W. *Salvation by Allegiance Alone: Rethinking Faith, Works, and the Gospel of Jesus the King*. Grand Rapids, MI: Baker Academic, 2017.

Bauckham, Richard. *Jesus and the God of Israel: God Crucified and Other Studies on the New Testament's Christology of Divine Identity*. Grand Rapids, MI: Eerdmans, 2008.

Bauckham, Richard. "Paul's Christology of Divine Identity." In *Jesus and the God of Israel*, 182–232. Grand Rapids, MI: Eerdmans, 2009.

Baur, Ferdinand Christian. *Paul the Apostle of Jesus Christ: His Life and Works, His Epistles and Teachings*. Vol. 2, translated by Eduard Zeller and A. Menzies. London: Williams & Norgate, 1876.

Barton, Carlin, and Daniel Boyarin. *Imagine No Religion: How Modern Abstractions Hide Ancient Realities*. New York: Fordham University Press, 2016

Barton, John. "Déjà Lu: Intertextuality, Method or Theory?" In *Reading Job Intertextually*. LHBOTS 574, edited by Katharine Dell and Will Kynes., 1–16. London: Bloomsbury, 2013.

Beard, Mary, John North, and Simon Price. *Religions of Rome: Vol 1: A History*. Cambridge: Cambridge University Press, 1998.

BeDuhn, Jason D. *The First New Testament: Marcion's Scriptural Canon*. Salem, OR: Polebridge, 2013.

Beker, J. Christiaan. *Paul the Apostle*. Minneapolis, MN: Fortress Press, 1980.

Beker, J. Christiaan. "The Dilemma of Sin and Death: Equivalent or Disparate Powers?" In *Paul the Apostle: The Triumph of God in Life and Thought*, 213–234. Minneapolis, MN: Fortress Press, 1980.

Beker, J. Christiaan. *Heirs of Paul: Paul's Legacy in the New Testament and in the Church Today*. Minneapolis, MN: Fortress Press, 1991.

Bertschmann, Dorothea H. *Bowing before Christ – Nodding to the State?: Reading Paul Politically with Oliver O'Donovan and John Howard Yoder.* London: T&T Clark, 2014.
Betz, Hans Dieter. *Galatians: A Commentary on Paul's Letter to the Churches in Galatia.* Philadelphia: Fortress Press, 1979.
Bird, Michael F. *Crossing over Sea and Land: Jewish Missionary Activity in the Second Temple Period.* Peabody, MA: Hendrickson, 2010.
Blackwell, Ben C. *Christosis: Pauline Soteriology in light of Deification in Irenaeus and Cyril of Alexandria.* Rev. ed. Grand Rapids, MI: Eerdmans, 2016.
Blanton, Ward. *A Materialism for the Masses: Saint Paul and the Philosophy of Undying Life.* New York: Columbia University Press, 2014.
Bockmuehl, Markus. "'The Form of God' (Phil. 2:6) Variations on a Theme of Jewish Mysticism." *Journal of Theological Studies* 48, no. 1 (1997): 1–23.
Bockmuehl, Markus. *The Epistle to the Philippians.* London: A & C Black, 1998.
Bohak, Gideon. "The Ibis and the Jewish Question: Ancient 'Anti-Semitism' in Historical Context." In *Jews and Gentiles in the Holy Land in the Days of the Second Temple, the Mishnah and the Talmud: A Collection of Articles,* 27–43. Jerusalem: Yad Ben-Zvi Press, 2003.
Boyarin, Daniel. *A Radical Jew: Paul and the Politics of Identity.* Berkeley, CA: University of California Press, 1997.
Boyarin, Daniel. *Judaism: The Genealogy of a Modern Notion.* New Brunswick, NJ: Rutgers University Press, 2018.
Brand, M. T. *Evil Within and Without: The Source of Sin and Its Nature as Portrayed in Second Temple Literature.* Göttingen: Vandenhoeck & Ruprecht, 2013.
Bremmer, Jan L., and István Czachesz, eds. *The Visio Pauli and the Gnostic Apocalypse of Paul.* Studies on Early Christian Apocrypha 9. Leuven: Peeters, 2007.
Bremmer, Jan L. *Initiation into the Mysteries of the Ancient World.* Berlin: De Gruyter, 2014.
Brooke, George J. "'The Canon within the Canon' at Qumran and in the New Testament." In *The Scrolls and the Scriptures: Qumran Fifty Years After.* JSPSup 26, edited by Stanley E. Porter and Craig A. Evans., 242–266. Sheffield: Sheffield Academic, 1997.
Bultmann, Rudolf. "δικαιοσύνη θεοῦ." *Journal of Biblical Literature* 83 (1964): 12–16.
Burkert, Walter. *Ancient Mystery Cults.* Cambridge, MA: Harvard University Press, 1987.
Campbell, Douglas A. *The Rhetoric of Righteousness in Romans 3:21–26.* Sheffield: Sheffield Academic Press, 1992.
Campbell, Douglas A. "The Narrative Dimensions in Paul's Gospel." In *Narrative Dynamics in Paul: A Critical Assessment,* edited by Bruce W. Longenecker, 97–124. Louisville, KY: Westminster John Knox, 2002.
Campbell, Douglas A. *The Deliverance of God: An Apocalyptic Rereading of Justification in Paul.* Grand Rapids, MI: Eerdmans, 2009.
Campbell, Douglas A. "An Attempt to Be Understood: A Response to the Concerns of Matlock and Macaskill with the Deliverance of God." *Journal for the Study of the New Testament* 34 (2011): 162–208.

Campbell, Douglas A. *Framing Paul: An Epistolary Biography*. Grand Rapids, MI: Eerdmans, 2014.

Campbell, Douglas A. *Paul: An Apostle's Journey*. Grand Rapids, MI: Eerdmans, 2018.

Carraway, George. *Christ Is God Over All: Romans 9:5 in the Context of Romans 9–11*. LNTS 489. London: T&T Clark, 2013.

Castelli, Elizabeth Anne. *Imitating Paul: A Discourse of Power*. Louisville, KY: Westminster John Knox, 1991.

Chaniotis, Angelos. "Megatheism: The Search for the Almighty God and the Competition of Cults." In *One God: Pagan Monotheism in the Roman Empire*, edited by Stephen Mitchell and Peter van Nuffelen, 112–140. Cambridge: Cambridge University Press, 2010.

Clark, Elizabeth A. *Reading Renunciation: Asceticism and Scripture in Early Christianity*. Princeton, NJ: Princeton University Press, 1999.

Clarke, John R. *Roman Life: 100 B.C. to A. D. 200*. New York: Harry N. Abrams, 2007.

Clauss, Manfred. *The Roman Cult of Mithras: The God and His Mysteries*. Edinburgh: Edinburgh University Press, 2000.

Colijn, Brenda B. *Images of Salvation in the New Testament*. Downers Grove, IL: IVP Academic, 2010.

Collins, Raymond F. "The Image of Paul in the Pastorals." *Laval Theologique et Philosophique* 31 (1975): 147–173.

Collins, Raymond F. *I & II Timothy and Titus*. Louisville, KY: Westminster John Knox, 2002.

Croasmun, Matthew. *The Emergence of Sin: The Cosmic Tyrant in Romans*. Oxford: Oxford University Press, 2017.

de Boer, Martinus C. *Galatians: A Commentary*. Louisville, KY: Westminster John Knox, 2011.

deSilva, David A. "Paul, Honor, and Shame." In *Paul in the Greco-Roman World: A Handbook*. 2nd ed. Vol. 2, edited by J. Paul Sampley, 26–47. London: Bloomsbury, 2016.

Dijkstra, Roald. *The Apostles in Early Christian Art and Poetry*. VCSup 134. Leiden: Brill, 2016.

Donaldson, Terence L. *Judaism and the Gentiles: Jewish Patterns of Universalism (to 135 CE)*. Waco, TX: Baylor University Press, 2007.

Donfried, Karl P., ed. *The Romans Debate*. Revised and expanded ed. Peabody, MA: Hendrickson, 1991.

Duff, Paul B. *Jesus Followers in the Roman Empire*. Grand Rapids, MI: Eerdmans, 2017.

Dunn, James D. G. *The Theology of Paul the Apostle*. Edinburgh: T&T Clark, 1998.

Eastman, David L. *The Ancient Martyrdom Accounts of Peter and Paul, Writings from the Greco-Roman World*. Atlanta, GA: Society of Biblical Literature, 2015.

Eastman, Susan Grove. *Paul and the Person: Reframing Paul's Anthropology*. Grand Rapids, MI: Eerdmans, 2017.

Ehrensperger, Kathy. *Paul and the Dynamics of Power: Communication and Interaction in the Early Christ-Movement*. London: T&T Clark, 2009.

Ehrman, Bart D. *Forgery and Counterforgery: The Use of Literary Deceit in Early Christian Polemics*. Oxford: Oxford University Press, 2012.

Ehrman, Bart D. *How Jesus Became God: The Exaltation of a Jewish Preacher from Galilee*. New York: HarperOne, 2014.

Eisenbaum, Pamela. *Paul Was Not a Christian: The Original Message of a Misunderstood Apostle*. New York: HarperOne, 2009.

Flew, A. *There Is a God: How the World's Most Notorious Atheist Changed His Mind*. San Francisco, CA: HarperOne, 2007.

Flower, Harriet I. *Dancing Lares and the Serpent in the Garden: Religion at the Roman Street Corner*. Princeton, NJ: Princeton University Press, 2017.

Fowl, Stephen E. *Philippians*. Grand Rapids, MI: Eerdmans, 2005.

Fowl, Stephen E. *Ephesians: A Commentary*. Louisville, KY: Westminster John Knox, 2012.

Fredriksen, Paula. "Paul and Augustine: Conversion Narratives, Orthodox Traditions, and the Retrospective Self." *Journal of Theological Studies* 37 (1986): 3–34.

Fredriksen, Paula. "If It Looks Like a Duck, and It Quacks Like a Duck . . . : On *Not* Giving Up the Godfearers." In *A Most Reliable Witness: Essays in Honor of Ross Shepard Kraemer*, edited by Susan Ashbrook Harvey, Nathaniel DesRosiers, Shira L. Lander, Jacqueline Z. Pastis, and Daniel Ullucci, 25–34. Providence, RI: Brown Judaic Studies, 2015.

Fredriksen, Paula. *Paul: The Pagans' Apostle*. New Haven, CT: Yale University Press, 2017.

Fredriksen, Paula. "How Jewish Is God? Divine Ethnicity in Paul's Theology." *Journal of Biblical Literature* 137 (2018): 193–212.

Fredriksen, Paula. *When Christians Were Jews. The First Generation*. New Haven, CT: Yale University Press, 2018.

Fredriksen, Paula. "Paul the 'Convert'?" In *The Oxford Handbook of Pauline Studies*, edited by B. Matlock and M. Novenson. Oxford: Oxford University Press, forthcoming.

Fredriksen, Paula. "'Circumcision is Nothing and Foreskin is Nothing': A Non-Reformation Reading of Paul's Letters." In *Protestant Bible Scholarship: Antisemitism, Philosemitism and Anti-Judaism*, edited Arjen Bakker, René Bloch, Yael Fisch, Paula Fredriksen and Hindy Najman. Leiden: Brill, forthcoming.

Friesen, Steven J. "Poverty in Pauline Studies: Beyond the So-Called New Consensus." *Journal for the Study of the New Testament* 26 (2004): 323–361.

Funk, Franz Xaver, Karl Bihlmeyer, and Molly Whittaker. *Die Apostolischen Väter, Griechische-Deutsche Parallelausgabe*. Tübingen: Mohr Siebeck, 1992.

Fuß, Barbara. *"Dies Ist Die Zeit, von Der Geschrieben Ist ..." Die Expliziten Zitate Aus Dem Buch Hosea in Den Handschriften von Qumran Und Im Neuen Testament*. Münster: Aschendorff, 2000.

Gamble, Harry Y. *Books and Readers in the Early Church: A History of Early Christian Texts*. New Haven, CT: Yale University Press, 1997.

Garroway, Joshua, and David Lincicum et al. "Paul: Within Judaism, Without Law." In *Law and Lawlessness in Early Judaism and Christianity*. Tübingen: Mohr Siebeck, 2019.

Gathercole, Simon J. *Defending Substitution: An Essay on Atonement in Paul*. Grand Rapids, MI: Baker Academic, 2015.

Gathercole, Simon J. "'Sins' in Paul." *New Testament Studies* 64, no. 2 (2018): 143–161.

Gaventa, Beverly Roberts. "The Cosmic Power of Sin in Paul's Letter to the Romans: Toward a Widescreen Edition." *Interpretation* 58, no. 3 (2004): 229–240.

Gaventa, Beverly Roberts. *Our Mother Saint Paul*. Louisville, KY: Westminster John Knox, 2007.

Gaventa, Beverly Roberts, ed. *Apocalyptic Paul: Cosmos and Anthropos in Romans 5–8*. Waco, TX: Baylor University Press, 2013.

Glancy, Jennifer A. *Slavery in Early Christianity*. New York: Oxford University Press, 2002; Minneapolis, MN: Fortress Press, 2006.

Goodman, Martin. "The Persecution of Paul by Diaspora Jews." In *The Beginnings of Christianity*, edited by Jack Pastor and Menachem Mor, 379–387. Jerusalem: Yad ben Zvi, 2005.

Gordley, Matthew E. *New Testament Christological Hymn: Exploring Texts, Contexts, and Significance*. Downers Grove, IL: InterVarsity Press, 2018.

Gorman, Michael J. *Inhabiting the Cruciform God: Kenosis, Justification, and Theosis in Paul's Narrative Soteriology*. Grand Rapids, MI: Eerdmans, 2009.

Gorman, Michael J. *Apostle of the Crucified Lord: A Theological Introduction to Paul and His Letters*. 2nd ed. Grand Rapids, MI: Eerdmans, 2017.

Graves, David E. "What Is the Madder with Lydia's Purple? A Re-examination of the Purpurarii in Thyatira and Philippi." *Near East Archaeological Society Bulletin* 62 (2017): 3–28.

Gray, Patrick. *Paul as a Problem in History and Culture: The Apostle and His Critics through the Centuries*. Grand Rapids, MI: Baker Publishing Group, 2016.

Gregory, Andrew F., and Christopher Tuckett, eds. *The Reception of the New Testament in the Apostolic Fathers*. Oxford: Oxford University Press, 2005.

Gruen, Erich S. *Heritage and Hellenism: The Reinvention of Jewish Tradition*. Berkeley, CA: University of California Press, 1998.

Gruen, Erich S. *Diaspora: Jews amidst Greeks and Romans*. Cambridge, MA: Harvard University Press, 2002.

Harding, Sarah. *Heritage and Hellenism: The Reinvention of Jewish Tradition*. Berkeley, CA: University of California Press, 1998.

Harding, Sarah. *Paul's Eschatological Anthropology: The Dynamics of Human Transformation*. Minneapolis, MN: Fortress Press, 2016.

Harink, Douglas, ed. *Paul, Philosophy, and the Theopolitical Vision: Critical Engagements with Agamben, Badiou, Zizek, and Others*. Eugene, OR: Wipf & Stock, 2010.

Harnack, Adolf von. *What Is Christianity?* Translated by Thomas Bailey Saunders. New York: Harper, 1957.

Harnack, Adolf von. "The Old Testament in the Pauline Letters and in the Pauline Churches." In *Understanding Paul's Ethics: Twentieth Century Approaches*, edited by Brian Rosner, 27–49. Grand Rapids, MI: Eerdmans, 1995.

Harrill, J. Albert. *Paul the Apostle: His Life and Legacy in Their Roman Context*. Cambridge: Cambridge University Press, 2012.

Harrison, James R. "The First Urban Churches: Introduction." In *The First Urban Churches 1: Methodological Foundations*, edited by James R. Harrison and L. L. Welborn, 1–40. Atlanta, GA: Society of Biblical Literature, 2015.

Harrison, James R., and L. L. Welborn, eds. *The First Urban Churches 3: Ephesus*. Atlanta, GA: Society of Biblical Literature, 2018.

Harvey, Anthony Ernest. "Forty Strokes Save One: Social Aspects of Judaizing and Apostasy." In *Alternative Approaches to New Testament Study*, 79–86. London: SPCK, 1985.

Hays, Richard B. "Psalm 143 and the Logic of Romans 3." *Journal of Biblical Literature* 99 (1980): 107–115.

Hays, Richard B. "'Have We Found Abraham to be Our Forefather according to the Flesh?' A Reconsideration of Rom 4:1." *Novum Testamentum* 27, no. 1 (1985): 76–98.

Hays, Richard B. *Echoes of Scripture in the Letters of Paul*. New Haven, CT: Yale University Press, 1989.

Hays, Richard B. "The Story of God's Son: The Identity of Jesus in the Letters of Paul." In *Seeking the Identity of Jesus: A Pilgrimage*, edited by Richard B. Hays and Beverly Roberts Gaventa, 180–199. Grand Rapids, MI: Eerdmans, 2008.

Häfner, Gerd. *'Nützlich Zur Belehrung' (2 Tim 3,16): Die Rolle Der Schrift in Den Pastoralbriefen Im Rahmen Der Paulusrezeption*. Freiburg: Herder, 2000.

Heilig, Christoph. *Hidden Criticism?: The Methodology and Plausibility of the Search for a Counter-Imperial Subtext in Paul*. Tübingen: Mohr Siebeck, 2015.

Heine, Ronald F. *The Commentaries of Origen and Jerome on Saint Paul's Epistle to the Ephesians*. Oxford: Oxford University Press, 2002.

Hellerman, Joseph H. *The Ancient Church as Family*. Minneapolis, MN: Fortress Press, 2001.

Hendrix, Holland L. "Philippi." In *Anchor Bible Dictionary*. Vol. 5, 313–317. New Haven, CT: Yale University Press, 2007.

Hiestermann, Heinz. *Paul and the Synoptic Jesus Tradition*. Leipzig: Evangelische Verlagsanstalt, 2017

Hill, Wesley. *Paul and the Trinity: Persons, Relations, and the Pauline Letters*. Grand Rapids, MI: Eerdmans, 2015.

Hockey, Katherine M., and David G. Horrell, eds. *Ethnicity, Race, Religion: Identities and Ideologies in Early Jewish and Christian Texts, and in Modern Biblical Interpretation*. New York: T&T Clark, 2018.

Holloway, Paul A. *Philippians*. Minneapolis, MN: Fortress Press, 2017.

Hooker, Morna D. "Interchange in Christ." *Journal of Theological Studies* 32, no. 2 (1971): 349–361. Reprint, *From Adam to Christ: Essays on Paul*, 13–69. Cambridge: Cambridge University Press, 1990. Reprint, Eugene, OR: Wipf and Stock, 2008.

Horbury, William. "Jewish and Christian Monotheism in the Herodian Age." In *Herodian Judaism and New Testament Study*, 2–33. Tübingen: Mohr Siebeck, 2006.

Horsley, Richard A., ed. *Paul and Empire: Religion and Power in Roman Imperial Society*. Harrisburg, PA: Trinity Press International, 1997.

Horsley, Richard A., *Paul and the Roman Imperial Order*. Harrisburg, PA: Trinity Press International, 2004.

Horrell, David G. *An Introduction to the Study of Paul*. New York: Bloomsbury T&T Clark, 2015.

Horrell, David G. "The Letters for All (Local) Christians: Were There Pauline Churches?" In *The Making of Christian Morality: Reading Paul in Ancient and Modern Contexts*, 15–26. Grand Rapids, MI: Eerdmans, 2019.

Hübner, Hans. *Law in Paul's Thought: A Contribution to the Development of Pauline Theology*. Translated by J. C. G. Greig. Edinburgh: T&T Clark, 1984.

Hultgren, Arland J. "The Pastoral Epistles." In *The Cambridge Companion to St Paul*, edited by James D. G. Dunn, 141–157. Cambridge: Cambridge University Press, 2003.

Hurtado, Larry W. *Lord Jesus Christ: Devotion to Jesus in Earliest Christianity*. Grand Rapids, MI: Eerdmans, 2005.

Hurtado, Larry W. *Why on Earth Did Anyone Become a Christian in the First Three Centuries*. Milwaukee, WI: Marquette University Press, 2016.

Hurtado, Larry W., and C. Keith. "Writing and Book Production in the Hellenistic and Roman Periods." In *The New Cambridge History of the Bible, Volume 1: From the Beginnings to 600*, edited by James Carleton Paget and Joachim Schaper, 63–80. Cambridge: Cambridge University Press, 2013.

Huttner, Ulrich. *Early Christianity in the Lycus Valley*. Translated by David Green. Leiden: Brill, 2013.

Isaac, Benjamin H. *The Invention of Racism in Classical Antiquity*. Princeton, NJ: Princeton University Press, 2004.

Jackson-McCabe, Matt, ed. *Jewish Christianity Reconsidered: Rethinking Ancient Groups and Texts*. Minneapolis, MN: Fortress Press, 2007.

Jaquette, James L. *Discerning What Counts: The Function of the Adiaphora Topos in Paul's Letters*. Atlanta, GA: Scholars Press, 1996.

Jennings, Willie James. *The Christian Imagination: Theology and the Origins of Race*. New Haven, CT: Yale University Press, 2011.

Jewett, Robert. "Tenement Churches and Communal Meals in the Early Church," *Biblical Research* 38 (1993): 23–43.

Jewett, Robert. *Romans: A Commentary*. Minneapolis, MN: Fortress Press, 2007.

Johnson, Luke Timothy. *Letters to Paul's Delegates: 1 Timothy, 2 Timothy, Titus*. Harrisburg, PA: Trinity Press International, 1996.

Johnson, Luke Timothy. *The First and Second Letters to Timothy*. New York: Doubleday, 2001.

Johnson Hodge, Caroline E. *If Sons, Then Heirs: A Study of Kinship and Ethnicity in the Letters of Paul*. Oxford: Oxford University Press, 2007.

Jones, Donald L. "Roman Imperial Cult." In *Anchor Bible Dictionary*. Vol. 5, 806–809. New Haven, CT: Yale University Press, 1992.

Käsemann, Ernst. *New Testament Questions of Today*. Philadelphia: Fortress Press, 1969.

Käsemann, Ernst. "On Paul's Anthropology." In *Perspectives on Paul*. Translated by J. Kohl, 1–31. Mifflintown, PA: Sigler, 1996.

Käsemann, Ernst. "The Cry for Liberty in the Worship of the Church." In *Perspectives on Paul*. Translated by M. Kohl, 122–137. Mifflintown, PA: Sigler, 1996.

Keener, Craig S. *The Mind of the Spirit: Paul's Approach to Transformed Thinking*. Grand Rapids, MI: Baker Academic, 2016.

Keesmaat, Sylvia C., and Brian J. Walsh. *Romans Disarmed: Resisting Empire, Demanding Justice*. Grand Rapids, MI: Brazos, 2019.

Klauck, Hans-Josef. *The Apocryphal Acts of the Apostles: An Introduction*. Translated by Brian McNeil. Waco, TX: Baylor University Press, 2008.

Kloppenborg, John S. "Gaius the Roman Guest." *New Testament Studies* 63 (2017): 534–549.

Koch, Dietrich-Alex. *Die Schrift Als Zeuge Des Evangeliums: Untersuchungen Zur Verwendung Und Zum Verständnis Der Schrift Bei Paulus*. Tübingen: Mohr Siebeck, 1986.

Kohler, Kaufmann. "Saul of Tarsus." In *The Jewish Encyclopedia*. Vol. 11, edited by Samson Talmid Hakam, 79–89. New York: Funk & Wagnalls, 1902.

Kovacs, Judith L. "Paul the Apostle." In *The Oxford Handbook of Early Christian Biblical Interpretation*, edited by Paul M. Blowers and Peter W. Martens, 614–625. Oxford: Oxford University Press, 2019.

Kujanpää, Katja. "From Eloquence to Evading Responsibility: The Rhetorical Functions of Quotations in Paul's Argumentation." *Journal of Biblical Literature* 136 (2017): 185–202.

Kujanpää, Katja. *The Rhetorical Functions of Scriptural Quotations in Romans*. Leiden: Brill, 2019.

Langton, Daniel R. *The Apostle Paul in the Jewish Imagination: A Study in Modern Jewish-Christian Relations*. Cambridge: Cambridge University Press, 2010.

Lampe, Peter. "Keine 'Sklavenflucht' des Onesimus." *Zeitschrift für die Neutestamentliche Wissenschaft* 76 (1985): 135–137.

Lampe, Peter. *From Paul to Valentinus: Christians at Rome in the First Two Centuries*. London: T&T Clark International, 2003.

Last, Richard. *The Pauline Church and the Corinthian Ekklēsia: Greco-Roman Associations in Comparative Context*. Cambridge: Cambridge University Press, 2016.

Levine, Lee I. *The Ancient Synagogue: The First Thousand Years*. New Haven, CT: Yale University Press, 2000.

Levinskaya, Irina. *The Book of Acts in Its Diaspora Setting*. Grand Rapids, MI: Eerdmans, 1996.

Lieu, Judith M. *Marcion and the Making of a Heretic: God and Scripture in the Second Century*. Cambridge: Cambridge University Press, 2015.

Lincicum, D. "Intertextuality, Effective History, and Memory: Conceptualizing Paul's Use of Scripture." In *Paulinische Schriftrezeption: Grundlagen – Ausprägungen – Wirkungen – Wertungen*, edited by Florian Wilk and Markus Öhler, 9–22. Göttingen: Vandenhoeck & Ruprecht, 2017.

Lincicum, D. *Paul and the Early Jewish Encounter with Deuteronomy*. Reprint, Grand Rapids, MI: Baker Academic, 2013.

Litwa, M. David. *Iesus Deus: The Early Christian Depiction of Jesus as a Mediterranean God*. Minneapolis, MN: Fortress Press, 2014.

Long, Frederick J. "Ephesians: Paul's Political Theology in Greco-Roman Context." In *Christian Origins and Greco-Roman Culture: Social and Literary Contexts for the New Testament*, edited by Stanley E. Porter and Andrew W. Pitts, 255–309. Leiden: Brill, 2012.

Long, Frederick J. "Roman Imperial Rule under the Authority of Jupiter-Zeus: Political-Religious Contexts and the Interpretation of 'The Ruler of the Authority of the Air' in Ephesians 2:2." In *The Language of the New Testament: Context, History, Development*, edited by Stanley E. Porter, 113–154. Leiden: Brill, 2013.

Longenecker, Bruce W. "Sharing in Their Spiritual Blessings? The Story of Israel in Galatians and Romans." In *Narrative Dynamics in Paul: A Critical Assessment*, edited by Bruce W. Longenecker, 58–84. Louisville, KY: Westminster John Knox, 2002.

Longenecker, Bruce W. *Rhetoric at the Boundaries: The Art and Theology of New Testament Chain-Link Transitions*. Waco, TX: Baylor University Press, 2005.

Longenecker, Bruce W. *Remember the Poor: Paul, Poverty, and the Greco-Roman World*. Grand Rapids, MI: Eerdmans, 2010.

Longenecker, Bruce W. *The Cross before Constantine: The Early Life of a Christian Symbol*. Minneapolis, MN: Fortress Press, 2015.

Longenecker, Bruce W. "Peace, Security, and Propaganda: Advertisement and Reality in the Early Roman Empire." In *An Introduction to Empire in the New Testament*, edited by Adam Winn, 15–46. Atlanta, GA: Society of Biblical Literature, 2016

Longenecker, Bruce W. "Faith, Works, and Worship: Torah Observance in Paul's Theological Perspective." In *The Apostle Paul and the Christian Life*, edited by Scot McKnight and Joe Modica, 47–70. Grand Rapids, MI: Baker Academic, 2016.

Longenecker, Bruce W. *The Crosses of Pompeii: Jesus-Devotion in a Vesuvian Town*. Minneapolis, MN: Fortress Press, 2016.

Longenecker, Bruce W. "Sin and the Sovereignty of God in Romans." In *Sin and Its Remedy in Paul*, edited by John K. Goodrich and Nijay K. Gupta. Eugene, OR: Cascade, forthcoming.

Longenecker, Bruce W., and Scott C. Ryan. "Presenting the Pauline Voice: An Appreciation of the Letter to the Laodiceans." *NTS* 62 (2016): 136–148.

Longenecker, Bruce W., and Todd D. Still. *Thinking through Paul: A Survey of His Life, Letters, and Theology*. Grand Rapids, MI: Zondervan, 2014.

MacDonald, Dennis R. *The Legend and the Apostle: The Battle for Paul in Story and Canon*. Louisville, KY: Westminster John Knox, 1983.

MacDonald, Margaret Y. *The Pauline Churches: A Socio-Historical Study of Institutionalization in Pauline and Deutero-Pauline Writings*. Cambridge: Cambridge University Press, 1988.

MacDonald, Margaret Y. *Colossians and Ephesians*. Collegeville, MN: The Liturgical Press, 2000.

MacDonald, Margaret Y. "Slavery, Sexuality and House Churches: A Reassessment of Colossians 3.18–4.1 in light of New Research on the Roman Family." *New Testament Studies* 53 (2007): 94–113.

Maier, Harry O. *Picturing Paul in Empire: Imperial Image, Text and Persuasion in Colossians, Ephesians and the Pastoral Epistles*. London: Bloomsbury T&T Clark, 2013.

Malina, Bruce J. *The New Testament World: Insights from Cultural Anthropology*. 3rd ed. Louisville, KY: Westminster John Knox, 2001.

Marchal, Joseph A. *The Politics of Heaven: Women, Gender, and Empire in the Study of Paul*. Minneapolis, MN: Fortress Press, 2008.

Marcos, Natalio Fernandez. *The Septuagint in Context: Introduction to the Greek Version of the Bible*. Translated by Wilfred G. E. Watson. Boston, MA: Brill, 2001.

Marshall, I. Howard. "Recent Study of the Pastoral Epistles." *Themelios* 23 (1997): 3–21.

Marshall, I. Howard. *The Pastoral Epistles*. Edinburgh: T&T Clark, 1999.

Martin, Dale B. *The Corinthian Body*. New Haven, CT: Yale University Press, 1995.

Martyn, J. Louis. "Apocalyptic Antinomies in Paul's Letter to the Galatians." *New Testament Studies* 31 (1985): 410–424.

Martyn, J. Louis. "Romans as One of the Earliest Interpretations of Galatians." In *Theological Issues in the Letters of Paul*, 37–46. Edinburgh: T&T Clark, 1997.

Martyn, J. Louis. *Galatians: A New Translation with Introduction and Commentary*. New York: Doubleday, 1997.

Mason, Steve. "Jews, Judaeans, Judaizing, Judaism: Problems of Categorization in Ancient History." *Journal for the Study of Judaism* 38 (2007): 457–512.

Mason, Steve. *Orientation to the History of Roman Judaea*. Eugene, OR: Cascade, 2016.

McLaughlin, Barbara Kelley. "Lydia (Place)." In *Anchor Bible Dictionary*. Vol. 6, 423–425. New Haven, CT: Yale University Press, 1992.

McNeel, Jennifer Houston. *Paul as Infant and Nursing Mother: Metaphor, Rhetoric and Identity in 1 Thessalonians 2:5–8*. Atlanta, GA: Society of Biblical Literature, 2014.

Meeks, Wayne A. *The First Urban Christians: The Social World of the Apostle Paul*. 2nd ed. New Haven, CT: Yale University Press, 2003.

Meggitt, Justin J. *Paul, Poverty and Survival*. SNTW. Edinburgh: T&T Clark, 1998.

Meyer, Marvin W., ed. *The Ancient Mysteries: A Sourcebook*. San Francisco, CA: Harper and Row, 1987.

Michel, Otto. *Paulus Und Seine Bibel*. Darmstadt: Wissenschaftliche Buchgesellschaft, 1972.

Migliore, Daniel. *Philippians and Philemon*. Louisville, KY: Westminster John Knox, 2014.

Millar, Fergus. "Condemnation to Hard Labour in the Roman Empire, from the Julio-Claudians to Constantine." In *Rome, the Greek World, and the East: Government, Society, and Culture in the Roman Empire*, edited by Hannah M. Cotton and Guy M. Rogers, 120–150. Chapel Hill, NC: University of North Carolina Press, 2004.

Mitchell, Margaret M. *Paul and the Rhetoric of Reconciliation: An Exegetical Investigation of the Language and Composition of 1 Corinthians*. Louisville, KY: Westminster John Knox, 1993.

Mitchell, Margaret M. "Pauline Accommodation and 'Condescension' (ΣΥΓΚΑΤΑΒΑΣΙΣ): 1 Cor 9:19–23 and the History of Influence." In *Paul beyond the Judaism/Hellenism Divide*, edited by Troels Engberg-Pedersen, 197–214. Louisville, KY: Westminster John Knox, 2001.

Mitchell, Margaret M. *The Heavenly Trumpet: John Chrysostom and the Art of Pauline Interpretation*. Louisville, KY: Westminster John Knox, 2002.

Mitchell, Margaret M. *Paul, the Corinthians, and the Birth of Christian Hermeneutics*. Cambridge: Cambridge University Press, 2010.

Mitchell, Margaret M. *Paul and the Emergence of Christian Textuality: Early Christian Literary Culture in Context*. Tübingen: Mohr Siebeck, 2018.

Mitchell, Stephen, and Peter Van Nuffelen, eds. *One God: Pagan Monotheism in the Roman Empire*. Cambridge: Cambridge University Press, 2010.

Moo, Douglas J. *The Letter to the Romans*. 2nd ed. Grand Rapids, MI: Eerdmans, 2018.

Morgan, Robert. "Sachkritik in Reception History." *Journal for the Study of the New Testament* 33, no. 2 (2010): 175–190.

Morgan, Teresa. *Roman Faith and Christian Faith: Pistis and Fides in the Early Roman Empire and Early Churches*. Oxford: Oxford University Press, 2015.

Morris, Helen. "The City as Foil (Not Friend nor Foe): Conformity and Subversion in 1 Corinthians 12:12–31." In *The Urban World of the First Christians*, edited by Steve Walton, Paul R. Trebilco, and David W. J. Gill, 141–159. Grand Rapids, MI: Eerdmans, 2017.

Moses, Robert. "Discerning the Body of Christ: Paul, Poverty, and the Powers." *Journal for the Study of the New Testament* 40, no. 4 (2018): 473–493.

Munck, Johannes. *Paul and the Salvation of Mankind*. Translated by Frank Clarke. Richmond, VA: John Knox Press, 1959.

Murphy-O'Connor, Jerome. *St Paul's Corinth: Texts and Archaeology*. 3rd ed. Collegeville, MN: Liturgical Press, 2002.

Murphy-O'Connor, Jerome. *Paul: His Story*. Oxford: Oxford University Press, 2004.

Myers, Ched, and Elaine Enns. *Ambassadors of Reconciliation: Vol. I: New Testament Reflections on Restorative Justice and Peacemaking*. Maryknoll, NY: Orbis, 2009.

Nanos, Mark D. *Paul within Judaism: Restoring the First-Century Context to the Apostle*. Edited by Magnus Zetterholm. Minneapolis, MN: Fortress Press, 2015.

Nasrallah, Laura Salah. *Archaeology and the Letters of Paul*. Oxford: Oxford University Press, 2019.

Neusner, Jacob. "Preface." In *Judaisms and Their Messiahs at the Turn of the Christian Era*, edited by Jacob Neusner, William S. Green, and Ernest Frerichs, ix–xiv. Cambridge: Cambridge University Press, 1987.

Newman, Carey. "Narrative Cross, Apocalyptic Resurrection: Ephesians and Reading Paul." In *One God, One People, One Future*, edited by John Anthony Dunne and Eric Lewellen, 493–512. Minneapolis, MN: Fortress Press, 2018.

Nongbri, Brent. "Pauline Letter Manuscripts." In *All Things to All Cultures: Paul among Jews, Greeks, and Romans*, edited by Mark Harding and Alanna Nobbs, 84–102. Grand Rapids, MI: Eerdmans, 2012.

Nongbri, Brent. *Before Religion: A History of a Modern Concept*. New Haven, CT: Yale University Press, 2015.

Novenson, Matthew V. *Christ among the Messiahs: Christ Language in Paul and Messiah Language in Ancient Judaism*. New York: Oxford University Press, 2012.

Novenson, Matthew V. "Paul's Former Occupation in Ioudaismos." In *Galatians and Christian Theology*, edited by Mark Elliott, Scott J. Hafemann, N. T. Wright, and John Frederick, 24–39. Grand Rapids, MI: Baker, 2014.

Novenson, Matthew V. "The Pauline Epistles in Tertullian's Bible." *Scottish Journal of Theology* 68, no. 4 (2015): 471–483.

Novenson, Matthew V. "The Self-Styled Jew of Romans 2 and the Actual Jews of Romans 9–11." In *The So-Called Jew in Paul's Letter to the Romans*, edited by Rafael Rodriguez and Matthew Thiessen, 133–162. Minneapolis, MN: Fortress Press, 2016.

Oakes, Peter. *Reading Romans in Pompeii: Paul's Letter at Ground Level*. Minneapolis, MN: Fortress Press, 2009.

Oakes, Peter. "Using Historical Evidence in the Study of Neronian Christian Groups and Texts." In *The Last Years of Paul's Life: Essays from the Tarragona Conference, June 2013*, edited by Armand Puig i Tàrrech, John M. G. Barclay, and Jörg Frey, 131–151. Tübingen: Mohr Siebeck, 2015.

Oakes, Peter. *Galatians*. Grand Rapids, MI: Baker Academic, 2015.

Oakes, Peter. "Pistis as Relational Way of Life in Galatians." *Journal for the Study of the New Testament* 40 (2018): 255–275.

Okland, Jorunn. *Women in Their Place: Paul and the Corinthian Discourse of Gender and Sanctuary Space*. London: T&T Clark, 2004.

Oliver, Isaac, and Gabriele Boccaccini, eds. *The Early Reception of Paul the Second Temple Jew: Text, Narrative, and Reception History*. New York: T&T Clark, 2018.

Osiek, Carolyn, and Margaret Y. MacDonald. *A Woman's Place: House Churches in Earliest Christianity*. Minneapolis, MN: Augsburg Fortress, 2006.

Peppard, Michael. *The Son of God in the Roman World: Divine Sonship in Its Social and Political Context*. New York: Oxford University Press, 2011.

Pervo, Richard. *Luke's Story of Paul*. Minneapolis, MN: Fortress Press, 1990.

Pervo, Richard. *Dating Acts: Between the Evangelists and the Apologists*. Santa Rosa, CA: Polebridge Press, 2006.

Pervo, Richard. *The Making of Paul: Constructions of the Apostle in Early Christianity*. Minneapolis, MN: Fortress Press, 2010.

Petersen, Norman. *Rediscovering Paul: Philemon and the Sociology of Paul's Narrative World*. Philadelphia: Fortress Press, 1985.

Pitre, Brant, Michael P. Barber, and John A. Kincaid. *Paul, a New Covenant Jew: Rethinking Pauline Theology*. Grand Rapids, MI: Eerdmans, 2019.

Pilhofer, Peter, and Philippi I. Band. *Die erste christliche Gemeinde Europas*. Tübingen: Mohr Siebeck, 1995.

Porter, Stanley E. "The Use of the Old Testament in the New: A Brief Comment on Method and Terminology." In *Early Christian Interpretation of the Scriptures of Israel: Investigations and Proposals*, edited by Craig A. Evans and J. A. Sanders, 79–96. Sheffield: Sheffield Academic, 1997.

Porter, Stanley E. *When Paul Met Jesus: How an Idea Got Lost in History*. Cambridge: Cambridge University Press, 2016.

Porter, Stanley E. "Pauline Techniques of Interweaving Scripture into His Letters." In *Paulinische Schriftrezeption: Grundlagen – Ausprägungen – Wirkungen – Wertungen*, edited by Florian Wilk and Markus Öhler, 23–55. Göttingen: Vandenhoeck & Ruprecht, 2017.

Price, S. R. F. *Rituals and Power: The Roman Imperial Cult in Asia Minor*. Cambridge: Cambridge University Press, 1984.

Puig i Tàrrech, Armand, John M. G. Barclay, and Jörg Frey, eds. *The Last Years of Paul*. Tübingen: Mohr Siebeck, 2015.

Reed, Annette Yoshiko. *Jewish-Christianity and the History of Judaism*. Tübingen: Mohr Siebeck, 2018.

Richards, E. Randolph. *Paul and First-Century Letter Writing: Secretaries, Composition and Collection*. Downers Grove, IL: InterVarsity Press, 2004.

Rives, James B. *Religion in the Roman Empire*. London: Routledge, 2007.

Robertson, Paul M. *Paul's Letters and Contemporary Greco-Roman Literature: Theorizing a New Taxonomy*. Leiden: Brill, 2016.

Roetzel, Calvin. *Paul: The Man and the Myth*. Personalities of the New Testament. Philadelphia: Fortress Press, 1999.

Roetzel, Calvin. *The Letters of Paul: Conversations in Context*. 5th ed. Louisville, KY: Westminster John Knox, 2009.

Rogers, Guy MacLean. "An Ephesian Tale: Mystery Cults, Reverse Theological Engineering, and the Triumph of Christianity in Ephesus." In *The First Urban Churches 3: Ephesus*, edited by James R. Harrison and L. L. Welborn, 69–91. Atlanta, GA: Society of Biblical Literature, 2018.

Rosner, Brian. *Paul, Scripture, and Ethics: A Study of 1 Corinthians 5–7*. Reprint, Grand Rapids, MI: Baker, 1999.

Rudolph, David J. *A Jew to the Jews: Jewish Contours of Pauline Flexibility in 1 Corinthians 9:19–23*. 2nd ed. Eugene, OR: Wipf and Stock, 2016.

Sampley, J. Paul, ed. *Paul in the Greco-Roman World: A Handbook*. 2nd ed. 2 vols. London: Bloomsbury, 2016.

Sanders, E. P. *Paul and Palestinian Judaism: A Comparison of Patterns of Religion*. Philadelphia: Fortress Press, 1977.

Sanders, E. P. *Paul, the Law, and the Jewish People*. Minneapolis, MN: Fortress Press, 1983.

Schoedel, William R. *Ignatius of Antioch: A Commentary on the Seven Letters of Ignatius*. Hermeneia. Philadelphia: Fortress Press, 1986.

Scholem, Gershom Gerard. *Sabbatai Sevi: The Mystical Messiah*. Translated by R. J. Zwi Werblowsky. Princeton, NJ: Princeton University Press, 1976.

Scholem, Gershom Gerard. *The Messianic Idea in Judaism: And Other Essays on Jewish Spirituality*. Reprint, New York: Schocken, 1995.

Scholem, Gershom Gerard. *Major Trends in Jewish Mysticism*. Reissue, New York: Schocken, 1995.

Schröter, Jens. "Paul the Founder of the Church: Reflections on the Reception of Paul in the Acts of the Apostles and the Pastoral Epistles." In *Paul and the Heritage of Israel: Paul's Claim upon Israel's Legacy in Luke and Acts in light of the Pauline Letters*, edited by David Moessner, Daniel Marguerat, Mikeal Parsons, and Michael Wolter, 195–219 New York: T&T Clark, 2012.

Schröter, Jens, Simon Butticaz, and Andreas Dettwiler, eds. *Receptions of Paul in Early Christianity: The Person of Paul and His Writings through the Eyes of His Early Interpreters*. Berlin: De Gruyter, 2018.

Schütz, John Howard. *Paul and the Anatomy of Apostolic Authority*. Cambridge: Cambridge University Press, 1975.

Schwartz, Seth. "How Many Judaisms Were There?" *Journal of Ancient Judaism* 2, no. 2 (2011): 208–238.

Schweitzer, Albert. *The Mysticism of Paul the Apostle*. London: A & C Black, 1931.

Scott, James C. *Domination and the Arts of Resistance: Hidden Transcripts*. New Haven, CT: Yale University Press, 1990.

Scott, James C. *Paul and the Nations: The Old Testament and Jewish Background of Paul's Mission to the Nations with Special Reference to the Destination of Galatians*. Tübingen: Mohr Siebeck, 1995.

Segal, Alan F. *Paul the Convert: The Apostolate and Apostasy of Saul the Pharisee*. New Haven, CT: Yale University Press, 1990.

Shum, Shiu-Lun. *Paul's Use of Isaiah in Romans: A Comparative Study of Paul's Letter to the Romans and the Sibylline and Qumran Sectarian Texts*. Tübingen: Mohr Siebeck, 2002.

Smith, Jonathan Z. *Drudgery Divine: On the Comparison of Early Christianities and the Religions of Late Antiquity*. Chicago: University of Chicago Press, 1990.

Smith, R. R. R. "The Imperial Reliefs from the Sebasteion at Aphrodisias." *Journal of Roman Studies* 77 (1987): 88–138.

Smith, R. R. R. "Simulacra Gentium: The Ethnē from the Sebasteion at Aphrodisias." *Journal of Roman Studies* 78 (1988): 50–77.

Soyars, Jonathan E. *The Shepherd of Hermas and the Pauline Legacy*. Leiden: Brill, 2019.

Sprinkle, Preston. *Law and Life: The Interpretation of Leviticus 18:5 in Early Judaism and Paul*. Tübingen: Mohr Siebeck, 2008.

Stanley, Christopher D. *Paul and the Language of Scripture: Citation Technique in the Pauline Epistles and Contemporary Literature*. Cambridge: Cambridge University Press, 1992.

Stanley, Christopher D. *Arguing with Scripture: The Rhetoric of Quotations in the Letters of Paul*. London: T&T Clark, 2004.

Stanley, Christopher D. *The Colonized Apostle: Paul in Postcolonial Eyes*. Minneapolis, MN: Fortress Press, 2011.

Stark, Rodney. *The Rise of Christianity: A Sociologist Reconsiders History*. Princeton, NJ: Princeton University Press, 1996.

Stendahl, Krister. "The Apostle Paul and the Introspective Conscience of the West." *Harvard Theological Review* 56 (1963): 199–215. Reprinted in *Paul among Jews and Gentiles*, 78–96.

Stendahl, Krister. *Paul among Jews and Gentiles*. Philadelphia: Fortress Press, 1976.

Still, Todd D., ed. *God and Israel: Providence and Purpose in Romans 9–11*. Waco, TX: Baylor University Press, 2017.

Stowers, Stanley K. "Friends and Enemies in the Politics of Heaven: Reading Theology in Philippians." In *Pauline Theology*. Vol. 1, edited by J. M. Bassler, 105–121. Minneapolis, MN: Fortress Press, 1991.

Stroumsa, Gedaliahu G. "Form(s) of God: Some Notes on Metatron and Christ." *Harvard Theological Studies* 76, no. 3 (1983): 269–288.

Stuckenbruck, Loren T. "'Angels' and 'God': Exploring the Limits of Early Jewish Monotheism." In *Early Christian and Jewish Monotheism*, edited by Wendy E. S. North, 45–70. London: T&T Clark, 2004.

Sumney, Jerry L. *Colossians: A Commentary*. Louisville, KY: Westminster John Knox, 2008.

Tamez, Elsa. *The Amnesty of Grace: Justification by Faith from a Latin American Perspective*. Translated by Sharon H. Ringe. Nashville, TN: Abingdon, 1993.

Tannehill, Robert. "Participation in Christ: A Central Theme in Pauline Soteriology." In *The Shape of the Gospel: New Testament Essays*, 223–227. Eugene, OR: Cascade, 2007.

Taussig, Hal. *In the Beginning Was the Meal: Social Experimentation and Early Christian Identity*. Minneapolis, MN: Fortress Press, 2009.

Thiessen, Matthew. *Paul and the Gentile Problem*. Oxford: Oxford University Press, 2016.

Thiselton, Anthony C. *The First Epistle to the Corinthians*. Grand Rapids, MI: Eerdmans, 2013.

Thompson, Michael B. *Clothed with Christ: The Example and Teaching of Jesus in Romans 12:1–15:13*. Eugene, OR: Wipf & Stock, 2011.

Torjesen, Karen Jo. *When Women Were Priests: Women's Leadership in the Early Church & the Scandal of their Subordination in the Rise of Christianity*. San Francisco, CA: Harper San Francisco, 1993.

Tov, Emanuel, Robert A. Kraft, and P. J. Parsons. *The Greek Minor Prophets Scroll from Naḥal Ḥever (8ḤevXIIgr)*. Oxford: Clarendon, 1989.

Towner, Philip H. *The Letters to Timothy and Titus*. Grand Rapids, MI: Eerdmans, 2006.

Trobisch, David. *Paul's Letter Collection: Tracing the Origins*. Philadelphia: Augsburg Fortress, 1994.

Tuckett, Christopher M. "Paul, Scripture and Ethics. Some Reflections." *New Testament Studies* 46, no. 3 (2000): 403–424.

Tomson, Peter J. *Paul and the Jewish Law: Halakhah in the Letters of the Apostle to the Gentiles*. Minneapolis, MN: Fortress, 1990.

van der Watt, Jan G., ed. *Salvation in the New Testament: Perspectives on Soteriology*, 163–358. Leiden: Brill, 2005.

Wagner, J. Ross. *Heralds of the Good News: Isaiah and Paul in Concert in the Letter to the Romans*. Leiden: Brill, 2002.

Walsh, Brian J., and Sylvia C. Keesmaat. *Colossians Remixed: Subverting the Empire*. Downers Grove, IL: Intervarsity Press, 2004.

Walsh, P. G. *Apuleius, The Golden Ass*. Oxford: Oxford University Press, 1995.

Wasserman, Emma. *Apocalypse As Holy War: Divine Politics and Polemics in the Letters of Paul*. New Haven, CT: Yale University Press, 2018.

Watson, Francis. *Paul and the Hermeneutics of Faith*. 2nd ed. New York: Bloomsbury T&T Clark, 2016.

Watson, Francis. "By Faith (of Christ): An Exegetical Dilemma and its Scriptural Solution." In *The Faith of Jesus Christ: Exegetical, Biblical, and Theological Studies*, edited by Michael F. Bird and Preston M. Sprinkle, 147–163. Peabody, MA: Hendrickson, 2009.

Webb, Natalie R. "Powers and Protection in Pompeii and Paul: The Apotropaic Function of the Cross in the Letter to the Galatians." In *Early Christianity in Pompeian Light: People, Texts, Situations*, edited by Bruce W. Longenecker, 93–121. Minneapolis, MN: Fortress Press, 2016.

Welborn, L. L. *Paul, the Fool of Christ: A Study of 1 Corinthians 1–4 in the Comic-Philosophic Tradition*. London: A&C Black, 2005.

Wendt, Heidi. *At the Temple Gates: The Religion of Freelance Experts in the Roman Empire*. Oxford: Oxford University Press, 2016.

Westerholm, Stephen. *Perspectives Old and New on Paul: The "Lutheran" Paul and His Critics*. Grand Rapids, MI: Eerdmans, 2004.

White, Benjamin L. *Remembering Paul: Ancient and Modern Contests over the Image of the Apostle*. Oxford: Oxford University Press, 2014.

Wiefel, Wolfgang. "The Jewish Community in Ancient Rome and the Origins of Roman Christianity." In *The Romans Debate*. Revised and expanded ed., edited by K. P. Donfried, 85–101. Peabody, MA: Hendrickson, 1991.

Wiles, Maurice. *The Divine Apostle: The Interpretation of St. Paul's Epistles in the Early Church*. Cambridge: Cambridge University Press, 1967.

Wilk, Florian. *Die Bedeutung Des Jesajabuches Für Paulus*. Göttingen: Vandenhoeck & Ruprecht, 1998.

Wink, Walter. *Engaging the Powers: Discernment and Resistance in a World of Domination*. Minneapolis, MN: Fortress Press, 1992.

Winter, Bruce W. *Seek the Welfare of the City: Christians as Benefactors and Citizens*. Grand Rapids, MI: Eerdmans, 1994.

Winter, Bruce W. *Divine Honours for the Caesars: The First Christians' Responses*. Grand Rapids, MI: Eerdmans, 2015.

Wire, Antoinette Clark. *The Corinthian Women Prophets: A Reconstruction through Paul's Rhetoric*. Minneapolis, MN: Fortress, 1990.

Wischmeyer, Oda. "Wie kommt Abraham in den Galaterbrief? Überlegungen zu Gal 3,6–29." In *Umstrittener Galaterbrief: Studien zur Situierung der Theologie des Paulus-Schreibens*, edited by Michael Bachmann and Bernd Kollmann, 119–163. Neukirchen-Vluyn: Neukirchener Verlag, 2010.

Wright, N. T. *The Climax of the Covenant: Christ and the Law in Pauline Theology*. Minneapolis, MN: Fortress Press, 1993.

Wright, N. T. *Paul and the Faithfulness of God*. Minneapolis, MN: Fortress Press, 2013.

Young, Frances M. *Biblical Exegesis and the Formation of Christian Culture*. Cambridge: Cambridge University Press, 1997.

Index of Biblical and Ancient Writings

Romans

1 Corinthians

2 Corinthians

Galatians

Ephesians

Philippians

Colossians

1 Thessalonians

2 Thessalonians

1 Timothy

Index of Modern Scholars

CAMBRIDGE COMPANIONS TO RELIGION *(continued from page iii)*

Other Titles in the Series

LIBERATION THEOLOGY Edited by Chris Rowland
MARTIN LUTHER Edited by Donald K. McKim
MEDIEVAL JEWISH PHILOSOPHY Edited by Daniel H. Frank and Oliver Leaman
MODERN JEWISH PHILOSOPHY Edited by Michael L. Morgan and Peter Eli Gordon
MOHAMMED Edited by Jonathan E. Brockup
THE NEW CAMBRIDGE COMPANION TO ST. PAUL Edited by Bruce W. Longenecker
NEW RELIGIOUS MOVEMENTS Edited by Olav Hammer and Mikael Rothstein
PENTECOSTALISM Edited by Cecil M. Robeck, Jr and Amos Yong
POSTMODERN THEOLOGY Edited by Kevin J. Vanhoozer
THE PROBLEM OF EVIL Edited by Chad Meister and Paul K. Moser
PURITANISM Edited by John Coffey and Paul C. H. Lim
QUAKERISM Edited by Stephen W. Angell and Pink Dandelion
THE QUR'AN Edited by Jane Dammen McAuliffe
KARL RAHNER Edited by Declan Marmion and Mary E. Hines
REFORMATION THEOLOGY Edited by David Bagchi and David C. Steinmetz
REFORMED THEOLOGY Edited by Paul T. Nimmo and David A. S. Fergusson
RELIGION AND TERRORISM Edited by James R. Lewis
RELIGIOUS STUDIES Edited by Robert A. Orsi
FREIDRICK SCHLEIERMACHER Edited by Jacqueline Mariña
SCIENCE AND RELIGION Edited by Peter Harrison
ST. PAUL Edited by James D. G. Dunn
SUFISM Edited by Lloyd Ridgeon
THE SUMMA THEOLOGIAE Edited by Philip McCosker and Denys Turner
THE TALMUD AND RABBINIC LITERATURE Edited by Charlotte E. Fonrobert and Martin S. Jaffee
THE TRINITY Edited by Peter C. Phan
HANS URS VON BALTHASAR Edited by Edward T. Oakes and David Moss
VATICAN II Edited by Richard R. Gaillardetz
JOHN WESLEY Edited by Randy L. Maddox and Jason E. Vickers

Made in United States
Troutdale, OR
02/23/2024

17916198R00216